Business
Plans
Handbook

Business Plans

A COMPILATION OF BUSINESS PLANS DEVELOPED BY INDIVIDUALS THROUGHOUT NORTH AMERICA

Handbook

VOLUME

42

GALE
A Cengage Company

Farmington Hills, Mich • San Francisco • New York • Waterville, Maine
Meriden, Conn • Mason, Ohio • Chicago

Business Plans Handbook, Volume 42

Project Editor: Donna Craft

Composition and Electronic Prepress: Evi Seoud

Manufacturing: Rita Wimberley

For product information and technology assistance, contact us at
Gale Customer Support, 1-800-877-4253.
For permission to use material from this text or product,
submit all requests online at **www.cengage.com/permissions.**
Further permissions questions can be emailed to
permissionrequest@cengage.com

Gale, A Cengage Company
27500 Drake Rd.
Farmington Hills, MI 48331-3535

ISBN-13: 978-1-4103-3848-8
1084-4473

Printed in Mexico
1 2 3 4 5 6 7 22 21 20 19 18

Contents

BUSINESS PLANS

CONTENTS

Highlights

Business Plans Handbook, Volume 42 (BPH-42) is a collection of business plans compiled by entrepreneurs seeking funding for small businesses throughout North America. For those looking for examples of how to approach, structure, and compose their own business plans, *BPH-42* presents 20 sample plans, including plans for the following businesses:

- Appliance Repair Business
- Cross-Stitch Business
- DIY Automotive Repair Businesss
- Driving School
- First-Aid Training
- Food Hall Business
- Gutter Cleaning Service
- Optometry Practice
- Small Engine Repair Facility
- Violence Prevention Consulting Firm

FEATURES AND BENEFITS

BPH-42 offers many features not provided by other business planning references including:

- Twenty business plans, each of which represent an attempt at clarifying (for themselves and others) the reasons that the business should exist or expand and why a lender should fund the enterprise.
- Two fictional plans that are used by business counselors at a prominent small business development organization as examples for their clients. (You will find these in the Business Plan Template Appendix.)
- A directory section that includes listings for venture capital and finance companies, which specialize in funding start-up and second-stage small business ventures, and a comprehensive listing of Service Corps of Retired Executives (SCORE) offices. In addition, the Appendix also contains updated listings of all Small Business Development Centers (SBDCs); associations of interest to entrepreneurs; Small Business Administration (SBA) Regional Offices; and consultants specializing in small business planning and advice. It is strongly advised that you consult supporting organizations while planning your business, as they can provide a wealth of useful information.
- A Small Business Term Glossary to help you decipher the sometimes confusing terminology used by lenders and others in the financial and small business communities.
- A cumulative index, outlining each plan profiled in the complete *Business Plans Handbook* series.
- A Business Plan Template which serves as a model to help you construct your own business plan. This generic outline lists all the essential elements of a complete business plan and their components, including the Summary, Business History and Industry Outlook, Market Examination,

Competition, Marketing, Administration and Management, Financial Information, and other key sections. Use this guide as a starting point for compiling your plan.

- Extensive financial documentation required to solicit funding from small business lenders. You will find examples of Cash Flows, Balance Sheets, Income Projections, and other financial information included with the textual portions of the plan.

Introduction

Perhaps the most important aspect of business planning is simply doing it. More and more business owners are beginning to compile business plans even if they don't need a bank loan. Others discover the value of planning when they must provide a business plan for the bank. The sheer act of putting thoughts on paper seems to clarify priorities and provide focus. Sometimes business owners completely change strategies when compiling their plan, deciding on a different product mix or advertising scheme after finding that their assumptions were incorrect. This kind of healthy thinking and re-thinking via business planning is becoming the norm. The Editor of *Business Plans Handbook, Volume 42 (BPH-42)* sincerely hopes that this latest addition to the series is a helpful tool in the successful completion of your business plan, no matter what the reason for creating it.

This volume, like each volume in the series, offers business plans created by real people. *BPH-42* provides 20 business plans. The business and personal names and addresses and general locations have been changed to protect the privacy of the plan authors.

NEW BUSINESS OPPORTUNITIES

As in other volumes in the series, *BPH-42* finds entrepreneurs engaged in a wide variety of creative endeavors. Examples include an appliance repair business, a cupcake studio, a gutter cleaning service, and an interpretation and translation service, among others.

Comprehensive financial documentation has become increasingly important as today's entrepreneurs compete for the finite resources of business lenders. Our plans illustrate the financial data generally required of loan applicants, including Income Statements, Financial Projections, Cash Flows, and Balance Sheets.

ENHANCED APPENDIXES

In an effort to provide the most relevant and valuable information for our readers, we have updated the coverage of small business resources. For instance, you will find a directory section, which includes listings of all of the Service Corps of Retired Executives (SCORE) offices; an informative glossary, which includes small business terms; and a cumulative index, outlining each plan profiled in the complete *Business Plans Handbook* series. In addition we have updated the list of Small Business Development Centers (SBDCs); Small Business Administration Regional Offices; venture capital and finance companies, which specialize in funding start-up and second-stage small business enterprises; associations of interest to entrepreneurs; and consultants specializing in small business advice and planning. For your reference, we have also reprinted the business plan template, which provides a comprehensive overview of the essential components of a business plan and two fictional plans used by small business counselors.

SERIES INFORMATION

If you already have the first forty-one volumes of *BPH*, with this forty-second volume, you will now have a collection of over 720 business plans (not including the updated plans); contact information for hundreds of organizations and agencies offering business expertise; a helpful business plan template; more than 1,500 citations to valuable small business development material; and a comprehensive glossary of terms to help the business planner navigate the sometimes confusing language of entrepreneurship.

ACKNOWLEDGEMENTS

The Editor wishes to sincerely thank the contributors to *BPH-42*, including:

- Francis R. Fletcher
- Moore Consulting Services
- Paul Greenland Communications, Inc.
- Zuzu Enterprises

COMMENTS WELCOME

Your comments on *Business Plans Handbook* are appreciated. Please direct all correspondence, suggestions for future volumes of *BPH*, and other recommendations to the following:

Project Editor
Business Plans Handbook
Gale, A Cengage Company
27500 Drake Rd.
Farmington Hills, MI 48331-3535
Phone: (248)699-4253
Toll-Free: 800-877-GALE
URL: www.gale.com

Appliance Repair Business

Apex Appliance Repair, Inc.

2355 J St.
Sacramento, CA 94256

Claire Moore

Apex Appliance Repair, Inc. (AAR) is a family owned and operated business offering repair services of major appliances, including refrigerators, ice makers, freezers, ovens, cooktops, dishwashers, microwaves, washers, dryers, and garbage disposals. AAR is based in Sacramento, California, and will provide appliance repair services for cities in the Sacramento area including: Elk Grove, Citrus Heights, and Carmichael. Company founder, Andy Cooper, has over 30 years' experience in appliance service and repair.

EXECUTIVE SUMMARY

According to Statista (Statista, 2017), the home appliance industry, which includes electrical or mechanical devices used in a household, is a multi-billion-dollar industry. The research company projects that the consumption of household appliances worldwide will generate nearly $590 billion in revenues by the year 2020.

The home appliance industry is divided into two sectors: major domestic appliances (such as freezers, stoves, and washing machines) and small domestic appliances (food processors, toasters, and coffee makers). Sales of major appliances generated almost $190 billion in revenue in 2016.

A growing sub-market within the home appliance industry is the smart appliance market. Smart appliances contain specialized equipment that enables them to be run from a central system, such as a laptop. Many are also connected to the manufacturer, which allows for monitoring of the need for repairs or maintenance.

Apex Appliance Repair, Inc. (AAR) is a family owned and operated business offering repair services of major appliances including, refrigerators, ice makers, freezers, ovens, cooktops, dishwashers, microwaves, washers, dryers, and garbage disposals. AAR is based in Sacramento, California, and will provide appliance repair services for cities in the Sacramento area including: Elk Grove, Citrus Heights, and Carmichael. Company founder, Andy Cooper, has over 30 years' experience in appliance service and repair.

AAR will serve primarily residential clients including homeowners, apartment buildings, and condominium complexes. In addition to growing the business through our marketing efforts, AAR has been successful in becoming an Independent Authorized Service Provider through a Home Depot store in the Natomas area of Sacramento. This "partnership" relationship will enable AAR to grow much faster than it otherwise would. We hope to gain contracts with other Home Depot locations in Sacramento and surrounding areas as we demonstrate our ability to provide quality service to Home Depot customers.

We have also secured several contracts with local property management companies to provide their rental units with prompt and affordable service.

The purpose of this business plan is to serve as a blueprint for operations. It is our intention to conduct business for the next fifteen years and then sell our assets, including our customer list and contracts, to a qualified operator.

OBJECTIVES

Company objective for years one through three include the following:

- Establish Apex Appliance Repair as a recognized brand.

- Develop a reputation for providing quality service and prompt attention to customer needs.

- Achieve a level of revenues that will allow for future growth.

- Acquire additional contracts with Home Depot locations in the Sacramento area.

KEYS TO SUCCESS

Keys to success for Apex Appliance Repair will include the following:

- Prompt replies to inquiries, courteous service, fair pricing, and quality service.

- Strong customer relationships that are maintained through print and online contact.

- Value-added service, such as diagnostics, advice, troubleshooting, and prompt price quotes.

- Our many years of experience in repairing electrical and mechanical appliances.

MISSION

Apex Appliance Repair is dedicated to providing five-star customer service and giving our customers the best repair service experience possible.

COMPANY SUMMARY

Andy Cooper is a veteran having served for twenty years in the U.S. Army. During that time, he trained and served in several job areas including, utilities equipment repairer, a job that is responsible for supervising and performing maintenance on equipment, such as air conditioner electrical systems, air conditioner vapor systems, refrigeration unit electrical systems, portable heater fuel/electrical systems, fire extinguisher recharging systems, and fire extinguishers/valves.

After retiring from the Army, Cooper completed an online course in appliance repair through Penn Foster Career School and obtained CFC certification and a contractor's license in HVAC and Residential Appliance.

Cooper then took a job with Sears, where he worked for the next ten years as an appliance service technician. Then, having achieved all that he felt he could, Andy began to long for more job satisfaction and considered self-employment as the solution.

He decided to go on his own and Apex Appliance Repair was born in the summer of 2016. Steps in starting Apex included acquiring a business license through California's Bureau of Electronic and Appliance Repair, Home Furnishings and Thermal Insulation (BEARHFTI). State registration is required for a business that conducts repairs on appliances and electronics.

Licensure adds credibility to the business, as potential customers can complete an online search and obtain information about actions that may have been taken against the company. The BEARHFTI's mission is to protect and serve consumers, while ensuring a fair and competitive market.

Building on his experience and contacts as an appliance technician with Sears, Cooper spent much of 2016 cultivating business clients. He was successful in becoming an Independent Authorized Service Provider through a Home Depot store in the Natomas area of Sacramento. This "partnership" relationship will enable AAR to grow much faster than it otherwise would. We hope to gain contracts with other Home Depot locations in Sacramento and surrounding areas as we demonstrate our ability to provide quality service to Home Depot customers.

Cooper also secured several contracts with property management companies in Sacramento and surrounding areas, such as Elk Grove and Roseville. By providing special services and rates to these customers, we expect to build a revenue base that is scalable and predictable.

AAR has engaged the services of an independent bookkeeper to assist in completing the monthly accounting and payroll tasks. The company uses QuickBooks Online and its Payroll service to allow for direct connect with our bank to download transactions, pay bills, invoice customers, issue paychecks, file payroll tax forms, pay taxes, and process payments from customers.

COMPANY OWNERSHIP

AAR is a California corporation owned by Andrew Cooper. The office and storage site for the company vehicles and parts inventory is located in Andrew's home in Sacramento, California.

STARTUP SUMMARY

Andrew Cooper has invested his personal funds during the startup phase of the business. We do not anticipate the need for additional funding at this time. Andrew has also secured a revolving line of credit based on the equity in his home. This HELOC will be used should he need additional funding.

List of Equipment Needed for Startup

Item	Estimated cost
Computer/printer/copier/scanner/fax	$ 1,500
Storage/filing/shelving	$ 125
Paper shredder	$ 50
Desk/table/chair/lamp	$ 125
Tablet computer	$ 500
Misc tools & safety equipment	$ 250
Van (used)	$15,000
Van customization	$ 1,500
Uniforms & shoes	$ 150
Misc. supplies	$ 200
Misc. tools	$ 120
Total non-cash assets for startup	**$19,520**

Start-up Expenses

Licenses	$ 350
Advertising	$ 550
Web site development	$ 800
Insurance deposit	$ 100
Office supplies	$ 180
Brochures, cards, flyers	$ 220
Legal and incorporation	$2,500
Total start-up expenses	**$4,700**

Startup Funding

Cash required	$ 5,000
Startup assets to fund	$19,520
Startup expenses to fund	$ 4,700
Total funding required	**$29,220**

SERVICES

Each AAR technician arrives at your home in a company-branded service vehicle, wearing a company uniform, and ready to work. When he knocks on your door, he will greet you and offer to wear shoe covers in your home. Plus, he'll have a tool bag in hand, all the necessary troubleshooting schematics, and the skills necessary to service your appliance.

Our service trucks are stocked with the most common appliance repair parts, which improves our ability to get the job done right the first time.

REPAIRS

Our list of repair services includes:

- Washer/Dryer
- Refrigerator/Ice Maker/Freezer
- Trash Compactor
- Oven/Range/Cooktop
- Oven/Micro Combo
- Garbage Disposal Install/Repair
- Range Hood
- Dishwasher Install/Repair
- Microwave
- Ice Machines
- Warming Drawers
- Air Conditioners/Dehumidifiers/Air Cleaners
- Fire Extinguisher Installation/Maintenance

At AAR, we recognize that some owners prefer to do their own repairs. For that reason, we can also sell you a variety of appliance parts. Just give us a call or complete the contact form at our web site, providing us with the part number, model, and serial number of the appliance, and we will expedite your request and ship the part to your home.

APPLIANCE BRANDS SERVICED

We offer an extensive warranty! Our warranty includes: 90 Days on the diagnosis, 90 days on repair labor, and 3 years on parts.

The list of brands that we can repair includes:

- Admiral
- Amana
- Bosch
- Frigidaire
- GE
- Jenn-Air
- Kenmore
- KitchenAid
- Miele
- Siemens
- Whirlpool
- Wolf

INSTALLATION

You get a full-service appliance installation experience that puts your safety and satisfaction first. We work with electrical, water, and ventilation to make sure that your appliance is properly aligned and connected to your home utility system.

Here's what we do for you:

- Unpack your appliance—Taking care not to damage anything
- Inspect appliance for defects and damages—Ensuring safety and warranty coverage
- Verify space is suitable for appliance installation—Thorough inspection of infrastructure including wiring and housing
- Connect your appliance to code-approved utilities—Safely and responsibly activating your appliance
- Level and secure your appliance—Ensuring your appliance is balanced and stable
- Test your appliance—Perform thorough testing to make sure all vital functions are responsive
- Clean up—We fully clean and dispose of debris in our workspace
- Provide our warranty—We provide a 90-day labor warranty on all of our appliance installations

PRICING

Our service charge ranges from $89.95 to $149.95, depending on how far away you are from our closest technician. This charge covers the cost of bringing a fully-trained technician, with a fully stocked mobile service shop to your home. Our technician will provide you an estimate for the cost of labor and parts, if needed. This service charge will be waived if you approve the estimate and have us repair the appliance.

Service quotes can be provided at the time of the service call at the customer's location. The quote includes parts and labor. The part replacement comes with our ninety-day labor warranty and our three-year parts warranty.

Labor charges are based on industry standards for each individual type of repair rather than on time spent on the repair. This method of billing takes into account the specialized training, equipment, and overhead required to complete the repair.

Any parts required in the repair will be billed in addition to the service charge and labor.

All fees are due at time of service unless the customer is a participant in our Preferred Vendor program. We accept MasterCard and Visa credit cards and electronic funds transfer.

HOURS OF OPERATION

Our hours of operation are: Monday through Friday 8 a.m. to 5 p.m., Saturday 9 a.m. to 1 p.m.

PROPERTY MANAGEMENT SERVICES

We have developed a program for our Preferred Vendors to receive special treatment and great rates.

Property Management Preferred Vendor Benefits:

- 50% off the cost of our regular service charge.
- Same day or next day service (Monday thru Friday), or you get an additional $10 off.
- 10% off parts.
- Free shipping on parts purchases over $75.
- Free technical support to you or your maintenance manager for any repairs you'd like to attempt yourself.

Property Management Preferred Vendor Qualifications:

- A minimum of 10 separate managed properties/condos/apartments.
- A minimum of 1 appliance repair per month, or 3 repairs within 3 consecutive months.
- Payment terms of NET 45.
- A personal payment guarantee with valid credit card authorization.

WARRANTY

Customer satisfaction is our top concern. We stand by our work and, to prove it, we offer the following warranty on our services:

- 5 years on non-electronic Parts (warranty valid for parts we supply and install, unless specifically noted)

- 90 days labor

- 90 days on service call

Our warranty only applies when you have paid us directly, otherwise your warranty is the duration of the warranty you have with the manufacturer and/or extended warranty company.

SERVICE AREA

Our service area includes Sacramento and surrounding cities including: Folsom, Elk Grove, Roseville, Citrus Heights, and Carmichael.

MARKET ANALYSIS

In a September 2017 report, IBISWorld (IBISWorld, 2017) projected that consumers will decide to replace rather than repair their appliances as their incomes increase. Their conclusion was that over the next five years, industry revenue will decline.

While there is some truth in this prediction, we feel that AAR is poised for success due to the following factors and strategies:

- We create and develop strong relationships with our customers by helping them to maintain their appliances from the time they are installed.

- We stress regular maintenance as a way to get the longest service life from their appliances.

- We continue to build stable property management clients, who certainly do not want to buy a new appliance every time one needs servicing.

- Our program of continuous training and improvement includes gearing up to install and service the new smart appliances.

COMPETITION

One of the biggest challenges to an appliance repair business is the competition from large companies, such as Sears, Home Depot, Lowes, and Best Buy. For this reason, we have secured our place among the Independent Authorized Service Providers with Home Depot. We are currently connected with their store in the Natomas area of Sacramento, and we hope to be added to other Home Depot stores in the future.

As a member of Home Depot's Service Provider Portal, AAR has achieved a boost in business credibility, gained access to a large customer base, and ensured a revenue stream with growth potential.

MARKETING STRATEGY

During the research and startup phase, Cooper contracted with an Internet marketing company that specializes in online branding, web site development, and ongoing marketing assistance for in-home service professionals. Services include: search engine optimization (SEO), pay-per-click advertising

(PPC), email marketing, and reputation management. The agency also helped Cooper to find an independent copywriter who will contribute content on a regular basis to the blog, web site, Facebook page, Twitter feed, and newsletter.

Our marketing strategy will also include the following:

The web: A web presence will be developed with the assistance of a professional web site creator. Cooper will add a blog to the site where he will post regular articles with information of interest to the public about how to care for their appliances, shopping for appliance repair services, information on the latest in-home appliance technology, and more.

The web site will also include:

- A listing and explanation of services, pricing, warranties, hours, and service areas.

- Testimonials from satisfied customers.

- An app to schedule service.

- Information on how to locate your model number.

Social media: Social media tools such as Facebook and Twitter will be used to ensure that AAR has an identifiable presence. Contact information including the company's toll-free phone number will be listed on all sites.

Networking: Cooper has joined a local networking group that operates on the principle of sharing leads. Other group members includes a realtor, insurance agent, and accountant. Networking with other business owners will be key to AAR's success. Not only will affiliations with other professionals, such as realtors and insurance agents be stressed; Cooper will also maintain and develop his relationships with complementary professionals in plumbing and HVAC specialties.

Newsletter: A quarterly newsletter will be e-mailed to existing customers in order to keep AAR top of mind. The newsletter will contain articles, tips, and fun facts of interest to homeowners. Web visitors who subscribe to our newsletter will receive a $15 discount coupon that can be applied to the labor charge on their next service repair.

Referrals: The ability to build trust with a customer through an accurate quote that creates no surprises will build a loyal following and, in turn, numerous happy referrals. Both paper and magnet business cards will be handed out liberally to help customers keep AAR top of mind.

Online service listings: A membership on ANGI Homeservices will be purchased so that customers can post comments. Posts will be monitored so that any customers who post unfavorable comments can be contacted and resolved.

Vehicles: All vehicles used by AAR will have a custom wrap that will include the company name, logo, phone number, web address, list of primary services, and geographic areas served.

Yellow pages: All but replaced by the web, yellow pages are still used by a segment of the population. A listing here on a year after year basis will help to establish the brand and build recognition.

PERSONNEL PLAN

Service technicians at AAR must have at least two years of experience in repairing residential appliances. They must also demonstrate excellent customer service skills, team cooperation, and problem-solving skills. Appliance Repair Technician candidates must be able to pass the pre-employment drug screen and criminal background check.

Our personnel plan for the first three years of operation is as follows:

Personnel	Year 1	Year 2	Year 3
Andrew Cooper	$36,000	$ 36,000	$ 36,000
Repair technician	$41,600	$ 41,600	$ 45,000
Repair technician		$ 24,000	$ 41,600
Totals	**$77,600**	**$101,600**	**$122,600**
Total people	**2**	**3**	**3**

FINANCIAL PLAN

Pro forma Profit and Loss

	Year 1	Year 2	Year 3
Sales	$135,000	$168,000	$205,000
Direct costs of sales	$ 6,750	$ 8,400	$ 10,250
Gross profit	$128,250	$159,600	$194,750
Gross profit margin	95%	95%	95%
Expenses			
Depreciation	$ 3,903	$ 6,403	$ 6,403
Phone/Internet	$ 2,100	$ 2,400	$ 2,800
Payroll	$ 77,600	$101,600	$122,600
Insurance: liability, property, auto	$ 4,200	$ 4,500	$ 6,200
Payroll taxes/benefits	$ 11,640	$ 15,240	$ 18,390
Professional dues/memberships	$ 400	$ 400	$ 400
Sales & marketing	$ 4,500	$ 4,500	$ 4,500
Office supplies	$ 425	$ 350	$ 400
Auto: gas & maintenance	$ 12,800	$ 14,500	$ 19,000
Accounting & legal	$ 2,600	$ 2,400	$ 2,400
Repairs & maintenance	$ 500	$ 600	$ 800
Business software/quickbooks online	$ 1,800	$ 1,800	$ 1,800
Other expenses	$ 1,200	$ 1,200	$ 1,500
Total operating expenses	**$123,668**	**$155,893**	**$187,193**
Earnings before interest and taxes	**$ 4,583**	**$ 3,708**	**$ 7,558**
Interest expense	**$ 291**	**$ 520**	**$ 395**
Net earnings	**$ 4,292**	**$ 3,188**	**$ 7,163**
Income tax	**$ 644**	**$ 478**	**$ 1,074**
Net profit	**$ 3,648**	**$ 2,709**	**$ 6,088**
Net profit/sales	**3%**	**2%**	**3%**

Projected Balance Sheet

Assets	Year 1	Year 2	Year 3
Cash in bank	$11,151	$ 4,337	$12,008
Accounts receivable			
Other current assets			
Total current assets	**$11,151**	**$ 4,337**	**$12,008**
Fixed assets			
Office furniture & equipment	$ 2,525	$ 2,525	$ 2,525
Van	$16,500	$16,500	$16,500
Trucks	$20,000	$45,000	$45,000
Less: depreciation	($ 3,903)	($10,305)	($16,708)
Total assets	**$46,274**	**$58,057**	**$59,326**
Liabilities			
Current liabilities			
Accounts payable	$ 500	$ 700	$ 1,500
Other current liabilities			
Total current liabilities	**$ 500**	**$ 700**	**$ 1,500**
Long term liabilities			
Truck loan	$12,126	$21,000	$15,380
Total liabilities	**$12,626**	**$21,700**	**$16,880**
Paid-in capital	$30,000	$30,000	$30,000
Retained earnings		$ 3,648	$ 6,357
Net profit	**$ 3,648**	**$ 2,709**	**$ 6,088**
Total capital	**$33,648**	**$36,357**	**$42,445**
Total liabilities & capital	**$46,274**	**$58,057**	**$59,325**

REFERENCES

IBISWorld. (2017, September 1). *Appliance Repair in the US: Market Research Report.* Retrieved December 16, 2017, from IBISWorld.com: https://www.ibisworld.com/industry-trends/market-research-reports/other-services-except-public-administration/repair-maintenance/appliance-repair.html

Statista. (2017, January 1). *Home Appliance Industry—Statistics & Facts.* Retrieved December 16, 2017, from The Statistics Portal: https://www.statista.com/topics/1068/home-appliances/

Cross-Stitch Business

Anika Esperanza Designs

1917 Maple Ave.
Oregon, IL 61195

Paul Greenland

Anika Esperanza Designs develops and sells cross-stitch patterns and creates highly personalized custom cross-stitch embroidery.

EXECUTIVE SUMMARY

Stitched goods have been a popular art form for thousands of years. In fact, some estimates claim that needlework dates back as far as the sixth century BC. Today, embroidery continues to experience strong demand. This especially is true of pieces that are personalized and unique. A form of counted-thread embroidery, cross-stitch creates pictures from a series of crossed or X-shaped stitches that are made by hand without the use of a sewing machine. Anika Esperanza Designs is a cross-stitching business that develops and sells cross-stitch patterns and creates highly personalized custom cross-stitch embroidery.

INDUSTRY ANALYSIS

Cross-stitching enthusiasts, whether stitching for pleasure or profit, have access to several organizations devoted to their craft. One is the Embroiderers' Guild of America (www.egausa.org), which serves "to inspire passion for the needle arts through education and the celebration of its heritage." The organization counts both beginners and professionals among its members, some of whom belong to local chapters or the organization's online chapter, Cyber Stitchers. The EGA, which itself is a member of the International Council of Needlework Associations, offers five certification programs in the areas of education, appraisal, and judging.

Another industry resource is the National NeedleArts Association (www.tnna.org), which "advances its community of professional businesses by encouraging the passion and leadership for needlearts through education, industry knowledge exchange, and a strong marketplace." The organization offers a retail membership geared toward members who operate home-based businesses, traditional storefronts, mail-order operations, and online stores.

MARKET ANALYSIS

Market Overview

Although data regarding the cross-stitching market, specifically, is not available, the United States is home to a lucrative arts and crafts industry. According to a report from Global Industry Analysts Inc., the U.S. arts and crafts market was worth approximately $40 billion during the mid-2010s.

Target Markets

The patterns and embroidery work produced by Anika Esperanza Designs will appeal to customers in search of items that are truly unique and have special meaning. However, while completing projects for family and friends, the owner has experienced especially strong demand for specific themes, including weddings, family history, and occupations. For this reason, Anika Esperanza Designs will emphasize these themes when engaging in marketing and promotional efforts.

Competition

Anika Esperanza Designs will compete with many other businesses that sell cross-stitch patterns and custom embroidery. The owner realizes that her creativity and the ability to connect with niche markets will differentiate her business in a highly competitive marketplace.

PRODUCTS & SERVICES

Anika Esperanza Designs will specialize in the following products and services:

1. Developing general cross-stitch patterns.

2. Developing custom/personalized patterns that customers can complete on their own.

3. Developing custom/personalized patterns and producing finished embroidery.

In the case of custom/personalized designs, Anika Esperanza will use source material (e.g. photographs, sketches, paintings, etc.) provided by the customer in digital format via e-mail.

Pricing

Anika Esperanza Designs, typically, will sell general cross-stitch patterns for $5-$10.

Customized patterns, developed using an image editing program and/or cross-stitch pattern software, generally will cost $35.

Finally, the business usually will charge $85-$100 for most finished embroidery work (in addition to the cost of a customized pattern).

Themes

Cross-stitching patterns are available in virtually every category imaginable. To maximize the efficiency of her pattern development efforts, Anika Esperanza will focus on themes that often have significant meaning for customers (e.g., people, hobbies, occupations, special places, etc.). Examples include, but are not limited to:

Pets:

- Birds
- Cats
- Dog
- Fish
- Horses

Buildings & Architecture:

- Bridges

- Churches

- Cottages

- Farms & Barns

- Houses

People:

- Children

- Famous Individuals

- Friends & Family

- Occupations

Special Events:

- Anniversary

- Birth Announcements

- Birthday

- Celebrations

- Graduations

- Memorials

- Weddings

Transportation:

- Aircraft

- Automobiles

- Maps

- Ships & Boats

- Trains

- Work Vehicles/Equipment

Stitching

Most of the business' finished embroidery will be produced using a basic cross-stitch. However, the owner is able to use other types of stitching, including:

- Basket Stitch

- Closed Herringbone Stitch

- Double Cross-stitch

- Herringbone Stitch

- Italian Cross-stitch

- Leaf Stitch

- Thorn Stitch

- Threaded Herringbone Stitch

- Tied Herringbone Stitch
- Trellis Stitch

OPERATIONS

Production

One key consideration for a cross-stitching business is the amount of time required to complete a piece of embroidery. This can be impacted by a variety of factors, including the number of stitches that one is able to perform on an hourly basis (depending on his or her skill level), the complexity of a given pattern, and the number of thread color changes needed.

Several cross-stitching resources indicate that 100 stitches per hour is an average pace for many cross-stitchers. Anika Esperanza estimates that she can complete most of her patterns at a pace of 150 stitches per hour. By taking a more minimalistic approach, Anika will be able to develop patterns and get them to market more quickly. Additionally, when performing actual embroidery work, she will be able to complete work at a faster pace. This will allow her to maintain reasonable price points and maximize profit margins through greater efficiency.

Location

Anika Esperanza Designs will operate as a home-based business. Anika Esperanza has designated space in her home that will be used exclusively for operating her business. In addition to a well-lit worktable, the space also includes a comfortable chair, a tablet computer that can be used in conjunction with a large monitor when needed, storage cabinets, a filing cabinet, and several shelving units.

Business Structure

Anika Esperanza Designs initially will operate as a sole proprietorship. As the business grows, the owner will consider establishing an S corporation, which offers certain tax advantages. As a sole proprietor, Anika Esperanza understands that she will be responsible for paying self-employment taxes on a quarterly basis.

Hours of Operation

As a home-based business, Anika Esperanza will enjoy flexible work hours. However, the owner acknowledges that she will need to respond to customer inquiries in a timely manner. Excellent customer service will enable the business to maximize customer satisfaction, word-of-mouth referrals, and repeat business. For this reason, Anika will attempt to respond to all customer inquiries within one business day.

Communications

The owner has obtained a dedicated phone line for Anika Esperanza Designs through a local Internet service provider. The service includes a mobile app that allows Anika to receive and make calls through her business number from any location. In addition, she has purchased a dedicated domain name for the business.

Bookkeeping & Billing

Anika Esperanza Designs will use a popular cloud-based accounting and invoicing service that allows business owners to generate invoices for customers with a credit card payment option. Customers will be required to pay for custom patterns and embroidery work in advance.

Shipping & Receiving

As a rule, Anika Esperanza Designs will only accept source material (e.g. photographs, sketches, paintings, etc.) in digital format via e-mail. Finished patterns also will be delivered to the customer via email, in PDF format. In the case of finished embroidery, the business will utilize a leading carrier service that allows package tracking and provides the customer with the option of insuring their shipment.

Supplies

Anika Esperanza Designs will require certain supplies on an ongoing basis. The owner estimates that she will need to purchase approximately $125 in supplies prior to start up. She has obtained wholesale pricing for several key items, including:

- Adjustable Bamboo Circle Cross-stitch Hoop Rings (3"-14") $12-$18 (wholesale, qty. 6)

- Premium Rainbow Cross-stitch Threads (105 Skeins/35 Colors Per Pack) $25

- Aida Cloth Cross-stitch Cloth (12 x 18, White, 14 Count) $10/4 pieces

Equipment

Because Anika Esperanza has been an avid cross-stitcher for many years, she already has the equipment needed to perform embroidery work and create new patterns. However, she has identified several items that will be purchased for operations, including:

- Cross-stitch Pattern Software: $55

- Universal Craft Stand: $40

- Cross-stitch Scroll Frame Set: $35

- Dimmable LED Magnifying Floor Lamp with Rolling Base: $100

- Plastic Floss Storage Boxes (4): $40

PERSONNEL

Anika Esperanza has a unique background that positions her for success as a small business owner. Anika learned how to cross-stitch from her mother at a young age, and has nearly 20 years of experience. Additionally, she has a background in graphic design and is highly skilled at using computer applications, including image editing software. Together, these skills will allow her to create visually appealing patterns for customers. In addition to her creative and technical skills, Anika recognizes the importance of good business management. For this reason, she took advantage of a small business certificate program at her local community college and read several books on the subject.

Professional & Advisory Support

Anika Esperanza Designs has established a business banking account with Oregon Community Bank, including a merchant account for accepting credit card payments. Tax advisement is provided by Williams and Associates.

GROWTH STRATEGY

Year One: Establish Anika Esperanza Designs as a sole proprietorship. Focus on brand building/ awareness and generating new business through word-of-mouth referrals. Establish a presence on the online marketplace, Etsy. Generate gross sales of $45,000 (40 percent from custom embroidery, 35 percent from custom patterns, and 25 percent from general patterns).

Year Two: Establish a dedicated online storefront on the platform, Shopify. Consider incorporating the business as an S-corporation in the state of Illinois. Generate gross sales of $55,000 (45 percent from custom embroidery, 40 percent from custom patterns, and 15 percent from general patterns).

Year Three: Begin investigating the use of independent contractors who can function as extenders to increase the business' capacity for custom embroidery work. Generate gross sales of $65,000. (50 percent from custom embroidery, 45 percent from custom patterns, and 5 percent from general patterns).

MARKETING & SALES

Anika Esperanza Designs will use a number of key marketing tactics to promote the business, including:

1. Online sales via the arts and crafts marketplace, Etsy.

2. A media relations strategy positioning Anika Esperanza as a source for magazine and blog articles focused on gift ideas for weddings, genealogy/family history, and specific occupations (e.g., police, fire, nursing, etc.).

3. An engaging Web site created on the e-commerce platform, Shopify.

4. A unique brand identity for Anika Esperanza Designs, helping the business to stand out in a crowded marketplace.

5. An online mailing list that will enable Anika Esperanza to stay visible with customers and encourage repeat business.

6. A referral program, offering a $10 discount to customers who refer someone else.

7. A presence on the social media platforms Instagram and Facebook.

8. Case studies that tell the story of select cross-stitch creations, which can be shared via Anika Esperanza Designs' Web site and social media channels.

9. A dedicated blog for Anika Esperanza Designs, as well as interviews/guest contributions to other blogs in the arts and crafts field.

10. Participation in select local, regional, and national craft shows, to create word-of-mouth buzz.

11. Development of an online portfolio that showcases examples of different patterns and embroidery work from Anika Esperanza Designs.

FINANCIAL ANALYSIS

After carefully considering several factors, including the number of overall (custom and general) patterns that she can realistically produce in a given year, the amount of passive income generated from the sale of general patterns, and her capacity for producing custom embroidery work, Anika Esperanza has established conservative sales targets for her business' first three years of operations:

- 2018: $45,000

- 2019: $55,000

- 2020: $65,000

SWOT ANALYSIS

Strengths: Anika Esperanza Designs will produce patterns and embroidery pieces that are creative and highly customized, yet simplistic enough that efficiency and production can be maximized.

Weaknesses: The owner must devote time to both production and administrative/business tasks, which may impact her availability/capacity if she is not efficient.

Opportunities: By establishing a strong presence within niche markets, Anika Esperanza Designs has the opportunity to gain an edge over competitors that focus on more general themes.

Threats: During difficult economic times, the business will be at risk because its products are discretionary in nature. In addition, Anika Esperanza is the only source of production, which may put the business at financial risk in the event of a lengthy illness or injury.

Cupcake Studio Business

Sweet Street LLC

2158 McHenry Avenue, SW
Miller Creek, PA 15004

Paul Greenland

Sweet Street LLC is a home-based cupcake studio with significant growth potential.

EXECUTIVE SUMMARY

Sweet Street LLC is a home-based cupcake studio. The business has been established by Jessica Streeter, who began baking cupcakes for fun and enjoyment at a young age when she learned the art from her grandmother. After sharpening her skills through a series of continuing education classes at a local community college and experimenting with recipes and new decorating techniques, Streeter began baking cupcakes for family and friends as a way of earning extra income while pursuing a degree in business administration. To her surprise, she quickly experienced demand that exceeded the capacity of a side business. To capitalize on this demand, and significant profit potential, Streeter established Sweet Street LLC as a formal part time, home-based business that she will slowly transition into a full-time enterprise.

MARKET ANALYSIS

Market Overview

Sweet Street is located in the Philadelphia suburb of Miller Creek, Pennsylvania, which has a thriving service economy and is home to many businesses and organizations. Specifically, the community included 2,473 business establishments in 2018.

Target Markets

Like cupcakes, cupcake businesses come in many varieties. Because she already has several existing business customers that order cupcakes on a regular basis, Jessica Streeter has decided to concentrate her marketing efforts on delivering cupcakes to businesses and organizations who order treats for special events, meetings, and gift giving.

The owner has classified key prospective customers as follows:

- Advertising Agencies (7)

- Health & Medical Service Providers (42)

- Legal Services (44)

- Membership Organizations (86)

- Professional Services (22)

In particular, Jessica Streeter has identified the following organizations as top prospects, and will make them a special focus of Sweet Street's sales and marketing efforts:

- Damien Engineering Services Inc.

- Engine Creative Co.

- Lane Enterprises Inc.

- Law Offices of Smith & Wakefield

- Lombardi Business Consulting Inc.

- Masters Insurance

- Miller Creek Chiropractic Care

- Miller Creek Community Hospital

- Mitchell & Anderson LP

- Nicholas Sign Co.

- RightWay Manufacturing Co.

- Thomas Financial Services LLC

Competition

Although several cupcake businesses operate in the suburban Philadelphia market, including Cupcake Heaven, Cupcakes by Sarah, and Miller Creek Bakery, Sweet Street will differentiate itself from the competition by focusing on business customers and their unique needs. For example, Jessica Streeter is especially skilled at reproducing corporate logos on cupcakes. This has created considerable buzz around Miller Creek, leading to several significant corporate orders. Additionally, the business will use its status as a home-based operation as a competitive advantage, allowing it to minimize the substantial overhead costs incurred by many competitors. By renting commercial kitchen space (described in the Operations section of this plan), Sweet Street has the option to quickly scale up its production capabilities when large orders are received.

PRODUCTS

Sweet Street makes cupcakes based on the recipes of Jessica Streeter, most of which are inspired by her grandmother's wildly popular recipes. She has perfected these over the years, adding her own unique selections of frostings that can be customized with unique designs (e.g., logos, phrases, images, etc.) based on a client's desires.

Flavors

Sweet Street offers cupcakes in the following flavors:

- Banana Split

- Birthday Cake

- Blueberry Lemonade

- Butterfinger

- Cannoli

- Chocolate
- Chocolate Chip Cookie Dough
- Chocolate Crunch
- Chocolate Toffee
- French Toast
- Mocha
- Peanut Butter
- Rainbow Sherbet
- Red Velvet
- Root Beer Float
- Strawberry
- Vanilla
- White Chocolate

Organic and gluten-free options are available upon request. Additional charges apply based on cost of ingredients.

Cost

The following pricing structure has been established for Sweet Street's cupcakes:

- Price per cupcake: $2.85 (six-cupcake minimum)
- Price per dozen: $33.00

All prices include free delivery within a five-mile radius of Miller Creek.

OPERATIONS

Location

Jessica Streeter will operate Sweet Street from her parents' home, located at 2158 McHenry Avenue, SW, in Miller Creek. Additionally, she has negotiated use of commercial kitchen space at Miller Creek Baptist Church for the production of large orders. The church has allowed her to rent the space for a very competitive fee in exchange for a deep discount on cupcakes for church functions and events. The arrangement has the added advantage of providing Jessica Streeter with exposure to members of the congregation, who likely will place their own individual cupcake orders or recommend her business to others.

Business Structure

Sweet Street is organized as a limited liability company (LLC), which provides the owner with certain liability protections without the complexity of forming a corporation. Jessica Streeter has the option to incorporate her business later if desired. She utilized a popular online legal document service to establish her LLC as cost-effectively as possible.

Equipment

To keep overhead costs low, Jessica Streeter has purchased a variety of bakeware from a local resale shop (cupcake pans, spatulas, spoons, mixing bowls, etc.). This has allowed her to expand her existing inventory of baking equipment, which includes an electric mixer, at a minimal cost.

Ingredients

Depending on the specific recipe, Sweet Street will utilize some or all of the following ingredients when producing cupcakes:

- Frosting
- Cake Mix
- Cream
- Baking cups
- Sugar
- Flour
- Eggs
- Oil

Jessica Streeter will begin operations by purchasing ingredients in bulk from a local warehouse club. She also will explore opportunities to purchase ingredients at wholesale from a national supplier. Streeter will purchase some ingredients from local sources.

Product Labeling

Sweet Street will list all ingredients directly on its bakery boxes. This is essential to protect individuals with food allergies.

Licensure

Although many states require cupcake businesses to operate from a commercial kitchen, the Commonwealth of Pennsylvania allows for the operation of home-based bakeries. Sweet Street will adhere to all guidelines established by the Pennsylvania Department of Agriculture, and will be subject to related licensure and inspection requirements.

Insurance

A liability policy has been obtained from a local insurance company in Miller Creek.

PERSONNEL

Jessica Streeter

Sweet Street LLC is a home-based cupcake studio. The business has been established by Jessica Streeter, who began baking cupcakes for fun and enjoyment at a young age when she learned the art from her grandmother. After sharpening her skills through a series of continuing education classes at a local community college and experimenting with recipes and new decorating techniques, Streeter began baking cupcakes for family and friends as a way of earning extra income while pursuing a degree in business administration. Currently a sophomore at the University of Pennsylvania, Streeter plans to gain valuable real-world business experience by operating Sweet Street, which eventually will become a full-time enterprise operating within its own dedicated space.

During the first three years of operations, Jessica will pay herself a salary of $15 per hour. Profits will be reinvested into the business, providing capital for eventual expansion.

Professional & Advisory Support

Sweet Street has established a business banking account with Miller Creek Bank, including a merchant account for accepting credit card payments. Tax advisement is provided by Paulson & McCloskey.

GROWTH STRATEGY

Year One: Begin operations with a focus on the business/organizational market. Concentrate on growing through word-of-mouth and social media (especially on Facebook and LinkedIn). Devote 750 hours to production (15 hours/week). Produce 1,500 dozen cupcakes, generating gross sales of $49,500.

Year Two: Focus on developing new recipes and maintaining exceptional quality and customer service. Continue to build the brand through word-of-mouth promotion and social media marketing. Devote 1,000 hours to production (20 hours/week). Produce 2,000 dozen cupcakes, generating gross sales of $66,000.

Year Three: Transition to full-time operations. Devote 1,500 hours to production (30 hours/week). Produce 3,000 dozen cupcakes, generating gross sales of $99,000. Enhance existing word-of-mouth/social media marketing with paid online advertising, as well as advertisements on local business Web sites. Begin searching for a dedicated facility for the business (relocate in year four) and making preparations to hire 1-2 additional staff people.

MARKETING & SALES

Sweet Street has developed a marketing strategy that includes the following main tactics:

1. Social media promotion/engagement, namely on Facebook, Instagram, and LinkedIn.

2. Word-of-mouth marketing, with 10 percent discounts provided to existing customers who make referrals to family, friends, and colleagues.

3. Publication of an online profile in *Miller Creek Today*, an online business directory maintained by the Miller Creek Chamber of Commerce.

4. Free cupcake samples to prospective customers, along with a one-time 15 percent discount off their first order.

5. A simple Web site with online ordering options, a listing of available cupcake flavors, and special online-only discounts.

6. A unique brand identity/logo, enabling Sweet Street to stand out in the local market.

7. Product packaging featuring the Sweet Street brand and contact information.

FINANCIAL ANALYSIS

Jessica Streeter has calculated base production costs for the business' cupcakes, which she can make at a rate of two dozen per hour:

Production Costs (per dozen)

Labor ($15/hour)	$ 7.50
Utilities	$ 1.00
Ingredients	$ 5.00
Total cost	**$13,50**

Based on a retail price of $33 per dozen, Streeter anticipates that she will generate a net profit of $19.50 per dozen. According to the production estimates outlined in the Growth Strategy section of this plan, Streeter has prepared the following basic sales projections:

	2018	2019	2020
Gross sales	$49,500	$66,000	$99,000
Profit	$29,250	$39,000	$58,500

Sales Forecast

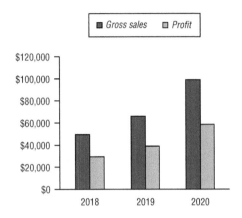

Following Sweet Street's first three years of operations, Jessica Streeter estimates that the business will have generated profits of $126,750. After taxes and basic expenses (packaging, marketing, etc.) of $42,900, this will leave $83,850 that can be used for expansion with the business transitioning to a dedicated location in year four.

DIY Automotive Repair Business

Gary's Garage Club Inc.

2267 Stevens Ave.
Louisville, KY 40202

Paul Greenland

Gary's Garage Club Inc. is a DIY automotive repair and education center located in Louisville, Kentucky.

EXECUTIVE SUMMARY

Gary's Garage Club Inc. is a DIY automotive repair and education center located in Louisville, Kentucky. The business provides both urban and suburban residents with access to fully-equipped automotive service bays on an hourly or daily basis. Customers can take advantage of a membership option that provides special perks and access to the facility at lower rates.

Gary's Garage Club Inc. is being established by Gary Lewis, an ASE-certified mechanic who operated Gary's Automotive Service in Louisville for more than 35 years. Instead of pursuing a traditional retirement, Lewis sold Gary's Automotive Service and is using a portion of the proceeds to establish Gary's Garage Club, which is located in space once occupied by a Kmart Automotive Center.

INDUSTRY ANALYSIS

Often associated with home repair and renovation, the do-it-yourself (DIY) concept transcends many other categories, including automotive repair. In recent years, DIY automotive repair centers have begun to appear in several urban markets, providing residents with limited work/tool storage space with a place to work on their vehicles. The concept is popular among a variety of target markets, including individuals with little or no automotive repair experience who desire to learn and build their skill base, as well as experienced car enthusiasts who either perform their own maintenance on everyday vehicles or restore classic cars.

MARKET ANALYSIS

Market Overview

According to research conducted by the owner at his public library, Louisville, Kentucky, had a population of 1.77 million people in 2017 (701,130 households).

Data from Experian Marketing Solutions indicated that Louisville residents owned 1.37 million vehicles (an average of two per household) in 2017. On a percentage basis, ownership broke down as follows:

- 0 Vehicles (7.44%)
- 1 Vehicle (33.23%)
- 2 Vehicles (38.06%)
- 3 Vehicles (14.96%)
- 4 Vehicles (4.58%)
- 5+ Vehicles (1.73%)

On average, total household automotive and transportation expenditures in Louisville totaled $12,069 in 2017. Vehicle repair and maintenance expenditures averaged $828, the third-largest category behind vehicle insurance ($1,020) and gasoline and motor oil ($2,046). By 2022, vehicle repair and maintenance expenditures were expected to average $955 per household.

Annual average household vehicle maintenance and repair expenditures, specifically, broke down as follows:

- Tires ($132)
- Oil Change & Lube ($93)
- Parts, Equipment & Accessories ($48)
- Motor Tune-ups ($38)
- Bodywork and Painting ($30)
- Auto Repair Service ($37)
- Front End Alignment & Balancing ($29)
- Shock Absorbers ($12)
- Coolant & Other Fluids ($8)

Competition

Because Gary's Garage Club is unique in the local market, it does not yet have any direct competitors. Indirectly, the business competes against automotive repair shops that are an alternative to DIY automotive repair, including:

- New Car Dealerships
- Chain Stores with Automotive Repair Facilities
- Gas Stations
- Quick Lube Centers
- Tire Stores

Examples of businesses in these categories include Aamco, Discount Tire, Firestone, Goodyear, Jiffy Lube, Kmart, Meineke, Midas, NAPA Auto Parts, and Walmart.

SERVICES

Gary's Garage Club provides customers with access to the tools and space they need to perform their own automotive maintenance and repairs. The business has four automotive workstations (two lift bays and two flat bays), which may be rented per hour or per day (hourly rentals are billed in 30-minute increments, with a 30-minute minimum). Each workspace is equipped with a complete selection of air tools and hand tools. Additionally, monitors with Internet connectivity are available for customers to stream how-to videos or access online repair manuals. Through arrangements with automotive parts distributors, customers may choose to order the parts they need and have them delivered directly to Gary's Garage Club. Alternatively, they may bring their own parts.

Via the ExpertAdvantage service, either Gary Lewis or the business' staff mechanic is available to provide customers with coaching and assistance for an additional fee.

Gary's Garage Club also provides educational experiences for Louisville area residents in the form of several basic how-to workshops called Automotive Fundamentals, including:

- Changing Your Oil

- Changing Your Tires

- Rotating Your Tires

- Changing Your Brakes (Pads & Rotors)

OPERATIONS

Location

Gary's Garage Club is located in space formerly occupied by a Kmart Automotive Center, which was vacated by the retailer. The majority of the former Kmart store has been occupied by a self-storage business. However, a portion of the space is still available for lease. This provides Gary's Garage Club with an option to occupy additional space and offer indoor vehicle storage (ideal for automotive enthusiasts working on classic cars) for an additional fee.

Hours

Gary's Garage Club will operate from 12 p.m. to 9 p.m., Monday through Friday, and 9 a.m. to 9 p.m. on Saturdays and Sundays.

Pricing

Gary's Garage Club has established the following workstation rental rates:

- Lift Bay ($40/hour; $300/day)

- Flat Bay ($30/hour; $225/day)

- ExpertAdvantage ($30/hour)

In addition to workstation rentals, Gary's Garage Club also has a limited selection of specialty tools and equipment available (fee schedule available upon request).

The business will charge $20/person for access to its Automotive Fundamentals workshops.

Memberships, available at an annual rate of $350, provide members with a 25 percent discount on all rental services, 35 percent off Automotive Fundamentals workshops, 2 hours of ExpertAdvantage assistance, and access to The Tool Crib, a private lounge space with access to complimentary bottled water, coffee, snacks, and a kitchenette space equipped with a refrigerator and microwave.

PERSONNEL

Gary Lewis, Owner

Gary's Garage Club Inc. is being established by Gary Lewis, an ASE-certified mechanic who operated Gary's Automotive Service in Louisville for more than 35 years. Instead of pursuing a traditional retirement, Lewis sold Gary's Automotive Service and is using a portion of the proceeds to establish Gary's Garage Club. Lewis' idea to establish this innovative business originated while operating Gary's Automotive. Twice per month, Lewis operated an automotive repair ministry on Tuesday evenings, allowing members of his church to repair donated automobiles and provide them to disadvantaged people in the community. Many of the volunteers in this program had no automotive repair skills, providing Gary with opportunities to teach and train them. During the process, Gary discovered that he had a knack for teaching others the ABCs of automotive repair. Additionally, he enjoyed serving as an expert resource for those who already had foundational automotive repair skills.

Staff

In addition to owner Gary Lewis, Gary's Garage Club will employ one ASE-certified mechanic who will assist with management duties and be on-hand to provide services for customers desiring ExpertAdvantage service. Additionally, the business will employ a receptionist who will answer phones, answer customer inquiries, register customers for classes, book automotive workstation rentals, and perform other duties as assigned.

Professional & Advisory Support

Gary's Garage Club has established a business banking account with Louisville Corners Credit Union, including a merchant account for accepting credit card payments. Tax advisement is provided by Michael Evans Tax Service.

GROWTH STRATEGY

Year One: Establish Gary's Garage Club in the Louisville, Kentucky, market. Secure 150 annual memberships and use 75 percent of total capacity for hourly/daily workstation rentals. Generate a net profit of $8,167 on gross revenue of $206,500.

Year Two: Begin exploring educational relationships with area public/private schools that do not already have vocational training programs. Secure 200 annual memberships and use 80 percent of total capacity for hourly/daily workstation rentals. Generate a net profit of $33,572 on gross revenue of $240,500.

Year Three: Evaluate opportunities for additional services/revenue streams, such as on-site indoor vehicle storage. Secure 300 annual memberships and use 85 percent of total capacity for hourly/daily workstation rentals. Generate a net profit of $69,477 on gross revenue of $285,500.

MARKETING & SALES

Gary's Garage Club has developed a marketing strategy that includes the following tactics:

1. A unique brand identity/logo for the business, developed in partnership with a local graphic designer.

2. A coupon promotion good for $5 off any Automotive Fundamentals class and 15 percent off an hourly automotive workstation rental. This coupon will be distributed in a local coupon pack that is distributed to households in the Louisville, Kentucky, area. Additionally, Gary's Garage Club will

offer this and other discounts on its Web site and social media outlets, in exchange for joining the company's mailing list.

3. A presence on social media outlets, including Facebook, Twitter, and YouTube.

4. A monthly direct-mail program to (1) car owners in a 25-mile radius surrounding the business and (2) new movers (e.g., individuals who have recently located to the area). The business has identified a reputable broker that can provide mailing list data (including information regarding vehicle ownership) along with a local mailing service to handle the mailings.

5. A Web site with complete details about Gary's Garage Club, including video clips and photos. The site will include details regarding the business' services, policies, and membership options, along with a bio of owner Gary Lewis.

6. A bi-monthly blog, written by Gary Lewis, offering basic automotive repair tips.

7. Eye-catching exterior signage to attract area consumers.

8. Paid advertising segments on local TV network affiliates, allowing Gary Lewis the opportunity to provide brief automotive maintenance and repair advice to the public while promoting Gary's Garage Club.

9. Vehicle graphics (a vinyl vehicle wrap) on Gary Lewis' vehicle, providing the business with free mobile advertising.

FINANCIAL ANALYSIS

Gary's Garage Club has prepared a complete set of pro forma financial statements, which are available upon request. Following are key highlights.

Startup Costs

Following is an overview of the business' expected startup costs:

Office Equipment

Alarm Equipment—$1,200

Cash Register—$450

Coffee Machine—$75

Deposit for Oxygen Tank—$150

Fax Machine—$374

Fire Extinguishers—$345

Incorporation—$1,380

Lounge & Office Furniture—$1,500

Phone System—$2,013

Safe—$400

Signage—$1,570

TOTAL—$9,456

Shop Equipment

Air Compressor—$2,300

Alignment Machine (wireless)—$11,500

Anti-Freeze Drum Cradle—$102

Arbor Press—$765

Battery Charger—$805

Bearing Packer—$403

Catch Pan—$17

Drain Pan—$28

Exhaust Analyzer—$4,485

Exhaust Hoses—$236

Lab Scope—$2,478

Oil Dispenser—$173

Parts Washer—$518

R134 Air-Conditioning Machine—$6,900

Strut Compressor—$874

Tall Jack Stand—$144

Tire Changer/Wheel Balancer—$2,760

Tire Spreader—$86

Tire Tank—$58

Trans Jack—$431

Volt Amp Tester—$518

Waste Oil Tank—$173

TOTAL—$51,931

Tool Sets

Four complete automotive tool sets, containing a wide variety of basic and specialized hand tools and diagnostic tools (420 pieces), will be purchased from a leading manufacturer at a cost of $5,150 each ($20,600). Additionally, four sets of common pneumatic power tools and impact socket sets/extensions (150 pieces) will be purchased for $3,400/each ($13,600). A complete inventory breakdown of these tools is available upon request. Total tool purchase costs will be $34,200.

Revenue & Expenses

	2018	2019	2020
Revenue			
Memberships	$ 52,500	$ 70,000	$105,000
Classes	$ 60,000	$ 70,000	$ 80,000
Hourly rentals	$ 94,000	$100,500	$100,500
	$206,500	**$240,500**	**$285,500**
Expenses			
Service expenses			
Dumpster	$ 720	$ 730	$ 740
Floor dry	$ 80	$ 85	$ 90
Floor soap	$ 200	$ 210	$ 220
Hand soap	$ 150	$ 160	$ 170
Shop towels	$ 500	$ 510	$ 520
Tire removal	$ 600	$ 610	$ 620
Waste anti-freeze removal	$ 185	$ 200	$ 215
Waste oil filters removal	$ 350	$ 375	$ 400
Waste oil removal	$ 600	$ 650	$ 675
Welding supplies	$ 800	$ 850	$ 900
Sub-total	**$ 4,185**	**$ 4,380**	**$ 4,550**
Office expenses			
Accountant	$ 1,950	$ 2,000	$ 2,250
Advertising	$ 14,500	$ 15,500	$ 16,500
Alarm service	$ 500	$ 500	$ 500
Miscellaneous	$ 1,500	$ 1,500	$ 1,500
Liability insurance	$ 3,500	$ 3,750	$ 4,000
Property lease	$ 25,500	$ 25,500	$ 25,500
Business loan	$ 11,698	$ 11,698	$ 11,698
Telephone	$ 1,500	$ 1,600	$ 1,700
Utilities	$ 3,500	$ 4,000	$ 4,500
Sub-total	**$ 64,148**	**$ 66,048**	**$ 68,148**
Salaries expenses			
Gary Lewis	$ 60,000	$ 63,000	$ 66,150
Ase mechanic	$ 45,000	$ 47,250	$ 49,613
Receptionist	$ 25,000	$ 26,250	$ 27,563
Sub-total	**$130,000**	**$136,500**	**$143,325**
Total expenses	**$198,333**	**$206,928**	**$216,023**
Net profit	**$ 8,167**	**$ 33,572**	**$ 69,477**

Financing

Gary Lewis will cover startup costs for Gary's Garage Club, using some of the proceeds from the sale of his automotive repair business. He is seeking a loan of $50,000 (60-month term, 6.35% interest) to cover operational costs.

DIY Project Plan Business

PlanPerfect Inc.

Rural Route 23
Schenectady, NY 12307

Paul Greenland

PlanPerfect Inc. develops and sells downloadable DIY project plans with step-by-step video and/or printed instructions.

EXECUTIVE SUMMARY

PlanPerfect Inc. develops and sells downloadable DIY project plans with step-by-step video and/or printed instructions. The business is being established by the husband-and-wife team of Larry and Juliet Swanson. Larry is an experienced general contractor and woodworker. A DIY enthusiast with a flair for home decoration and organization, Juliet has a professional background in e-commerce and marketing. After extensive planning and research, including small business management training at a local community college, the Swansons are ready to launch a part-time enterprise with full-time potential.

MARKET ANALYSIS

Overview

Toward the end of the decade, the DIY market was experiencing rapid growth thanks to programming on entertainment networks such as HGTV (Home & Garden Television), blogs, social media channels such as Pinterest, and online marketplaces like Etsy, which originated with the sale of a single coin purse in 2005 and evolved into a multi-billion-dollar enterprise within 10 years.

According to data from Statistica, the value of the global DIY market was expected to reach $40.7 billion in 2017 and $43.7 billion in 2018. This was a substantial increase from an estimated $35.0 billion in 2015. The researcher indicated that baby boomers, in particular, were an important market for home improvement projects, specifically. In 2016 sales of existing homes, which are prime candidates for home improvement projects, reached their highest levels since the Great Recession, according to a 2017 report from Euromonitor International.

Geographic Focus

As an online business, PlanPerfect will market plans to DIY enthusiasts worldwide.

Competition & Differentials

Larry and Juliet Swanson realize that many free DIY plans are available online. PlanPerfect will stand out from the competition by offering extremely detailed content that is essentially foolproof. The owners will go to great lengths to ensure that their photography, videography, instructions, and schematics are of the highest quality. PlanPerfect will offer all of its customers a 90-day money-back guarantee if they are not completely satisfied with instructional content. To ensure complete satisfaction, the Swansons also will engage with customers who have questions or concerns regarding any of PlanPerfect's plans.

PRODUCTS

PlanPerfect's mission is to develop high-quality instructional DIY plans in three main categories (home decoration, storage & organization, and home-improvement) that are creative and unique. For organization and home improvement projects, the company will focus on offering practical, but innovative solutions to everyday problems. The following list provides a snapshot of the categories and subcategories in which PlanPerfect will offer instructional content:

Home Decoration

- Seasonal
- Holiday
- Rustic Chic
- Country Chic

Storage & Organization

- Kitchen
- Garage
- Bedroom
- Bathroom
- Workshop
- Laundry Room

Home Improvement

- Maintenance and Repair
- Roofing
- Concrete and Masonry
- Painting
- Fences
- Plumbing
- Electrical
- Windows & Doors

OPERATIONS

Location

PlanPerfect will operate from the home of Larry and Juliet Swanson. The owners have designated space on their rural property for business operations, including an area in their basement, as well as a large outbuilding that is suitable for producing home-improvement-related content.

Business Structure

The Swansons have structured their new business as an S Corporation in the state of New York, which offers certain liability and tax advantages. The owners established their corporation in partnership with a local business attorney.

Content Development Process

The Swansons will begin operations with a solid foundation of DIY plans. Leading up to the formation of PlanPerfect, the owners spent the previous 12 months developing 45 different plans (15 in each category), based on the most popular projects they have done personally over the years. While developing these plans, the Swansons gained valuable experience using photography, videography, and architectural software, and developed and refined an effective plan/content development process, which is outlined below.

The Swansons realize that research and development will be the lifeblood of their enterprise. For PlanPerfect to be successful, the owners will need to build upon their existing content library and produce a steady stream of new project plans that inspire customers, generate positive word-of-mouth, and encourage repeat business.

The owners will take the following approach when developing new project plans:

1. *Concepting*: Larry and Juliet Swanson will hold regular brainstorming sessions to develop new project plan ideas in each of the business' core categories.

2. *Feedback*: Each month, the Swansons will develop a shortlist of new products. A brief description of each project, along with 2-3 conceptual sketches/renderings, will be produced and shared with PlanPerfect's Plan Development Squad (a group of 10 DIY enthusiasts in the owners' local market who have agreed to serve as a sounding board in exchange for free access to the company's DIY content). Using an online polling tool, the Plan Development Squad will help the owners determine which new plan ideas will be developed.

3. *Development*: Once new project plan ideas have been agreed upon, the Swansons will move forward with the development process. This step typically will involve the creation of rough draft plans, which the owners will then follow to actually build a rough prototype of the featured item/solution. After going through the prototyping step, enhancements and adjustments will be made, leading to the creation of a more detailed set of plans. The owners will then build a final prototype, documenting the process with photography and videography.

4. *Production*: After the owners have verified the reliability of their test plans, a final set of project plans will be developed using a popular architectural software application. Instructional videos, combining narration, still photography, and videography, will be produced to accompany the instructional plans. All of the content will then be uploaded to PlanPerfect's online forum for review by the Plan Development Squad, which will provide criticism and feedback within two weeks. Using this feedback, the owners will make final tweaks and adjustments to all plan materials.

5. *Rollout*: On a monthly basis, PlanPerfect will introduce 4-6 new projects on their site, which will be available for online purchase.

On average, the Swansons estimate that each project, from concept to rollout, will take approximately 40 hours of development time.

Technology Platform

PlanPerfect's owners developed their own Web site for the business using a popular online service that offers customizable templates and a scalable hosting plan based on their unique needs (e.g., number of pages, bandwidth, etc.). Because PlanPerfect focuses exclusively on the sale of digital goods, the owners knew that they needed to have a reliable solution for managing the entire content hosting/sales process. The owners have selected a reputable online partner that will host all of their downloadable DIY plan content and handle multiple forms of payment in various global currencies.

Equipment

The Swanson's have invested in the following equipment, which is necessary for routine operations and content development purposes:

Dell Laptops (2): $1,975

Microsoft Surface Tablets (2): $2,250

Office 365 Subscription: $150

Camera Equipment:

—Sony HXR-MC2500 Shoulder Mount AVCHD Camcorder: $1,160

—0.5x Hi-Res Wide Angle Lens: $150

—Hi-Res 2X Telephoto Lens: $150

—3 Piece Multicoated Filter Kit: $120

—HDFX 32GB Ultra High Speed SDHC SD Card: $120

—HDFX High Speed SD/ Micro SD Card Reader: $10

—Photo & Video Tripod: $150

—HDMI Cable: $60

—Led Ultra Bright Video Light: $70

—Deluxe Camera Starter Kit: $20

—Large Deluxe Case HDDFX: $50

Total startup equipment cost: $6,435

PERSONNEL

Larry and Juliet Swanson

PlanPerfect is being established by the husband-and-wife team of Larry and Juliet Swanson. Larry is an experienced general contractor and woodworker. A DIY enthusiast with a flair for home decoration and organization, Juliet has e-commerce and marketing experience, following a seven-year career with the leading online retailer, PowerStore. After extensive planning and research, including small business management training at a local community college, the Swansons are ready to launch their new enterprise.

For years, Larry and Juliet have enjoyed working together on projects in their own home. Juliet has a gift for envisioning possibilities, which Larry helps to translate into real-world creations. Based on Juliet's creative vision, Larry is adept at choosing the right materials and sketching out plans for a variety of DIY projects. The results, which Juliet shares on her Facebook page, typically receive many "likes" and positive comments. More often than not, the Swansons receive requests for instructions from friends who are interested in tackling similar projects, along with lots of questions. This phenomenon was the inspiration to establish PlanPerfect as a dedicated part-time business with full-time potential.

Plan Development Squad

PlanPerfect will rely upon a core group of 10 DIY enthusiast volunteers who have agreed to provide feedback on new projects/concepts in exchange for free access to the company's DIY content.

Professional & Advisory Support

PlanPerfect has established a business banking account with Market Avenue Bank, including a merchant account for accepting credit card payments. Tax advisement is provided by Schenectady Tax Advisory.

GROWTH STRATEGY

Year One: Begin operations part-time, beginning with a base of 45 different downloadable DIY project plans in three categories (Home Decoration, Storage & Organization, and Home Improvement). Generate net income of $11,870 on gross revenue of $53,820.

Year Two: Transition to full-time operations. Expand content through the addition of at least 48 new DIY plans, equally divided among the Home Decoration, Storage & Organization, and Home Improvement categories, bringing the company's total library to 93 plans. Generate net income of $16,440 on gross revenue of $107,640.

Year Three: Expand content offerings through the addition of at least 48 new DIY plans, equally divided among the Home Decoration, Storage & Organization, and Home Improvement categories, bringing the company's total library to 141 plans. Generate net income of $17,010 on gross revenues of $161,460.

Following the first three years of operations, the owners will conduct customer research and evaluate sales data to identify the best opportunities for expansion into additional niche/hobby categories (e.g., crafts, sewing, woodworking, etc.).

MARKETING & SALES

PlanPerfect will rely on the following tactics to promote its offerings:

1. A distinctive logo, providing the business with a unique brand identity.

2. A Web site with an extensive gallery of DIY projects that customers can browse by category and order via online payment.

3. A social media strategy that involves a presence on Facebook and Instagram.

4. A DIY blog, where the Swansons will share their insights on topics of interest to customers.

5. Highly targeted online advertising/paid search using Google AdWords.

6. An online DIY newsletter, providing the Swansons with a regular means of communication with current and prospective customers.

FINANCIAL ANALYSIS

Once PlanPerfect gains a base of regular customers and attains a certain level of brand awareness, the owners anticipate that the business will generate substantial revenues from its library of proprietary content, which will generate a significant passive income stream as the Swansons focus on new content development opportunities.

PlanPerfect has prepared a complete set of pro forma financial statements, which are available upon request. Following is a breakdown of projected revenue and expenses for the business' first three years of operations:

	2018	2019	2020
Revenue	**$53,820**	**$107,640**	**$161,460**
Expenses			
Salaries	$20,000	$ 60,000	$100,000
Payroll tax	$ 3,000	$ 9,000	$ 15,000
Insurance	$ 1,550	$ 1,650	$ 1,750
Accounting & legal	$ 1,500	$ 1,600	$ 1,700
Office supplies	$ 450	$ 500	$ 550
Equipment	$ 6,500	$ 3,500	$ 3,500
Marketing & advertising	$ 5,500	$ 10,500	$ 16,500
Service provider fees	$ 2,350	$ 3,350	$ 4,350
Home office deduction	$ 600	$ 600	$ 600
Misc.	$ 500	$ 500	$ 500
Total expenses	**$41,950**	**$ 91,200**	**$144,450**
Net income	**$11,870**	**$ 16,440**	**$ 17,010**

Driving School
Victors Driving School

3365 Washtenaw Ave.
Ann Arbor, MI 48108

Zuzu Enterprises

Victors Driving School offers driving lessons for students of all ages, whether they're just learning to drive or have been driving for years. Our patient, friendly, professional instructors provide comprehensive behind-the-wheel training and are approved by the Road Safety Educators' Association and accredited by the Driving School Association of the Americas.

EXECUTIVE SUMMARY

Victors Driving School offers driving lessons for students of all ages, whether they're just learning to drive or have been driving for years. Our patient, friendly, professional instructors provide comprehensive behind-the-wheel training and are approved by the Road Safety Educators' Association and accredited by the Driving School Association of the Americas.

Victors Driving School features:

- Professional Driving Instructors
- Certified and Licensed
- Competitive Service Rates
- Effective Driver Education Lessons
- Excellent Customer Service
- Fully Insured
- Locally Owned Business
- Open Daily from 9am-9pm

INDUSTRY ANALYSIS

The Automobile Driving Schools Industry consists of firms that primarily offer driving instruction to new drivers and those who have experienced accidents or problems while driving; bus and truck driving are excluded from this industry.

The Automobile Driving Schools Industry currently employs more than 51,000 people at over 9,000 establishments and has an annual payroll of over $1 billion dollars.

The driving school business can be very lucrative due to the fact that it requires minimal capital to start. A successful business can begin with a few reliable vehicles, necessary business licenses and insurance, classroom space, and an experienced and patient instructor. Second-handed vehicles are preferred not only because they are cheaper to purchase and cost less to insure, but because it is less stressful and costly when they get minor dings and dents. The business is also scalable and can easily accommodate expansion as needed and warranted for the customer base.

MARKET ANALYSIS

Market Overview

The population of the city of Ann Arbor is just over 120,000 people, with 15-19-year-olds comprising 11.5 percent of the population. Another 13.5 percent of the market is age 60 or above. All of theses segments are the focus and potential market for the services of Victors Driving School. This equates to approximately 30,000 people in the city that are eligible for and likely to use our driving instruction services.

Competition

There are a total of seven driving schools located within the Ann Arbor metropolitan area. All but one restrict their services to beginning driver's education for new, young drivers. Only one other business offers assessment services for older adults or those with medical conditions that may affect driving, and none offer either corporate defensive driving courses or stick shift training. These additional services will set Victors Driving School apart from the competition and offer a competitive advantage for long-term success.

PRODUCTS/SERVICES

Victors Driving School offers a comprehensive driving program. Classes include:

- Teen Driver's Education Segment One
- Teen Driver's Education Segment Two
- Adult Driving Lessons
- Road Skills Test
- Corporate Defensive Driving Course
- Stick Shift Training
- Professional Driving Skills Assessments

Teen Driver's Education Segment One

Segment One courses provide classroom instruction using the State of Michigan's curriculum focusing on traffic laws, rules, and safety. All students must be 14 years and 8 months old by the first day of class. This class includes:

- 24 hours of classroom instruction
- 6 hours behind-the-wheel driving instruction
- 4 hours observation (viewing others drive)

Teen Driver's Education Segment Two

Segment Two courses are a defensive driving-based class focusing on problems specific to new drivers, road rage/aggressive driving, distractions, problems with alcohol/drugs, and more. Classes run for three (3) consecutive days for two (2) hours per day and provide classroom instruction covering laws of the road and safely. This class:

- Prepares students for the road test

- Prepares new drivers for the challenges of the road

- Includes 6 hours of classroom instruction

Requirements for this class include:

- Student must have received their permit from the Secretary of State a minimum of ninety (90) days before the first day of class.

- Student must provide a driving log showing at least 30 hours of practice driving on or before the first day of class (including a minimum of 2 hours at night).

- Student must show a total of 50 hours of practice driving by the time they schedule a road test (including a minimum of 10 hours at night).

Adult Driving Lessons

Adult driving lessons are intended for those individuals who did not receive training as teenagers. This may include people who didn't have the need or desire to learn to drive earlier or for those who would like to improve their driving skills. People who are new to the country or those who have incurred driving violations or accidents are also eligible for this type of training. Training includes behind-the-wheel instruction and customized programs to fit each client's individual needs. Students can sharpen their skills with one-on-one instruction from our certified driving instructor. Adult Driving Lessons feature:

- Training session tailored to improving where you need it the most.

- Private training session with just yourself and one of our certified instructors.

- Discounted multiple session packages are available.

Road Skills Test

The Road Skills Test is the last step for students before getting their license. We are state approved to give automobile road tests for both teenagers and adults. Requirements for this test include:

Auto Road Tests for Teens

1. A level one license that is 180 days old or older

2. A segment II certificate

3. A signed driving log by your parents that states you have 50 hours of drive time, 10 of them being at night

4. Up-to-date insurance and registration in your car

5. Minor safety vehicle inspection (i.e. brake lights, mirrors, turn signals and horn)

Auto Tests for Adults

1. Your temporary instructor's permit that is 30 days old, but less than 180 days old, or stamped with "Waive 30-day waiting period"

2. Up-to-date insurance and registration

3. Minor safety vehicle inspection (i.e. brake lights, mirrors, turn signals and horn)

Vehicle rentals are available upon request for the Road Skills Test for an additional fee.

Corporate Defensive Driving Course

Some companies may benefit from hiring Victors Driving School to train their employees. The Defensive Driving Course has proven to be an effective solution to:

- Control liability costs associated with work-related vehicle crashes.

- Reduce insurance premiums and fleet repair bills.

- Reduce motor vehicle incident rates.

- Decrease workers' compensation claims.

- Improve productivity by keeping employees safe, both on and off the job.

- Protect your brand by improving public perception of your employees' driving practices.

Employees who complete the training will be motivated to change their behind-the-wheel behaviors and attitudes. Students will learn coping techniques for handling speeding, distracted driving, impaired driving, hazardous traffic conditions, and more. The result will be a responsible driver who better understands the best ways to prevent injury and death while driving a motor vehicle. This course provides key understanding of the skills and techniques needed to avoid collisions, reduce traffic violations and change driver behaviors and attitudes. Employees may also benefit from insurance reduction, ticket dismissal and point reduction in many states.

Stick Shift Training

Driving a vehicle with manual transmission, also known as a stick shift, can be intimidating for many drivers, young and old. Many motorists go through life without owning or ever even driving a stick shift, but it is a good skill to have as these types of vehicles are popular. Once you learn how to do it, and after a little practice, driving a stick shift is fairly easy. It becomes a habit and also becomes, for many, a more exciting and exhilarating way to drive a car or truck.

Training will take place in our parking lot or somewhere else with plenty of space and time for stalls. When students are comfortable accelerating and decelerating while they shift the gears of the vehicle, and they can comfortably start in first, put the car in reverse and back up, and stop and go, they are almost ready for the real road. Stick shift driving experience may also help to become a CDL driver.

Professional Driving Skills Assessments

Behind the wheel evaluations are conducted in one of our specially equipped automobiles or high-tech vans. A clinical pre-driver assessment will be required. Our evaluators are friendly, patient, and knowledgeable. They will do everything possible to assist you with your driving needs.

Professional Driving Skills Assessments generally fall into two categories: driving skills evaluations and clinical driving assessments. A driving skill evaluation includes an in-car evaluation of your driving abilities and a recommendation regarding any further specialized driver's training. Clinical driving assessments are used to identify underlying medical causes of any driving performance deficits and offer ways to address them, so driving remains a safe option.

The comprehensive driving skills evaluation or clinical driving assessment is essential if:

- You have been diagnosed with a medical condition known to impact driving ability (e.g., impaired vision, dementia, diabetes, seizures, sleep disorders, stroke).

- You have experienced a recent increase in near misses or minor crashes (fender benders).

- Friends and/or family have suggested that you may not be fit to drive.

Instructors for the Professional Driving Skills Assessments are Occupational Therapists, Certified Driving Instructors, and Certified Driver Rehabilitation Specialists who have been board certified by Association for Driver Rehabilitation Specialists (ADED).

Requirements for Skills Assessments include:

- A physician's prescription (Physician Statement or Vision Statement).

- Students must be seizure-free for at least 6 months.

- Students must meet state requirements for licensing.

OPERATIONS

Location
Victors Driving School is located at 3365 Washtenaw Ave. in Ann Arbor. The facility is approximately 3,000 square feet and includes a reception area, classroom, and small office. A spacious parking lot is adjacent to the building and includes enough room for parking the company vehicles, client parking, and room for basic instruction.

Hours of Operation
Open daily from 9 a.m. to 9 p.m. Various services are available at different times. For example, most Segment One and Segment Two classes are offered in the late afternoons or evenings to accommodate high school schedules. Corporate Defensive Driving Courses and Professional Driving Skills Assessments are typically scheduled during the day to accommodate business schedules and a less-hectic atmosphere for training. Most road tests are scheduled in the evenings or on weekends to accommodate teenage drivers using their parents' car. Specific schedules and availabilities are noted below.

SCHEDULE AND PRICING

Teen Driver's Education Segment One
Segment One classes typically run for three weeks, with class being held for two hours a day, four days a week. Class times during the school year are generally:

- 2:30 p.m. to 4:30 p.m.

- 5:00 p.m. to 7:00 p.m.

- 8:00 p.m. to 10:00 p.m.

During the summer months, classes may also be offered from:

- 9:00 a.m. to 11:00 a.m.

- 1:00 p.m. to 3:00 p.m.

The cost for Segment One class is $275.

Teen Driver's Education Segment Two
Segment Two classes run consecutively for three days, with two hours of instruction each day. Class times during the school year are generally:

- 2:30 p.m. to 4:30 p.m.

- 5:00 p.m. to 7:00 p.m.

- 8:00 p.m. to 10:00 p.m.

During the summer months, classes may also be offered from:

- 9:00 a.m. to 11:00 a.m.

- 1:00 p.m. to 3:00 p.m.

The cost for Segment Two class is $40.

Adult Driving Lessons

The cost for adult driving lessons varies based on the level and duration of training needed. The rates for this type of training includes:

- $43 for (1) one-hour lesson

- $125 for (3) one-hour lessons

- $229 for (6) one-hour lessons

Lessons are scheduled based on each individual's needs and availability.

Road Skills Test

Victors Driving School also offers road tests and certification for those ready to obtain their license. The cost for this test includes:

- Monday thought Saturday, $40

- Sunday, $45

Rental cars are available for the road test at a cost of $25.

Corporate Defensive Driving Course

Corporate Defensive Driving Courses are quoted on a case-by-case basis, based on employee count and the customized instruction that is predetermined by the client and Victors Driving School.

Stick Shift Training

Stick shift training is offered at the following rates:

- $135 for 1-hour training

- $250 for 2 hours of training

Lessons are scheduled based on each individual's needs and availability.

Professional Driving Skills Assessments

Professional Driving Skills Assessments typically cost $200 for a full assessment, including recommendations for additional training or adaptive devices. Assessment usually lasts for 1 1/2 hours.

Payment

Payment is accepted via cash, checks (corporate and government only; no personal checks), money order, or major credit card.

PERSONNEL

All instructors at Victors Driving School are certified by the State of Michigan and the National Safety Council.

Instructors performing professional driving skills assessments are Occupational Therapists, Certified Driving Instructors, and Certified Driver Rehabilitation Specialists, who have been board certified by Association for Driver Rehabilitation Specialists (ADED).

INSURANCE

Victors Driving School has secured all of the necessary insurance policies for the business. These insurance policies include:

- *Motor Vehicle Insurance*: This type of insurance covers damages or theft of the training vehicles, as well as potential damages to client's vehicles.

- *Approved Driving Instructor Insurance (ADI)*: Driving instructor insurance covers things including negligent tuition, loss of earnings, and personal liability in case the business ever gets sued for compensation. Basically, it covers for anything that poses a threat to your means of livelihood as a driving instructor.

- *Public Liability Insurance*: This covers the business in the eventuality that a member of the public is harmed or suffers a loss due to the activities of the business. Sometimes, accidents and damages are inevitable when training inexperienced drivers, so this type of insurance is essential.

- *Employer's Liability Insurance*: This insurance covers possible negligence on the part of employees.

- *GAP Insurance*: Driving School GAP insurance helps cover for the difference between the valuation amount and the amount outstanding on finance of the company vehicles.

AFFILIATIONS

Victors Driving School is a member of/accredited by the following organizations:

The American Driver and Traffic Safety Education Association (ADTSEA)

The American Occupational Therapy Association (AOTA)

Association of Driver Rehabilitation Specialists

Driving School Association of the Americas

Michigan Driver and Traffic Safety Education Association

National Highway Traffic Safety Administration (NHTSA)

National Mobility Equipment Dealers Association

National Safety Council (NSC)

Road Safety Educators' Association

Factory Tours
Made in Detroit Tours

4803 Harvard Rd.
Detroit, Michigan 48224

Zuzu Enterprises

Made in Detroit Tours is capitalizing on the past and future manufacturing success in Detroit by offering custom factory tours. The business is owned and operated by Amie Duncan.

EXECUTIVE SUMMARY

Factory tours have become extremely popular in the past decade, as more and more people are seeking different and interesting ways to spend their hard-earned vacation dollars. What better place to enjoy a wide variety of factory tours than the Detroit area, known for its rich history in manufacturing and now experiencing a small business and manufacturing revitalization!

Made in Detroit Tours is capitalizing on the past and future manufacturing success in Detroit by offering custom factory tours. Agreements already exist with a number of different businesses to coordinate and provide the tours, with more tours to be added every week.

INDUSTRY ANALYSIS

The tour operator business in Detroit is steadily expanding as more and more people discover the many gems Detroit has to offer. Lonely Planet, one of the largest travel book publishers in the world, named Detroit the second-best city in the world to visit in 2018. This is only one of the the latest national distinctions in a growing list that adds up to significant focus on the city, including an article about the city's many amenities in *The New York Times*.

Competition
Other tour operators in the area utilize bikes, boats, buses, and even feet (walking tours) to explore the food, architecture, and history of the area. Some of our favorite tours include:

- Detroit Rolling Pub—riders provide the horsepower by pedaling this passenger "bike" while enjoying the various sights and attractions of Detroit and a tasty beverage or two.

- Feet on the Street Tours—explores the wonders of Eastern Market.

- Detroit Bus Company—offers tours on buses that are also used to provide free transportation to local kids.

- Motor City Photography Workshops—explores both the architecture and abandoned spaces in Detroit by offering photography trips.
- City Tour Detroit—offers signature walking tours such as See The D, Incredible Journey to Midnight, Notorious 313, Solid Gold Detroit: Soundtrack to the City, and Taste of the Town foodie tours.

All of these are fantastic tours, but none offer what Made in Detroit Tours can—a glimpse into what made the city great before and is helping to make it great once again.

MARKET ANALYSIS

Michigan is the eighth largest state in the United States and the city of Detroit is the 18th largest city. Wayne, Oakland, and Macomb counties are among the largest counties in the United States by population. According to the Bureau of Economic Analysis, the 2016 population in the Detroit Metropolitan Statistical Area was 4,297,617, making it the 14th highest in the United States.

The sheer number of people working, living, and visiting the area make the market for our tours strong. Adding in the business community by offering corporate team building experiences, and our potential client list grows even more.

TOURS

Made in Detroit already has agreements in place to offer and advertise tours for the following factories:

- Better Made Snack Food Company, 10148 Gratiot Ave, Detroit, MI 48213, https://bettermade snackfoods.com/
- Faygo, 3579 Gratiot Ave, Detroit, MI 48207, https://www.faygo.com/
- Ford Rouge Factory, Village Road and Oakwood Boulevard, Dearborn, MI 48120, https://www.the henryford.org/visit/ford-rouge-factory-tour/
- Germack Pistachio Company, 2140 Wilkins St, Detroit, MI 48207, https://www.germack.com/
- Jiffy Mix, 201 W. North Street, Chelsea, MI 48118, http://www.jiffymix.com/index.php/tours/
- Morley Candy Makers and Sanders Candy Factory, 23770 Hall Road (M-59), Clinton Township, MI 48036, https://www.sanderscandy.com/factory-tours
- The Parade Company, 9500 Mt. Elliott, Studio A, Detroit, MI 48211, https://theparade.org/
- Pewabic Pottery, 10125 E Jefferson Ave, Detroit, MI 48214, http://www.pewabic.org/
- Rochester Mills Beer Co. Brewpub, 400 Water Street Suite 101, Rochester, MI 48307, http://www.beercos.com/
- WeatherGard Windows, 14350 W. 8 Mile Rd., Oak Park, MI 48237, https://weathergard.com

A description of each is below.

Better Made Snack Food Company

Although created in 1853, the potato chip did not catch on as a snack food until after World War I. In 1930, two entrepreneurial Detroiters, Cross Moceri and Peter Cipriano, decided they could make a better chip than any on the market and Better Made was born. More than three quarters of a century later, it is firmly established as Detroit's Potato Chip.

Surviving in the snack food business has not been easy. At one time there were 24 potato chip manufacturers in Detroit. By 1999 only one was still in business, earning the Better Made company tremendous regional loyalty. Competing head-to-head with national brands, Better Made relies on quality ingredients and superb freshness. Serious chip connoisseurs can buy their products directly from the factory, just hours old, or have them shipped anywhere in the world.

Many Detroiters have driven by the Better Made plant on Gratiot Avenue and marveled to see full size semi-trailers lifted to the sky; when it comes to efficiently emptying a truck full of potatoes, there is no better way.

Over time Better Made has diversified its product base, offering three different cuts of potato chips—original, wavy, and kettle—in numerous flavors. The plant also makes several types of corn chips, pork rinds, popcorn, pretzels, cheese puffs, and dips and salsas to go with them. They recently became the largest producer of shoestring potatoes in the country.

Better Made prides itself on its commitment to customer satisfaction. It became not only a brand name but a way of doing business. Even in the early days of the company, only the best ingredients and methods were used. At first, production was simple. Burlap bagged, select potatoes were cooked in the best oil available, weighed, and hand packed into crude, greaseless bags. Distribution was chiefly through the company's own store outlets, which later grew into small delivery routes.

Today, Better Made uses 60 million pounds of chip potatoes every year and the entire process is a little more complex. The potatoes are purchased in bulk (45,000 to 85,000 pounds per truck load) and unloaded from delivery trucks, which are lifted by a hydraulic lift. The potatoes are then transported by conveyors to storage bins. As needed, the potatoes are automatically conveyed to the fryers where they are washed, peeled, sliced, and inspected. Next, the potato slices are conveyed to temperature-controlled cookers where only 100 percent cottonseed oil is used. The cooked chips are then lightly salted and automatically advanced by an overhead vibrating conveyor system to automatic packaging machines that weigh, form, fill, and seal the finished bags. The entire process only takes seven minutes from the bin to the bag. Better Made Potato Chips uses all-natural resources and are untouched by human hands from the time the potatoes leave the farm until customers bring the crunchy chips to their mouth.

Tours are available Tuesday through Friday from 9:00 am until 5:00 pm and Saturday from 8:30 am until 4:30 pm.

Faygo

In 1907, Ben and Perry Feigenson started bottling lager beer, mineral water, and soda water. Recent Russian immigrants to Detroit, the brothers were trained as bakers. While packaging their soda water, they began playing around with the idea of creating soft drinks based on their frosting flavors.

Their carbonated soda "pop"—nicknamed because of the sound it made when the lid popped off—was bottled in a small plant on Benton Street. The initial flavors were fruit punch, strawberry, and grape, which they sold fresh from a horse-drawn wagon the day after it was made.

The brothers formed the Feigenson Brothers Bottling Works, and in 1920 changed the name to Feigenson Brothers Company. In a clever marketing move, "Faygo" was adopted as the brand name in 1921. They moved their growing bottle works to Gratiot Avenue in 1935, where Faygo pop is still created today.

The brothers ran the company until the mid-1940s, when they ceded control to their sons. In the 1950s Faygo was sold only in Detroit, Michigan, because it had a limited shelf life. At that time, chemists determined that impurities in the water prevented the pop from staying carbonated. A new water filtration system was installed, improving shelf life to more than a year.

Faygo became popular outside of Michigan in the late 1960s when the company began advertising during televised Detroit Tigers games. Ads featuring the "Faygo Kid" and heartwarming jingles became instantly recognizable and very popular.

In 1985, the Feigenson family sold the Faygo Beverage Inc. to National Beverage Company, based in Florida. National Beverage, which also owns the Shasta soda pop brand, still operates the Detroit bottling works. Many of the employees have worked for Faygo for over 30 years. Today, Faygo comes in over 30 flavors and is sold in many states east of the Mississippi River. The most popular Faygo flavor remains one of the Feigenson brothers' earliest creations: Redpop.

Tours are scheduled on a case-by-case basis.

Ford Rouge Factory

Game-changing technology, sustainable design, and sheer American grit meet at America's greatest manufacturing experience. Immerse yourself in the awe-inspiring scale of the real factory floor where the F-150 is made, and pop the hood on Ford's rich design and manufacturing history during this one-of-a-kind tour. This is innovation on wheels.

Ford Rouge Factory Tour is normally available only as a self-guided tour, but Made in Detroit Tours adds the element of a docent to guide people and answer questions; it also schedules tours only when the Dearborn Truck Plant is actually building vehicles so that participants can see the assembly line in full operation. The seven-part experience that includes:

Legacy Theater

Discover the Rouge Complex's long history of triumphs, tragedies, and innovations, from Henry Ford's pioneering vision of vertical integration to today's sustainable manufacturing, much of it told through rare, never-before-seen historic footage. Theater shows begin every 20 minutes, from 9:20 a.m. until 4:00 p.m. Approximate time: 13 minutes.

Manufacturing Innovation Theater

Experience a multisensory exploration of the vehicle manufacturing process, filled with jaw-dropping special effects, including a 360-degree look at how automobiles are made! Theater seating is limited to 79 guests per show; shows run continuously until 4:00 p.m. and are seated on a first come, first serve basis. Approximate time: 10 minutes.

Observation Deck Tour

Get a bird's-eye view of environmental innovations: the mammoth living roof, naturalized habitat, solar arrays, and energy-saving photovoltaic panels from our 80-foot-high Observation Deck. Variable time: 5-15 minutes.

Assembly Plant Walking Tour

Travel the elevated walkway above the Dearborn Truck Plant's lean and flexible assembly line. Visitors will have the opportunity to view the final assembly process from an elevated walkway. Variable time: 30-45 minutes.

Legacy Gallery

Explore the vehicles made at the Rouge, including the groundbreaking V-8, the classic Thunderbird and the Mustang. See the 20,000,000th Ford, hop in a new F-150, and visit our Factory Store.

Living Laboratory Walking Tour

See sustainable design in action. Discover how natural processes help manage the Rouge's water, soil, and air. This outdoor tour runs May 1 through September 30, weather permitting.

Living Roof

Planted with a drought-resistant groundcover called sedum, the Living Roof spans 454,000 square feet (or 10.4 acres) and it is one of the largest living roofs in the world. Offering many advantages over conventional tar and metal roofs, the sedum plants grow in a four-layer, vegetated mat, rather than in loose soil. The plants collect and filter storm water runoff.

Tours are available Monday through Saturday, 9:30 a.m. to 5 p.m.

Germack Pistachio Company

Like many young enterprises, Germack Pistachio Company started as a family business. In the early 1900s, three brothers, Elias, John, and Frank Germack, emigrated from Syria to New York, where they worked together as wholesale grocers. In 1924, John and Frank moved to Detroit and opened another wholesale operation specializing in imported Turkish pistachios and other Middle Eastern foods.

In 1935 the firm took the name Germack Brothers and moved to a building on Russell Street. The company thrived on the edge of Eastern Market, one of the oldest and largest farmers markets in the country. Their high-quality pistachios, roasted in small batches, distinguished the company internationally. The business was so successful that John moved back to New York in 1939 and bought the Zenobia Nut Company, also a pistachio processor.

Eventually, Frank, Jr. began directing operations at Germack Pistachio Co. and the firm branched out and expanded production. Besides creating some of the finest gourmet nuts available, the staff began drying and selling squash seeds, pumpkin seeds, and various fruits. The company was sold briefly to Acton Corporation, but the Germacks bought it back and retain ownership today.

The Germack Pistachio Co. is credited with being the first to add the famous red coloring to pistachios. Still located in historic Eastern Market, the Germack family continues to prepare nuts the "old school" way—in small batches and according to the roasting methods perfected decades ago by Frank, Sr.

With changing consumer tastes, Germack Pistachio has added over 100 new products, including dried fruits and healthy mixes, in addition to gourmet chocolate covered nuts and special Christmas items. They are also one of the nation's largest producers of squash (pumpkin) and sunflower seeds.

Germack is proud to partner with Detroit's professional sports teams by supplying peanuts for the Tigers, Red Wings, Pistons, and Lions home games. They are a QVC Network vendor and work with various distributors and direct sales partners to service their expanding business. That's a sure formula for becoming a respected household name, not to mention a Detroit snack food superstar.

Tours are scheduled on a case-by-case basis.

JIFFY Mix

Chelsea Milling Company is operated by a family whose roots in the flour milling business date back to the early 1800s. They have been milling flour in Chelsea for over one hundred years. Mabel White Holmes, grandmother of Jiffy President, Howdy S. Holmes, developed and introduced consumers to the first prepared baking mix product, JIFFY Baking Mix, in the spring of 1930.

Chelsea Milling Company is a complete manufacturer. They store wheat, mill wheat into flour, and use that flour for their own mixes. They even make their own "little blue" boxes. The company currently offers 18 JIFFY Mixes. Products are shipped out to all 50 states, as well as some foreign countries through the United States Military. JIFFY is the market share leader in retail prepared muffin mixes and, in addition to their retail products, they produce mixes for the foodservice and institutional markets.

Tours last approximately one and a half hours and consist of an educational and informative video presentation, a product sample, refreshments, and a walk through their packaging plant. Tours are scheduled between the hours of 9:00 a.m. and 2:00 p.m. Monday through Friday.

Morley Candy Makers and Sanders Candy Factory

It all started with a passionate dream and a borrowed barrel of sugar on June 17, 1875. That's the day Fred Sanders Schmidt, commonly known as Fred Sanders, opened his first chocolate shoppe in Detroit.

By the 1940's and 1950's, Sanders products and stores were woven into the lives of Michigan families. Sanders soon became the leading purveyor of confections in the region and started selling directly to national supermarket chains, as well as to other retailers in the area. Eventually, there were more than 57 locations in the Great Lakes Region offering candy, ice cream toppings, and baked goods. These early shoppes were also known for providing light lunches and an assortment of fountain counter specialties including ice cream sodas, hot fudge sundaes, and (the now iconic) Sanders Hot Fudge Cream Puffs.

In 2002, Morley Candy Makers, Inc. purchased the Sanders brand and original recipes, adding to its own rich history dating back to 1919.

Today Morley Candy Makers is the largest producer of chocolates and confections in Michigan and is among the largest in the United States, as well. Each year Morley Candy Makers use over 1,000,000 pounds of their own blend of milk and dark chocolate, as well as eleven other blends, such as sugar-free and ivory chocolate.

The flagship Sanders Chocolate & Ice Cream Shoppe is located inside the chocolate factory and corporate headquarters on Hall Road (M-59) in Clinton Township between Groesbeck Highway and Gratiot Avenue. It's a one-of-a-kind experience filled with real chocolate waterfalls and plenty of seating to stay awhile. You can also watch bakers at work and take a walk down their observation hallway during production hours to see candy makers in action.

The tour includes a video presentation, the factory observation walkway, a visit to their Chocolate & Ice Cream Shoppe, and free chocolate samples. The tour lasts approximately one hour and is scheduled on a case-by-case basis.

The Parade Company

Venture into magical ParadeLand and experience a behind-the-scenes look at America's Thanksgiving Parade presented by Art Van. Learn more about the Parade's fascinating history, explore the 200,000 square-foot storyland of floats, and see how their award-winning artisans bring them to life. Take a journey through their unique creative kingdom, marvel at the world's largest collection of paper mache heads that resemble local icons and famous characters, and view The Parade Company costume shop that warehouses over 3,000 costumes. Designed and created in their Detroit studio, these costumes make a colorful array of characters come to life. Parade Company studios is one the most interactive and family-friendly things to do in Detroit.

Tours are available Monday through Friday from 9 a.m. to 3 p.m. and Saturdays from 9 a.m. to 2 p.m. The tours are a walking guided tour through the 200,000 square foot studio. They are wheelchair and walker friendly, and strollers are always welcome. The tours last approximately one hour.

Pewabic Pottery

Pewabic Pottery was founded in 1903 by Mary Chase Perry (later Mary Chase Perry Stratton) and her partner, Horace Caulkins (developer of the Revelation Kiln), at the height of the Arts & Crafts movement in America. The Pottery's first home was a stable on Alfred Street in Detroit. Four years later, Pewabic Pottery moved to a new facility on East Jefferson designed by architect William Buck Stratton in the Tudor Revival style. In 1991, the building (which still houses the Pottery) and its contents were designated a National Historic Landmark and today is Michigan's only historic pottery.

Under the direction of Mary Chase Perry Stratton, Pewabic Pottery produced nationally renowned vessels, tiles, and architectural ornamentation for public and private installations and later, when the Depression reduced the demand for costlier wares, ceramic jewelry featuring Pewabic's unique iridescent glazes. Works fabricated by Pewabic Pottery can be seen throughout the United States in such places as the National Shrine of the Immaculate Conception in Washington, D.C., the Nebraska State Capitol, the Science Building at Rice University in Houston, and the Herald Square installation commissioned by the New York Metro Transit Authority.

Stratton is a member of the Michigan's Women Hall of Fame. In Michigan, Pewabic installations can be found in countless churches (including Christ Church at Cranbrook, Holy Redeemer Church, and St. Paul Cathedral in Detroit), schools, commercial buildings, and public facilities (such as Detroit's Guardian Building, Northwest Terminal, the Detroit Public Library, and Comerica Ballpark,) public spaces (Detroit People Mover Stations) and private residences (particularly in Detroit's Indian Village and nearby Bloomfield Hills and Grosse Pointe.) Pewabic art pottery can also be found in many private and public collections including the Detroit Institute of Arts, the Shedd Aquarium in Chicago, and the Freer Gallery at the Smithsonian Institution in Washington, D.C.

Guided tours are docent-led and will take you through Pewabic's storied history beginning with its founding. In addition to its history, you will go behind the scenes in their fabrication space to see staff pressing tiles, glazing bisque objects, and (un)loading kilns. The docent will also take you for a quick visit to their education studio where they will share the methods and tradition of making ceramics.

Tours last approximately one hour. They are scheduled on a case-by-case basis.

Rochester Mills Beer Co. Brewpub

The Rochester Mills Beer Co. opened its doors in 1998 and began brewing a wide selection of handcrafted Lagers and Ales for the residents of Rochester, Michigan, and the emerging craft beer enthusiast in the surrounding communities. The brewpub is located on Water Street, just two blocks east of Downtown Rochester's Main Street in the historic Western Knitting Mill. Preserving the original character of the building, the brewpub features original hardwood floors, columns, beams, and exposed brick walls. The Pub's menu features a broad selection of eclectic American cuisine, all prepared with the freshest ingredients. From delectable appetizers, fresh salads, pizzas, and pastas to delicious entrees and unique sandwiches, the menu has something for everyone, even the kids. Special amenities include an outdoor patio, pool tables, and live entertainment every Thursday, Friday, and Saturday night. In 2012 they expanded operations and opened a Production Brewery just five miles down the road in Auburn Hills to take the beers beyond the brewpub. Today you can find the beers of Rochester Mills on draft and packaged in 16 oz. cans across Michigan and beyond.

The Rochester Mills Beer Co. has grown to be one of the largest beer producing brew pubs in Michigan, consistently brewing over 1,500 bbl annually leading to the opening of our Rochester Mills Production Brewery in Auburn Hills. This microbrewery is focused on brewing and distributing high quality craft beer, equipped with a Taproom open for the public to come enjoy.

Tours are scheduled on a case-by-case basis.

WeatherGard Windows

WeatherGard began in 1988 when its founder, Albert Benezra, began designing and building windows to sell and install. He started in the Empire Iron Works factory on Prarie St. in Detroit, and in October of the same year, WeatherGard Window Company was incorporated.

WeatherGard is still a family owned and operated business. It has strived to be the number one innovator of new technology as it applies to the vinyl window business. Based in Southeast Michigan, it's always been their mission to design and build a window that's perfect for Michigan's uniquely challenging climate—something tough, efficient, and affordable. To that end, WeatherGard was the first vinyl window manufacturer to offer a fully welded window lineup, the first to offer Warm Edge Technology for the glass units, and the first to offer standard Low-E/Argon glass units in all windows.

Tours are available Monday through Friday from 8:00 a.m. to 4:30 p.m. and Saturday from 8:00 a.m. until noon.

Other

New tours may be added as interest and availability dictates.

PERSONNEL

Made in Detroit Tours is owned and operated by Amie Duncan. Amie has lived in the Detroit area her entire life and bought and renovated her current home in the city. She has worked in the manufacturing industry for fifteen years and has always been fascinated by the process of making things. With the renewed interest in the city, she saw a way to add income and share her love of the industrious city with others.

OPERATIONS

Location

To begin, operations will be on a part-time basis and business will be conducted from Amie's Detroit home. A dedicated home office is equipped with computer, printer/copier/fax machine, and business phone. Everything she needs to book and schedule tours is available in the office.

Hours

Hours will vary according to interest and availability, but it is expected that most will occur on Saturday mornings.

FINANCIAL ANALYSIS

Startup costs for Made in Detroit Tours is minimal, consisting mainly of outfitting the office, advertising, and insurance and other fees. Amie will use her current vehicle for both personal and business purposes and will keep track of business mileage for tax purposes. The vehicle will be outfitted with a car wrap to take advantage of mobile advertising. A breakout of these costs is below:

Office furniture—$1,000

Office equipment—$1,250

Phone and data plan—$1,000

Website—$250

Advertising (online and printed)—$2,500

Car wrap—$3,000

Insurance—$500

Legal and business fees—$500

TOTAL—$10,000

First-Aid Training

Superior Health & Safety Education (SHSE)

PO Box 5567
Romulus, MI 48184

Zuzu Enterprises

The first-aid training program developed by Superior Health & Safety Education (SHSE) is an excellent choice for both the community and workplace setting and conforms to all federal and state requirements. Because employees may encounter unique medical emergencies or injuries, depending on the industry, training programs are tailored to fit each client's specific needs and is done entirely onsite.

EXECUTIVE SUMMARY

"The outcome of occupational injuries depends not only on the severity of the injury, but also on the rendering of first-aid care. Prompt, properly administered first-aid care can mean the difference between life and death, rapid vs. prolonged recovery and temporary vs. permanent disability" (OSHA, 1991 *Guidelines for Basic First Aid Training Programs.*)

The U.S. Bureau of Labor Statistics reports that there were a total of 5,190 fatal work injuries recorded in the United States in 2016, a 7-percent increase from the 4,836 fatal injuries reported in 2015. There were approximately 2.9 million nonfatal workplace injuries and illnesses reported by private industry employers in 2016. In the manufacturing and warehousing industries specifically, more than 325 people were killed during this time, and there were 35,000 injuries requiring medical attention. Workers in manufacturing who sustained occupational injuries and illnesses resulting in days away from work in 2016 required a median of 9 days to return to work. In addition to workplace injuries, more than 360,000 sudden cardiac arrests occur annually in the United States, with about 10,000 of them happening at work, according to the Sudden Cardiac Arrest Foundation.

The good health and resulting productivity of employees is one area that is often overlooked as a means of improving a company's profitability. Lost work time due to injury or illness costs employers billions of dollars annually—money that comes directly off the bottom line. Conducting regular first aid and safety training helps keep employees up-to-date on how to respond in emergency situations. In addition, you can reduce your costs by minimizing unnecessary on-the-job injuries and emergencies.

First-aid training helps employees develop the basic skills and confidence they will need to respond effectively in emergency situations. The training program developed by Superior Health & Safety Education (SHSE) is an excellent choice for both the community and workplace setting and conforms to all federal and state requirements. Because employees may encounter unique medical emergencies or injuries depending on the industry, training programs are tailored to fit each client's specific needs and is done entirely onsite.

MARKET ANALYSIS

According to a search done in Reference USA, there are 9,385 active manufacturing companies in the metropolitan Detroit area. More than 4,300 of these have between 10 and 500 employees. In all, there are more than 250,000 people employed in the manufacturing industry, which equates to 14 percent of all jobs in Southeastern Michigan.

County	2014	
	# of Jobs	% of Jobs
Livingston	7,839	16.3%
Macomb	70,040	25.6%
Monroe	5,287	14.8%
Oakland	61,573	9.5%
St. Clair	7,540	19.9%
Washtenaw	14,024	11.3%
Wayne	84,205	13.8%
Southeast Michigan	**250,508**	**14.1%**

SOURCE: Quarterly Census of Employment Wages estimates as researched by Don Grimes, University of Michigan

These companies and their employees are the target market for Superior Health & Safety Education (SHSE).

Workplace Injuries

The manufacturing and warehousing industries saw more than 325 people killed and 35,000 injuries that required medical attention during 2016. Workers in manufacturing, who sustained occupational injuries and illnesses resulting in days away from work, required a median of 9 days to return to work. Clearly, making the right first-aid response when incidents happen is critical. It could literally save someone's life.

Whether employees work in a high-hazard or low-hazard environment, they face a variety of risks. Shock, bleeding, poisonings, burns, temperature extremes, musculoskeletal injuries, bites and stings, medical emergencies, and distressed employees in confined spaces are just a sampling of the first-aid emergencies that might be encountered. These risks are compounded when employees don't feel well. Their lack of concentration can result in costly injuries.

If employees aren't prepared to handle these types of injuries on all shifts and their coworkers are left untreated until an ambulance arrives, a victim's condition may worsen and injuries can become far more debilitating, which leads to greater medical costs and lost productivity.

It makes good business sense to provide first-aid and appropriate training to all employees. By making an investment in keeping employees safe and well-trained, businesses can net big returns, along with a competitive advantage.

That's where Superior Health & Safety Education (SHSE) come in. SHSE focuses primarily on the manufacturing and warehouse industries. With our industry-specific training scenarios, the content is more relevant to the specific incidents employees will face, and the scenarios discussed can even be customized by the instructor to highlight risks or add content to reinforce compliance issues without adding extra classroom time. SHSE provides first-aid training that gives employees the skills they need to save lives and avoid injuries. We train directly at our clients' workplace location and all training exceeds OSHA requirements.

Competition

The American Red Cross is our primary competitor in first-aid, CPR, and AED training. While they are clearly the premier provider of such training, Superior Health & Safety Education (SHSE) offers the competitive advantage of decades of manufacturing experience and staff that can easily relate to workers. With our industry-specific training scenarios, the content is more relevant to the specific incidents employees will face, and the scenarios discussed can even be customized by the instructor to highlight risks or add content to reinforce compliance issues.

SERVICES

Superior Health & Safety Education (SHSE) offers customizable training programs tailored to fit each client's specific needs. The course meets OSHA workplace requirements and teaches:

- Basic First Aid including burns; cuts; head, neck and back injuries; and more
- Adult CPR
- How to use an Automated External Defibrillator (AED)
- Blood Borne Pathogens

First Aid, CPR, and AED

Our First-Aid, CPR, and AED certification programs are typically combined, giving clients the opportunity to get certified in three important areas during one convenient class. Adult CPR training gives employees the information and skills they need to help adults during breathing and cardiac emergencies. AED (automated external defibrillator) training shows employees how to use the sophisticated, yet easy-to-use, medical device that can analyze the heart's rhythm and, if necessary, deliver an electrical shock to help the heart re-establish an effective rhythm for those people experiencing sudden cardiac arrest. First-Aid training helps employees develop basic first-aid knowledge, skills, and the confidence to respond in an emergency situation.

First-aid class topics include:

- Recognizing an Emergency
- Deciding to Help
- Personal Safety
- Infectious Bloodborne Diseases
- Standard Precautions
- Personal Protective Equipment
- Consent
- Implied Consent
- Abandonment
- Good Samaritan Laws
- Emergency Medical Services (EMS)
- Emergency Action Plans
- Poison Help Line
- Emergency Moves
- Primary Assessment
- Recovery Position
- Compression-only CPR

- Choking

- Control of Bleeding

- Tourniquets

- Hemostatic Dressings

- Internal Bleeding

- Shock

- Amputation

- Impaled Objects

- Open Chest/Abdominal Injuries

- Spinal Injury

- Brain Injury

- Concussion

- Nosebleed

- Injured Tooth

- Burns (Thermal, Electrical or Chemical)

- Fainting

- Stroke

- Hypoglycemia

- Seizure

- Breathing Difficulty

- Asthma and Inhalers

- Severe Allergic Reaction

- Pain, Severe Pressure, or Discomfort in Chest

- Ingested or Inhaled Poisoning

- Heat Exhaustion

- Heat Stroke

- Hypothermia

- Frostbite

Blood Borne Pathogens

This optional add-on course meets OSHA's revised Bloodborne Pathogens Standard and goes into more depth on the topic than is covered in the basic first-aid class. It teaches participants how bloodborne pathogens are spread, how to prevent exposures, and what to do if exposed to infectious materials. This is ideal for housekeeping and janitorial staff and anyone with potential for exposure to blood or body fluids.

Certification Period

All students who successfully complete the course will be certified. Certification for First-Aid/CPR/AED training is two years, while the certification for Blood Borne Pathogens is one year.

Course Length

The length of the class varies based on topics covered and discussion. Typically, First-Aid/CPR/AED class lasts about three hours, while the Blood Borne Pathogens training can add another 45 minutes.

Classroom Requirements

Superior Health & Safety Education (SHSE) maintains a strict student to instructor ratio of 10 to 1. This allows instructors to ensure all participants are actively engaged in the process and have the attention and instruction they require to succeed. The student to Equipment Ratio is 2 to 1, thus ensuring that all participants are able to practice their skills on the equipment at their own pace and until they feel completely comfortable.

Upon completion of the course, all participants are required to complete both a written evaluation and a skills evaluation where they perform required skills competently without assistance. Individual certification will only be awarded when these requirements are successfully met.

Training Materials

All participants will receive a Basic First-Aid Student book (one per participant, print or digital). Extra copies may be left with the organization for distribution to new employees or those absent from training. Other materials to be left with the organization include First-Aid/CPR/AED ready reference guides, DVDs demonstrating the techniques covered in training, and various safety posters.

First-aid supplies that will be used in training and demonstrated to participants, include:

- CPR masks
- Gloves
- First-aid kits
- Face shields
- Bandages
- AED training pads
- Fluid spill cleanup materials
- Emergency eye and face wash

OSHA

OSHA mandates compliance for CPR and First-Aid Training in the workplace. OSHA requirements include:

- Employers are required by OSHA standard 29 CFR 1910.151 to have a person or persons adequately trained to render first aid for worksites that are not in near proximity to an infirmary, clinic, or hospital.
- It is advised that the first-aid program for a particular workplace be designed to reflect the known and anticipated risks of the specific work environment. Consultation with local emergency medical experts and providers of first-aid training is encouraged when developing a first-aid program.
- The program must comply with all applicable OSHA standards and regulations.
- OSHA requires certain employers to have CPR-trained rescuers on site. Sudden cardiac arrest is a potential risk at all worksites, regardless of the type of work.
- First-aid supplies must be available in adequate quantities and be readily accessible.

- First-aid training courses should include instruction in general and workplace hazard-specific knowledge and skills.

- CPR and First-Aid training should incorporate AED training if an AED is available at the worksite.

- CPR and First-Aid training should be repeated periodically to maintain and update knowledge and skills.

- Management commitment and worker involvement is vital in developing, implementing, and assessing a workplace first-aid program.

Superior Health & Safety Education (SHSE) helps companies meet or exceed these requirements.

OPERATIONS

Policies

Class Deposit
A class deposit of $100 is required at the time of reservation. The class deposit is non-refundable and will be applied to the balance due on the final invoice.

Payment
Unless prior arrangements have been made, final payment is due at the time service is rendered. We accept business checks (no personal checks) and credit cards: Visa, MasterCard, Discover, and Amex. Payment by credit card must be made prior to the class date by completing the credit card authorization form.

Rescheduling Policy
Classes rescheduled prior to 48 hours of the scheduled class date may be rescheduled free of charge. For classes rescheduled with less than 48 hours' notice, a fee of $50 is due at the time of the reschedule.

Cancellation Policy
There is a $100 cancellation fee for all canceled classes.

Participant Count
A final participant count is due at least 48 hours prior to the scheduled class date so that we can ensure adequate instructors and training materials as well as adjust the invoice accordingly. If less than 48 hours prior to the class date, a $15 drop fee will be charged per person. If a participant is a no-show at the time of the class, the full invoiced amount is due.

Equipment
Superior Health & Safety Education (SHSE) will require considerable equipment for training. The equipment needed for each class of ten participants includes:

CPR manikins (5)—$700

AED training machines and pads (5)—$500

Kneeling mats—$50

Gym or yoga mats (for students to use)—$100

Bandages of various types—$50

CPR masks/face shields—$50

Gloves—$20

First-aid kit—$150

Fluid spill cleanup materials—$25

Emergency eye and face wash—$40

Laptop computer—$500

Projector—$125

IT and extension cables—$50

Flipchart easel—$150

Flipchart paper and pens—$50

TOTAL—$2,560

Location

Superior Health & Safety Education (SHSE) will maintain a small office and storage area in Romulus. This is a central location and convenient for travel to all client sites, as all training will be done directly at the client site. This is a convenience factor for clients, minimizing work disruption and travel time and expenses. It also saves SHSE the cost of renting, outfitting, and maintaining a large training room that may or may not be used.

Hours

The core business hours for Superior Health & Safety Education (SHSE) are Monday through Friday, 8 a.m. to 5 p.m.. All business communications and most training will be completed during this time. However, SHSE is also available to deliver training 24-hours-a-day, 7-days-a-week, thus accommodating any and all manufacturing schedules.

Pricing

Pricing may vary depending on location, number of participants, and custom-tailored training options. Our basic pricing model includes:

$400 class minimum for up to 8 people

9-15 people $45 per person

16-20 people $43 per person

21-29 people $40 per person

30 or more people $37 per person

Add Bloodborne Pathogens for $10 per person

PERSONNEL

Owner-Operator

The primary instructor is Jake Dominquez. Jake spent 20 years in the manufacturing industry, with his most recent position as Materials Manager for a tier-one automotive supplier. He is at home on the shop floor and has a first-hand understanding of the risks and consequent health and safety needs of the staff. Coupled with his 15 years' experience as a volunteer firefighter and related first-aid training, Jake was in a unique position to see a need and fill it.

Jake is a certified instructor by the Health & Safety Institute (HSI), the National Safety Council, and the American Red Cross. Proof of certifications and background check are available upon request.

Jake is also fluent in Spanish and is able to deliver both bilingual and Spanish-only classes as needed.

Instructors

Additional instructors will be added on an ad-hoc basis. Jake has a network of other firefighters and EMS personnel that are able to step in as needed to meet client schedules and needs. All instructors are required to adhere to our effective quality assurance standards and must pass a background check and verification of their qualifications before training. Once the business is established and the number of clients exceeds the capacity of Jake and the ad-hoc staff, an additional 1-2 staff will be hired on a more permanent basis.

GROWTH STRATEGY

Expansion may be considered into the Toledo, Ohio, metropolitan area. In that area alone, there are an additional 1,391 manufacturing businesses, with more than 700 fitting the profile of 10 and 500 employees. With less than an hour drive from the office to the Toledo area, this seems a likely and profitable market in which to expand.

Flight School

A-1 Flight School and Rentals

Cobb County Airport (KRYY)
49958 Airport Rd.
Kennesaw, Georgia 30144

Zuzu Enterprises

A-1 Flight School and Rentals was founded in 2017 by Andrew Collins. Through efficient, highly-focused training towards FAA pilot certification, A-1 Flight prepares men and women for the wonderful world of flying for fun and recreation or for the start of a professional pilot career.

EXECUTIVE SUMMARY

A-1 Flight School and Rentals was founded in 2017 by Andrew Collins. Through efficient, highly-focused training towards FAA pilot certification, A-1 Flight prepares men and women for the wonderful world of flying for fun and recreation or for the start of a professional pilot career. A-1 Flight School and Rentals offers many different types of programs and services, including:

- Discovery Flights
- Recreational Pilot Certificate
- Private Pilot Certificate
- Flight Ground School
- Aircraft Rentals

Our most poplar program is the Private Pilot Certificate; this is the first certificate you receive if you're becoming a pilot as a career and, thus, the most versatile.

INDUSTRY ANALYSIS

The U.S. Bureau of Labor Statistics reports that airline and commercial pilots make an average of $105,720 per year, with airline pilots making a median wage of $127,820 and commercial pilots making $77,200. There are more than 124,000 people employed as pilots, with the job outlook expected to increase 4.4 percent over the next 10 years as many pilots are expected to retire as they reach the required retirement age of 65.

The Atlanta-Sandy Springs-Roswell, Georgia Metropolitan Area is the second highest area for employment in the Airline Pilot, Copilot, and Flight Engineer Industry with over 6,700 people employed with an average salary of $89,850, according to the Bureau of Labor Statistics.

This economic forecast and the need to train pilots to replace those retiring in the near future bodes well for those people wishing to enter the market as a pilot.

Learning to fly and training for the Private Pilot Certificate is the first step in this process and gives students a glimpse at what such a job would entail.

Of course, becoming a commercial or airline pilot is not the only reason to learn to fly. It can also be an exhilarating hobby or a simple mode of transportation.

MARKET ANALYSIS

Competition
There are two primary competitors in the Kennesaw, Georgia area, including:

1. Superior Flight School
2. Aero Atlanta Flight Center

Both are well-known and respected in the area. However, demand is high for this area and we feel A-1 Flight school can compete from both a schedule and cost perspective, as well as providing superior instructors.

SERVICES

We offer many different types of programs and services, including:

- Discovery Flights
- Recreational Pilot Certificate
- Private Pilot Certificate
- Flight Ground School
- Aircraft Rentals

Discovery Flights
Whether the participant has never flown before or has had some first-hand experience, a Discovery Flight is an actual flight lesson and will count towards a license if they choose to continue. A Discovery Flight is the perfect opportunity to learn about A-1 Flight School and Rentals, meet our instructors, and experience the difference that is A-1 Flight training.

Upon arrival, participants will meet their instructor and discuss the steps toward becoming a pilot, be introduced to the A-1 Flight program, be familiarized with the airplane, preview and participate in the preflight checks, and taken on their first flight lesson where they will actually get to take the controls and fly the airplane.

Recreational Pilot Certificate
The recreational pilot certificate may be right for you if you plan to fly for fun in your local area. It generally takes less time to earn than the private pilot certificate and can serve as a stepping stone should you decide to move on to the private pilot certificate later.

There are many restrictions to the Recreational Pilot License, including:

- Must remain within 50 nautical miles of your home base.
- Can carry only one passenger in single-engine aircraft of 180 horsepower or less with up to four seats.

- Flying must be during daylight hours in good weather.

- Can fly no higher than 10,000 feet unless you happen to be flying over terrain, such as a mountain, that is higher than 10,000 feet.

- If you go more than 180 days without logging any flight time, you'll need to take an instructor with you to establish your currency.

Recreational Pilot FAA Requirements
- 30 in-flight hours minimum; this is the minimum required by the FAA. The average in the United States is 40-50 hours, but at A-1 Flight we average about 35 hours of in-flight training.

- Minimum age is 17 to obtain your license, however, you can begin training and solo at age 16.

- You must pass at least a class III medical examination by an Aviation Medical Examiner prior to solo flight.

- You must be able to read, speak, write, and understand English.

Private Pilot Certificate

Most people start by obtaining their Private Pilot certificate. While there are other certificates you can start with, the Private Pilot certificate is the most useful. As long as you have three miles of visibility, it will allow you to fly day or night with no distance limitations. Private Pilot is the first certificate you receive if you're becoming a pilot as a career.

Private Pilot FAA Requirements
- 40 in-flight hours minimum; this is the minimum required by the FAA. The average in the United States is 60-70 hours, but at A-1 Flight we average about 55 hours of in-flight training. This includes 20 dual hours with an instructor and 10 solo hours.

- 8 hours cross-country flight time; cross-country means landing at an airport more than 50 nautical miles away.

- 10 takeoffs and landings performed to a full stop.

- 3 hours of simulated or actual instrument flight.

- 3 hours of practical test prep in the previous 60 days.

- 3 hours instrument or simulated instrument flight time.

- 3 hours night flight time.

- Minimum age is 17 to obtain your license, however, you can begin training and solo at age 16.

- You must pass at least a class III medical examination by an Aviation Medical Examiner prior to solo flight.

- You must be able to read, speak, write, and understand English.

Flight Ground School

Along with hands-on flight instruction to prepare for the check ride, you'll take ground school to prepare for the required FAA knowledge test. The traditional method is to attend a class taught by a certified flight instructor, where you will have the opportunity to learn from questions and discussions that take place between the instructor and the student. You attend class on your schedule and go at your own pace. All students must attend flight ground school to prepare for the FAA written exam, whether seeking either the Recreational Pilot Certificate or the Private Pilot Certificate. The test is a quick 50-question test, and you must score a 70 percent or higher to pass; it must be completed before you can take the final private pilot check ride for your certificate.

Aircraft Rentals

We have several different aircraft available for rent, either for students or licensed pilots. All are meticulously maintained aircraft to meet or exceed FAA requirements. These aircraft include:

- 2-seat Diamond DA20

- 2-seat Diamond DA-40

- 4-seat Cessna 172

- 5-seat Cirrus SR20

Routine maintenance is performed on each of the aircraft. After every 50 hours of flight, the aircraft will receive an oil-change, and after every 100 hours, the aircraft will receive a full inspection. We are extremely meticulous about aircraft maintenance. Each plane is taken to maintenance shops that specialize in their specific manufacturer. We fix every issue, even if it is cosmetic, to reduce any distraction to the pilots.

Pricing

Pricing for the various services offered by A-1 Flight School and Rentals are noted below.

Discovery Flights
- Diamond DA20 (2 seat)—$165 for one hour

- Diamond DA-40 (4 seat)—$185 for one hour

- Cessna Skyhawk 172 (4 seat)—$185 for hour

- Cirrus SR20 (5 seat)—$280 for 1 hour

If you are fairly confident that you would like to obtain your Private Pilot rating, we recommend a one-hour discovery flight as it will be more like a full flight lesson.

Flight Instruction and Ground School
- Private, with A-1 Flight-owned aircraft—$49.00 per Hour

- Private, in student-provided, privately-owned aircraft—$42.00 per Hour

Generally, if you are consistently flying once or twice a week in one of our DA20 aircraft then the overall total cost for a Private Pilot Certificate will be around $8,500-$10,000.

All the rates listed are all-inclusive and include gas, oil, taxes, and insurance. There are no extra, hidden costs or surcharges.

Aircraft Rentals
Block Discounted Rates

Cessna Skyhawk 172—$109 per hour

Diamond DA20—$120 per hour

Diamond DA-40—$136 per hour

Cirrus SR20 (5 seat)—$220 per hour

Regular Pay-As-You-Go Rates

Cessna Skyhawk 172—$119 per hour

Diamond DA20—$130 per hour

Diamond DA-40—$146 per hour

Cirrus SR20 (5 seat)—$230 per hour

Participant Requirements

There are two primary certificates offered by A-1 Flight, commonly called licenses, that you can earn in order to enjoy the privileges, challenges, and beauty of flying: the recreational pilot and private pilot certificates. To be eligible to receive either certificate in a single-engine airplane, you must meet a few minimum requirements for aeronautical knowledge, flight proficiency, and experience.

You must:

• Be 16 years old to fly solo.

• Be 17 years old to receive your pilot certificate.

• Read, speak, and understand English.

• Hold at least a third-class medical certificate for private and recreational certificates.

Perfect vision is not required. However, a pilot's vision needs to be correctable to 20/20.

To begin taking lessons with A-1 Flight, all participants must present a birth certificate, passport, and/or any government-issued identification. The Transport Security Administration (TSA) requires flight schools to verify citizenship of every student beginning flight training for recreational pilot, sport pilot, private pilot certificate, multiengine rating, commercial certificate, and instrument rating. Non U.S. Citizens will need to successfully complete a background check with TSA before being eligible to participate.

Current students can only fly solo (without an instructor) after training with us and obtaining approximately 15-25 hours of instructor-led flight.

Supplies

Each student will be required to purchase and use the following supplies before beginning flight lessons with A-1 Flight School and Rentals. The supplies include:

• *Training syllabus*—The syllabus will guide you through the entire process. Each lesson includes a required pre-study section, which will tell you exactly what you need to study in preparation for each flight training lesson. Once you have completed all ground and flight lessons in the syllabus, you will have logged about 55 hours of flight time and have met all the FAA requirements for the Private Pilot rating.

• *Logbook*—This is your official FAA logbook where you will record all your logged flight time.

• *FAR/AIM Book*—This is a book containing the Federal Aviation Regulations and Aeronautical Information Manual. You will use this book to understand the regulations for a Private Pilot in detail and will be required as a reference throughout your training.

• *Airplane Flying Handbook/Pilot's Handbook of Aeronautical Knowledge Combo*—The FAA's Airplane Flying Handbook introduces the basic pilot skills and knowledge essential for piloting airplanes. It benefits student pilots just beginning their aviation endeavors, as well as those pilots wishing to improve their flying proficiency and aeronautical knowledge, pilots preparing for additional certificates or ratings, and flight instructors engaged in the instruction of both students and licensed pilots.

• *Georgia Aeronautical Chart*—This is the Georgia VFR (Visual Flight Rules) chart showing local topography and elevation for Georgian public use airports. You will use the VFR chart throughout your training.

• *ASA Composite E6B Computer*—This is a slide-rule type computer to calculate crosswind landing components, wind and heading calculations, time en-route, and fuel calculations.

- *Plotter*—This is for measuring distance and heading on your Aeronautical Chart for your planned flight route.

- *GLEIM Private Pilot FAA Knowledge Test Book*—The primary purpose of the Gleim Private Pilot FAA Knowledge Test book is to provide you with the easiest, fastest, and least-expensive means of passing the FAA knowledge test.

- *Private Pilot Practical Test Standards*—This details the type and levels of skill and knowledge that must be demonstrated before an examiner can issue a certificate or rating to an applicant, and describes background study and reference materials.

- *Private Oral Exam Guide*—The Private Oral Exam Guide is designed for student pilots training for the Private Pilot Certificate. All the subjects a Private Pilot candidate will be tested on during checkrides and review flights are covered.

Flight Scheduler

We use an Online Scheduling System at A-1 Flight. Once participants have gone through the sign up process and obtained all their required materials, A-1 will approve their scheduling system ID and they can log in to the scheduling system to schedule their flight lessons at their convenience. Participants will schedule a 2-hour block of time in the aircraft of their choice with their instructor for each lesson. A-1 Flight staff are always available by phone to schedule flights, as well if students are not at a computer or prefer to schedule by phone.

Written, Oral and Practical Exams

After completing all the ground lessons and having completed a final review of the material, your instructor will sign-off that you are ready for the written exam. The written exam will be given at a designated FAA testing center.

Once you have completed all flight lessons, successfully demonstrated all the required skills to your instructor, and passed the written exam, your instructor will sign-off that you are ready for the Recreational or Private Pilot check-ride with an FAA Designated Pilot Examiner (DPE). Your instructor will help you schedule your check-ride for a time that is convenient for you.

Time Frames

How often you fly will determine how quickly you get your license. If you can commit to training every day for three weeks straight, you can achieve your license in as little as three weeks. Most of our clients schedule their flight lessons about two times per week with study time in-between flights. Students who follow this schedule generally complete their flight in about four to six months.

OPERATIONS

Location

A-1 Flight School and Rentals operates out of the Cobb County Airport (KRYY), and is located at 49958 Airport Rd., Kennesaw, Georgia. The location includes hangar space for all aircraft, a front reception area and office, back office, classroom, locker room, and bathroom facilities.

Hours

Our normal business office hours are weekdays from 9 a.m. until 5 p.m. However, we fly by appointment seven days a week, early morning to late evening. Each instructor's schedule is posted to our online scheduler with their availability. We try to accommodate all schedules and make it easy for our clients to schedule their flights. Most of our instructors are willing to fly as early as 7:00 a.m. and as late as 11:00 p.m. As all of our aircraft are fully-equipped with heated cabins and stored in our heated hanger, the time of year does not affect the schedule or availability of instruction times. Some may think of flying as primarily a summer occupation, but during the winter the air is smoother, and the airplanes perform very well in the colder temperatures. For many pilots, winter is their favorite time to fly.

PERSONNEL

The owner and lead instructor is Andrew Collins. Andrew graduated from Western Michigan University with a Bachelor's degree in Aviation Administration and Science. After graduating from Western, he moved back to the Metro Atlanta area and worked for InagineAir in the operations department. He then decided to attend Middle Georgia State University where he obtained his flight instructor certificate. After working for a local flight training company, Andrew decided to venture out on his own to form A-1 Flight School and Rentals.

All instructors at A-1 Flight School and Rentals are FAA Certificated Flight Instructors, including Certified Flight Instrument Instructors, Multi-Engine Instructors, and Advanced Ground Instructors.

Food Hall Business

Spencer Park Market

Manchester Development Partners Inc.
3651 Market St., Ste. 209
Burlington Ridge, IN 46000

Paul Greenland

Spencer Park Market is a trendy food hall business located in downtown Burlington Ridge, Indiana.

EXECUTIVE SUMMARY

Business Overview

Spencer Park Market is a trendy food hall business located in downtown Burlington Ridge, Indiana. Food halls, which were experiencing explosive growth during the late 2010s, are facilities that feature a mix of high-quality food and beverage vendors with seating in a common area. The facility, which is part of the revitalization occurring in the city's Market Square District, initially will feature ten different food and beverage vendors.

This business plan has been prepared by Manchester Development Partners, which plans to acquire the former Stanley Brothers Furniture facility. Constructed in 1905, the historic three-story building has been unoccupied for nearly twenty years. It formerly was home to a furniture retail business on the main level, with warehouse and office space on the upper floors.

If funding is received, the owners anticipate that renovations will be completed in late 2018. Manchester Development Partners has established a subsidiary named Spencer Park Market Inc. to operate the food hall business, which will open its doors in early 2019. This following business plan focuses on Spencer Park Market Inc.'s first three years of operations.

INDUSTRY ANALYSIS

Food halls are part of the food and beverage industry. According to the National Restaurant Association, industry revenues were expected to reach $798.7 billion in 2017, up significantly from $586.7 billion in 2010 and $379.0 million in 2000. The industry's more than one million restaurants provide employment for 14.7 million people. By 2027, the industry is expected to create an additional 1.6 million jobs. Most restaurants (90%) have fewer than 50 employees, and about 70 percent are single-unit operations.

Food halls originated in Britain. Although the concept continues to evolve in the United States, the firm Cushman & Wakefield provided some definition in a 2016 report, explaining: "While the historic model of the food hall in the U.S. has been that of the larger, tourism- or transit-oriented property featuring a mix of food-related proprietors, the modern definition has changed somewhat. The overwhelming focus of the modern food hall is on quality, authentic food offerings offered by a mix of vendors. Typically, this is a variety of restauranteurs offering everything from sit-down white-linen tablecloth, upscale dining experiences to urban street foods. These tenants range from world-renowned Michelin star chef-driven concepts to relatively unknown start-ups. Additionally, modern food hall concepts typically feature a strong contingent of artisanal food vendors selling unprepared items like gourmet meats and cheeses, mushrooms, caviar, chocolates, etc."

In an April 6, 2017, *Restaurant Hospitality* article, Liz Barrett added: "Unlike a food court, which typically offers familiar fast-food options to feed hungry shoppers at a mall, food halls bring together a unique collection of local restaurant concepts and food purveyors under one roof, reaching more consumers and providing, in theory, a more-elevated dining experience with lower overhead and higher foot traffic for operators."

While traditional retailers and shopping centers have suffered in recent years, Cushman & Wakefield indicated that the opposite was true of food-related retail generally, and food halls particularly. After slow growth between 2010 and 2013, during which time roughly 25 food halls opened per year, data from the firm revealed that food halls began experiencing stronger growth in 2014, when about 50 locations opened their doors. The strong growth continued through the middle of the decade, with 100 locations expected to open in 2016. Cushman & Wakefield projected that annual food hall openings would approach 150 in 2017 and continue growing into the latter part of the decade, with about 200 locations expected to open annually by 2019.

Although some "mini food halls" are as small as 7,000 square feet, and a few locations exceed 150,000 square feet, most food halls in the United States are between 10,000 and 50,000 square feet in size. Food halls tend to be situated in business districts, feature spaces for vendors that range between 200 and 400 square feet, and offer communal seating (sometimes outdoors). Some food halls offer areas for entertainment and games, as well as retail space where items such as sauces, olive oil, and locally grown organic produce are sold.

Food halls offer a mix of permanent and temporary tenants, who often can secure short lease terms of one to three years. They provide up-and-coming food retailers (especially food cart operators) with an affordable means of experimenting with a permanent retail location. Tenants benefit from the ability to share janitorial, security, maintenance, electricity, landscaping, and marketing/promotional costs. A location providing generous foot traffic is a key ingredient for success.

MARKET ANALYSIS

Overview

For decades, Burlington Ridge, Indiana, was a hotbed for manufacturing. However, like the fate of other Rust Belt cities, Burlington Ridge experienced a rapid decline in manufacturing activity as several leading employers relocated operations to countries where more affordable labor was available. Unable to compete, many smaller and mid-sized manufacturers closed their doors or were acquired by larger competitors.

Following especially difficult times during the Great Recession, conditions have significantly improved in Burlington Ridge, which is quickly becoming a technology hub in the Midwest. For example, a leading tech company recently established an "idea lab" downtown, attracting tech startups seeking operational space and access to unique development resources. Several mobile technology, design, and law firms also have established operations downtown, which has, in turn, attracted new restaurants, entertainment businesses, and retailers.

According to a recent analysis conducted by the city of Burlington Ridge, Manchester Development Partners has compiled the following snapshot of establishments in the downtown area:

- Colleges & Universities (3 establishments)
- Large Companies (11 establishments)
- Mid-Sized Companies (53 establishments)
- Small Businesses (198 establishments)
- Hospitals (2 establishments)
- Health & Medical Services (179 establishments)
- Membership Organizations (63 establishments)
- Museums & Zoos (2 establishments)
- Churches & Religious Organizations (44 establishments)

Competition

Because no other food halls currently operate in Burlington Ridge, Spencer Park Market will have no direct competitors. However, its tenants will compete against one another for wallet share, and with other local restaurants and mobile food carts that do not have a presence in Spencer Park Market.

SERVICES

Vendor Stalls

Spencer Park Market will lease 350-square-foot stalls to prospective food and beverage vendors. Each stall will be equipped with the following:

- Cooktops
- Front Counter
- Fryer
- Grill/Oven
- Point-of-Sale System
- Sinks

Vendors can provide additional equipment, unique to their specific operation, but will be liable for any associated costs.

Food Types

Spencer Park Market initially will feature ten vendors. Via a request for proposal process, the owners have had conversations with prospective vendors in the following food and beverage categories, which illustrates the incredible possibilities associated with a food hall business:

- Barbecue
- Breakfast Food
- Chicken Sandwiches
- Chinese Noodles
- Churros

- Cocktail Bar
- Coffee
- Craft Beer
- Crepe's
- Desserts
- Donuts
- Fish and Chips
- Greek Food
- Hamburgers
- Healthy Bowls
- Italian
- Japanese Sliders
- Juice
- Lobster
- Popsicles
- Rolled Ice Cream
- Rotisserie Chicken
- Seafood
- Smoothies
- Southern Cuisine
- Sushi
- Tacos
- Tapas Bar
- Tex-Mex
- Vietnamese Cuisine
- Waffles
- Wine Bar
- Woodfire Pizza

Entertainment & Special Events

Utilizing open space within Spencer Park Market, the owners occasionally will book live entertainment engagements and host special events, typically in cooperation with at least some tenant food and beverage vendors. For example, companies may wish to host special events or private parties within flexible space on the facility's main level. In some cases, events may be held on Sundays, when the facility is typically closed. Spencer Park Market will negotiate an agreeable rental fee with customers, based on their specific requirements.

OPERATIONS

Facility Summary

Spencer Park Market will be located within the former Stanley Brothers Furniture facility, which has been unoccupied for nearly 20 years. Constructed in 1905, the three-story, 75,000-square-foot building formerly was home to a furniture retail business on the main level, with warehouse and office space on the upper floors. The space will feature a large open area, with rustic/industrial decor that reflects the community's heritage.

Vendor spaces will be on the main level (25,000 square feet), in a perimeter around a large open floor plan featuring four-foot and eight-foot tables with a combination of bench-style seating and traditional chairs. Following renovations, the building will have the capacity to accommodate up to twenty vendors on the main level. However, expansion is possible on the upper levels to accommodate future growth. In addition to the common area, the main level includes two 5,000-square-foot flexible-use spaces for hosting special events, live entertainment, and private parties.

New Vendor Process

Manchester Development Partners/Spencer Park Market Inc. will require all prospective tenants/vendors to submit a detailed business plan, including certain financial projections (startup expenses and capitalization, sales forecast, and wage cost analysis). This will enable the partners to assess factors such as the uniqueness of the food/beverage concept, sample menu and pricing, and the vendor's financial position. If accepted, the vendor will be required to pay a conditionally refundable $15,000 security deposit and agree to a three-year lease, after which time the concept will be reevaluated and potentially renewed. Annual lease terms are $22,750 ($65/square foot) for a 350-square-foot stall.

Hours

Catering mainly to employees and the entertainment crowd in the downtown area, Spencer Park Market will operate from 7 a.m. to 7 p.m., Monday through Thursday, 7 a.m. to 11 p.m. on Friday, and 11 a.m. to midnight on Saturday. The facility may open outside of these timeframes for special events and functions.

PERSONNEL

Ownership

Manchester Development Partners Inc. is a partnership including real estate developer Lindsay Zimmerman, general contractor Glenn Thomas, and attorney Ander Schering. Well-established business-people in Burlington Ridge, the owners have excellent reputations in the community. Together, they have invested in several buildings over the previous five years that, collectively, have served as a catalyst for the Market Square District's resurgence. Along with the efforts of other developers and city government, the restoration of previously vacant historic buildings has added new residential, commercial, and mixed-use space to the area, which has attracted new residents and businesses, stimulating job growth in the process.

Employees

Spencer Park Market will employ a full-time business manager, whose responsibilities will include managing relationships and business dealings with both third-party service providers and vendors/tenants, as well as responding to customer service issues. Additionally, this position will be responsible for managing an operational budget for Spencer Park Market established by Manchester Development Partners/Spencer Park Market Inc.

Service Providers

Spencer Park Market will contract with reputable third-party providers for assistance with operational functions, including building maintenance, janitorial services, security, and landscaping.

Professional and Advisory Support

The company has retained Denton Accounting Inc., a local accounting firm, to assist with the preparation of our financial statements. A commercial checking account has been established with Midway Community Bank. Legal services will be provided by attorney Ander Schering of Manchester Development Partners.

GROWTH STRATEGY

Year One: Begin operations with ten food and beverage vendors. Focus on establishing Spencer Park Market as the food and beverage destination of choice in downtown Burlington Ridge. Emphasize incentives in marketing activities to encourage new customer visits.

Year Two: Add an additional five food and beverage vendors (total of fifteen). Emphasize Spencer Park Market's expanding selection of vendors in marketing activities. Recoup owners' initial investment. Explore the feasibility and associated costs of expanding operations to the facility's second level in year four.

Year Three: Add an additional five food and beverage vendors (total of twenty). Continue to emphasize the growing selection of vendors in all marketing activities. Based on the feasibility study conducted in year two, potentially move forward with construction and renovation of the second level to accommodate expanded services in year four.

MARKETING & SALES

In addition to the individual marketing efforts of its tenants, a marketing plan has been developed for Spencer Park Market that includes several key tactics, including:

- *Social Media*: Guests will be able to follow the Spencer Park Market on Facebook and Twitter and take advantage of exclusive special offers.

- *Mobile Marketing*: The business has identified a service that will enable it to send text alerts to customers interested in receiving information about special discounts and upcoming events.

- *Web Site*: A site with key information about Spencer Park Market and its tenants will be developed.

- *Advertising*: The business will run regular print ads in *Go Downtown!*, a monthly print/online publication serving businesses and residents in Burlington Ridge's Market Square District.

- *Incentives*: To encourage prospective customers to visit Spencer Park Market, the business will distribute 2,000 coupons good for $2 off any purchase at any of the venue's vendors.

- *Media Relations*: The owners will attempt to secure stories from local TV network affiliates, as well as the *Burlington Ridge Gazette*, which typically profiles new businesses that have been established in the city.

- *Direct Marketing*: Manchester Development Partners will send monthly mailings and e-mailing's to key prospects in Burlington Ridge to secure bookings for special events.

- *Sales Calls*: Spencer Park Market's business manager will make at least five sales calls per month to key prospects in Burlington Ridge to secure bookings for special events. Additionally, the owners will promote the venue to their associates and colleagues in the business community.

During the first three years of operation, Spencer Park Market's owners will evaluate the business' marketing plan on a semi-annual basis. Adjustments will be made as needed.

FINANCIAL ANALYSIS

Manchester Development Partners/Spencer Park Market Inc. have negotiated a purchase price of $225,000 for the former Stanley Brothers Furniture facility. The owners have determined that $250,000 will be needed for renovations and capital purchases. They have applied for $125,000 in related economic development funds from the City of Burlington Ridge. These matching funds (e.g., corresponding to their own personal investment) may be provided in the form of a three-year forgivable grant. Manchester Development Partners will provide $350,000 of the total funds needed for this project, less the $125,000 grant.

The business is expected to generate more than $900,000 in profits within its first three years of operations, and the owners anticipate that they will recoup their investment during the second year. Following is an overview of projected revenue and expenses for 2019-2021:

	2019	2020	2021
Revenue			
Vendor leases	$227,500	$341,250	$455,000
Entertainment	$ 35,000	$ 40,000	$ 45,000
Special events	$ 60,000	$ 70,000	$ 80,000
Total revenue	**$322,500**	**$451,250**	**$580,000**
Expenses			
Accountant	$ 2,500	$ 3,000	$ 3,500
Marketing & advertising	$ 27,500	$ 32,500	$ 37,500
Security	$ 2,500	$ 3,000	$ 3,500
Miscellaneous	$ 1,000	$ 1,000	$ 1,000
Liability insurance	$ 1,100	$ 1,300	$ 1,500
Maintenance & repair	$ 15,000	$ 17,500	$ 20,000
Telecommunications & Internet	$ 1,500	$ 1,600	$ 1,700
Office supplies	$ 700	$ 750	$ 800
Utilities	$ 7,000	$ 8,000	$ 9,000
Salaries	$ 65,000	$ 70,000	$ 75,000
Payroll taxes	$ 9,750	$ 10,500	$ 11,250
Total expenses	**$133,550**	**$149,150**	**$164,750**
Net profit	**$188,950**	**$302,100**	**$415,250**

Group Fitness Business

Midtown Movement Inc.

Midtown Mall
4307 N. 2nd St.
Johnstown, ND 58992

Paul Greenland

Midtown Movement Inc. is a mall-based, group fitness instruction business that makes fitness fun and easy.

EXECUTIVE SUMMARY

Midtown Movement Inc. is a mall-based, group fitness instruction business that makes fitness fun and easy. Established by Harper Smith and Lisa Monroe, certified group fitness instructors, the business will offer group fitness classes in several categories for adults, children/teens, and senior citizens. The following business plan outlines Midtown Movement's strategy for its first three years of operations.

INDUSTRY ANALYSIS

According to the U.S. Department of Labor, approximately 299,200 people worked as fitness trainers and instructors in 2016. Between 2016 and 2026, the profession is expected to experience faster-than-average growth of 10 percent, resulting in the addition of 29,300 jobs. Most fitness trainers and instructors hold a high school diploma or equivalent and earn salaries of $38,160 per year. According to the Department of Labor's *Occupational Outlook Handbook:* "As businesses, government, and insurance organizations continue to recognize the benefits of health and fitness programs for their employees, incentives to join gyms or other types of health clubs are expected to increase the need for fitness trainers and instructors."

The fitness industry is served by several leading organizations, including the American Council on Exercise (ACE), which describes itself as "an established resource for health and fitness professionals, and the public, providing comprehensive, unbiased research and validating ourselves as the country's trusted authority on health and fitness." With roots dating back to 1985, the nonprofit ACE is the nation's largest provider of health and fitness education, certification, and training. The organization has certified more than 70,000 professionals in the fitness industry. The certifications provided by ACE include: Health Coach, Personal Trainer, and Group Fitness Instructor. Certifications such as these are required by many leading fitness centers and studios.

MARKET ANALYSIS

Market Overview

Midtown Movement is in the Midtown District of Johnstown, North Dakota. In 2016 the community was home to 156,329 people (49,780 households). In recent years, Johnstown has experienced an economic revival, thanks in large part to expansion initiatives at several local and regional companies. Continued progress is expected as several key suppliers to these companies establish new manufacturing and support-related operations in and around Johnstown.

However, the community is not without its challenges. Particularly concerning are levels of obesity and diabetes that are significantly higher than the national average. Not only will Midtown Movement provide a service that is much needed by local residents, it will be positioned to capitalize on wellness-related benefits provided by local employers (namely reimbursement for fitness and nutrition programs, and potentially the establishment of on-site group fitness classes).

The owners of Midtown Movement will actively market their services to households with income of $35,000 or more. According to research conducted by the owners at their local public library, the household income of prospects in Johnstown breaks down as follows:

- $35,000 - $49,999—14.6%

- $50,000 - $74,999—19.2%

- $75,000 - $99,999—11.6%

- $100,000 - $124,999—7.9%

During its first three years of operations, the services provided by Midtown Movement will grow to include programming for customers in the following age groups:

- Children & Teens (ages 5-17)

- Adults (ages 18-64)

- Seniors (ages 65+)

The owners' research reveals that prospects in the local market break down by age as follows:

- Children & Teens (21.8%)

- Adults (57.9%)

- Seniors (13.4%)

Competition

Midtown Movement's main competition will come from the following local businesses and organizations:

- Johnstown Fitness

- Planet Fitness

- Johnstown YMCA

The business will differentiate itself from the competition by focusing exclusively on "drop-in" group fitness classes and offering an environment that is less intimidating (e.g., smaller, more easily accessible, etc.). Despite the drop-in nature of its business model, the staff of Midtown Movement will attempt to develop relationships with customers, helping them to feel welcome and comfortable and achieve their fitness goals.

SERVICES

Midtown Movement's group fitness classes typically will fall into one of three main categories, including:

- **Cardiorespiratory:** With a goal of elevating participants' heart rates through moderate-to-high-intensity exercise, courses in this category may include hi-lo and step/platform aerobics and kickboxing.

- **Strength Training:** Courses in this category utilize kettle bells, barbells, dumbbells, and resistance bands to increase endurance and muscular strength.

- **Mind/Body:** Emphasizing balance, core strength, and flexibility, with a mind-body connection, examples of classes in this category include Pilates and yoga.

Midtown Movement will begin operations by offering classes in these categories for adults between the ages of 18 and 64. Courses for children and teens (ages 5-17) will be introduced during the second year, followed by programming for senior citizens (ages 65+) in year three.

Pricing

Customers will be able to take advantage of several different pricing options at Midtown Movement:

- **Introductory Lesson ($20):** On a one-time basis, prospective customers are welcome to participate in any group fitness class to determine if regular participation is of interest to them.

- **The Six Pack ($199):** This package provides customers with the ability to participate in 6 group fitness classes of their choice per month (90-day commitment and prepayment required).

- **The Perfect 10 ($149):** This package provides customers with the ability to participate in 10 group fitness classes of their choice per month (90-day commitment and prepayment required).

- **Unlimited ($125/month):** This package, which requires an annual commitment and is billed in 4 installments of $375, provides customers with the ability to participate in an unlimited number of group fitness classes throughout the year.

OPERATIONS

Location

Midtown Movement will occupy space in the Midtown Mall, a strip mall that recently has experienced the exit of several retailers. The owners have negotiated an agreeable lease for a period of three years, securing a location that is conveniently located near several of the community's largest employers, as well as two elementary schools, one middle school, one high school, and a large retirement community.

The facility includes four 800-square-foot, climate-controlled spaces, which feature high ceilings and sound systems. Locker room facilities for men and women, as well as a small office area for the owners, also is included. The owners have hired a contractor to perform a number of required facility modifications at a cost of $8,500.

Policies

- Midtown Movement can accommodate a maximum of 20 customers in each group exercise class at any time. If maximum capacity is reached, customers must wait for the next session.

- Lessons are provided on a "drop-in" basis, with no scheduling required.

- Staff members reserve the right to decline customers who are disruptive, or who wear attire that is considered to be inappropriate.

- Guests are encouraged, but not required, to wear loose-fitting, comfortable clothing.

- For safety reasons, customers may be asked to remove their jewelry during lessons.

PERSONNEL

Owners

Harper Smith, President—A Johnstown native, Harper Smith graduated from Johnstown High School. While pursuing an associate's degree from Lawrence Community College, where she graduated in 2013, Harper became certified as a group fitness instructor and began teaching courses at a local fitness club. This experience prompted her to establish Midtown Movement, which fulfills her desire to help people achieve their fitness goals while experiencing the satisfaction of running her own business.

Lisa Monroe, Vice President & Treasurer—Also a Johnstown native and Johnstown High School graduate, Lisa Monroe has been a certified group fitness instructor for fifteen years. For most of that time, she has led classes on an independent basis for several local companies, including her own employer, where she worked in corporate finance. Ready for a career change and equally excited about running her own business, Lisa is excited to establish Midtown Movement. Her financial background and undergraduate business degree will allow her to handle many of the administrative responsibilities at Midtown Movement.

Midtown Movement has developed a personnel plan for its first three years of operations, which is summarized in the following table:

FTE	Position	2018	2019	2020
1.0	Owner	$ 50,000	$ 60,000	$ 70,000
1.0	Owner	$ 50,000	$ 60,000	$ 70,000
0.5	Fitness instructor	$ 19,080	$ 20,034	$ 21,036
0.5	Fitness instructor	$ 19,080	$ 20,034	$ 21,036
0.5	Fitness instructor	$ 0	$ 19,080	$ 20,034
0.5	Fitness instructor	$ 0	$ 0	$ 19,080
1.0	Fitness instructor	$ 38,160	$ 40,068	$ 42,071
1.0	Fitness instructor	$ 38,160	$ 40,068	$ 42,071
1.0	Fitness instructor		$ 38,160	$ 40,068
1.0	Fitness instructor	$ 0	$ 0	$ 38,160
1.0	Receptionist	$ 20,000	$ 21,000	$ 22,050
0.5	Receptionist	$ 10,000	$ 10,500	$ 11,025
		$244,480	**$328,944**	**$416,631**

The business will begin operations with a staff consisting of its two owners (who will share administrative duties in addition to serving as fitness instructors), two full-time fitness instructors, two part-time fitness instructors, one full-time receptionist, and one part-time receptionist.

Independent Contractors

To provide operational flexibility, including coverage in the event of illnesses, vacations, unexpected demand, etc., the owners of Midtown Movement have identified several independent fitness instructors in the local market who meet the business' standards for certification and experience. These instructors have agreed to provide services on an as-needed basis.

Professional & Advisory Support

Midtown Movement has established a business banking account with Stillman Ridge Bank, including a merchant account for accepting credit card payments. Tax advisement is provided by Parkview & Associates.

GROWTH STRATEGY

Year One: Begin operations with a core offering of group fitness classes for adults. Achieve 50 percent of maximum capacity (10 participants per class). Generate net income of $6,856 on gross revenue of $432,000.

Year Two: Introduce group fitness classes for children. Begin developing a strategy to offer on-site group fitness classes to the corporate market. Generate net income of $68,202 on gross revenue of $622,080.

Year Three: Introduce group fitness classes for seniors and begin offering on-site group fitness classes to area employers. Generate net income of $281,362 on gross revenue of $967,680.

MARKETING & SALES

Midtown Movement has developed a marketing strategy that includes the following tactics:

1. A presence on social media outlets, including Facebook, Twitter, YouTube, and Instagram.

2. A quarterly direct-mail program to prospects in the business' target market.

3. A Web site with complete details about Midtown Movement, including video clips and photos. The site also will provide customers with the ability to purchase various levels of membership packages and read bios of the business' owners and staff.

4. Advertising on Johnstown's local light rock station, WJHT, including fitness class giveaways and semi-annual on-site broadcasts.

5. An e-mail newsletter with tips on fitness, nutrition, and staying healthy.

6. Drop-In Days, which allows prospective customers who follow Midtown Movement on Facebook to experience one lesson free of charge. Drop-In Days will be announced exclusively on Facebook.

7. Eye-catching exterior signage to attract the attention of passersby.

8. Paid search advertising, to connect with local and regional customers seeking a fitness program.

9. Periodic sales calls to human resources professionals at local employers and insurance companies, to promote employee/participant discounts and the development of on-site group fitness classes.

10. Promotional premiums (e.g., pens, water bottles, magnetic business cards, etc.), to spread awareness of the business in the local market.

FINANCIAL ANALYSIS

Midtown Movement has prepared a complete set of pro forma financial statements, which are available upon request. Following is a detailed breakdown of projected revenue and expenses for the business' first three years of operations:

	2018	2019	2020
Revenue			
General group fitness	$432,000	$497,664	$677,376
Children's group fitness	$ 0	$ 93,312	$145,152
Seniors group fitness	$ 0	$ 31,104	$ 96,768
Corporate group fitness	$ 0	$ 0	$ 48,384
Total revenue	**$432,000**	**$622,080**	**$967,680**
Expenses			
Telecommunications	$ 1,450	$ 1,650	$ 1,850
Maintenance & repairs	$ 500	$ 500	$ 500
Insurance	$ 10,500	$ 15,500	$ 20,500
Business loan	$ 16,992	$ 16,992	$ 16,992
Accounting & legal	$ 2,150	$ 2,300	$ 2,450
Payroll	$244,480	$328,944	$416,631
Payroll taxes	$ 36,672	$ 49,342	$ 62,495
Independent contractors	$ 35,000	$ 45,000	$ 55,000
Janitorial services	$ 9,750	$ 10,000	$ 10,250
Utilities	$ 7,500	$ 8,500	$ 9,500
Miscellaneous	$ 1,500	$ 1,500	$ 1,500
Marketing & promotion	$ 30,000	$ 45,000	$ 60,000
Facility lease	$ 28,650	$ 28,650	$ 28,650
Total expenses	**$425,144**	**$553,878**	**$686,318**
Net income	**$ 6,856**	**$ 68,202**	**$281,362**

Startup Costs

The owners of Midtown Movement anticipate startup cost of $20,000, which they will divide equally and pay from personal savings:

Facility Improvements—$8,500

Sound Systems—$2,135

DVD Players—$300

Video Monitors—$4,250

Office Supplies—$450

Decor—$600

Office Furniture—$1,750

Equipment—$2,865

TOTAL—$20,850

Financing

Midtown Movement is expecting to be profitable during its first year. However, the business' owners are requesting a business loan of $60,000 (48-month term, 6.25% interest) from Stillman Ridge Bank to provide working capital.

Gutter Cleaning Service

Five Star Cleaning Services, Inc.

2715 Folsom Blvd.
Sacramento, CA 94207

Claire Moore

Five Star Cleaning Services, Inc. (FSCLI) is a full service residential and commercial gutter cleaning, repair, and installation company. We specialize in all aspects of the gutter industry, including gutter installation, clog-free leaf protection, gutter cleaning, and repair services of any nature.

EXECUTIVE SUMMARY

Revenues for contract (non-proprietary) cleaning services are forecast to grow by 3.2 percent annually to $65 billion in 2019 (Freedonia Group, 2015). In Sacramento County alone, there are 555,932 housing units. Of these, 55.4 percent are owner-occupied. The common home has an average of 200 feet of gutters, which need to be cleaned at least twice a year. These routine maintenance tasks are essential for protecting a homeowner's investment and overall health. Clean gutters protect against roof and structural damage; prevent dampness, mold and water damage; and prevent pest infestation.

Five Star Cleaning Services, Inc. (FSCLI) is a full service residential and commercial gutter cleaning, repair, and installation company. We specialize in all aspects of the gutter industry, including gutter installation, clog-free leaf protection, gutter cleaning, and repair services of any nature.

OBJECTIVES

Five Star Cleaning Services, Inc.'s objectives for the first three years of operations include:

- Establish a list of contract clients who we service on a regular basis
- Develop a base of commercial clients comprising at least 40 percent of our business
- Achieve profitability by the end of year two
- Cultivate a brand that is recognized for quality service and customer satisfaction
- Develop a stable of trained and certified staff who adhere to our commitment to customer satisfaction

KEYS TO SUCCESS

As a service business we know that good work often goes unnoticed, but a bad job can lose you a customer immediately.

Our keys to success will include:

- A commitment to customer satisfaction that includes soliciting customer feedback after every job and regular communication through our blog/newsletter

- Hiring of qualified staff and continuous training in technical and customer relation skills

- Background checks of job applicants

- Utilization of Green cleaning techniques

- Cost containment through the use of computer technology and apps to automate scheduling, bidding, time-keeping, and billing tasks

MISSION

Our mission at FSCLI is to provide the highest quality cleaning and repair services to our customers, to establish long-term relationships with our vendors and customers, and to maintain a roster of qualified staff who share our commitment to customer satisfaction.

COMPANY SUMMARY

FSCLI was established by John and Cindy Miller in 2017 to offer residential and commercial gutter cleaning, installation, and repair services to Northern California. The business office is located in the home of John and Cindy Miller in Sacramento, California. Cindy Miller will maintain the scheduling of services, answer phones and emails, perform basic data entry, and banking activities.

The company has engaged the services of an independent bookkeeper who will oversee the preparation of monthly financial statements, review billing and accounts receivables, as well as payroll. QuickBooks Online is the software being used for accounting and full-service payroll recordkeeping, thus saving time and money while ensuring accuracy and timeliness of filing and paying of payroll taxes.

Apps that interface with QuickBooks will facilitate the preparation of estimates, billing, and scheduling.

COMPANY OWNERSHIP

FSCLI is a California Corporation owned by John and Cindy Miller.

STARTUP SUMMARY

During the startup phase, FSCLI incurred the following costs:

Start-up Expenses

Licenses	$ 150
Advertising	$ 250
Web site development	$ 850
Legal fees & incorporation	$2,200
Magnetic truck signs	$ 100
Insurance deposit	$ 400
Office supplies	$ 100
Brochures, cards, flyers	$ 130
BioRenewable® cleaners	$ 500
Total start-up expenses	**$4,680**

List of Equipment Needed for Startup

Item	Estimated cost
Computer/printer/copier/scanner/fax	$ 1,500
Storage/filing/shelving	$ 300
Paper shredder	$ 50
Desk/table/chair/lamp	$ 350
Brushes/scoops/gloves	$ 700
Misc tools & safety equipment	$ 450
Uniforms & shoes	$ 350
Misc. supplies	$ 350
Misc. tools	$ 1,250
Window cleaning tools/supplies	$ 850
Yard signs	$ 400
Ladders & ladder hooks	$ 1,250
Pole kit tuckers	$ 1,100
Water reclaiming system	$ 2,550
Hoses	$ 250
Hose reels	$ 550
Water fed pole system	$ 3,000
Truck used	$15,000
Truck customization	$ 1,500
Total non-cash assets for startup	**$31,750**

Startup Funding

Cash required	$ 5,000
Startup assets to fund	$31,750
Startup expenses to fund	$ 4,680
Total funding required	**$41,430**

MARKET ANALYSIS

Nonresidential markets account for the vast majority of cleaning service revenues, making up almost eighty percent of the total in 2014. In general, demand for cleaning services in the nonresidential market is more inelastic than in the residential market because cleaning functions are often essential to presenting a safe and clean facility for customers and employees. The cleaning services industry is expected to experience a growth rate of 6.2 percent by the year 2022 (Freedonia Group, 2015).

Factors affecting this industry include:

- Growth in the number of dual income households.

- An increase in disposable income.

- Increased new construction.

- An aging population who desire assistance in completing home maintenance tasks.

In Sacramento County alone, there are 555,932 housing units. Of these, 55.4 percent are owner-occupied. The common home has an average of two hundred feet of gutters, which need to be cleaned at least twice a year. These routine maintenance tasks are essential for protecting a homeowner's investment and overall health. Clean gutters protect against roof and structural damage; prevent dampness, mold, and water damage; and prevent pest infestation.

MARKET SEGMENTATION

FSCLI will focus on developing commercial and residential contracts with the majority of contracts as commercial locations, such as offices and rental units. The reason for this emphasis on commercial contracts is that commercial locations are required to maintain a clean and safe environment for their residents, employees, and customers. Therefore, the demand for services exists in spite of economic changes.

We will also pursue residential contracts, especially in areas where the home value is in excess of $300,000 because home owners must maintain the value of their homes.

In order to reach this market, we will engage in advertising in local newspapers and in mailer packets, such as the ValuePak that is sent to specific zip code areas. Our advertisement will offer a $50 discount on the first scheduled service and a free estimate. Mailings and ads will be scheduled on a monthly basis from September through December each year.

We will also rent and staff a booth at the Sacramento and the Placer County Home and Garden Shows, where we can meet potential clients face-to-face and describe our services and their benefits. Our booth will include a video that illustrates services and benefits running on a loop, flyers, brochures, cards, and a discount coupon.

SERVICES

Five Star Cleaning Services, Inc. provides services to residential homes, condos, townhouses, businesses, industrial buildings, apartment buildings, commercial buildings, schools, churches, and temples.

We specialize in gutter protection services with our Preventative Maintenance Contracts. We are licensed and we carry General Liability and Worker's Compensation Insurance on all of our fully-trained, qualified, and experienced gutter crews. Our technicians have received Safety Certification through the International Window Cleaning Association (IWCA) Safety Certification Program in accordance with IWCA/ANSI I-14 Safety Standard.

Five Star Cleaning Services, Inc. begins by cleaning gutters by hand. The high pressure of a leaf blower or pressure washer can damage your gutters, roof, wood fascia, and more. These both also make an incredible mess that someone (usually the homeowner) has to clean up.

We then follow up by flushing gutters and downspouts with water to check for proper flow and for obstructions that need to be addressed.

Finally, our technicians gather, bag, and remove all debris from the site.

Our list of services includes:

- *Gutter cleaning*: Clogged gutters can lead to water leaks into the home. We provide gutter cleaning to both commercial and residential buildings.
- *Window/screen/window track cleaning*: We clean windows both interior and exterior. Window cleaning is usually needed after gutter cleaning or pressure washing.
- *Pressure washing*: House, roof, deck, driveway, and much more. We also specialize in restaurant hood cleaning. Pressure washing can safely be used to clean mold, dust, rust, algae, and other dirt and grime from a wide variety of surfaces.
- *Solar panel cleaning*: Solar panel cleaning increases production up to 30%.
- *Gutter screening*: Effective screening can significantly reduce the frequency of gutter maintenance.
- *Moss removal*: Accumulation of moss on the roof can attract and hold water, causing deterioration and leaks. Removing the moss allows for proper drainage.

Prices

- For a typical single-story home of 1,500 square feet, cleaning can run between $145 and $196.
- For a two-story home in the 2,500-square foot range, the price goes up to $163 to $216 for a normal cleaning.

- A three-story home or a two-story home with a high reach (maybe in the rear of the house from ground level at a basement level to the gutter in addition to other lower roof areas) can range from $233 to $422 or more.

Factors that can affect the total cost of cleaning include:

- Cleaning under screens or 'gutter guards' requires extra labor and can add as much as $100 to the price of gutter cleaning.

- Clearing an obstruction in a downspout (like a branch or toy that has become wedged in the pipe) can also add $50 to $100 to the price plus any replacement parts or downspout sections.

- Length of time since the last gutter cleaning can really influence price when you consider that instead of scooping out leaves and twigs, the technician is pulling out grass and even small trees that may have grown!

- Larger square footage or unusual roof pitch homes can also cost more simply because of the amount of labor required.

Package Deals

Customers can save up to twenty percent off of regular prices when they buy a service package.

Our service packages are defined as follows:

Square footage	Bronze	Silver	Gold
Up to 3,000	$450	$ 525	$ 750
Up to 4,000	$650	$ 800	$1,000
Up to 5,000	$800	$1,000	$1,250

Bronze:
1. Window Cleaning—Exterior Only, screens
2. House Wash or Gutter Cleaning

Silver:
1. Window Cleaning—Interior and Exterior, screens & tracks
2. House Wash or Gutter Cleaning

Gold:
1. Window Cleaning—Interior and Exterior, screens & tracks
2. House Wash
3. Gutter Cleaning

Note: Window Cleaning does not include sun rooms, houses with French windows, or additional detached garages, shops, or guest quarters.

Note: Gutter Cleaning does not include removing and reinstalling gutter guards or cleaning the roof.

Preventive Maintenance Contracts

Our customers can save time and money by signing up for regular service on a monthly, quarterly, or semi-annual basis.

Savings come in the form of discounts based on frequency of service:

- 25% off your residential window cleaning if we provide service within 1 months' time
- 20% off your residential window cleaning if we provide service within 3 months' time
- 10% off your residential window cleaning if we provide service within 6 months' time

A "RAINY DAY GUARANTEE"

Professionally cleaned windows really shouldn't spot if it rains within a few days of the cleaning. Dirt makes your windows dirty, not rain. When the dust from landscapers, tree pollen, exhaust, etc. settles on your windows, rain drops move the dirt around, and after the rain dries the dirt becomes much more visible. However, clean windows remain clean after the rain because once the pure rain water dries there is nothing to obscure your view.

In the unlikely event that there are spots or marks left on your windows due to rain within seven days of our professional cleaning, if you have purchased our Silver or Gold Package, we will return to re-clean those windows at no charge to you. Think of it as free insurance for your windows.

SERVICE AREA

Our service area includes Sacramento County, Sutter County, Placer County, and El Dorado County. Cities and towns served include: Davis, Granite Bay, Folsom, El Dorado Hills, Roseville, Lincoln, and Rocklin.

MARKETING STRATEGY

Our marketing efforts will be focused in the following areas:

- *Web site*: Pages will cover services offered, service areas, contact information, testimonials, articles on home maintenance issues, and a Request for Quote input form.

- *Blog (updated weekly)*: Short postings of interest to local area residents, periodic focus on sales and specials.

- *Social media*: A presence on Facebook, Pinterest, and YouTube.

- *Yelp listing*: According to Vivial Marketing (Vivial Marketing, 2015), 79 percent of people trust online reviews as much as personal recommendations and 44 percent of customers reach their decision on who to hire after reading a review. We have contracted with a social marketing expert who will assist us in optimizing our Yelp profile and in responding to our Yelp reviews, both positive and negative.

- *Angie's List*: The typical Angie's List member has a median income of $75,000 and a home value over $300,000. More than three million households check Angie's List for their service needs before they hire.

- *Print advertising*: Local publications, Yellow Pages ad, post card reminders for annual gutter cleaning to previous customers, and direct mail services, such as ValuePak, which mails a packet of coupons quarterly to specific zip code areas.

- *Google Adwords*: Ads can be targeted to Internet users based on their location and their search terms.

- *Craiglist*: Ads will be run during the fall and winter season. The ads can be tracked with the use of a custom email address so that we know the effectiveness of this marketing tool.

- *Trade shows/Home shows*: The Northern California Home & Landscape Expo is the largest show of its kind on all of California. It will be held in Sacramento in January 2018. The Sacramento Home & Garden Show will be held in March 2018.

Having a web site is crucial to business success today. Our site integrates with our customer management software to help us do a number of essential tasks.

- Set up appointments

- Receive requests for quotes and then follow up

- Scheduling jobs

- Billing and collections

By automating key administrative functions, we will be able to provide optimal customer service at an affordable cost.

An independent web specialist has been contracted to design, set up, and maintain our web site and social media accounts. Cindy will create the content for web pages, blog postings, and much of the social media activity. Cindy will also monitor emails and online contact submissions and will respond within two business days.

All of our marketing materials will contain our phone number and web site address in order to increase the ability of our target market to learn about us and set up appointments.

COMPETITIVE EDGE

There are many other companies in the greater Sacramento area that offer gutter-related services. In the near term, FSCSI plans to focus on gutter cleaning, installation, repair, and leaf guard protection services. Once we are established, we will examine the feasibility of adding other specialties, such as roof repair or solar installation.

By focusing on gutter services for high-value and commercial properties, we expect to fine-tune our systems. In this way, we can really get to know our customers and their needs in order to better serve them. We will be able to schedule regular service and anticipate any related services that they may need. Our business will grow because we will build on our customer base in addition to seeking new customers.

While property owners may recognize the benefits of regular gutter maintenance, it is the type of task that is often forgotten or left until the situation becomes a problem. We will send an email newsletter to our customers on a quarterly basis. It will contain links to articles on our blog on topics such as: home shows, spring cleaning checklist, what to look for when buying a new home, what's growing in your gutters, and more.

Our system of regular contact with customers and our convenient Protective Maintenance Contracts will help us to cultivate valuable and enduring relationships with our customers. These will be the kind of relationships that lead to referrals.

PERSONNEL PLAN

A critical factor in the success of FSCSI will be our staff of trained and certified professionals. We project our staffing needs for the first three years as follows.

Personnel	Year 1	Year 2	Year 3
John Miller	$20,000	$36,000	$ 42,000
Cleaning technician	$30,000	$36,000	$ 36,000
Cleaning technician		$18,000	$ 30,000
Cleaning technician			$ 30,000
Totals	**$50,000**	**$90,000**	**$138,000**
Total people	**2**	**3**	**4**

FINANCIAL PLAN

We expect to see steady growth as we cultivate repeat customers, develop service contracts, and generate referrals from satisfied customers. As we grow, we will add trained staff, equipment, and vehicles.

Pro forma Profit and Loss

	Year 1	Year 2	Year 3
Sales	$92,000	$145,000	$220,000
Direct costs of sales	$ 4,600	$ 7,250	$ 11,000
Gross profit	$87,400	$137,750	$209,000
Gross profit margin	95%	95%	95%
Expenses			
Depreciation	$ 2,950	$ 2,950	$ 6,670
Phone/Internet	$ 2,100	$ 2,400	$ 2,800
Payroll	$50,000	$ 90,000	$138,000
Insurance: liability, property, auto, wcomp	$ 5,200	$ 5,500	$ 6,500
Payroll taxes	$ 5,000	$ 9,000	$ 13,800
Professional dues/memberships	$ 700	$ 700	$ 700
Sales & marketing	$ 3,500	$ 3,500	$ 2,500
Office supplies	$ 420	$ 420	$ 420
Auto: gas & maintenance	$ 6,000	$ 7,500	$ 8,400
Accounting & legal	$ 2,400	$ 2,400	$ 2,400
Repairs & maintenance	$ 1,200	$ 1,200	$ 1,600
Accounting & legal	$ 1,800	$ 1,800	$ 2,000
Business software/quickbooks online	$ 1,800	$ 1,800	$ 1,800
Other expenses	$ 1,200	$ 1,200	$ 1,500
Total operating expenses	**$84,270**	**$130,370**	**$189,090**
Earnings before interest and taxes	**$ 3,130**	**$ 7,380**	**$ 19,910**
Interest expense			$ 1,500
Net earnings	**$ 3,130**	**$ 7,380**	**$ 18,410**
Income tax	$ 470	$ 1,107	$ 2,762
Net profit	**$ 2,660**	**$ 6,273**	**$ 15,648**
Net profit/sales	**3%**	**4%**	**7%**

Projected Balance Sheet

Assets	Year 1	Year 2	Year 3
Cash in bank	$ 5,410	$14,533	$14,751
Accounts receivable	$ 1,200	$ 1,500	$ 2,200
Other current assets			
Total current assets	**$ 6,610**	**$16,033**	**$16,951**
Fixed assets			
Office furniture & equipment	$ 2,200	$ 2,200	$ 2,200
Tools & equipment	$10,800	$10,800	$18,000
Truck 1	$16,500	$16,500	$16,500
Truck 2			$30,000
Less: depreciation	($ 2,950)	($ 5,900)	($12,570)
Total assets	**$33,160**	**$39,633**	**$71,081**
Liabilities			
Current liabilities			
Accounts payable	$ 500	$ 700	$ 1,500
Current maturities loan			
Total current liabilities	**$ 500**	**$ 700**	**$ 1,500**
Long term liabilities loan	$ 0	$ 0	$15,000
Total liabilities	**$ 500**	**$ 700**	**$16,500**
Paid-in capital	$30,000	$30,000	$30,000
Retained earnings		$ 2,660	$ 8,933
Net profit	**$ 2,660**	**$ 6,273**	**$15,648**
Total capital	**$32,660**	**$38,933**	**$54,581**
Total liabilities & capital	**$33,160**	**$39,633**	**$71,081**

REFERENCES

Freedonia Group. (2015, December 31). *Contract Cleaning Services.* Retrieved November 9, 2017, from Freedonia Group: https://www.freedoniagroup.com/industry-study/contract-cleaning-services-3371.htm

Vivial Marketing. (2015, April 22). *Managing Yelp Reviews.* Retrieved November 13, 2017, from Vivial Resources: https://vivial.net/blog/managing-yelp-reviews/

Home Weatherization/Energy Conservation Business

Brown Mechanical, Inc.

2875 Rocklin Rd.
Rocklin, CA 95677

Claire Moore

Brown Mechanical, Inc. is a home improvement contractor specializing in updating older homes to utilize today's more effective and efficient weatherization materials and methods. Services provided include: cellulose insulation, replacement windows, weather stripping, and thermal imaging. The company is structured as a California corporation and will be led by owners Samson Brown and Kent Smith. Brown and Smith each have extensive experience in the home building industry and each has training and certification in specialties relating to home energy performance.

EXECUTIVE SUMMARY

According to an October 2017 report published by the U.S. Energy Information Administration (EIA), one in three U.S. households faced challenges in paying energy bills or in sustaining adequate heating and cooling in their homes in 2015 (the most recent survey year). Households experiencing energy insecurity were more likely to live in homes built before 1990.

California leads the country in creating home energy efficiency programs and setting standards for the building industry. Since 1975, the California Energy Commission has been responsible for reducing the state's electricity and natural gas demand primarily by adopting new Building and Appliance Energy Efficiency Standards that have contributed to keeping California's per capita electricity consumption relatively low. These standards—coupled with the Energy Commission's programs to reduce energy consumption in existing buildings—are saving consumers money, reducing energy use and greenhouse gas (GHG) emissions, and creating clean energy jobs in California.

Brown Mechanical, Inc. is a home improvement contractor specializing in updating older homes to utilize today's more effective and efficient weatherization materials and methods. Services provided include: cellulose insulation, replacement windows, weather stripping, and thermal imaging. We employ only C-2 Insulation and Acoustical licensed contractors.

The company is structured as a California corporation and will be lead by owners Samson Brown and Kent Smith. Brown and Smith each have extensive experience in the home building industry and each has training and certification in specialties relating to home energy performance.

Brown Mechanical has forecast gross sales in year two of $255,000 rising to $305,000 in year three. Startup funding, vehicles, and equipment have been provided by the company's owners. The planned purchase of another vehicle in year two will be financed by the company. We do not anticipate the need for addition financing at this time.

MISSION

At Brown Mechanical our mission is to ensure that our customers achieve a comfortable environment that is in compliance with California energy standards, saves them money on their energy bills, and is affordable to install.

KEYS TO SUCCESS

Our keys to success are grounded in the background, experience, and expertise of founders Samson Brown and Kent Smith, who have worked in the Sacramento building industry for over twenty years.

Other keys to success include:

- Our ability to consult with customers on government rebates and energy efficiency financing.
- Our knowledge of California energy standards.
- Our ability to help our customers to economically achieve compliance with state energy standards.

OBJECTIVES

Brown Mechanical has identified three objectives to be achieved for our long-term success:

- Hire and uphold a high level of certification for all of our technicians and the team as a whole.
- Assist our customers in securing rebates and financing that will help them to afford energy upgrades.
- Achieve profitability by the end of year three.

COMPANY SUMMARY

Brown Mechanical is a Sacramento-based company specializing in building performance and energy efficiency services. Structured as a California corporation, Brown Mechanical is owned by founders Samson Brown and Kent Smith.

The company offers energy audits, consultations, energy upgrades, and assistance with financing to owners of residential properties in the greater Sacramento area.

STARTUP SUMMARY

Startup funding and a company van have been provided by the owners, Brown and Smith.

Costs involved in starting the company include:

List of Equipment Needed for Startup

Item	Estimated Cost
Computers/printer/copier/scanner/fax	$ 4,500
Tablet computers	$ 1,500
Thermal imaging equipment	$ 2,400
Office furniture	$ 850
Storage/filing/shelving	$ 300
Adding machine	$ 50
Paper shredder	$ 50
Ladders	$ 1,250
Measuring devices	$ 325
Misc tools & safety equipment	$ 250
Uniforms, shoes, work gear	$ 850
Misc. supplies	$ 200
	$12,525

Start-up Expenses

Licenses	$ 550
Advertising	$ 750
Web site development	$1,500
Legal fees incorporation	$1,500
Truck customization/signage	$ 550
Insurance	$ 700
Van customization	$1,250
Total start-up expenses	**$6,800**

Startup Funding

Cash required	$ 5,000
Startup assets to fund	$12,525
Startup expenses to fund	$ 6,800
Total funding required	**$19,325**

COMPANY LOCATION

Company office and storage of vehicles and equipment is located in an industrial park in Sacramento, California.

SERVICES

Brown Mechanical technicians are highly trained in home insulation, saving customers money for years to come. All the insulation products we install are highly durable, safe, and cost-effective home upgrades, and some contain post-consumer recycled materials.

Energy Audit

Our energy audits involve examining how the home performs from an energy-efficiency standpoint. In addition to physical assessment of exterior walls, insulation, ductwork, and HVAC system, we also use tools to assess its performance. We rely on data to make strategic recommendations to make the biggest impact on energy usage and comfort.

Energy Upgrades

Home heating and cooling systems account for about forty-three percent of the home energy bill according to the Department of Energy. Energy Star estimates that a homeowner can save thirty percent on cooling costs by replacing the central air conditioning unit if it is more than twelve years old. Brown Mechanical can help customers achieve energy savings with a new, energy-efficient HVAC system.

Weatherization & Air Sealing

According to Energy Star, most homes have significant leaks and inadequate insulation. All the leaks, gaps, and holes in an average home's building envelope are equivalent to having a window open every day of the year, even on the coldest and hottest days.

From the basement and crawl spaces to the attic, we can air seal leaks and holes. In some cases, such projects can qualify for financing or government incentives, making these money-saving improvements more affordable.

Radiant Barriers

This effective energy-efficiency product helps reduce cooling costs by keeping summer heat gains down. Radiant barriers reflect radiant heat, instead of absorbing heat. Applying a radiant barrier acts similarly to having the roof in the shade, when in fact it is in full sun.

Insulation

We can apply attic insulation, cellulose insulation around pipes and wiring, and spray foam to seal cracks and irregularly shaped building elements.

Ductwork problems, such as air leaks, improper sizing, or obstructions can cause uneven temperatures, high energy bills, and issues with indoor air quality. Ductwork must be well-sealed, insulated, and sized to ensure the home's heating and cooling systems are working as efficiently as possible.

Energy Monitoring

We can set up a home energy monitoring system that provides convenient, real-time data on household energy consumption and that communicates with the smart meter, clearly displaying the actual usage data. The monitoring system also determines how much is being paid for electricity. Because our electricity rates in California are difficult to calculate, this feature adds great insight into energy expenditures for your Sacramento-area home.

Service Areas

Our service areas include: Sacramento, El Dorado Hills, Elk Grove, Folsom, Galt, Auburn, Davis, Yuba City, Granite Bay, Rocklin, and Roseville.

Rebates & Financing

Brown Mechanical offers customers consultation on government rebates and energy efficiency financing for a full range of government rebates, manufacturer rebates, and energy efficiency financing products to help make your home or building improvements a reality. We're lucky to be in a state with so much available—from the $6,500 PG&E Home Upgrade program to mPower and HERO energy efficiency financing.

We can help our customers to navigate the following programs:

Energy Efficient Mortgages (EEM): In many cases, home buyers can include the cost of energy efficiency upgrades in their mortgage. Learn from our experience in this area.

Ygrene Energy Fund: Clean Energy Sacramento, managed and funded by Ygrene, provides 100 percent financing to commercial and residential property owners for energy efficiency, renewable energy, and water conservation improvements. Financing is repayable over the long term through your property tax bill.

Hero: This California-based program offers flexible, low-barrier financing for a full range of home energy products and services.

California First: California leads the way in financing products to help homeowners.

GEO Smart Financing Clearinghouse: We can provide you with a range of financing options available through GEO Smart and the Electric & Gas Industries Association. One of these options, the EGIA Fresh Start Program, is a great choice for homeowners who have marginal credit and do not want the loan tied to their home.

mPower: mPower is an energy efficiency financing tool available to the cities of Auburn, Colfax, Folsom, Lincoln, Loomis, Rocklin, Roseville, and the unincorporated areas of Placer County. Payments are included in your property tax.

MARKET ANALYSIS

The Department of Energy's sub-agency, the Energy Information Administration (EIA), collects and disseminates energy data on a daily basis so that anyone interested can get the information they need. The residential sector accounts for approximately a third of California's electric and gas usage.

According to an October 2017 report published by the EIA, one in three U.S. households faced challenges in paying energy bills or in sustaining adequate heating and cooling in their homes in 2015 (the most recent survey year). Households experiencing energy insecurity were more likely to live in homes built before 1990.

The demand for insulation and weatherization services has grown and profit margins have improved as the real estate market has recovered from the subprime mortgage crisis of 2008. The industry has also benefited from federal tax credits that encourage the installation of energy-efficient insulation.

The Freedonia Group predicts that U.S. insulation demand will rise 6.6 percent annually through 2019 to $10.3 billion. The residential market will grow the fastest, while the nonresidential market will recover from recent declines. Factors contributing to gains include: the increased number of new dwellings, the installation of more insulation in structures as more areas of the United States begin to comply with the 2012 IECC. The 2012 International Energy Conservation Code required more insulation, a tighter envelope, tighter ducts, better windows, and more efficient lighting than the 2009 code. As homeowners seek to reduce energy bills, demand will grow for insulation upgrades and retrofitting insulation in attics and walls of existing homes.

MARKETING PLAN

Our marketing plan is aimed at owners of residential property in the greater Sacramento area. We are particularly interested in targeting those owners of older homes, especially if they are likely to qualify for grants and rebates available in our state.

To summarize, our target market consists of several customer groups:

- Homeowners, especially older homes in need of energy upgrades.

- Owners of residential rental units.

We have contracted with a local web development firm to help us set up and manage our web site, blog, and social media sites. In order to reach our target markets, we plan to focus our advertising and marketing efforts in the following areas:

- **The web**: A web presence will be developed with the assistance of a professional web site creator. A blog to the site will contain articles with information of interest to the public about energy efficiency, energy-saving products, tips on saving on energy bills, and more. Each page of the site will include a contact form where a prospect provides their name, phone number, email address, and a question or comment. Contact form submissions will be answered within two business days. Our telephone number will be a prominent feature on each web page.

- **Social media**: Social media, such as Facebook and Instagram, will be used to ensure that Brown Mechanical has an identifiable presence. Contact information will be listed on all sites.

- **Networking**: Brown and Smith will participate in networking events where they can form and maintain contacts with other professionals related to the housing industry such as: realtors, insurance agents, and home repair professionals.

- **Direct mail**: A program of direct mail will be used to regularly send flyers to realtors and insurance agents in the county. Mailings will rotate with one city being targeted each month. We will also conduct bulk mailings to specific zip code areas twice a year, in the fall and spring. These campaigns will encourage homeowners to prepare for the extreme weather conditions of summer and fall when utility bills tend to rise.

- **Referrals**: The ability to build trust with a customer through an accurate quote that creates no surprises will build a loyal following and, in turn, numerous happy referrals. Both paper and magnet business cards will be handed out liberally to help customers keep Brown Mechanical top of mind. A membership on Angie's List will be purchased so that customers can post comments. Posts will be monitored so that any customers who post unfavorable comments can be contacted and resolved.

- **Vehicles**: All vehicles used by Brown Mechanical will have a custom paint job that will include the company name, logo, phone number, web address, list of primary services, and geographic areas served.

- **Yellow pages**: All but replaced by the web, yellow pages are still used by a segment of the population. A listing here on a year after year basis will help to establish the brand and build recognition.

- **Home Shows**: Fall and spring home shows in Sacramento County and nearby Placer County provide the perfect venue to meet with prospects face-to-face and explain how they can save money while upgrading the energy efficiency of their dwellings.

MANAGEMENT SUMMARY

The company will be managed by owners Samson Brown and Kent Smith, both native Sacramento residents.

Samson attended college at Sacramento State University and earned his tuition by working in construction during the summer. After graduation, Samson continued to work in construction. The recession that impacted the industry in 2009 prompted Samson to become a sales person for a major home improvement retailer.

In 2013, Samson became a certified HVAC (heating, cooling, and ventilation) technician and earned his license with the California State License Board (CSLB). He began working on construction jobs as a subcontractor while continuing his sales job.

Kent Smith also earned his college tuition by working in construction. He attended Sacramento State University where he earned a bachelor's degree in engineering. After graduation Kent went to work for a large construction company in Sacramento as a construction engineer. His duties included cost analysis, assisting with pre-construction activities, procurement, pricing, and managing potential changes in scope of work.

When Kent got the urge to go out on his own, he became a certified building analyst allowing him to perform comprehensive, whole-home assessments, identify problems at their root cause, and prescribe and prioritize solutions based on building science. Through the Building Performance Institute, Inc. (BPI) Kent also earned certification as an Energy Auditor (EA), which qualifies him to perform an evaluation of the home's performance, including using more advanced diagnostic equipment and modeling software.

PERSONNEL PLAN

Staffing needs for the company will increase to keep pace with increasing business.

Personnel	Year 1	Year 2	Year 3
Salary, Samson Brown	$20,000	$ 40,000	$ 40,000
Salary, Kent Smith	$20,000	$ 40,000	$ 40,000
Technician	$24,000	$ 30,000	$ 36,000
Technician		$ 32,000	$ 36,000
Office manager/ bookkeeper	$24,000	$ 24,000	$ 24,000
Totals	**$88,000**	**$166,000**	**$176,000**
Total people	**5**	**4**	**5**

FINANCIAL PLAN

Pro forma Profit and Loss

	Year 1	Year 2	Year 3
Sales	$165,000	$255,000	$305,000
Direct costs of sales	$ 18,150	$ 28,050	$ 33,550
Gross profit	$146,850	$226,950	$271,450
Gross profit margin	89%	89%	89%
Expenses			
Depreciation	$ 4,605	$ 7,105	$ 7,105
Phone/Internet	$ 2,100	$ 2,400	$ 2,800
Payroll	$ 88,000	$150,000	$176,000
Insurance: liability, property, auto, wcomp	$ 3,200	$ 3,500	$ 4,700
Payroll taxes/benefits	$ 13,200	$ 22,500	$ 26,400
Professional dues/memberships	$ 400	$ 400	$ 400
Sales & marketing	$ 5,500	$ 4,500	$ 4,500
Office supplies	$ 425	$ 350	$ 400
Accounting & legal	$ 2,600	$ 2,400	$ 2,400
Business software/quickbooks online	$ 1,800	$ 1,800	$ 1,800
Rent/utilities	$ 19,000	$ 19,000	$ 19,000
Other expenses	$ 1,200	$ 1,200	$ 1,500
Total operating expenses	**$142,030**	**$215,155**	**$247,005**
Earnings before interest and taxes	**$ 4,820**	**$ 11,795**	**$ 24,445**
Interest expense	**$ 291**	**$ 520**	**$ 395**
Net earnings	**$ 4,529**	**$ 11,275**	**$ 24,050**
Income tax	**$ 785**	**$ 1,797**	**$ 3,713**
Net profit	**$ 3,744**	**$ 9,478**	**$ 20,337**
Net profit/sales	**2%**	**4%**	**7%**

Projected Balance Sheet

Assets	Year 1	Year 2	Year 3
Cash in bank	$ 3,125	$ 3,082	$25,004
Accounts receivable	$ 1,800	$ 2,500	$ 3,200
Other current assets			
Total current assets	**$ 4,925**	**$ 5,582**	**$28,204**
Fixed assets			
Office furniture & equipment	$ 9,550	$ 9,550	$ 9,550
Van	$16,500	$16,500	$16,500
Trucks	$20,000	$45,000	$45,000
Less: depreciation	($ 4,605)	($11,710)	($18,815)
Total assets	**$46,370**	**$64,922**	**$80,439**
Liabilities			
Current liabilities	$ 500	$ 700	$ 1,500
Accounts payable			
Other current liabilities			
Total current liabilities	**$ 500**	**$ 700**	**$ 1,500**
Long term liabilities			
Truck loan	$12,126	$21,000	$15,380
Total liabilities	**$12,626**	**$21,700**	**$16,880**
Paid-in capital	$30,000	$30,000	$30,000
Retained earnings		$ 3,744	$13,222
Net profit	**$ 3,744**	**$ 9,478**	**$20,337**
Total capital	**$33,744**	**$43,222**	**$63,559**
Total liabilities & capital	**$46,370**	**$64,922**	**$80,439**

Indoor Sports and Athletic Training Facility

Top-Tier Sports Training, Inc.

48297 Eastern Pkwy, NW
Iron Ridge, MN 68339

Paul Greenland

Top-Tier Sports Training helps young athletes maximize performance and prevent avoidable injuries.

EXECUTIVE SUMMARY

Located in Iron Ridge, Minnesota, within close proximity to five school districts, two private colleges, and Iron Ridge University, Top-Tier Sports Training helps young athletes maximize performance and prevent avoidable injuries. The business offers athletic training services for youth, adolescents, and young adults through a series of age-based general conditioning programs, as well as private lessons geared specifically toward the sports of ice hockey and track and field. Top-Tier Sports Training is being established by Certified Athletic Trainers Lewis Foster and Samantha Williams, in conjunction with the equity firm, Eustis Capital Partners.

MARKET ANALYSIS

Top-Tier Sports Training is located in Iron Ridge, Minnesota, within close proximity to five school districts, two private colleges, and Iron Ridge University. The region is home to thousands of competitive youth and adolescent athletes, and hundreds of teams in a variety of sports.

In partnership with the graduate business program at Iron Ridge University, the owners of Top-Tier Sports Training conducted an analysis of the local market. Consisting of a survey distributed to area families, coaches, and athletic directors, the analysis sought to identify specific sports training-related opportunities in the Iron Ridge market. The results of the analysis identified three challenges that Top-Tier Sports Training will address, including:

1. A lack of general athletic training and conditioning programs for youth and adolescents (beyond instruction provided through team sports participation).

2. Hockey practice facility demand that exceeds supply, due to limited availability of indoor natural ice.

3. The need for indoor track and field practice facilities during the cold winter months, when outdoor facilities are inaccessible due to ice and snow.

SERVICES

Top-Tier Sports Training will offer athletic training services for youth, adolescents, and young adults. Services typically will be provided in one of two formats, including:

General Conditioning Programs (12 weeks)

Super Start (ages 7-9): Focuses on developing strong athletic foundations needed to compete in a variety of sports, with an emphasis on developing proper movement patterns, body mechanics, and coordination. $350

Rising Stars (ages 10-12): Builds upon and reinforces the principles established during the Super Start program, with an emphasis on developing movement skills (e.g., jumping and landing, etc.), endurance, and physical strength. $350

Strong Foundations (Ages 13-14): While reinforcing the concepts and principles established in previous programs, this program incorporates additional skills that pertain to specific sports, with an emphasis on developing a competitive edge through superior endurance, speed, and strength. Individualized opportunities will be provided to athletes preparing to compete at the collegiate level. $450

Peak Performers (Ages 15-17): Same as Strong Foundations, but geared to older students. $450

Private Lessons (Ages 7-21)

Hockey players and athletes participating in track and field will benefit from customized, goal-based strength and conditioning programs. Lessons will include both individualized instruction and small group participation when appropriate. Programming is intended to complement, and not interfere with, team-based instruction/conditioning. $550/12 weeks.

The owners anticipate that the Peak Performers program and private lessons will account for more than half of business volume during the first year of operation:

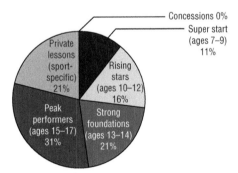

OPERATIONS

Location

Top-Tier Sports Training is located at 48297 Eastern Pkwy. NW in Iron Ridge, Minnesota, within close proximity to five school districts, two private colleges, and Iron Ridge University. The business occupies a 10,500-square-foot space that formerly was home to a leading retail chain.

Facility Features

Top-Tier Sports Training's facility includes:

1. Turf Space (2,000 square feet) for practicing jumps and throws.

2. Pole Vault Pit

3. Weight Training Area

4. Fitness/Cardio Area

5. Hockey/Skating Treadmill

6. Four-Lane Shooting Gallery (Synthetic Ice)

7. Locker Rooms

8. Speed Development & Conditioning Center (two three-lane straightaways, long enough to accommodate hurdle and sprint workouts)

9. Waiting Area (Concessions & Free Wi-Fi)

PERSONNEL

Ownership

Top-Tier Sports Training is being established by Lewis Foster and Samantha Williams. Both certified athletic trainers, the owners are passionate about teaching foundational athletic training and conditioning principles. The owners believe that this approach will enable young athletes to make the most of their athletic careers, regardless of the sports in which they participate. Importantly, Foster and Williams believe that proper training and conditioning are essential for avoiding preventable injuries and maximizing athletic performance.

Foster, who holds a degree in health fitness and recreation from Minnesota State University, will serve as president of Top-Tier Sports Training. A certified strength and conditioning specialist, he is a long-time hockey player who competed at the collegiate level and has worked as a trainer with two National Hockey League teams.

Williams, who will serve as Top-Tier Sports Training's vice president, graduated from the University of Central Oklahoma, where she earned degrees in exercise physiology and kinesiology. A competitive runner, she has extensive experience working with indoor and outdoor track teams at the collegiate level. Additionally, Williams holds an undergraduate business degree from Parker College and has seven years of experience managing locations for a national fitness center franchise.

Staff

Foster and Williams will hire several staff members, as outlined in the following staffing plan for the business' first three years of operations. An additional athletic trainer will be hired during the first year, and eventually will function as a front-line supervisor when the business adds personal trainers to the staff during years two and three.

Staffing	2018	2019	2020
Lewis Foster, president	$ 95,000	$105,000	$115,000
Samantha Williams, vice president	$ 95,000	$105,000	$115,000
Athletic trainer	$ 45,000	$ 47,250	$ 49,613
Personal trainer	$ 0	$ 36,000	$ 37,800
Personal trainer	$ 0	$ 0	$ 36,000
Administrative assistant	$ 25,000	$ 26,250	$ 27,563
	$260,000	**$319,500**	**$380,976**

Professional & Advisory Support

Top-Tier Sports Training has established a business banking account at Iron Ridge Community Bank, including a merchant account for accepting credit card payments. Tax advisement is provided by Northern Frontiers Financial LLC.

GROWTH STRATEGY

Top-Tier Sports Training has established the following growth strategy for its first three years of operations:

Year One: Establish Top-Tier Sports Training in conjunction with Eustis Capital Partners. Focus on building awareness of the business and the services it provides, among families, athletes, and sports teams in the local market. Generate a net profit of $140,948 on gross revenue of $533,750.

Year Two: Continue to emphasize brand building activities. Recoup owners' startup investments. Generate a net profit of $464,373 on gross revenues of $932,925.

Year Three: Evaluate opportunities to add additional training programs and services for other sports. Generate a net profit of $552,847 on gross revenues of $1,099,350.

MARKETING & SALES

Top-Tier Sports Training will rely upon the following marketing tactics to build the business:

1. *Branding*. In partnership with a local graphic designer, the owners have developed an eye-catching logo and color scheme for Top-Tier Sports Training.

2. *Discount Pricing*. The business will offer customers a twenty percent discount in exchange for committing to an annual membership contract, as opposed to paying for lessons/training in twelve-week increments.

3. *Sales Calls*. To generate referrals, the owners have developed a detailed schedule of promotional calls (available upon request), which they will make to coaches and athletic directors in the local market. Based on the success of this tactic, the owners will consider the eventual employment of dedicated sales representatives.

4. *Content Marketing*. Top-Tier Sports Training's owners will produce an e-mail newsletter and blog, which will allow them to stay visible with families, athletes, coaches, and athletic directors in the local market.

5. *Advertising & Sponsorships*. The business will pursue sponsorship advertising opportunities with regional school districts and sports teams. This may include advertisements in ice rinks, gymnasiums, and sports programs, as well as special event sponsorships (e.g., banner advertising at tournaments and competitions).

6. *Media Relations*. Top-Tier Sports Training's owners will position themselves as local expert sources for news stories pertaining to athletic training and conditioning. Seasonal opportunities include the need for experts to conduct brief television interviews about topics, such as training in hot or cold weather conditions, concussions, etc.

7. *Web Site*. Top-Tier Sports Training will develop a search-engine-friendly Web site that includes descriptions of its facility, owners, staff, and classes, along with case studies from athletes who have benefited from the business' programming.

8. *Social Media*. An active presence will be maintained on several social media channels, including Facebook, Twitter, and YouTube.

FINANCIAL ANALYSIS

Startup Costs

Top-Tier Sports Training will require approximately $200,000 in capital to cover the following startup costs:

Startup Costs

Turf	$ 2,665
Netting	$ 780
Synthetic ice	$ 4,000
Lockers	$ 1,650
Signage	$ 1,450
Fitness equipment	$ 10,250
Sporting goods	$ 850
Skating treadmill	$ 25,000
Polevault pit	$ 16,500
Furniture	$ 3,000
Facility improvements	$ 65,500
Rubber fitness mats	$ 475
Mortgage down payment	$ 70,000
	$202,120

Projected Revenues & Expenses

In partnership with their accounting firm, the owners have prepared a complete set of pro forma financial statements, which are available upon request. The following table provides an overview of expected revenue and expenses for the first three years of operations:

	2018	2019	2020
Revenue			
Super start	$ 56,000	$ 98,000	$ 115,500
Rising stars	$ 84,000	$147,000	$ 173,250
Strong foundations	$112,000	$196,000	$ 231,000
Peak performers	$168,000	$294,000	$ 346,500
Private lessons	$112,000	$196,000	$ 231,000
Concessions	$ 1,750	$ 1,925	$ 2,100
Total revenue	**$533,750**	**$932,925**	**$1,099,350**
Expenses			
Telecommunications	$ 1,650	$ 1,700	$ 1,750
Maintenance & repairs	$ 5,500	$ 6,000	$ 6,500
Accounting & legal	$ 3,200	$ 3,500	$ 3,700
Payroll	$260,000	$319,500	$ 380,976
Payroll taxes	$ 39,000	$ 47,925	$ 57,146
Janitorial services	$ 7,500	$ 7,750	$ 8,000
Security	$ 1,500	$ 1,650	$ 1,800
Utilities	$ 11,500	$ 12,075	$ 12,679
Miscellaneous	$ 1,500	$ 1,500	$ 1,500
Equipment	$ 12,000	$ 12,000	$ 12,000
Food & beverage	$ 5,000	$ 5,500	$ 6,000
Marketing & promotion	$ 25,000	$ 30,000	$ 35,000
Facility mortgage	$ 19,452	$ 19,452	$ 19,452
Total expenses	**$392,802**	**$468,552**	**$ 546,503**
Net profit	**$140,948**	**$464,373**	**$ 552,847**

Financing

The equity firm, Eustis Capital Partners, has agreed to provide $150,000 in startup capital for Top-Tier Sports Training in exchange for a 35 percent ownership stake in the company. Eustis Capital, which has extensive experience investing in sports-related businesses, such as health clubs and indoor sports centers, will provide valuable management and operations guidance. Lewis Foster and Samantha Williams will contribute $70,000 and $50,000, respectively, from personal savings and investments, jointly controlling the remaining 65 percent. The business will begin operations with $270,000 in total funding.

Interpretation and Translation Services

Defender Interpreting Services

15567 Beach Blvd.
Pensacola, Florida 32505

Fran Fletcher

Defender Interpreting Services (DIS) provides interpreting and translation services in Pensacola, Florida. DIS is owned and operated by Lydia Lopez.

BUSINESS OVERVIEW

Defender Interpreting Services (DIS) provides interpreting and translation services in Pensacola, Florida. DIS is owned and operated by Lydia Lopez.

Ms. Lopez got the idea for her business while working at the local hospital. She became a valuable asset to the hospital by helping doctors and nurses better communicate with its Spanish-speaking patients. Ms. Lopez began working at a food processing facility after completing her biology degree. While working in the Quality Assurance laboratory, she saw a great need for her company to provide policies and procedures in Spanish for its workers who may not grasp English instructions in its entirety. Ms. Lopez was allowed to translate the policies and procedures, and the company saw an increase in productivity and a decrease in mistakes and accidents. She wants to start her own business and work with various industries providing these services. Ms. Lopez will work from her home office. She will provide onsite services and will also be available to interpret over the phone or Internet. Hospitals, medical offices, court systems, and various businesses that do not wish to hire a full-time employee, specifically for this task, will benefit from Ms. Lopez's services.

There are currently no other local businesses that provide interpreting and translation services. There is an increasing need for this type of service due to the expansion of industry in the region, which has brought in workers from all over the world. Some of these workers and members of their families do not speak English well and need help, especially when dealing with medical and legal terms. Ms. Lopez will also work with local industries to transcribe policies and procedures and conduct training.

Advertising will include placing ads in multiple industry trade journals. Ms. Lopez will also call and send brochures to industries in the Florida panhandle that will benefit from her services.

Ms. Lopez hopes to quickly build clientele. Eventually, she has plans to hire additional personnel as she expands her services for translating policies and procedures for local industries. A long-term goal is to provide services to companies across the United States.

Fortunately, Ms. Lopez does not need to seek outside financing at this time. She is currently employed and will remain at her current place of employment on a part-time basis until her new venture gets off the ground.

COMPANY DESCRIPTION

Location

Defender Interpreting Services (DIS) is located in Pensacola, Florida. Ms. Lopez will operate her business from her home office.

Hours of Operation

Monday through Friday, 9 a.m. to 5 p.m.

Additional Hours by Appointment

Personnel

Lydia Lopez (owner/interpreter/translator)

Ms. Lopez received a B.S. in Biology with a minor in chemistry from Florida State University.

While completing her degree, she worked at the local hospital pharmacy for five years. She became a valuable resource to the hospital by serving as an interpreter for Spanish-speaking patients. After completing her biology degree, Ms. Lopez began working at a local food processing facility in the Quality Assurance laboratory. She has been employed at this facility for two years.

Additionally, Ms. Lopez has been performing online freelance translation for five years.

Interpreter/Translator

Additional employees will be hired as business volume necessitates.

Products and Services

The company will initially offer the following services:

- Medical interpreting

- Court interpreting

- Industrial interpreting (Orientation, Safety meetings, etc.)

- Document translation

- Editing document translation

MARKET ANALYSIS

Industry Overview

The interpreting and translating industry is steadily growing across the United States. According to the Bureau of Labor Statistics, jobs in this industry are expected to remain steady over the next decade.

The Florida panhandle is currently experiencing industrial growth. The area has a diverse population, mostly due to construction and farm laborers. This diversity will continue to grow as new businesses come to the area. As the population continues to grow, there will be a need for more medical facilities and schools to service this growth.

Target Market

The target market for DIS will be any area industry that requires interpreting or translation services. These industries include, but are not limited to:

- Healthcare

- Education

- Legal

- Insurance

- Local government

- Manufacturing

Competition

Ms. Lopez is not aware of any local businesses in the Florida panhandle that provide interpreting and translating services at this time.

GROWTH STRATEGY

The overall growth strategy of DIS is to obtain interpreting and translating jobs in the Pensacola area.

Referrals are imperative for the company's growth. Ms. Lopez's primary focus will be tailoring her services to the specific needs of each individual customer. She wants them to contact her every time they need interpreting or translation services and refer her to their colleagues.

Ms. Lopez will specifically target the local courthouse, hospital, attorney offices, and schools to increase awareness of her interpreting services.

Ms. Lopez will also target local industries that are in need of Spanish policies, procedures, and documents for her document translation services.

A long-term goal is to expand the business and provide document translation services to companies across the United States.

Sales and Marketing

Ms. Lopez has identified key tactics to support the company's growth strategy.

Advertising and marketing will include:

- Mailing business brochures to local industries.

- Visiting with local industries to showcase services.

- Advertising in industry trade journals.

FINANCIAL ANALYSIS

Start-up Costs

The start-up costs for this business are minimal. The majority of start-up related costs are for new office supplies.

Start-up Costs

Business license	$ 250
Business cards	$ 150
Laptop computer	$1,000
Misc. office supplies	$2,000
Total	**$3,400**

Estimated Monthly Expenses

DIS will initially be operated as a sole proprietorship. Profits made each month will be considered Ms. Lopez's salary. She will use her personal vehicle for work and will maintain a mileage/maintenance log as required by the Internal Revenue Service.

Monthly Expenses

Phone/Internet	$150
Advertising	$150
Total	**$300**

Estimated Monthly Income

The number of clients will determine estimated income. Ms. Lopez believes that her time will be split into the following service segments:

Service Segments

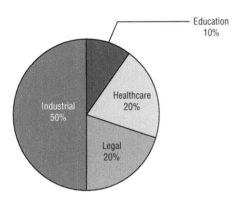

Education 10%
Healthcare 20%
Industrial 50%
Legal 20%

Price Schedule

Prices for translation projects will be negotiated between the company and each client. The base prices for services are as follows:

Service	Price
Interpreting in person	$45/hour
Interpreting via phone	$35/hour
Translation	$60/hour
Training sessions/meeting interpretation	$75/hour
Translation editing	$35/hour

Profit/Loss

Ms. Lopez is using conservative estimates to determine monthly profit/loss. She is estimating that she will not have any clients for the first month, during which time she will concentrate on meeting with potential clients and advertising her services.

During the second and third months, it is estimated that Ms. Lopez will interpret three days per month at the courthouse, eight hours per month at the local hospital, and five hours per month interpreting for local attorneys by phone. Additionally, she estimates that she will gain a one-week translation project.

Ms. Lopez expects business to remain steady from the second to the sixth month, and then increase in the third quarter by gaining an additional translation project every other month, gaining an additional three days per month at an additional courthouse, an additional five hours per month translating by phone, and one hour per week interpreting at industry safety meetings.

Therefore, these conservative figures show DIS making a small profit for the first and second quarters and making a considerable profit for the third and fourth quarters. Profits are expected to remain steady for the second and third years of operation.

Monthly Profit/Loss

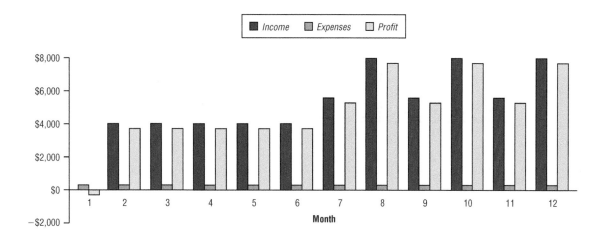

Monthly Profit/Loss

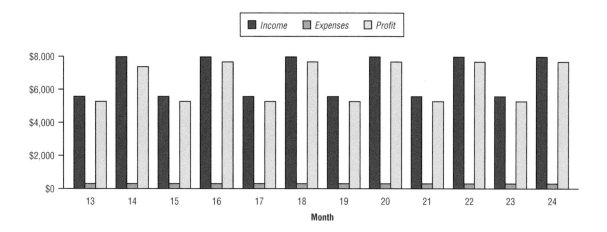

Profit projections assume that the company's income will remain constant for years two and three.

Year 1–3 Profit Projection

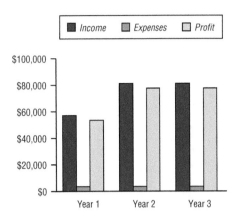

Financing

Ms. Lopez is personally financing this business venture. She will take $4,000 from her savings account to start the business and cover expenses for the first two months.

Optometry Practice

Ledgewood Eye Care Center

2296 Eastern Pkwy.
Ledgewood, WI 53000

Paul Greenland

Ledgewood Eye Care Center is a family-centered optometry business in Ledgewood, Wisconsin, which is being established through the acquisition of an existing practice.

EXECUTIVE SUMMARY

Ledgewood Eye Care Center is a family-centered optometry business in Ledgewood, Wisconsin, which is being established through the acquisition of an existing practice. The business will be led by Drs. Roger Greene and Samantha Adams. Dr. Greene recently graduated from optometry school, while Dr. Adams is an optometrist with seven years of experience working for a leading retail chain. The owners plan to build upon the practice's loyal patient base and increase revenue from new and existing patients through expanded service offerings and the use of new technology.

Mission Statement

Ledgewood Eye Care Center is committed to providing comprehensive eye health services to patients and their families by maintaining stringent quality standards, offering the very latest optometry expertise, utilizing advanced techniques and instrumentation, and maintaining a clean, professional environment.

INDUSTRY ANALYSIS

In the United States, optometrists generated revenues of $15.2 billion in 2016, according to a November 2017 report from Kentley Insights. The industry researcher found that revenues had increased at an annual rate of five percent over the previous three years. There were approximately 20,279 optometry businesses operating in the United States, which generated average annual sales of $700,000. Most of these operations were small businesses. An October 2017 report from First Research Inc. indicated that the fifty largest companies generated less than ten percent of industry revenues. An October 2017 article in *Digital Journal* found that several factors are propelling demand for optometry treatments and products, including the continued aging of the population and diabetes-related visual disorders.

MARKET ANALYSIS

Local Demographics

The community of Ledgewood was home to an estimated 26,823 people (10,656 households) in 2017. Through 2022, the population was projected to grow by 3.2 percent. Average household income, which totaled $59,751 in 2017, was expected to reach $72,513 by 2022 (an increase of 21.4 percent). In 2017, household income in Ledgewood broke down as follows:

$0-$15000—17.30%

$15,000-$24,999—13.60%

$25,000-$34,999—11.10%

$35,000-$49,999—13.40%

$50,000-$74,999—19.30%

$75,000-$99,999—10.70%

$100,000-$149,999—9.60%

$150,000 +—5.00%

Ledgewood Household Income Breakdown

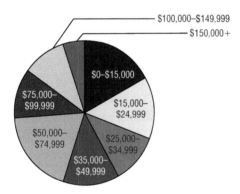

According to an October 2017 article in *Digital Journal*, several factors are propelling demand for optometry treatments and products, including the continued aging of the population and diabetes-related visual disorders. Demographic data reveal that 31.6 percent of the Ledgewood population was over the age of 45 in 2017. By 2022, this figure was projected to reach 31.9 percent. Especially strong growth (11.9%) was expected in the 65-to-74 age category, followed by individuals between the ages of 75 and 84 (9.9%).

In 2017 Ledgewood residents spent $3.1 million on eye care-related services. This total was divided almost equally between purchases of eyeglasses and contacts (53.9%) and eye care services (46.0%).

Competition

The Ledgewood market features several key competitors. In addition to an optical department at Walmart, Ledgewood is home to several independent optometrists. Like the practice that Drs. Greene and Adams are acquiring (from Dr. Charles McRae), most of these practices are very mature, having been in business for 20 years or more. They are very traditional and conservative in their approach to marketing, and typically do not have a strong focus on the latest eye care technology or innovative approaches to practice management/patient communications. Additionally, their retail eyewear selection tends to be more dated/traditional. Drs. Greene and Adams will use these factors to their advantage when competing in the local market.

SERVICES

Ledgewood Eye Care Center offers comprehensive eye exams to patients in Ledgewood and the surrounding area. In addition to assessing a patient's current vision and determining their best corrected vision, the eye exams provided by the practice will evaluate the overall health and functionality of patients' eyes and assess:

- Blood Pressure
- External and Internal Ocular Health
- Glaucoma
- Peripheral Vision
- Retinal Health

Beyond eye exams, the practice will offer several other services, including:

- Optical Dispensary
- Contact Lens Dispensary
- Vision Therapy

Additionally, Ledgewood Eye Care Center's providers will treat a variety of eye conditions, including:

- Amblyopia
- Cataract
- Conjunctivitis
- Diabetic Retinopathy
- Dry Eye Syndrome
- Eye Allergies
- Eye Infections
- Eye Injuries/Foreign Body Removal
- Glaucoma
- Keratoconus
- Macular Degeneration
- Styes and Chalazia
- Uveitis

OPERATIONS

Location

Ledgewood Eye Care Center is located at 2296 Eastern Pkwy. in Ledgewood, Wisconsin, in the heart of the community's retail district. The practice is situated in a 2,000-square-foot, freestanding building that currently is owner-occupied. Along with two fully-equipped examination rooms, the practice features a pre-test room, bathroom facilities, provider offices, a breakroom, and retail space for selling eyeglasses and contact lenses. The building has ample parking space and can accommodate physical expansion in the future.

Equipment

Ledgewood Eye Care Center's operations will utilize a variety of equipment and instruments, including:

- Computerized Autorefractor
- Computerized Ketatometer
- Digital Retinal Scanner
- Retinal Thickness Analyzer
- Visual Field Analyzer

Hours

The business will maintain the following hours:

> Monday (8 a.m.-6 p.m.)
>
> Tuesday (8 a.m.-6:30 p.m.)
>
> Wednesday (8 a.m.-6 p.m.)
>
> Thursday (8 a.m.-6:30 p.m.)
>
> Friday (8 a.m.-6 p.m.)
>
> Saturday (8 a.m.-12 p.m.)

Payment

Patients are required to pay for services on the date of their appointment. Ledgewood Eye Care Center accepts the following forms of payment:

- Cash
- Personal Checks
- Debit Card
- American Express
- Master Card
- Visa
- Discover

Forms

For the convenience of its patients, Ledgewood Eye Care Center has a variety of documents and forms available on its Web site that can be reviewed, completed, and/or submitted prior to appointments. These include:

- HIPPA
- Medical History
- Notice of Privacy Practices
- State School Exam
- Welcome/New Patient Intake

Insurance Plans

Ledgewood Eye Care Center participates in a variety of insurance plans, including Medicare, Blue Cross Blue Shield, and United Healthcare.

Legal

The owners of Ledgewood Eye Care Center have obtained adequate liability and malpractice coverage (policies available upon request). As a new graduate, Roger Greene received a fifty-percent discount on his malpractice policy premiums for the first year of operations, followed by a twenty five- percent discount for the second year. Additionally, the practice has obtained cyber liability insurance to cover costs associated with potential data breaches/computer hacking. Finally, the practice is EMR/EHR certified.

PERSONNEL

Ledgewood Eye Care Center is led by Drs. Roger Greene and Samantha Adams.

Dr. Roger Greene

A native of Wisconsin, Dr. Roger Greene recently graduated magna cum laude from the Illinois College of Optometry in Chicago. He then completed a post-doctoral residency in Ocular Disease at the Ridgeway VA Medical Center. Dr. Greene is a member of the American Optometric Association. He specializes in primary eye care including eyeglass and contact lens prescriptions.

Dr. Samantha Adams

Dr. Samantha Adams is an optometrist with seven years of experience working for a leading retail chain. A graduate of Ohio State University College of Optometry, Dr. Adams completed additional clinical training at North Side Veterans Administration Hospital and the Ohio Eye Institute. She specializes in the diagnosis and management of ocular diseases.

Professional & Advisory Support

The owners of Ledgewood Eye Care Center have established a business banking account with Ledgewood Community Bank, along with a merchant account for accepting credit card payments. An adequate level of liability insurance has been obtained from AOAExcel. Additionally, Greene and Adams have chosen to partner with Bank of America Practice Solutions, a leading provider of financial solutions for optometrists seeking to purchase or expand an existing practice. In addition to providing financing, Bank of America Practice Solutions offers other useful services, including a complimentary program to "help new optometrists develop the management, analytical, and competitive skills crucial to growth."

BUSINESS STRATEGY

Drs. Greene and Adams plan to build upon the practice's loyal patient base and increase revenue from new and existing patients through several key strategies. These include, but are not limited to:

1. The expansion of service offerings to include vision therapy (a service currently lacking in the local market) for patients with conditions such as amblyopia.

2. The use of new technology, including appointment confirmation/reminder messages (via phone, e-mail, and/or text message) to reduce no-show rates.

3. The revitalization of the practice's retail eyewear business by offering more contemporary styles and refreshing inventory more frequently.

4. The introduction of more patient-friendly amenities, including complementary bottled water, coffee, and snacks in the waiting room.

MARKETING & SALES

Ledgewood Eye Care Center has developed a marketing plan that includes the following key tactics:

1. Development of a new brand identity that reflects the practice's new ownership.

2. Semi-annual direct mailings to patients' homes, featuring discounts/special offers as a call to action.

3. High-impact exterior signage to promote the clinic's new branding/ownership.

4. Four-color, trifold brochures promoting the practice and the services provided.

5. Social media promotion (Facebook).

6. A mobile-friendly Web site.

7. A PR strategy (focused on major television network affiliates and regional newspapers) that positions Drs. Greene and Adams as eye care experts in Ledgewood and the surrounding region.

8. An eye health blog, with bimonthly postings from Drs. Greene and Adams.

9. A referral program that offers existing patients a fifteen percent discount off their next exam (or contact lens/eyeglass purchase) for each successful referral made.

10. Print, radio, and online/social advertising.

11. Imprinted promotional premiums (e.g., pens, notepads, mini flashlights, refrigerator magnets, etc.).

FINANCIAL ANALYSIS

Overview

Drs. Roger Greene and Samantha Adams are preparing to acquire an existing practice in the community of Ledgewood that has been operating since 1982. The practice, which has an asking price of $250,000, has annual revenues of approximately $550,000 and performs approximately 2,000 eye exams each year, with average patient revenue of $300. Additionally, the practice has approximately 1,200 frames in its inventory. Comprehensive financial statements, which have been inspected by the buyers and their business advisor, are available from the seller (Dr. Charles McRae).

Funding

The owners of Ledgewood Eye Care Center will provide $75,000 in funding (equal investments of $37,500) from personal savings and investments. They are seeking financing for the remaining $175,000 from Bank of America Practice Solutions, as well as an additional $35,000 in capital for purchasing new equipment and making enhancements to the practice.

Print/Copy/Design Business

On-Target Marketing & Express Printing Inc.

25773 Williams Pkwy. NW
Indianapolis, IN 46154

Paul Greenland

On-Target Marketing & Express Printing is a marketing solutions company that works with newly established small businesses. The company is especially focused on professional services providers.

EXECUTIVE SUMMARY

On-Target Marketing & Express Printing is a marketing solutions company that works with newly established small businesses. The company is especially focused on professional services providers, such as attorneys, accountants, insurance professionals, etc. Instead of taking a "commodity approach" to graphic design and printed materials production, On-Target Marketing & Express Printing will position itself as a provider of turnkey solutions that new businesses need to start strong and maintain momentum. By bundling basic marketing planning and brand/identity development with common printed collateral that virtually all businesses need, as well as simple Web/social media development, On-Target Marketing & Express Printing will help newly established businesses get "down the field" quickly when it comes to marketing.

INDUSTRY ANALYSIS

An analysis from the firm, Supplier Relations US LLC, indicated that revenues in the quick printing industry totaled $2.3 billion in 2015, with estimated gross profits of 29.05 percent. The traditional quick printing industry has suffered declines, as a growing number of small businesses and consumers take advantage of technology that has enabled them to produce a wider range of marketing materials in their home or office. Additionally, the industry has suffered from a movement toward digital communication. Nevertheless, small businesses continue to need traditional printed materials and companies, such as On-Target Marketing & Express Printing Inc., which also provide marketing services (e.g., brand/logo development, marketing planning, etc.) and digital (e.g., Web site/social media) development are in a much stronger position than traditional "copy shops" with a commodity focus.

MARKET ANALYSIS

Geography

On-Target Marketing & Express Printing will market its services throughout the continental United States.

Target Markets

One mistake that many newly established businesses make is trying to be all things to all customers. On-Target Marketing & Express Printing will focus on providing a core group of marketing and printing services, and doing them extremely well, for professional service providers, including:

- Accountants

- Attorneys

- Chiropractors

- Financial Advisors

- Insurance Agents

- Physicians

- Realtors

By maintaining a sharp focus, On-Target Marketing & Express Printing will have the advantage of gaining a deep understanding of its customers' business models and the marketing challenges they face. By concentrating its efforts mainly on professional service providers and small business startups, the company will develop collective knowledge regarding best case marketing practices and solutions, which will benefit all customers without breaching client confidentiality. For example, strategies that work well for a new attorney in one market will likely work equally well for a new law practice in another part of the country.

Market Research

On-Target Marketing & Express Printing's owners conducted basic market research to understand the needs of the business' prospects. This was accomplished through a series of informal conversations with both new and established professional service providers. Additionally, in collaboration with a business class at Mount Hubley Community College, the owners also distributed a national survey to the same types of service providers. The results of this research, which are available upon request, shaped the development of the product and service packages offered by On-Target Marketing & Express Printing.

Competitive Differential

Most quick/rapid print businesses have a commodity mindset, and often a local/regional focus. On-Target Marketing & Express Printing will differentiate itself in the market by positioning itself as a national provider of marketing solutions, as opposed to one of many providers of graphic design/printing services. Accordingly, the business will bundle many of its offerings into standard, but customizable, turnkey packages (summarized in the Services section of this plan) that meet the needs of professional service providers preparing to launch their business and sustain ongoing promotions. Additionally, the business will become a trusted advisor/resource by providing affordable marketing/strategic planning services. In this way, On-Target Marketing & Express Printing will help new businesses succeed by developing a solid marketing plan that considers goals and objectives, as opposed to focusing solely on tactics (e.g., brochures, etc.).

PRODUCTS & SERVICES

Categories

The products and services provided by On-Target Marketing & Express Printing will fall into three general categories:

Planning—More than just a "copy/print shop," On-Target Marketing & Express Printing will be able to assist new small businesses by (1) developing a simple branding/marketing strategy; (2) designing and producing business cards, letterhead, envelopes, flyers, postcards, etc.; and (3) creating a simple but highly effective Web site and social media presence.

Graphic Design—The business will offer comprehensive graphic design services, including logo design, pagination, illustration, etc.

Printing/Copying—Services in this category include:

- Broadsheet and Tabloid Printing
- Coil Binding
- Color Copying
- Comb Binding
- Cutting
- Digital File Transfer
- Digital Imaging
- Folding
- Lamination
- Perforation
- Saddle Stitching
- Scoring
- Shrink-wrapping
- Variable Data Printing

The types of products in this category include, but are not necessarily limited to:

- Announcements
- Binders/Index Tabs
- Booklets
- Brochures
- Business Cards
- Calendars
- Color Copies
- Coupons
- Black and White Copies
- Digital Color Printing
- Direct Mail Printing
- Envelopes
- Flyers
- Labels
- Letterhead

- Manuals
- Employee Handbooks
- Memo Pads
- Newsletters
- Notebooks
- Notepads
- Postcards
- Posters
- Presentation Materials
- Programs
- Raffle Tickets
- Reply Cards
- Report Covers
- Sales Kits
- Sales Sheets
- Tickets
- Training Materials

Marketing Solutions Packages

On-Target Marketing & Express Printing will bundle many of its solutions into standard, but customizable, packages that meet the needs of professional service providers preparing to launch their business and sustain ongoing promotions. Examples of packages include, but are not limited to:

1. *Business Startup*: Aimed at newly established professional service providers, this package includes (1) a basic marketing plan; (2) development of a logo/brand identity; (3) two hours of related consulting services; (4) an initial supply of business cards, letterhead, and envelopes (500 pieces/each); (5) a simple Web site (3-5 pages); and (6) guidance establishing a presence on to social media platforms. Cost: $2,499

2. *Creative Campaigns*: This package includes (1) development of a marketing campaign plan with measurable objectives; (2) two hours of related consulting services; and (3) basic campaign collateral (e.g., social media graphics, postcards, direct mailers, ad layout, etc.). The package includes three different types of printed collateral, with a base quantity of 1,000 pieces/each. Additional quantities can be bundled into the package for an additional fee. Cost: $1,999

3. *Successful Events*: This package helps small businesses plan and host a successful event through (1) development of simple event plan; (2) two hours of related consulting/planning services; and (3) the design and production of invitations, flyers/handouts, and social media graphics. The package enables the customer to choose from a selection of pre-designed invitations and flyers, which can be customized to meet their needs. A base quantity of 1,000 pieces/each is included. Additional quantities can be bundled into the package for an additional fee. Cost: $1,499

OPERATIONS

Location

On-Target Marketing & Express Printing maintain offices at 25773 Williams Pkwy. NW in Indianapolis, Indiana. The owners have identified a facility that is close to a U.S. Postal Service hub and routes serviced by leading carriers such as UPS and FedEx, which will allow it to ship printed collateral to customers quickly and easily. The facility features a large open work area with plenty of space for graphic design and production activities. Additionally, it offers a small kitchenette for staff, bathroom facilities, space for storing customer orders prior to shipment, overhead door access for receiving shipments, and off-street parking. Terms have been negotiated with the building's owner, who has agreed to lease the facility for $11,000/year (three-year term).

Hours of Operation

On-Target Marketing & Express Printing will maintain hours of 8 a.m. to 5 p.m. (EST) Monday through Friday, but will provide convenient self-service tools (described below) to facilitate customer orders/reorders at any time.

Communications

Customers can contact the business at any time via e-mail or toll-free voice. Additionally, consultative services also are provided via toll-free voice or video chat, through a popular online meeting service. In-person consultations will be offered to customers in the Indianapolis market.

Vendors & Suppliers

The business has identified a regional office equipment distributor that offers competitive service rates. Additionally, accounts have been established with several suppliers for ink, paper, etc.

Customer Portal & Mobile App

Using a simple login, customers will be able to access order/invoice information, as well as PDF samples of previously ordered materials at any time via On-Target Marketing & Express Printing's online portal. Additionally, customers can submit new project requests, pay invoices, upload project content/files, and place reorders through the portal. On-Target Marketing & Express Printing also has developed a mobile app for Android and Apple platforms, providing customers with convenient mobile access to most of the portal's functions.

Policies

On-Target Marketing & Express Printing has developed simple policies and procedures (available upon request) based on common North American printing industry standards.

PERSONNEL

Owners

On-Target Marketing & Express Printing is being established by Jonathan Vitelli, Dottie Lewandowski, and Rick Turner.

- Jonathan Vitelli is a marketing strategist who assisted many small business startups during an eighteen-year career with Action Design Works, a leading advertising agency in Indianapolis that he founded with three other partners. Vitelli recently left the agency, which was acquired by a large national competitor.

- Dottie Lewandowski is a graphic designer with eight years of freelance experience, along with sixteen years at several advertising agencies throughout the Midwest.

- Rick Turner is a production specialist with ten years of print/copy shop experience.

Staff

In addition to the owners, On-Target Marketing & Express Printing eventually will employ two customer service specialists whose primary responsibility will be communicating with new and existing customers and project management. The business will attempt to hire customer service staff with basic desktop publishing and social media skills so that they can assist with projects when needed.

Staffing Summary

Following is an overview of the business' staffing plan for its first three years of operations:

Position	2018	2019	2020
Jonathan Vitelli	$ 85,000	$100,000	$115,000
Dottie Lewandowski	$ 65,000	$ 80,000	$ 95,000
Rick Turner	$ 65,000	$ 80,000	$ 95,000
Customer service specialist	$ 25,000	$ 26,250	$ 27,563
Customer service specialist	$ 0	$ 25,000	$ 26,250
	$240,000	**$311,250**	**$358,813**

GROWTH STRATEGY

Year One: Establish On-Target Marketing & Express Printing as a national provider of marketing solutions and print/copy/design services for newly established professional service providers. Begin offering three marketing solutions packages for small business owners. Generate a net profit of $63,472 on adjusted gross revenue of $415,000.

Year Two: Hire a second customer service specialist based on business volume. Develop two new marketing solutions packages for small business owners. Generate a net profit of $68,557 on adjusted gross revenue of $505,000.

Year Three: Introduce an additional two marketing solutions packages for small business owners. Recoup the owners' collective $100,000 startup investment. Begin evaluating the need for additional equipment/larger facilities. Generate a net profit of $97,950 on adjusted gross revenue of $595,000.

MARKETING & SALES

On-Target Marketing & Express Printing will focus on reaching newly established small businesses in the professional services category. Following are some of the key tactics that the owners will employ to promote their products and services:

Web Site: A Web site, with complete details about the businesses and the products and services it provides, will be developed by the business' owners. Significant resources will be invested into development of the site, which will be a critical aspect of its operations. In addition to basic information, the site will feature a robust customer portal, described in the Operations section of this plan.

Mobile Marketing: Through its mobile app, On-Target Marketing & Express Printing will push out special offers to existing customers (e.g., cross-sell opportunities, reorder discounts, mobile-only coupons, etc.).

Search Engine Marketing (SEM): The business will employ a combination of organic and paid search engine tactics to reach new business owners.

Social Media Marketing: Because On-Target Marketing & Express Printing is a business-to-business enterprise, the company will utilize LinkedIn to connect with new business owners.

Direct Marketing: On-Target Marketing & Express Printing will obtain mailing lists from a leading list broker, using state data, to identify newly established businesses (e.g., limited liability companies, corporations, etc.). The business will work with a local mail house to send monthly mailings (featuring special new customer discounts) to key prospects.

Blog: The owners will blog regularly on topics of interest to small business startups in order to share their marketing expertise.

FINANCIAL ANALYSIS

Startup Costs

The owners expect to incur startup charges for the following items prior to beginning operations:

5 Apple 27 Inch IMacs with Retina Displays: $7,200

Xerox Tabloid Network Color Laser Printer: $5,999

Konica Minolta Bizhub C754E Color Copier Printer Scanner: $16,300

Martin Yale 1611 Folding Machine: $650

Swingline GBC CombBind C210E Electric Punch Comb Binding Machine: $339

Akiles CoilMac ER 4:1 Coil Binding Machine: $430

Formax FD120 Card Cutter: $4,765

VoIP Telephone System: $350

Office Furniture: $2,500

Lighting Fixtures: $425

Facility Improvements: $13,600

Total startup costs: $52,558

Projected Revenue & Expenses

The following projections have been developed for the business' first three years of operations:

	2018	2019	2020
Revenue			
Consulting/planning services	$200,000	$250,000	$300,000
Graphic design	$125,000	$150,000	$175,000
Printing/copying	$300,000	$350,000	$400,000
Cost of goods sold	($210,000)	($245,000)	($280,000)
Adjusted gross revenue	**$415,000**	**$505,000**	**$595,000**
Expenses			
Adobe creative cloud subscriptions	$ 1,680	$ 2,520	$ 2,520
Accountant	$ 1,950	$ 2,000	$ 2,250
Marketing & advertising	$ 46,698	$ 51,698	$ 56,698
Alarm service	$ 600	$ 600	$ 600
Miscellaneous	$ 1,500	$ 1,500	$ 1,500
Liability insurance	$ 650	$ 650	$ 650
Facility lease	$ 11,000	$ 11,000	$ 11,000
Equipment maintenance & repair	$ 1,250	$ 1,500	$ 1,750
Telecommunications & Internet	$ 1,500	$ 1,600	$ 1,700
Office supplies	$ 700	$ 750	$ 800
Utilities	$ 4,250	$ 4,500	$ 4,750
Salaries	$240,000	$311,250	$358,813
Payroll taxes	$ 39,750	$ 46,875	$ 54,019
Total expenses	**$351,528**	**$436,443**	**$497,050**
Net profit	**$ 63,472**	**$ 68,557**	**$ 97,950**

Funding

Jonathan Vitelli, Dottie Lewandowski, and Rick Turner have agreed to collectively invest $100,000 in On-Target Marketing & Express Printing, including $52,558 in startup costs and an additional $47,442 for operations. Vitelli will contribute 45.0 percent of the overall funding ($45,000), and Lewandowski and Turner will each contribute 27.5 percent ($27,500), respectively. Vitelli's funding will come from the sale of his stake in the advertising agency, Action Design Works, and Lewandowski and Turner will obtain their funding from personal savings and investments.

Small Engine Repair Facility

Steel's Small Engine Repair

3025 Hwy. 19 S
Camilla, Georgia 31730

Fran Fletcher

Steel's Small Engine Repair is located in Camilla, Georgia, and will provide area customers with service on all types of small engines. The facility owned is and operated by John Steel.

EXECUTIVE SUMMARY

Steel's Small Engine Repair is a small engine repair facility owned and operated by John Steel. Steel's Small Engine Repair is located in Camilla, Georgia, and will provide area customers with service on all types of small engines.

Mr. Steel, a native of Camilla, Georgia, has fifteen years' experience repairing small engines. He has been repairing everything from four-wheelers to weed-eaters for family and friends since he was a teenager. A popular small engine repair business has recently gone out of business due to the owner retiring. Mr. Steel thinks that the timing is perfect to start his own small engine repair business. He hopes he can fill the void left by the recent closure and continue to offer this important service to the community.

Mr. Steel plans to rent a facility on US 19, a major roadway, to increase visibility and for customer convenience. Mr. Steel, with assistance from a service technician, will perform maintenance and repairs on:

- ATVs
- UTVs
- Golf Carts
- Lawn Mowers
- Water Craft
- Power Equipment
- Motorcycles

According to the Bureau of Labor Statistics, jobs in the small engine repair industry are expected to increase six percent over the next decade.

Local residents are the target market for Steel's Small Engine Repair. There are currently 8,000 households in the county. It is estimated that each household has at least one small engine, and half of the households have two or more small engines. There are plenty of customers in the area to sustain this new business.

There are two other small engine repair shops in Mitchell County. The owner plans to set himself apart by offering loaner equipment while the repairs are being made.

The owner estimates that it will take him approximately one year to become established. During the second year of operation, he will pursue becoming a certified warranty repair facility for several major brands.

Mr. Steel would like to acquire a business line of credit for the amount needed to cover the start-up costs and the first month's operating expenses. This loan would be in the amount of $23,800. Mr. Steel estimates that it will take him five years to repay the business loan, if income and expenses remain constant.

COMPANY DESCRIPTION

Location
Steel's Small Engine Repair is located on US 19 S, a major roadway, and will make the business highly visible to passing motorists. This space has a large fenced area, parking lot, and a large metal building.

Hours of Operations
Monday through Friday, 8 a.m.—6 p.m.

Saturday, 8 a.m.—12 p.m.

Personnel

John Steel (Owner/Operator)
Mr. Steel has fifteen years of experience working on small engines.

Engine Repair Technician
One part-time technician will be hired.

Products and Services

Products
- Lawnmower belts
- Lawnmower blades
- Weed eater
- Chainsaw blades
- Batteries
- Oil

Services
Repair services will be performed on the following types of equipment:
- Golf carts
- All-terrain vehicles
- Utility Vehicles
- Motorcycles
- Outboard motors
- Jet skis

- Riding lawnmowers
- Push lawnmowers
- Weed Eaters
- Edgers
- Chainsaws

MARKET ANALYSIS

Industry Overview

According to the Bureau of Labor Statistics, jobs in the small engine repair industry are expected to increase six percent over the next decade.

Steel's Small Engine Repair will be located just outside the city limits of Camilla. Camilla is the county seat of Mitchell County, which has a population of 23,868. There are currently 8,000 households in Mitchell County. It is estimated that each household owns at least one small engine, and half of the households own two or more small engines.

Target Market

The target market for Steel's Small Engine Repair will be residents of Mitchell County and surrounding areas needing repair or maintenance performed on their small engines.

Competition

There are two other small engine repair shops in Mitchell County. The owner plans to set himself apart from the competition by offering loaner equipment while the repairs are being made.

1. Jones Small Engines, 1477 River Rd., Camilla, Georgia. Specializes in outboard motors.

2. Greenough Small Engines, 123 N Dairy Rd., Greenough, Georgia. Specializes in power equipment.

GROWTH STRATEGY

The overall strategy of the company is to attract new customers and to keep them coming back by offering quick turnaround times and exceptional customer service. Steel's Small Engine Repair wishes to achieve strong financial growth during the first three years of operation by making a name for itself in the community.

The owner estimates that it will take him approximately one year to become established. During the second year of operation, he will pursue becoming a certified warranty repair facility for several major brands.

Sales and Marketing

According to the Small Business Development Center, referrals serve as the main advertising method for engine repair facilities.

Advertising

Advertising will consist of:

- Running ads in the *Camilla Post*.
- Mailing fliers to the residents of Mitchell County.

In addition to conventional advertising, the company will rely on quality work, great customer service, and fair prices to generate customers by word-of-mouth.

FINANCIAL ANALYSIS

Start-up costs

Estimated Start-up Costs

Rent – 1 month advance	$ 1,000
Business license	$ 250
Repair equipment	$ 5,000
Supplies/tools	$ 5,000
Inventory	$ 5,000
Office equipment	$ 1,000
Total	**$17,250**

Estimated Monthly Income

The owner estimates that his time will be divided into the following service sectors.

Service sectors

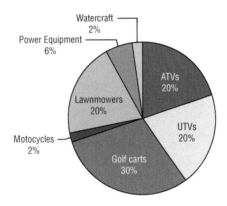

The number of repairs performed will determine monthly income. Mr. Steel estimates that the volume of income from golf carts, ATVs, UTVs, and motorcycles, which makes up seventy-two percent of his estimated business, will remain constant throughout the year. Lawnmower, power equipment, and watercraft repair, which make up twenty-eight percent of his estimated business, will primarily be in the months of April through October.

Price Schedule

Minimum Prices for General Repair Services

Golf carts	$100
UTVs	$100
ATVs	$100
Lawnmowers	$ 50
Power equipment	$ 50
Watercraft	$100
Motorcycles	$100

Estimated Monthly Expenses

Expenses are expected to remain steady.

Estimated Monthly Expenses

Bank loan	$ 400
Electricity	$ 500
Water	$ 50
Phone/Internet	$ 100
Advertising	$ 100
Insurance	$ 200
Wages for Mr. Steel (est.)	$4,000
Wages for technician (est.)	$1,200
Total	**$6,550**

Profit/Loss

Mr. Steel takes a conservative approach and uses the base price for services when estimating monthly income. During peak season, he estimates making a profit of $4,000 per month. During non-peak season months, he estimates that he could have a $550 deficit each month, but plans to use the profits from the peak months to make up the difference. At the end of the year, he should have approximately $21,400 profit.

Estimated Profits (Peak Season)

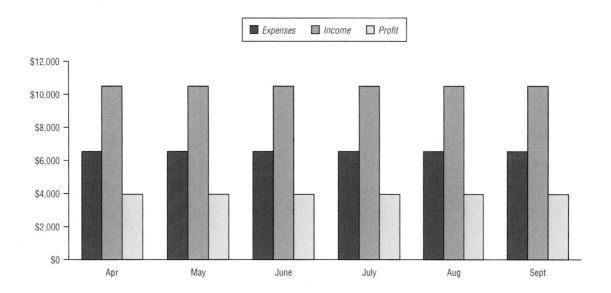

Estimated Profits (Non- Peak Season)

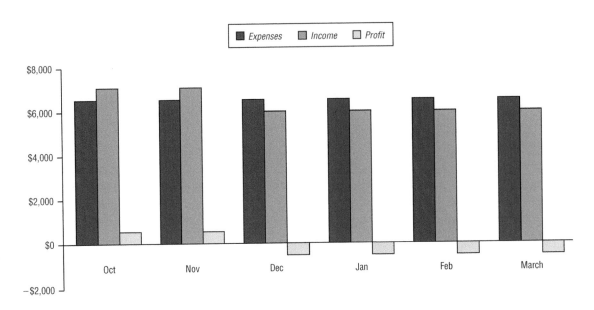

Estimated Profits Year 1

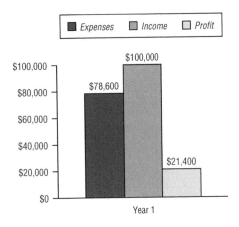

Financing

Mr. Steel would like to take out a business line of credit for the amount needed to cover the start-up costs and the first month operating expenses. This loan would be in the amount of $23,800.

Loan Repayment Plan

Mr. Steel estimates that it will take him five years to repay the business loan, if income and expenses remain constant.

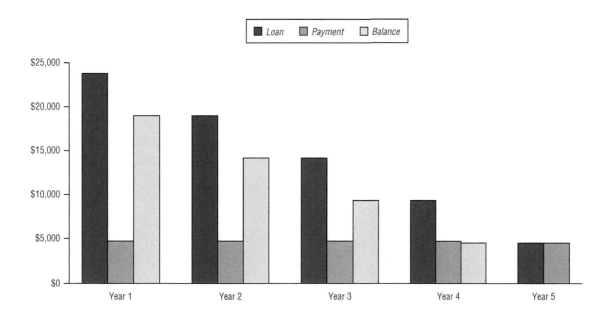

Trucking Company

Lone Star Trucking, Inc.

271 Sacramento St.
Waco, TX 76705

Claire Moore

Lone Star Trucking, Inc. (LSTI) is a Texas-based owner-operator trucking company that provides long-haul transportation services. LSTI will serve primarily the agricultural industry by hauling produce, livestock, and refrigerator freight from the field to the seller. We specialize in Midwest regional lanes ranging from Dallas to Chicago and points in between.

EXECUTIVE SUMMARY

According to the American Trucking Associations (ATA), over 70 percent of all the freight and tonnage moved in the United States moves on trucks. That translates into 10.4 billion tons of freight requiring over 3.6 million heavy-duty Class 8 trucks and over 3.5 million truck drivers.

Trucking is an industry made up of small businesses: 91 percent of motor carriers operate six or fewer trucks and 97.3 percent operate fewer than twenty. One in nine drivers are independent, a majority of which are owner-operators. In 2016, trucking generated $676.2 billion, or 79.8 percent of the nation's freight bill.

In "ATA Freight Transportation Forecast 2017" (Sean McNally 2017), ATA projects freight volumes to grow 2.8 percent in 2017, and then follow that up with 3.4 percent annual growth through 2023. In 2017, ATA projects that 15.18 billion tons of freight will be moved by all modes—a figure that rises 36.6 percent to 20.73 billion tons in 2028.

Lone Star Trucking, Inc. (LSTI) is a Texas-based owner-operator trucking company that provides long-haul transportation services. LSTI will serve primarily the agricultural industry by hauling produce, livestock, and refrigerator freight from the field to the seller. We specialize in Midwest regional lanes ranging from Dallas to Chicago and points in between.

LSTI will obtain loads through brokers, load boards, and by developing clients through personal contacts. Marilyn Messman, a trucking company dispatcher, is completing her studies to become a freight broker.

OBJECTIVES

Our objectives for the next three years include the following:

- Establish a roster of clients for whom we regularly haul product.
- Achieve profitability.
- Commence providing broker services for load scheduling.

KEYS TO SUCCESS

Making sure that every mile driven produces revenue is a constant challenge for a trucking company. We have identified the following strategies to ensure maximum revenues.

- Working with a team of brokers and shippers with whom we have developed a relationship.
- Traveling the same routes and knowing where to secure the best revenues and fuel prices.
- Established relationships with truck service and repair facilities for the best service and prices.
- The ability to perform most basic repairs and maintenance on our own.

MISSION

Our mission at Lone Star Trucking, Inc. is to deliver value to our customers by providing the highest level of transportation services that reflect our commitment to quality and professionalism.

COMPANY SUMMARY

Lone Star Trucking, Inc. is a Texas corporation with an office location at the home of owners Ted and Marilyn Messman in Waco, Texas. The home is located on five acres and includes storage structures to house the company's vehicles. Ted and Marilyn are majority owners. Other investors include Jim Messman, Ted's father, and John Kirkpatrick, Marilyn's father.

COMPANY HISTORY

Ted's professional career includes five years in the U.S. Army serving in Germany, the United States, and Iraq. After the Army, Ted earned an Associate's degree in business and began to work in construction.

Ted Messman worked for twenty years in construction in Waco, Texas, where he made a good living as a general contractor until the recession of 2009. Falling real estate prices and a tight economy led to a shortage of work with little relief in sight. Seeking a new career, Ted studied at a truck driving school and obtained certification and a commercial driving license.

After three years as a team driver for a large, national trucking company, Ted decided that it was time to go out on his own. LSTI has been in business for six months. Building on his contacts in the community, Messman developed several direct contracts with Texas growers. He also created relationships with brokers specializing in produce hauling.

His plan is to develop LSTI over the next fifteen to twenty years and then sell his equipment and contracts to a qualified trucker.

In order to help with his plans for developing a profitable business, Marilyn, who has fifteen years' experience as a truck dispatcher, is training to become a freight broker. A freight broker is an intermediary between a shipper who has goods to transport and a carrier who has capacity to move that freight.

Marilyn will continue to work as a dispatcher for the next five years. During that time, she will gradually increase her activity as a broker to secure loads for LSTI at the best rates. We project that Marilyn will then retire from her job and become a full-time broker working primarily for LSTI.

Marilyn's dispatcher salary will be crucial to the success of LSTI as the company is financing its vehicle over the next five years. Marilyn includes Ted in her health insurance coverage through her job.

The company is carrying life insurance policies on both Ted and Marilyn as a security to ensure loan payments will be covered in the event of either owner's death.

STARTUP SUMMARY

LSTI has incurred the following costs during its startup phase.

Startup Costs

Licenses	$ 350
Advertising	$ 750
Legal fees & incorporation	$ 2,500
Insurance deposit	$ 3,000
Authority: MC and DOT	$ 600
Unified Carrier Registration (UCR)	$ 85
IRP Truck plate	$ 1,600
BOC3	$ 200
Truck letters	$ 100
Software	$ 450
HRT 2290 tax	$ 550
State permits	$ 500
Office supplies	$ 300
Furniture	$ 600
Computer equipment	$ 2,400
Total start-up expenses	**$13,985**

Vehicles

2005 Kenworth W900B truck tractor	$38,500
2007 Great dane trailer reefer van refrigerated	$18,900
2000 Cornhusker convertible trailer	$10,900
Truck improvements	$ 4,000
Total vehicles	**$72,300**

COMPETITIVE ANALYSIS

Factors that directly influence the trucking business include:

- Variable fuel prices
- Fluctuation in the production of product
- Competition from large carriers
- Regulations
- Payment delays

According to the National Association of Small Trucking Companies (NASTC), only fifteen percent of new trucking companies will survive to their second year of operations. Net profit percentages were projected at between five and eight percent.

Estimates show an operating ratio of 95.2. This means for every dollar in revenue the trucking company has a cost of 95.2 cents, leaving them with a profit of 4.8 cents of every dollar. Apex Capital, a factoring company for the trucking industry, estimated in 2016 that the average operating cost per mile was $1.59.

Income figures from clients of the American Truck Business Services (ATBS), including independents three quarters of the way through the year, showed an annualized business income after expenses of $60,887, based on income averages through September.

A crucial factor for success is the company's ability to schedule loads for every mile driven. This means that a load delivered to Memphis must have a load scheduled for pickup in Memphis in order to avoid driving empty to the next destination.

COMPETITIVE EDGE

LSTI has adopted defined practices to help control costs and contribute to maximized profit. These practices include:

- We run a set number of regular routes or lanes.

- We run on a regular basis.

- We specialize in hauling certain goods (agriculture/refrigerated/food products).

- We have secured several long-term contracts with shippers, thus locking in the amount to be made on each run.

- We make use of sophisticated load board services that allow us to analyze the revenue per load and the credit worthiness of the shipper.

- By using our skills in freight brokering, we can better schedule loads for the return trips.

MARKET ANALYSIS

According to the American Trucking Associations (ATA), "The ATA U.S. Freight Transportation Forecast to 2028 projects continued growth for freight transportation overall and for the trucking industry. In 2017, ATA Projects that 15.18 billion tons of freight will be moved by all modes—a figure that rises 36.6 percent to 20.73 billion tons in 2028."

In 2017 the industry is experiencing a scarcity of drivers due to several factors including:

- A resurgence of construction jobs in the wake of hurricanes in Texas and Florida.

- Difficulty obtaining insurance for newer drivers.

- Low appeal of trucking due to wages and quality of life issues.

If the Trump administration is successful in pushing its national infrastructure initiative, the pool of drivers is expected to shrink even more as potential drivers are attracted to construction.

The ATA predicted that the driver shortfall could reach 50,000 positions by the end of 2017. If the trend continues, the shortfall could grow to more than 174,000 by 2026.

In response to the shortage in qualified drivers, fleets are raising pay and offering other incentives to attract drivers. Driver wages now top fuel as the biggest operating expense for motor carriers.

Currently, drivers are paid by the load which means a fee per mile. Industry observers speculate that pressures on driver wages will lead to a change to hourly pay, a move that will likely result in higher shipping charges. The federal mandate that requires truckers to use electronic logging devices (ELDs) to monitor their driving hours could add more pressure for a switch to an hourly wage.

Technological changes that are increasing efficiency in the industry include:

- An increase in the use of automatic transmissions, which increase fuel economy because they are lighter and they are easier to use.

- Increased use of laptops, email, electronic platforms, and GPS systems.

- The SmartWay program developed by the Environmental Protection Agency, which provides valuable insight into fuel use through tracking and monitoring as well as EPA-verified retrofits for clean diesel technologies.

  SmartWay helps companies to increase fuel efficiencies and reduce their carbon and diesel emissions.

ELD MANDATE

An ELD synchronizes with a vehicle engine to automatically record driving time for easier, more accurate hours of service (HOS) recording. Its use is intended to help create a safer work environment for drivers and make it easier and faster to accurately track, manage, and share records of duty status (RODS) data.

The ELD Rule applies to most motor carriers and drivers who are currently required to maintain records of duty status (RODS). The rule applies to commercial buses as well as trucks. The ruling does not apply to drivers of vehicles manufactured before the year 2000.

Carriers must evaluate and select ELDs, ensure they are installed, and ensure that drivers and administrative staff are trained to use them by the deadline that applies (December 16, 2019 for carriers using and automatic onboard recording device (AOBRD) or December 18, 2017 for those using paper logs or logging software).

Drivers must understand and be able to use ELDs by the required deadline, including how to annotate and edit RODS, certify RODS, and collect required supporting documents. They will also need to know how to display and transfer data to safety officials when requested.

SERVICES

LSTI provides hauling services for companies who wish to transport goods within the continental United States. We specialize in hauling agricultural products and temperature-controlled freight.

Cargo hauled by LSTI includes:

- Fresh Produce

- General Freight

- Livestock

- Grain Feed Hay

- Meat

- Dry Bulk

- Refrigerated Food

- Beverages

LSTI vehicles are in compliance with the ELD mandate having installed and trained on the required devices in our vehicles.

SERVICE AREA

LSTI hauls on truck lanes between Dallas, Texas, and Chicago, Illinois.

MARKETING STRATEGY

LSTI will focus its marketing efforts on personal contact, the Internet, and social media to reach potential customers.

Listings on the Internet will include:

- B2B Yellow pages
- Facebook
- LinkedIn

We will also take advantage of listing services through free online load boards including the following sites:

- Quick Transport Solutions
- Trucking Planet
- Hot Shot Carrier

The company web site will include a blog where Ted will regularly post articles from the road. The site will also house pages that highlight photos of our vehicles, information about our services, USDOT and FMCSA numbers, liability insurance information, as well as contact information.

Our web site and blog will link to our Facebook page and LinkedIn page. Visitors can "Like" us on Facebook and get notifications of our postings, which will be about our company.

Other marketing strategies that we will use include:

- Company vehicles that list our name, company address, phone number, web site address.
- Company shirts and hats that contain company logo and contact info.
- A tri-fold flier, pens with contact information, and business cards to hand out to contacts.
- Maintaining vehicles that are always clean and in good repair.
- Annual mailings of a Christmas card to clients.
- Membership as an industry service provider in industry organizations, such as the United Fresh Produce Association, and attendance at events where we can meet and develop client relationships.

Ted and Marilyn have developed their own special chili recipe, which has gained something of a reputation in the trucking community. Ted carries a supply with him on the road and makes sales to other truckers and customers. He often makes a gift of his famous chili to prospective clients.

The chili is an effective marketing device because it helps LSTI to stand out from the crowd.

PERSONNEL PLAN

We have developed the following plan for staffing.

Personnel plan	Year 1	Year 2	Year 3
Ted Messman	$12,000	$20,000	$30,000
Marilyn Messman	$ —	$ —	$ —
Total people	**2**	**2**	**2**
Total payroll	**$12,000**	**$20,000**	**$30,000**

MILESTONES

Task	Delivery date
Begin business plan	Jun. 2016
Corporation formed, IRS EIN obtained	Jul. 2016
Finalized logo design and registration of trademark	Aug. 2016
Apply for USDOT (Dept. of transportation) number	Sept. 2016
Apply for operating authority MC (Motor carrier) number	Sept. 2016
Purchase truck	Sept. 2016
BOC3	Sept. 2016
Obtain insurance file MCS90 form to FMCSA	Sept. 2016
Obtain IFTA (Internat'l fuel tax agreement) license	Oct. 2016
Obtain unified carrier registration	Oct. 2016
Set up IRT (Internat'l registration plan) accounts	Oct. 2016
File 2290 heavy road tax	Oct. 2016
Obtain truck plate	Oct. 2016
Finalize truck lease/log book	Nov. 2016
Create maintenance sheet	Nov. 2016
Drug consortium	Nov. 2016
Mileage sheet	Nov. 2016
Haul first load	Feb. 2017
Achieve profitability	Dec. 2018

FINANCIAL PLAN

Financial projections of revenues and expenses are based on a projected annual mileage of 100,000 per year.

Pro forma Profit and Loss

	Year 1	Year 2	Year 3
Trucking revenues	$110,000	$150,000	$170,000
Less: dispatch/broker fees	$ (5,500)	$ (7,500)	$ (8,500)
Gross profit	$104,500	$142,500	$161,500
Gross profit %	95%	95%	95%
Expenses			
Payroll	$ 12,000	$ 20,000	$ 30,000
Employment taxes/benefits	$ 2,640	$ 4,400	$ 6,600
Depreciation	$ 7,530	$ 7,530	$ 7,530
Fuel	$ 40,000	$ 50,000	$ 53,000
Repairs/maintenance	$ 11,000	$ 16,000	$ 16,000
Load boards	$ 720	$ 720	$ 720
Insurance	$ 12,000	$ 12,000	$ 12,000
License and permit renewals	$ 1,000	$ 1,000	$ 1,000
Tolls, fines, citations, tows	$ 1,300	$ 3,000	$ 3,400
Legal, accounting	$ 2,000	$ 2,000	$ 2,000
Supplies	$ 1,200	$ 1,400	$ 1,500
Misc tools	$ 700	$ 700	$ 700
Cell phone wireless network	$ 2,400	$ 2,400	$ 2,400
Meals lodging	$ 6,000	$ 10,000	$ 14,000
Profession dues	$ 800	$ 800	$ 800
Other	$ 1,000	$ 1,000	$ 1,000
Total operating expenses	**$102,290**	**$132,950**	**$152,650**
Earnings before interest and taxes	**$ 2,210**	**$ 9,550**	**$ 8,850**
Interest expense	**$ 1,429**	**$ 1,131**	**$ 824**
Net earnings	**$ 781**	**$ 8,419**	**$ 8,026**
Income tax	**$ 117**	**$ 1,263**	**$ 1,204**
Net profit	**$ 664**	**$ 7,156**	**$ 6,822**
Net profit/sales	**1%**	**5%**	**4 %**

Projected Balance Sheet	Year 1	Year 2	Year 3
Assets			
Current assets			
Cash in bank	$ 1,772	$ 3,951	$ 6,533
Accounts receivable	$ 7,000	$ 10,000	$ 12,000
Other current assets			
Total current assets	**$ 8,772**	**$ 13,951**	**$ 18,533**
Long term assets			
Vehicles	$72,300	$ 72,300	72,300
Furniture/equipment	$ 3,000	$ 3,000	$ 3,000
Less: depreciation	$ (7,530)	$(15,060)	$(22,590)
Total long term assets	**$67,770**	**$ 60,240**	**$ 52,710**
Total assets	**$76,542**	**$ 74,191**	**$ 71,243**
Liabilities & capital			
Current liabilities			
Accounts payable	$ 264	$ 440	$ 660
Current maturities loan			
Total current liabilities	**$ 264**	**$ 440**	**$ 660**
Long term liabilities			
Vehicle loans	40,614	30,931	20,941
Total liabilities	**$40,878**	**$ 31,371**	**$ 21,601**
Paid-in capital	$35,000	$ 35,000	$ 35,000
Retained earnings		$ 664	$ 7,820
Net profit	**$ 664**	**$ 7,156**	**$ 6,822**
Total capital	**$35,664**	**$ 42,820**	**$ 49,642**
Total liabilities & capital	**$76,542**	**$ 74,191**	**$ 71,243**

REFERENCES

Sean McNally. 2017. *ATA Forecasts Continued Growth for Trucking, Freight Economy*. July 19. Accessed October 21, 2017. http://www.trucking.org/article/ATA-Forecasts-Continued-Growth-for-Trucking-and-Freight-Economy.

Violence Prevention Consulting Firm

Weston & Kirby Associates Inc.

1736 Prestwick Blvd., Ste. 245
Lakewood, MA 01005

Paul Greenland

Weston & Kirby Associates Inc. is a consulting firm focused on developing violence prevention training programs and multimedia products for schools.

EXECUTIVE SUMMARY

Weston & Kirby Associates Inc. is a consulting firm focused on developing violence prevention training programs and multimedia products for schools. The firm is being established by Training and Development Specialist, Peter Weston and School Social Worker, Samantha Kirby, who will leverage their extensive professional experience to establish a successful consultancy that provides high-impact violence prevention strategies and solutions to school administrators and educators. The firm initially will provide services in the Greater Boston region, and then gradually expand throughout the Commonwealth of Massachusetts. Long-term, Weston & Kirby Associates plans to serve school districts along the entire eastern seaboard.

INDUSTRY ANALYSIS

Overview

According to the U.S. Department of Labor, Bureau of Labor Statistics, employment in the field of education and training was expected to experience growth of nine percent between 2016 and 2026, during which time 876,800 new jobs were expected to be created.

Professional Organizations

Many professionals in the training field pursue membership in the Association for Talent Development (https://www.td.org). Formerly known as the American Society for Training & Development, the ATD describes itself as "a professional membership organization supporting those who develop the knowledge and skills of employees in organizations around the world." ATD counts a variety of professionals from approximately one hundred and twenty different countries among its membership base, including trainers and instructional designers. It offers a variety of resources, including conferences, research, education programs, and certification opportunities.

MARKET ANALYSIS

Overview

Violence is a major public health issue, impacting people of all ages and economic backgrounds. In addition to physical injury and harm, violence has related socioeconomic costs, ranging from low productivity and lost wages to mental illness and suicide. Violence among youth, specifically, is an especially pressing problem that impacts thousands of people every day.

According to a 2016 report from the Centers for Disease Control and Prevention's Division of Violence Prevention, National Center for Injury Prevention and Control, "Youth violence occurs when young people between the ages of ten and twenty-four years intentionally use physical force or power to threaten or harm others. Youth violence typically involves young people hurting other peers who are unrelated to them and who they may or may not know well. Youth violence can take different forms. Examples include fights, bullying, threats with weapons, and gang-related violence. A young person can be involved with youth violence as a victim, offender, or witness."

The CDC's report indicated that twelve young people are homicide victims every day, and approximately 1,374 receive medical treatment in emergency rooms for injuries related to nonfatal physical assault. More than 500,000 medically treated physical injuries are attributed to youth violence every year. Furthermore, medical and lost productivity costs associated with both nonfatal physical assault-related injuries and youth homicides total approximately $18.2 billion annually. This figure does not take into account the economic impact related to incarcerations, arrests, prosecutions, etc.

Target Markets

Weston & Kirby Associates initially will focus its marketing efforts on educational institutions in the Greater Boston area, including:

- Private Schools
- Public School Districts
- Community Colleges
- Universities

Using a combination of publicly available data, as well as information purchased from a reputable mailing list broker, the owners have developed a detailed list of school administrators and personnel in the Boston market that will be used for marketing purposes, as outlined in the Marketing & Sales section of this plan.

Schools will typically utilize a combination of budgeted funds, as well as grant funding, to pay for the services offered by Weston & Kirby Associates.

Future Markets

As outlined in the Growth Strategy section of this plan, Weston & Kirby Associates will eventually begin marketing violence prevention consulting services and training programs in other regions of Massachusetts, and finally to school districts along the entire eastern seaboard.

PRODUCTS & SERVICES

Consulting & Training

Weston & Kirby Associates will utilize a combination of proprietary and third-party resources to offer school safety and violence prevention programs in several categories, including:

- Afterschool Program Development

- Classroom Management

- Code of Conduct Development

- Dispute Management/Conflict Resolution

- Districtwide Risk Factor Assessments

- Emergency Preparedness Strategies

- Mentoring Program Development

- Positive Behavior Support

The firm's training and consulting services will address specific issues, including:

- Bullying

- Dating Violence

- General Violence

- Problem Behaviors

Weston & Kirby Associates will customize its services to meet the unique needs of its customers (private schools, public school districts, colleges, and universities). Services typically will be provided at an hourly rate of $150 per consultant. This rate will be considered when developing topical training packages, which will be offered for a flat fee that includes preparation time, training, handouts, and travel/lodging expenses. Training packages will range in length and scope, including brief presentations and half-day, all-day, and multi-day programs. Trainings may be geared toward an administrative-level audience, teachers, paraprofessionals, support staff, general audiences, and students (e.g., classroom and/or general assembly presentations).

Although service-level scenarios may vary considerably, one example of an extensive situation would be a school district that contracts with the firm for fifteen days of consulting time for a given school year. During the summer months, the firm might work with principals, assistant principals, and other staff to plan the rollout of a program for the upcoming school year. This may involve an analysis of school- or district-wide data and the development of specific violence prevention strategies and tactics, which would be the focus of staff training throughout the year on school improvement days. Additionally, consultants also would make themselves available on an as-needed basis throughout the academic year.

Multimedia Products

In addition to consulting and training services, Weston & Kirby Associates will also develop and market a series of multimedia products that educators may use for training and development purposes. The partners plan to develop three different multimedia products per year, which typically will include components such as video presentations, printed materials, and self-scoreable assessment tools. The owners have developed three initial products that they will sell during the business' first year of operations.

1. *Bullying Prevention*: Successful Elementary School Strategies ($1,295)

2. *Next-Generation Conflict Resolution*: Proven Tools for Today's Educator ($1,595)

3. *On the Bus*: Violence Prevention Methods for School Transportation ($1,795)

Price points for the above products were established considering the cost of similar programs on the market, as well as production and marketing costs. A twenty-percent discount will be offered to clients that choose to purchase digital/downloadable versions of training products.

Product & Service Benefits

Regardless of the scope/format, the types of consulting services and evidence-based training programs offered by Weston & Kirby Associates have a proven track record of success. For example, in mid-2017 the Centers for Disease Control and Prevention indicated that "universal school-based violence prevention programs provide students and school staff with information about violence, change how youth think and feel about violence, and enhance interpersonal and emotional skills such as communication and problem solving, empathy, and conflict management." The CDC also indicated that "a systematic review of fifty-three studies found that universal school-based violence prevention programs were associated with reductions in violent behavior at all grade levels."

Additionally, the services offered by Weston & Kirby Associates help schools and school districts take a proactive approach to violence prevention. Beyond making schools and communities safer, this has the added advantage of helping educational organizations avoid litigation.

OPERATIONS

Location

Weston & Kirby Associates' partners will maintain home offices to keep overhead low during the firm's formative years. This situation is ideal, since the partners will meet with clients in schools and district offices and a dedicated physical location will not be required.

Communications

Weston & Kirby Associates has secured a low-cost, toll-free number with auto attendant capabilities and dedicated extensions for each of the partners. Additionally, the firm has retained the services of a virtual assistant who also is accessible at a dedicated extension and can assist with scheduling meetings, fielding calls, and reaching partners urgently when needed.

Business Structure

Weston & Kirby Associates is structured as an S corporation, which provides its owners with certain tax and liability advantages. The firm's partners established their corporation as cost-effectively as possible by using a popular online legal document service.

PERSONNEL

Peter Weston

Peter Weston has fifteen years of experience in the training and development field. After graduating from the University of Massachusetts, Peter began working as a training specialist for the Monticello Consolidated School District. After holding this position for seven years, he was promoted to a supervisory training specialist, and ultimately director of training and development. These positions collectively allowed Peter to gain invaluable assistance in the areas of training needs assessment, conducting focus groups, consulting with administrators/educators, and developing and implementing training programs (including training manuals, guides, videos, and other course materials). Peter is a gifted presenter with excellent written and verbal communication skills.

Samantha Kirby

Samantha Kirby has worked as a school social worker for twenty-five years. During that timeframe, she developed extensive experience working with students, families, and other school professionals. Kirby has first-hand experience counseling students involved in bullying situations. Additionally, she has been involved in the implementation of several violence prevention training programs for both students and educators. Kirby earned her Master's in Social Work degree from the University of Montana. Additionally, she has small business management experience that will be useful to Weston & Kirby Associates, having helped her father manage his accounting practice while pursuing her college education.

Professional & Advisory Support

Weston & Kirby Associates has established a business banking account with Lakewood Bank. Legal representation is provided by Trenton, Ashton & Drake, which has developed a set of basic business agreements that the firm can use with its clients. Additionally, tax advisory services are provided by Midway Financial Services LP.

GROWTH STRATEGY

Weston & Kirby Associates has established the following growth targets for its first three years of operations:

Year One: Focus on establishing Weston & Kirby Associates in the Greater Boston market. Introduce three initial multimedia training products. Generate net income of $10,362 on gross revenue of $300,000.

Year Two: Expand consulting services beyond Greater Boston to include Northeast, Southeast, and Central Massachusetts. Introduce three additional multimedia training products. Generate net income of $30,025 on gross revenue of $375,000.

Year Three: Continue to expand the firm's geographic footprint by offering services in the Pioneer Valley, Berkshires, and Cape & Islands regions of Massachusetts. Introduce three additional multimedia training products. Generate net income of $47,687 on gross revenue of $450,000.

Long-range: In year four, Weston & Kirby Associates will began evaluating the prospect of hiring an additional consultant to expand the firm's capacity and extend services to other markets along the eastern seaboard.

MARKETING & SALES

Weston & Kirby Associates will include the following tactics in the firm's marketing mix:

1. A monthly podcast on school violence prevention, featuring guest interviews with front-line educators and administrators.

2. A content marketing strategy featuring free checklists, guides, and articles that school administrators and educators can download in exchange for joining the firm's mailing list.

3. A media relations strategy that promotes the firm's partners as thought leaders and expert sources to industry publications, as well as consumer-focused media such as popular magazines, blogs, and newspapers.

4. A bi-annual direct marketing campaign targeting administrators at both private and public schools throughout the Boston area.

5. A social media strategy focusing on LinkedIn, including posting occasional guest articles.

6. A Web site featuring downloadable content, including articles and podcasts; bios of Peter Weston and Samantha Kirby; testimonials and success stories; an opt-in newsletter; social media links; and complete details about the firm and the services it provides.

7. Networking and presentations at important education conferences and events.

8. The submission of expert articles to key publications in the education field.

FINANCIAL ANALYSIS

Weston & Kirby Associates' partners have prepared the following projections, showing estimated revenues and expenses for the firm's first three years of operations:

	2018	2019	2020
Revenue			
Consulting & training	$235,000	$280,000	$325,000
Multimedia products	$ 65,000	$ 95,000	$125,000
Total revenue	**$300,000**	**$375,000**	**$450,000**
Expenses			
Salaries	$165,000	$200,000	$235,000
Payroll tax	$ 24,750	$ 30,000	$ 35,250
Insurance	$ 8,338	$ 9,488	$ 10,638
Accounting & legal	$ 2,875	$ 3,450	$ 4,025
Office supplies	$ 800	$ 850	$ 900
Multimedia production	$ 45,000	$ 50,000	$ 55,000
Equipment	$ 5,000	$ 3,000	$ 3,000
Marketing & advertising	$ 15,000	$ 20,000	$ 25,000
Telecommunications & Internet	$ 2,300	$ 2,588	$ 2,875
Professional development	$ 4,000	$ 4,000	$ 4,000
Unreimbursed travel	$ 15,000	$ 20,000	$ 25,000
Subscriptions & dues	$ 575	$ 600	$ 625
Misc.	$ 1,000	$ 1,000	$ 1,000
Total expenses	**$289,638**	**$344,975**	**$402,313**
Net income	**$ 10,362**	**$ 30,025**	**$ 47,687**

Financing

Peter Weston and Samantha Kirby will each provide $20,000 in capital to establish Weston & Associates. The partners are seeking a short-term loan in the amount of $60,000 to cover initial multimedia production and marketing costs.

Business Plan Template

USING THIS TEMPLATE

A business plan carefully spells out a company's projected course of action over a period of time, usually the first two to three years after the start-up. In addition, banks, lenders, and other investors examine the information and financial documentation before deciding whether or not to finance a new business venture. Therefore, a business plan is an essential tool in obtaining financing and should describe the business itself in detail as well as all important factors influencing the company, including the market, industry, competition, operations and management policies, problem solving strategies, financial resources and needs, and other vital information. The plan enables the business owner to anticipate costs, plan for difficulties, and take advantage of opportunities, as well as design and implement strategies that keep the company running as smoothly as possible.

This template has been provided as a model to help you construct your own business plan. Please keep in mind that there is no single acceptable format for a business plan, and that this template is in no way comprehensive, but serves as an example.

The business plans provided in this section are fictional and have been used by small business agencies as models for clients to use in compiling their own business plans.

GENERIC BUSINESS PLAN

Main headings included below are topics that should be covered in a comprehensive business plan. They include:

Business Summary

Purpose

Provides a brief overview of your business, succinctly highlighting the main ideas of your plan.

Includes

- Topic Headings and Subheadings
- Page Number References

Table of Contents

Purpose

Organized in an Outline Format, the Table of Contents illustrates the selection and arrangement of information contained in your plan.

Includes

- Name and Type of Business
- Description of Product/Service
- Business History and Development
- Location
- Market

- Competition
- Management
- Financial Information
- Business Strengths and Weaknesses
- Business Growth

Business History and Industry Outlook

Purpose

Examines the conception and subsequent development of your business within an industry specific context.

Includes

- Start-up Information
- Owner/Key Personnel Experience
- Location
- Development Problems and Solutions
- Investment/Funding Information

- Future Plans and Goals
- Market Trends and Statistics
- Major Competitors
- Product/Service Advantages
- National, Regional, and Local Economic Impact

Product/Service

Purpose

Introduces, defines, and details the product and/or service that inspired the information of your business.

Includes

- Unique Features
- Niche Served
- Market Comparison
- Stage of Product/Service Development
- Production

- Facilities, Equipment, and Labor
- Financial Requirements
- Product/Service Life Cycle
- Future Growth

Market Examination

Purpose

Assessment of product/service applications in relation to consumer buying cycles.

Includes

- Target Market
- Consumer Buying Habits
- Product/Service Applications
- Consumer Reactions
- Market Factors and Trends

- Penetration of the Market
- Market Share
- Research and Studies
- Cost
- Sales Volume and Goals

Competition

Purpose

Analysis of Competitors in the Marketplace.

Includes

- Competitor Information
- Product/Service Comparison
- Market Niche

- Product/Service Strengths and Weaknesses
- Future Product/Service Development

Marketing

Purpose

Identifies promotion and sales strategies for your product/service.

Includes

- Product/Service Sales Appeal
- Special and Unique Features
- Identification of Customers
- Sales and Marketing Staff
- Sales Cycles

- Type of Advertising/ Promotion
- Pricing
- Competition
- Customer Services

Operations

Purpose

Traces product/service development from production/inception to the market environment.

Includes

- Cost Effective Production Methods
- Facility
- Location

- Equipment
- Labor
- Future Expansion

Administration and Management

Purpose

Offers a statement of your management philosophy with an in-depth focus on processes and procedures.

Includes

- Management Philosophy
- Structure of Organization
- Reporting System
- Methods of Communication
- Employee Skills and Training

- Employee Needs and Compensation
- Work Environment
- Management Policies and Procedures
- Roles and Responsibilities

Key Personnel

Purpose

Describes the unique backgrounds of principle employees involved in business.

Includes

- Owner(s)/Employee Education and Experience
- Positions and Roles

- Benefits and Salary
- Duties and Responsibilities
- Objectives and Goals

Potential Problems and Solutions

Purpose

Discussion of problem solving strategies that change issues into opportunities.

Includes

- Risks
- Litigation
- Future Competition

- Economic Impact
- Problem Solving Skills

Financial Information

Purpose

Secures needed funding and assistance through worksheets and projections detailing financial plans, methods of repayment, and future growth opportunities.

Includes

- Financial Statements
- Bank Loans
- Methods of Repayment
- Tax Returns

- Start-up Costs
- Projected Income (3 years)
- Projected Cash Flow (3 Years)
- Projected Balance Statements (3 years)

Appendices

Purpose

Supporting documents used to enhance your business proposal.

Includes

- Photographs of product, equipment, facilities, etc.
- Copyright/Trademark Documents
- Legal Agreements
- Marketing Materials
- Research and or Studies

- Operation Schedules
- Organizational Charts
- Job Descriptions
- Resumes
- Additional Financial Documentation

Fictional Food Distributor

Commercial Foods, Inc.

3003 Avondale Ave.
Knoxville, TN 37920

This plan demonstrates how a partnership can have a positive impact on a new business. It demonstrates how two individuals can carve a niche in the specialty foods market by offering gourmet foods to upscale restaurants and fine hotels. This plan is fictional and has not been used to gain funding from a bank or other lending institution.

STATEMENT OF PURPOSE

Commercial Foods, Inc. seeks a loan of $75,000 to establish a new business. This sum, together with $5,000 equity investment by the principals, will be used as follows:

- Merchandise inventory $25,000
- Office fixture/equipment $12,000
- Warehouse equipment $14,000
- One delivery truck $10,000
- Working capital $39,000
- Total $100,000

DESCRIPTION OF THE BUSINESS

Commercial Foods, Inc. will be a distributor of specialty food service products to hotels and upscale restaurants in the geographical area of a 50 mile radius of Knoxville. Richard Roberts will direct the sales effort and John Williams will manage the warehouse operation and the office. One delivery truck will be used initially with a second truck added in the third year. We expect to begin operation of the business within 30 days after securing the requested financing.

MANAGEMENT

A. Richard Roberts is a native of Memphis, Tennessee. He is a graduate of Memphis State University with a Bachelor's degree from the School of Business. After graduation, he worked for a major manufacturer of specialty food service products as a detail sales person for five years, and, for the past three years, he has served as a product sales manager for this firm.

B. John Williams is a native of Nashville, Tennessee. He holds a B.S. Degree in Food Technology from the University of Tennessee. His career includes five years as a product development chemist in gourmet food products and five years as operations manager for a food service distributor.

Both men are healthy and energetic. Their backgrounds complement each other, which will ensure the success of Commercial Foods, Inc. They will set policies together and personnel decisions will be made jointly. Initial salaries for the owners will be $1,000 per month for the first few years. The spouses of both principals are successful in the business world and earn enough to support the families.

They have engaged the services of Foster Jones, CPA, and William Hale, Attorney, to assist them in an advisory capacity.

PERSONNEL

The firm will employ one delivery truck driver at a wage of $8.00 per hour. One office worker will be employed at $7.50 per hour. One part-time employee will be used in the office at $5.00 per hour. The driver will load and unload his own trucks. Mr. Williams will assist in the warehouse operation as needed to assist one stock person at $7.00 per hour. An additional delivery truck and driver will be added the third year.

LOCATION

The firm will lease a 20,000 square foot building at 3003 Avondale Ave., in Knoxville, which contains warehouse and office areas equipped with two-door truck docks. The annual rental is $9,000. The building was previously used as a food service warehouse and very little modification to the building will be required.

PRODUCTS AND SERVICES

The firm will offer specialty food service products such as soup bases, dessert mixes, sauce bases, pastry mixes, spices, and flavors, normally used by upscale restaurants and nice hotels. We are going after a niche in the market with high quality gourmet products. There is much less competition in this market than in standard run of the mill food service products. Through their work experiences, the principals have contacts with supply sources and with local chefs.

THE MARKET

We know from our market survey that there are over 200 hotels and upscale restaurants in the area we plan to serve. Customers will be attracted by a direct sales approach. We will offer samples of our products and product application data on use of our products in the finished prepared foods. We will cultivate the chefs in these establishments. The technical background of John Williams will be especially useful here.

COMPETITION

We find that we will be only distributor in the area offering a full line of gourmet food service products. Other foodservice distributors offer only a few such items in conjunction with their standard product line. Our survey shows that many of the chefs are ordering products from Atlanta and Memphis because of a lack of adequate local supply.

SUMMARY

Commercial Foods, Inc. will be established as a foodservice distributor of specialty food in Knoxville. The principals, with excellent experience in the industry, are seeking a $75,000 loan to establish the business. The principals are investing $25,000 as equity capital.

The business will be set up as an S Corporation with each principal owning 50% of the common stock in the corporation.

Fictional Hardware Store

Oshkosh Hardware, Inc.

123 Main St.
Oshkosh, WI 54901

The following plan outlines how a small hardware store can survive competition from large discount chains by offering products and providing expert advice in the use of any product it sells. This plan is fictional and has not been used to gain funding from a bank or other lending institution.

EXECUTIVE SUMMARY

Oshkosh Hardware, Inc. is a new corporation that is going to establish a retail hardware store in a strip mall in Oshkosh, Wisconsin. The store will sell hardware of all kinds, quality tools, paint, and housewares. The business will make revenue and a profit by servicing its customers not only with needed hardware but also with expert advice in the use of any product it sells.

Oshkosh Hardware, Inc. will be operated by its sole shareholder, James Smith. The company will have a total of four employees. It will sell its products in the local market. Customers will buy our products because we will provide free advice on the use of all of our products and will also furnish a full refund warranty.

Oshkosh Hardware, Inc. will sell its products in the Oshkosh store staffed by three sales representatives. No additional employees will be needed to achieve its short and long range goals. The primary short range goal is to open the store by October 1, 1994. In order to achieve this goal a lease must be signed by July 1, 1994 and the complete inventory ordered by August 1, 1994.

Mr. James Smith will invest $30,000 in the business. In addition, the company will have to borrow $150,000 during the first year to cover the investment in inventory, accounts receivable, and furniture and equipment. The company will be profitable after six months of operation and should be able to start repayment of the loan in the second year.

THE BUSINESS

The business will sell hardware of all kinds, quality tools, paint, and housewares. We will purchase our products from three large wholesale buying groups.

In general our customers are homeowners who do their own repair and maintenance, hobbyists, and housewives. Our business is unique in that we will have a complete line of all hardware items and will be able to get special orders by overnight delivery. The business makes revenue and profits by servicing our customers not only with needed hardware but also with expert advice in the use of any product we sell. Our major costs for bringing our products to market are cost of merchandise of 36%, salaries of $45,000, and occupancy costs of $60,000.

159

Oshkosh Hardware, Inc.'s retail outlet will be located at 1524 Frontage Road, which is in a newly developed retail center of Oshkosh. Our location helps facilitate accessibility from all parts of town and reduces our delivery costs. The store will occupy 7500 square feet of space. The major equipment involved in our business is counters and shelving, a computer, a paint mixing machine, and a truck.

THE MARKET

Oshkosh Hardware, Inc. will operate in the local market. There are 15,000 potential customers in this market area. We have three competitors who control approximately 98% of the market at present. We feel we can capture 25% of the market within the next four years. Our major reason for believing this is that our staff is technically competent to advise our customers in the correct use of all products we sell.

After a careful market analysis, we have determined that approximately 60% of our customers are men and 40% are women. The percentage of customers that fall into the following age categories are:

Under 16: 0%
17-21: 5%
22-30: 30%
31-40: 30%
41-50: 20%
51-60: 10%
61-70: 5%
Over 70: 0%

The reasons our customers prefer our products is our complete knowledge of their use and our full refund warranty.

We get our information about what products our customers want by talking to existing customers. There seems to be an increasing demand for our product. The demand for our product is increasing in size based on the change in population characteristics.

SALES

At Oshkosh Hardware, Inc. we will employ three sales people and will not need any additional personnel to achieve our sales goals. These salespeople will need several years experience in home repair and power tool usage. We expect to attract 30% of our customers from newspaper ads, 5% of our customers from local directories, 5% of our customers from the yellow pages, 10% of our customers from family and friends, and 50% of our customers from current customers. The most cost effect source will be current customers. In general our industry is growing.

MANAGEMENT

We would evaluate the quality of our management staff as being excellent. Our manager is experienced and very motivated to achieve the various sales and quality assurance objectives we have set. We will use a management information system that produces key inventory, quality assurance, and sales data on a weekly basis. All data is compared to previously established goals for that week, and deviations are the primary focus of the management staff.

GOALS IMPLEMENTATION

The short term goals of our business are:

1. Open the store by October 1, 1994
2. Reach our breakeven point in two months
3. Have sales of $100,000 in the first six months

In order to achieve our first short term goal we must:

1. Sign the lease by July 1, 1994
2. Order a complete inventory by August 1, 1994

In order to achieve our second short term goal we must:

1. Advertise extensively in Sept. and Oct.
2. Keep expenses to a minimum

In order to achieve our third short term goal we must:

1. Promote power tool sales for the Christmas season
2. Keep good customer traffic in Jan. and Feb.

The long term goals for our business are:

1. Obtain sales volume of $600,000 in three years
2. Become the largest hardware dealer in the city
3. Open a second store in Fond du Lac

The most important thing we must do in order to achieve the long term goals for our business is to develop a highly profitable business with excellent cash flow.

FINANCE

Oshkosh Hardware, Inc. Faces some potential threats or risks to our business. They are discount house competition. We believe we can avoid or compensate for this by providing quality products complimented by quality advice on the use of every product we sell. The financial projections we have prepared are located at the end of this document.

JOB DESCRIPTION-GENERAL MANAGER

The General Manager of the business of the corporation will be the president of the corporation. He will be responsible for the complete operation of the retail hardware store which is owned by the corporation. A detailed description of his duties and responsibilities is as follows.

Sales

Train and supervise the three sales people. Develop programs to motivate and compensate these employees. Coordinate advertising and sales promotion effects to achieve sales totals as outlined in budget. Oversee purchasing function and inventory control procedures to insure adequate merchandise at all times at a reasonable cost.

Finance

Prepare monthly and annual budgets. Secure adequate line of credit from local banks. Supervise office personnel to insure timely preparation of records, statements, all government reports, control of receivables and payables, and monthly financial statements.

Administration

Perform duties as required in the areas of personnel, building leasing and maintenance, licenses and permits, and public relations.

Organizations, Agencies, & Consultants

A listing of Associations and Consultants of interest to entrepreneurs, followed by the Small Business Administration Regional Offices, Small Business Development Centers, Service Corps of Retired Executives offices, and Venture Capital and Finance Companies.

Associations

This section contains a listing of associations and other agencies of interest to the small business owner. Entries are listed alphabetically by organization name.

American Business Women's Association
9820 Metcalf Ave., Ste. 110
Overland Park, MO 66212
(800)228-0007
Fax: (913)660-0101
E-mail: webmail@abwa.org
Website: http://www.abwa.org
Rene Street, Exec. Dir.

American Franchisee Association
53 W Jackson Blvd., Ste. 1256
Chicago, IL 60604
(312)431-0545
Fax: (312)431-1469
E-mail: spkezios@franchisee.org
Website: http://www.franchisee.org
Susan P. Kezios, Pres.

American Independent Business Alliance
222 S Black Ave.
Bozeman, MT 59715
(406)582-1255
Website: http://www.amiba.net
Jennifer Rockne, Co-Dir.
Jeff Milchen, Co-Dir.

American Small Business Coalition
PO Box 2786
Columbia, MD 21045
(410)381-7378
Website: https://www.theasbc.org
Margaret H. Timberlake, Pres.

American Small Business League
3910 Cypress Dr., Ste. B
Petaluma, CA 94954
(707)789-9575

Fax: (707)789-9580
E-mail: jspatola@asbl.com
Website: http://www.asbl.com
Lloyd Chapman, Founder

American Small Business Travelers Alliance
3112 Bent Oak Cir.
Flower Mound, TX 75022
(972)836-8064
E-mail: info@asbta.com
Website: http://www.asbta.com/
Chuck Sharp, Pres./CEO

America's Small Business Development Center
8990 Burke Lake Rd., 2nd Fl.
Burke, VA 22015
(703)764-9850
Fax: (703)764-1234
E-mail: info@americassbdc.org
Website: http://americassbdc.org
Charles Rowe, Pres./CEO

Association for Enterprise Opportunity
1310 L St NW, Ste. 830
Washington, DC 22209
(202)650-5580
E-mail: cevans@aeoworks.org
Website: http://www.aeoworks.org
Connie Evans, Pres./CEO

Association of Printing and Data Solutions Professionals
PO Box 2249
Oak Park, IL 60303
(708)218-7755
E-mail: ed.avis@irga.com
Website: http://www.apdsp.org
Ed Avis, Mng. Dir.

Association of Publishers for Special Sales
PO Box 9725
Colorado Springs, CO 80932-0725

(719)924-5534
Fax: (719)213-2602
E-mail: BrianJud@bookapss.org
Website: http://community.bookapss.org
Brian Jud, Exec. Dir.

BEST Association
17701 Mitchell N
Irvine, CA 92614-6028
866-706-2225
Website: http://www.beassoc.org

Business Planning Institute, LLC
580 Village Blvd., Ste. 150
West Palm Beach, FL 33409
(561)236-5533
Fax: (561)689-5546
E-mail: info@bpiplans.com
Website: http://www.bpiplans.com

Coalition for Government Procurement
1990 M St. NW, Ste. 450
Washington, DC 20036
(202)331-0975
Fax: (202)521-3533
E-mail: rwaldron@thecgp.org
Website: http://thecgp.org
Roger Waldron, Pres.

Ewing Marion Kauffman Foundation
4801 Rockhill Rd.
Kansas City, MO 64110
(816)932-1000
Website: http://www.kauffman.org
Wendy Guillies, Pres./CEO

Family Business Coalition
PO Box 722
Washington, DC 20044
(202)393-8959
E-mail: info@familybusinesscoalition.org
Website: http://familybusinesscoalition.org
Palmer Schoening, Chm.

Family Firm Institute, Inc.
200 Lincoln St., Ste. 201
Boston, MA 02111
(617)482-3045
Fax: (617)482-3049
E-mail: ffi@ffi.org
Website: http://www.ffi.org
Judy Green, Pres.

Film Independent
9911 W Pico Blvd., 11th Fl.
Los Angeles, CA 90035
(310)432-1200
Fax: (310)432-1203
E-mail: jwelsh@filmindependent.org
Website: http://www.filmindependent.org
Josh Welsh, Pres.

HR People and Strategy
1800 Duke St.
Alexandria, VA 223142
(703)535-6056
Fax: (703)535-6490
E-mail: info@hrps.org
Website: http://www.hrps.org
Lisa Connell, Exec. Dir.

Independent Visually Impaired Entrepreneurs
2121 Scott Rd., No. 105
Burbank, CA 91504-1228
(818)238-9321
E-mail: abazyn@bazyncommunications .com
Website: http://www.ivie-acb.org
Ardis Bazyn, Pres.

International Council for Small Business
Funger Hall, Ste. 315
2201 G St. NW
Washington, DC 20052
(202)994-0704
Fax: (202)994-4930
E-mail: icsb@gwu.edu
Website: http://www.icsb.org
Dr. Ayman El Tarabishy, Exec. Dir.

LearnServe International
PO Box 6203
Washington, DC 20015
(202)370-1865
Fax: (202)355-0993
E-mail: info@learn-serve.org
Website: http://learn-serve.org
Scott Rechler, Dir./CEO

National Association for the Self-Employed
PO Box 241
Annapolis Junction, MD 20701-0241
800-232-6273
800-649-6273 (Alaska and Hawaii only)
E-mail: media@nase.org
Website: http://www.nase.org
Keith R. Hall, CPA, Pres./CEO

National Association of Business Owners
1509 Green Mountain Dr.
Little Rock, AR 72211
(501)227-8423
Website: http://nabo.org

National Association of Small Business Contractors
700 12th St. NW, Ste. 700
Washington, DC 20005
Free: 888-861-9290
Website: http://www.nasbc.org
Cris Young, Pres.

National Business Association
15305 Dallas Pkwy., Ste. 300
Addison, TX 75001
800-456-0440
Fax: (972)960-9149
E-mail: database@nationalbusiness.org
Website: http://www.nationalbusiness.org

National Federation of Independent Business
1201 F St. NW
Washington, DC 20004
(615)872-5800
800-NFIBNOW
Fax: (615)872-5353
Website: http://www.nfib.org
Juanita Duggan, Pres./CEO

National Small Business Association
1156 15th St. NW, Ste. 502
Washington, DC 20005
800-345-6728
E-mail: info@nsba.biz
Website: http://www.nsba.biz
Todd McCracken, Pres.

Professional Association of Small Business Accountants
6405 Metcalf Ave., Ste. 503
Shawnee Mission, KS 66202
866-296-0001
E-mail: director@pasba.org
Website: http://community.pasba.org/ home
Jordan Bennett, Exec. Dir.

Rainbow PUSH Wall Street Project
1441 Broadway, Ste. 5051
New York, NY 10018
(646)569-5889
(212)425-7874
E-mail: info@rainbowpush.org

Website: http://www.rainbowpush.org
Chee Chee Williams, Exec. Dir.

Root Cause
11 Avenue de Lafayette
Boston, MA 02111
(617)492-2300
E-mail: info@rootcause.org
Website: http://www.rootcause.org
Andrew Wolk, Founder/CEO

Sales Professionals USA
1400 W 122nd Ave., No. 101
Westminster, CO 80234
(303)578-2020
E-mail: support@dmdude.com
Website: http://www.salesprofessionals-usa.com
Peter Brissette, Pres.

Score Association
1175 Herndon Pkwy., Ste. 900
Herndon, VA 20170
(202)205-6762
800-634-0245
E-mail: help@score.org
Website: http://www.score.org
W. Kenneth Yancey, Jr., CEO

Seedco
22 Cortlandt St., 33rd Fl.
New York, NY 10007
(212)473-0255
E-mail: info@seedco.org
Website: http://www.seedco.org
Barbara Dwyer Gunn, Pres./CEO

Small Business and Entrepreneurship Council
301 Maple Ave. W, Ste. 690
Vienna, VA 22180
(703)242-5840
Website: http://www.sbecouncil.org
Karen Kerrigan, Pres./CEO

Small Business Council of America
Brandywine East
1523 Concord Pike, Ste. 300
Wilmington, DE 19803
(302)691-SBCA
E-mail: lredstone@shanlaw.com
Website: http://sbca.net
Leanne Redstone, Exec. Dir.

Small Business Exporters Association of the United States
1156 15th St. NW, Ste. 502
Washington, DC 20005
(202)552-2903
800-345-6728
E-mail: info@sbea.org
Website: http://www.sbea.org
Jody Milanese, VP, Government Affairs

Small Business Investor Alliance
1100 H St. NW, Ste. 1200
Washington, DC 20005
(202)628-5055
E-mail: info@sbia.org
Website: http://www.sbia.org
Brett Palmer, Pres.

Small Business Legislative Council
4800 Hampden Ln., 6th Fl.
Bethesda, MD 20814
(301)652-8302
Website: http://www.sblc.org
Paula Calimafde, Pres.

Small Business Service Bureau, Inc.
554 Main St.
PO Box 15014
Worcester, MA 01615-0014
800-343-0939
E-mail: info@sbsb.com
Website: http://www.sbsb.com
Lisa M. Carroll, MS, MPH, RN, Pres.

Support Services Alliance
165 Main St.
Oneida, NY 13421
(315)363-65842
Website: http://www.oneidachamberny
.org/supportservices.html
Michele Hummel, Contact

**United States Association for Small
Business and Entrepreneurship**
University of Wisconsin
Whitewater College of Business and
Economics
Hyland Hall
809 W Starin Rd.
Whitewater, WI 53190
(262)472-1449
E-mail: psnyder@usasbe.org
Website: http://www.usasbe.org
Patrick Snyder, Exec. Dir.

Consultants

*This section contains a listing of consultants
specializing in small business development.
It is arranged alphabetically by country,
then by state or province, then by city, then
by firm name.*

Canada

Alberta

Dark Horse Strategies
20 Coachway Rd. SW, Ste. 262
Calgary, AB, Canada T3H 1E6
(403)605-3881

E-mail: info@darkhorsestrategies.com
Website: http://www.darkhorse
strategies.com

Kenway Mack Slusarchuk Stewart L.L.P.
333 11th Ave. SW, Ste. 1500
Calgary, AB, Canada T2R 1L9
(403)233-7750
Fax: (403)266-5267
E-mail: info@kmss.ca
Website: http://www.kmss.ca

Kenway Mack Slusarchuk Stewart L.L.P.
714 10 St., Ste. 3
Canmore , AB, Canada T1W 2A6
(403)675-1010
Fax: (403)675-6789
Website: http://kmss.ca/about-us/
canmore-office/

Tenato Strategy Inc.
1229A 9th Ave. SE
Calgary, AB, Canada T2G 0S9
(403)242-1127
E-mail: info@tenato.com
Website: http://www.tenato.com

Nichols Applied Management Inc.
10104 103rd Ave. NW, Ste. 2401
Edmonton, AB, Canada T5J 0H8
(780)424-0091
Fax: (780)428-7644
E-mail: info@nicholsapplied
management.com
Website: http://nicholsconsulting.com/WP

Abonar Business Consultants Ltd.
240-222 Baseline Rd., Ste. 212
Sherwood Park, AB, Canada T8H 1S8
(780)862-0282
Fax: (866)405-4510
E-mail: info@abonarconsultants.com
Website: http://www.abonarconsultants
.com/index.html

AJL Consulting
52312 Range Rd. 225, Ste. 145
Sherwood Park, AB, Canada T8C 1E1
(780)467-6040
Fax: (780)449-2993
Website: http://www.ajlconsulting.ca

Taylor Warwick Consulting Ltd.
121 Courtenay Terr.
Sherwood Park, AB, Canada T8A 5S6
(780)669-1605
E-mail: info@taylorwarwick.ca
Website: http://www.taylorwarwick.ca

British Columbia

Stevenson Community Consultants
138 Pritchard Rd.

Comox, BC, Canada V9M 2T2
(250)890-0297
Fax: (250)890-0296
E-mail: dagit@island.net

Andrew R. De Boda Consulting
1523 Milford Ave.
Coquitlam, BC, Canada V3J 2V9
(604)936-4527
Fax: (604)936-4527
E-mail: deboda@intergate.bc.ca

Reality Marketing Associates
3049 Sienna Ct.
Coquitlam, BC, Canada V3E 3N7
(604)944-8603
Fax: (604)944-4708
E-mail: info@realityassociates.com
Website: http://www.realityassociates.com

**Landmark Sq. II, 1708 Dolphin Ave.,
Ste. 806**
Kelowna, BC, Canada V1Y 9S4
(250)763-4716
Fax: (877)353-8608
Free: 877-763-4022
E-mail: steve@burnsinnovation.com
Website: http://www.burnsinnovation
.com

Kuber Business Consultants Ltd.
3003 Saint John's St., Ste. 202
Port Moody, BC, Canada V3H 2C4
(604)568-3055
Fax: (604)608-2903
E-mail: info@kuberbiz.ca
Website: http://www.kuberbiz.ca

Seajay Consulting Ltd.
800-15355 24th Ave., Ste. 527
Surrey, BC, Canada V4A 2H9
(604)541-0148
E-mail: chris@seajayconsulting.ca
Website: http://www.seajayconsulting.ca

Einblau and Associates Ltd.
999 W Broadway, Ste. 720
Vancouver, BC, Canada V5Z 1K5
(604)684-7164
Fax: (604)873-8256
E-mail: office@einblau.com
Website: http://www.einblau.com

Pinpoint Tactics Business Consulting
5525 West Blvd., Ste. 330
Vancouver, BC, Canada V6M 3W6
(604)263-4698
Fax: (604)909-4916
E-mail: info@pinpointtactics.com
Website: http://www.pinpointtactics.com

Synergy Complete Management Consulting
1489 Marine Dr., Ste. 317
West Vancouver, BC, Canada V7T 1B8
(604)260-5477
Free: 866-866-8755
E-mail: info@synergy-cmc.com
Website: http://www.synergy-cmc.com

Nova Scotia

The Marketing Clinic
1384 Bedford Hwy.
Bedford, NS, Canada B4A 1E2
(902)835-4122
Fax: (902)832-9389
Free: 877-401-9398
E-mail: office@themarketingclinic.ca
Website: http://www.themarketing clinic.ca

Thyagrissen Consulting Ltd.
35 Talon Ct.
Bible Hill, NS, Canada B2N 7B4
(902)895-1414
Fax: (902)895-5188
E-mail: yvonne@thyagrissenconsulting.ca
Website: http://www.thyagrissen consulting.ca

Coburg Consultants Ltd.
6100 University Ave.
Halifax, NS, Canada B3H 3J5
E-mail: info@coburgconsultants.ca
Website: http://www.coburgconsultants.ca

MacDonnell Group Consulting Ltd.
1505 Barrington St., Ste. 1100
Halifax, NS, Canada B3J 3K5
(902)425-3980
Fax: (902)423-7593
Website: http://www.macdonnell.com

Ontario

The Cynton Co.
17 Massey St.
Brampton, ON, Canada L6S 2V6
(905)792-7769
Fax: (905)792-8116
E-mail: cynton@cynton.com
Website: http://www.cynton.com

Fresh Insights Consulting
901 Guelph Line
Burlington, ON, Canada L7R 3N8
(905)634-6500
E-mail: info@freshinsightsconsulting.ca
Website: http://freshinsightsconsulting.ca

Globe Consult Corp.
34 Willow Shore Way
Carleton Place, ON, Canada K7C 0B1
(613)257-8265
Fax: (613)253-2436
E-mail: infoid@globeconsult.ca
Website: http://www.globeconsult.ca

KLynn Inc.
4421 Hwy. 45
Cobourg, ON K9A 4J9
(905)373-4909
Free: 888-717-2220
E-mail: info@klynnbusiness consulting.com
Website: www.klynnbusiness consulting.com

Heaslip Associates
50 West St., Unit 2
Collingwood, ON, Canada L9Y 3T1
(613)537-8900
E-mail: info@heaslipassociates.com
Website: http://www.heaslipassociates .com

JThomson & Co. CPA
645 Upper James St. S
Hamilton, ON, Canada L9C 2Y9
(905)388-7229
Fax: (905)388-3134
Website: http://www.jthomsonco.com

Queen's Business Consulting
Queen's University
Stephen J.R. Smith School of Business
Goodes Hall, Rm. LL201
Kingston, ON, Canada K7L 3N6
(613)533-2309
Fax: (613)533-2744
E-mail: qbc@business.queensu.ca
Website: http://smith.queensu.ca/ centres/business-consulting/index.php

Fronchak Corporate Development Inc.
23-500 Fairway Rd. S, Ste. 209
Kitchener, ON, Canada N2C 1X3
(519)896-9950
E-mail: mike@fronchak.com
Website: http://www.fronchak.com

Eigenmacht Crackower
345 Renfrew Dr., Ste. 202
Markham, ON, Canada L3R 9S9
(905)305-9722
(905)607-6468
Fax: (905)305-9502
E-mail: jack@eigenmachtcrackower.com
Website: http://www.eigenmacht crackower.com

JPL Consulting
236 Millard Ave.
Newmarket, ON, Canada L3Y 1Z2
(416)606-9124
E-mail: jplbiz1984@gmail.com
Website: http://www.jplbiz.ca

Roger Hay & Associates Ltd.
1272 Elgin Cres.
Oakville, ON, Canada L6H 2J7
(416)848-0997
E-mail: info@rogerhay.ca
Website: http://www.rogerhay.ca

Comgate Engineering Ltd.
236 1st Ave.
Ottawa, ON, Canada K1S 2G6
(613)235-4778
Fax: (613)248-4644
E-mail: info_eng@comgate.com
Website: http://www.comgate.com

PMC Training
858 Bank St., Ste. 109
Ottawa, ON, Canada K1S 3W3
(613)234-2020
Fax: (613)569-1333
E-mail: info@pmctraining.com
Website: http://pmctraining.com/

Arbex Forest Resource Consultants Ltd.
1555 Scotch Line Rd. E
Oxford Mills, ON, Canada K0G 1S0
(613)798-3099
Website: http://www.arbex.ca

G.R. Eagleson Consulting Inc.
69436 Mollard Line
RR3
Parkhill, ON, Canada N0M 2K0
(519)238-2676
Fax: (519)238-1224
E-mail: eagleson@hay.net
Website: http://www.eagleson.com/ consulting

Mark H. Goldberg & Associates Inc.
91 Forest Lane Dr.
Thornhill, ON, Canada L4J 3P2
(905)882-0417
Fax: (905)882-2219
E-mail: info@mhgoldberg.com
Website: http://www.mhgoldberg.com

Petersen Consulting
136 Cedar St. S
Timmons, ON, Canada P4N 2G8
(705)264-5323
E-mail: pcmanage@nt.net
Website: http://www.petersenconsulting.ca

Care Concepts & Communications
21 Spruce Hill Rd.
Toronto, ON, Canada M4E 3G2
(416)420-8840
E-mail: info@cccbizconsultants.com
Website: http://www.cccbizconsultants
.com

FHG International Inc.
99 Crown's Ln., 1st Fl.
Toronto, ON, Canada M5R 3P4
(416)402-8000
E-mail: info@fhgi.com
Website: http://www.fhgi.com

KLynn Inc.
6 Bartlett Ave., Ste. 8
Toronto, ON M6H 3E6
Free: 888-717-2220
E-mail: info@klynnbusinessconsulting
.com
Website: www.klynnbusinessconsulting
.com

PWR Health Consultants, Inc.
720 Spadina Ave., Ste. 303
Toronto, ON, Canada M5S 2T9
(416)467-1844
Fax: (416)467-5600
Fax: (416)323-3166
E-mail: ldoupe@pwr.ca
Website: http://www.pwr.ca

Ryerson Consulting Group
575 Bay St., Ste. 2-005
Toronto, ON, Canada M5G 2C5
(416)979-5059
E-mail: info@rcginsight.com
Website: http://www.rcginsight.com

David Trahair CPA, CA
15 Coldwater Rd., Ste. 101
Toronto, ON, Canada M3B 1Y8
(416)420-8840
Fax: (416)385-3813
Website: http://www.trahair.com

Quebec

PGP Consulting
17 Linton
Dollard-des-Ormeaux, QC, Canada H9B
1P2
(514)796-7613
(514)862-5837
Fax: (866)750-0947
E-mail: pierre@pgpconsulting.com
Website: http://www.pgpconsulting.com

Conseil Saint-Paul
400 Blvd. Saint-Martin Ouest, Bureau 121
Laval, QC, Canada H7M 3Y8

(450)664-4442
Fax: (450)664-3631
E-mail: info@spaul.ca
Website: http://spaul.ca

KLynn Inc.
2025 Rue de la Visitation
Montreal, QC H2L 3C8
Free: 888-717-2220
E-mail: info@klynnbusiness
consulting.com
Website: www.klynnbusiness
consulting.com

Komand Consulting Inc.
1250 Rene Levesque Blvd. W, Ste. 2200
Montreal, QC, Canada H3B 4W8
(514)934-9281
E-mail: info@komand.ca
Website: http://www.komand.ca

Lemay-Yates Associates Inc.
2015 Peel St., Ste. 425
Montreal, QC, Canada H3A 1T8
(514)288-6555
E-mail: lya@lya.com
Website: http://www.lya.com

Groupe Dancause Inc.
3175 Chemin des Quatre-Bourgeois,
Ste. 375
Quebec, QC, Canada G1W 2K7
(418)681-0268
E-mail: groupe@dancause.net
Website: http://www.dancause.net

Saskatchewan

Abonar Business Consultants Ltd.
3110 8th St. E, Ste. 8B-376
Saskatoon, SK, Canada S7H 0W2
Fax: (866)405-4510
Free: 866-405-4510
E-mail: info@abonarconsultants.com
Website: http://www.abonarconsultants
.com/index.html

Banda Marketing Group
3-1124 8th St. E
Saskatoon, SK, Canada S7H 0S4
(306)343-6100
E-mail: brent.banda@bandagroup.com
Website: http://www.bandagroup.com

Hoggard International
435 McKercher Dr.
Saskatoon, SK, Canada S7H 4G3
(306)374-6747
Fax: (306)653-7252
E-mail: bhoggard@shaw.ca
Website: http://hoggardinternational
.com

United states

Alabama

Accounting & Business Consultants Inc.
1711 9th Ave. N
Bessemer, AL 35020
E-mail: tclay@abcconsultants.com
Website:http://www.abcconsultants.com

Accounting & Business Consultants Inc.
4120 2nd Ave. S
Birmingham, AL 35222
(205)425-9000
E-mail: tclay@abcconsultants.com
Website: http://www.abcconsultants.com

MILBO, LLC
2214 3rd Ave. N, Ste. 204
Birmingham, AL 35203
(205)543-0645
Website: http://www.milbollc.com

Jackson Thorton Dothan Office
304 Jamestown Blvd.
Dothan, AL 36301
(334)793-7001
Fax: (334)793-7004
Website: http://www.jacksonthornton.com

Mason, Bearden & Diehl, Inc.
4100 Bob Wallace Ave.
Huntsville, AL 35805
(256)533-0806
Fax: (256)533-7742 fax
E-mail: mbd@mbdaccounting.com
Website: http://www.mbdaccounting.com

SEL & Associates
103 Cabot Circ., Ste. 201
Madison, AL 35758
(256)325-9809
Fax: (256)325-9809
E-mail: steven@stevenlevyassociates.com
Website: http://www.stevenlevy
associates.com

Jackson Thorton Montgomery Office
200 Commerce St.
Montgomery, AL 36104
(334)834-7660
Fax: (334)956-5090
Website: http://www.jacksonthornton.com

Jackson Thorton Auburn/Opelka Office
100 N 9th St.
Opelika, AL 36801
(334)749-8191
Fax: (334)749-9358
Website: http://www.jacksonthornton
.com

Jackson Thorton Prattville Office
310 S Washington St.
Prattville, AL 36067
(334)365-1445
Fax: (334)956-5066
Website: http://www.jacksonthornton
.com

Jackson Thorton Wetumpka Office
194 Fort Toulouse
Wetumpka, AL 36092
(334)567-3400
Fax: (334)956-5005
Website: http://www.jacksonthornton
.com

Alaska

Agnew::Beck Consulting
441 W 5th Ave., Ste. 202
Anchorage, AK 99501
(907)222-5424
Fax: (907)222-5426
E-mail: admin@agnewbeck.com
Website: http://agnewbeck.com

McDowell Group
1400 W Benson Blvd., Ste. 510
Anchorage, AK 99503
(907)274-3200
Fax: (907)274-3201
E-mail: info@mcdowellgroup.net
Website: http://www.mcdowellgroup.net

The Foraker Group
161 Klevin St., Ste. 101
Anchorage AK 99508
(907)743-1200
Fax: (907)276-5014
Free: 877-834-5003
Website: http://www.forakergroup.org

Consulting Professionals of Alaska
17137 Park Place St.
Eagle River, AK, 99577
(907)694-0105
Fax: (907)694-0107
Website: http://www.cpalaska.com

McDowell Group
9360 Glacier Hwy., Ste. 201
Juneau, AK 99801
(907)586-6126
Fax: (907)586-2673
E-mail: info@mcdowellgroup.net
Website: http://www.mcdowellgroup.net

Sheinberg Associates
1107 W 8th St., Ste. 4
Juneau, AK 99801
(907)586-3141
Fax: (907)586-2331

Website: http://www.sheinbergassociates
.com

Arizona

Comgate Telemanagement Ltd.
428 E Thunderbird Rd., Ste. 133
Phoenix, AZ 85022
(602)485-5708
Fax: (602)485-5709
E-mail: info_telemgmt@comgate.com
Website: http://www.comgate.com

Kalil & Associates, LLC
245 S Plumer Ave., Ste. 16
Tucson, AZ 85719
(520)628-4264
Fax: (520)903-0347
E-mail: info@kalilassociates.com
Website: https://www.kalilassociates.com

California

Cayenne Consulting, LLC
155 N Riverview Dr.
Anaheim Hills, CA 92808
Website: https://www.caycon.com

Fessel International, Inc.
20 E Foothill Blvd., Ste. 128
Arcadia, CA 91006
(626)566-3500
Fax: (626)566-3875
Free: 877-432-8380
Website: http://www.fessel.com/
default.asp

Streamline Planning Consultants
1062 G St. Suite I
Arcata, CA 95521
(707)822-5785
Fax: (707)822-5786
Website: http://streamlineplanning.net

The One Page Business Plan Co.
1798 Fifth St.
Berkeley, CA 94710
(510)705-8400
Fax: (510)705-8403
E-mail: info@onepagebusinessplan.com
Website: http://www.onepagebusiness
plan.com

Business Consulting Group
30 Landing Cir. 300
Chico, CA 95973
(530)864-5980
E-mail: info@bcgca.com
Website: http://www.bcgca.com

Go Jade Solutions
9808 Valgrande Way
Elk Grove, CA 95757

(916)538-7561
E-mail: info@gojadesolutions.com
Website: http://gojadesolutions.com

La Piana Consulting
5858 Horton St., Ste. 272
Emeryville, CA 94608-2007
(510)601-9056
Fax: (510)420-0478
E-mail: info@lapiana.org
Website: http://lapiana.org

Norris Bernstein, CMC
9309 Marina Pacifica Dr. N
Long Beach, CA 90803
(562)493-5458
Fax: (562)493-5459
E-mail: norris@norrisbernstein.com
Website: http://www.norrisbernstein.com

Blue Garnet Associates L.L.C.
8055 W Manchester Ave., Ste. 430
Los Angeles, CA 90293
(310)439-1930
E-mail: hello@bluegarnet.net
Website: http://www.bluegarnet.net

Edeska LLC (dba Go Business Plans)
Bldg. D, Fl. 3
12777 W Jefferson Blvd., Ste. 3119
Los Angeles, CA 90066
Free: 855-546-0037
Website: http://edeska.com

Growthink Inc.
12655 W Jefferson Blvd.
Los Angeles, CA 90045
Free: 800-647-6983
E-mail: services@growthink.com
Website: http://www.growthink.com

Paul Yelder Consulting
3964 Hubert Ave.
Los Angeles, CA 90008-2620
(323)295-7652
E-mail: email: consulting@yelder.com
Website: http://www.yelder.com

BizplanSource
1048 Irvine Ave., Ste. 621
Newport Beach, CA 92660
Free: 888-253-0974
Fax: (800)859-8254
E-mail: info@bizplansource.com
Website: http://www.bizplansource.com

MakeGreenGo!
240 3rd St., Ste. 2A
Oakland, CA 94607
(510)250-9890
Website: http://makegreengo.com

Accessible Business, LLC
18325 Keswick St.
Reseda, CA 91335
(818)264-7830
Free: 800-490-8362
Fax: (818)264-7833
E-mail: info@accessiblebusiness.com
Website: https://www.accessible
business.com

International Business Partners
8045 Darby Pl.
Reseda, CA 91335
(714)875-3604
E-mail: admin@IBPconsultants.com
Website: http://www.ibpconsultants
.com/home.html

Jackson Law Firm, P.C.
979 Golf Course Dr., Ste. 300
Rohnert Park, CA 94928
(707)584-4529
(707)584-9033
E-mail: shawnjackson@business
developmentattorney.com
Website: http://jacksonlawfirm.net/

Business Performance Consultants
9777 Caminito Joven
San Diego, CA 92131
(858)583-4159
E-mail: larrymiller@businessperformance
consultants.com
Website: http://businessperformance
consultants.com/

The Startup Garage
San Diego, CA 92109
(858)876-4597
E-mail: info@thestartupgarage.com
Website: https://thestartupgarage.com

Venture Builder, Inc.
1286 University Ave., Ste. 315
San Diego, CA 92103
(619)563-1841
Website: http://www.venturebuilderinc
.com

Growthink Inc.
55 2nd St., Ste. 570
San Francisco, CA 94105
Free: 800-647-6983
E-mail: services@growthink.com
Website: http://www.growthink.com

San Francisco Management Group
1048 Union St., Ste. 7
San Francisco, CA 94133
(415)775-3405
E-mail: info@sfmanagementgroup.com

Website: http://www.sfmanagement
group.com/

The Wright Consultants
835 Market St.
San Francisco, CA 94105
(415)928-2071
Website: http://www.thewright
consultants.com

Business Group
369-B 3rd St., Ste. 387
San Rafael, CA 94901
(415)491-1896
Fax: (415)459-6472
E-mail: mvh@businessgroup.biz
Website: http://www.businessowners
toolbox.com

Manex Inc.
2010 Crow Canyon Pl., Ste. 320
San Ramon, CA 94583
(925)807-5100
Free: 877-336-2639
Website: http://www.manexconsulting
.com

Bargain Business Plan, Inc.
12400 Ventura Blvd., Ste. 658
Studio City, CA 91604
Free: 800-866-9971
Fax: (800)866-9971
E-mail: info@bargainbusinessplan.com
Website: http://www.bargainbusiness
plan.com

Out of Your Mind...and Into the Marketplace
13381 White Sands Dr.
Tustin, CA 92780-4565
(714)544-0248
Fax: (714)730-1414
Free: 800-419-1513
E-mail: lpinson@aol.com
Website: http://www.business-plan.com

Colorado

Comer & Associates, LLC
5255 Holmes Pl.
Boulder, CO 80303
(303)786-7986
E-mail: info@comerassociates.com
Website: http://www.comerassociates
.com

McCord Consulting Group
2525 Arapahoe Ave., Ste. 515
Boulder, CO 80302
(720)443-0894
E-mail: nikki@mcconsultgroup.com
Website: http://mcconsultgroup.com/

The Startup Expert
661 Eldorado Blvd. Ste. 623
Broomfield, CO 80021
(303)534-1019
Website: http://thestartupexpert.com/

Ameriwest Business Consultants, Inc.
PO Box 26266
Colorado Springs, CO 80936
(719)380-7096
Fax: (719)380-7096
E-mail: email@abchelp.com
Website: http://www.abchelp.com

GVNW Consulting Inc.
2270 La Montana Way, Ste. 200
Colorado Springs, CO 80918
(719)594-5800
E-mail: jushio@gvnw.com
Website: http://www.gvnw.com

Wilson Hughes Consulting LLC
2100 Humboldt St., Ste. 302
Denver, CO 80205
(303)680-7889
E-mail: bhughescnm@gmail.com
Website: http://wilsonhughesconsulting
.com/

Extelligent Inc.
8400 E Crescent Pky., Ste. 600
Greenwood Village, CO 80111
(720)201-5672
E-mail: clientrelations@extelligent.com
Website: http://www.extelligent.com

The Schallert Group, Inc.
321 Main St.
Longmont, CO 80501
(303)774-6522
Website: http://jonschallert.com/

Vaughn CPA
210 E 29th St.
Loveland, CO 80538
(970)667-2123
E-mail: vaughn@vaughncpa.com
Website: http://vaughncpa.com/
loveland-cpa-firm

Connecticut

Alltis Corp.
PO Box 1292
Farmington, CT 06034-1292
(860)255-7610
Fax: (860)674-8168
E-mail: info@alltis.com
Website: http://www.alltis.com

Christiansen Consulting
56 Scarborough St.
Hartford, CT 06105

(860)586-8265
Fax: (860)233-3420
E-mail: Francine@Christiansen
Consulting.com
Website: http://www.christiansen
consulting.com/

Musevue360
555 Millbrook Rd.
Middletown, CT 06457
(860)463-7722
Fax: (860)346-3013
E-mail: jennifer.eifrig@musevue360.com
Website: http://www.musevue360.com

Kalba International Inc.
116 McKinley Ave.
New Haven, CT 06515
(203)397-2199
Fax: (781)240-2657
E-mail: kas.kalba@kalbainter
national.com
Website: http://www.kalbainternational.com

Delaware

Doherty & Associates
Stoney Batter Office Bldg.
5301 Limestone Rd., Ste. 100
Wilmington, DE 19808
(302)239-3500
Fax: (302)239-3600
E-mail: info@dohertyandassociates.com
Website: http://www.dohertyand
associates.com

Gunnip & Co. LLP
Little Falls Centre 2
2751 Centerville Rd., Ste. 300
Wilmington, DE 19808-1627
(302)225-5000
Fax: (302)225-5100
E-mail: info@gunnip.com
Website: http://www.gunnip.com

Master, Sidlow & Associates, P.A.
2002 W 14th St.
Wilmington, DE 19806
(302)652-3480
Fax: (302)656-8778
E-mail: imail@mastersidlow.com
Website: http://www.mastersidlow.com

Florida

BackBone, Inc.
20404 Hacienda Ct.
Boca Raton, FL 33498
(561)470-0965
Fax: (561)908-4038
E-mail: che@backboneinc.com
Website: http://www.backboneinc.com

Dr. Eric H. Shaw & Associates
500 S Ocean Blvd., Ste. 2105
Boca Raton, FL 33432
(561)338-5151
E-mail: ericshaw@bellsouth.net
Website: http://www.ericshaw.com

Professional Planning Associates, Inc.
1440 NE 35th St.
Oakland Park, FL 33334
(954)829-2523
Fax:(954)537-7945
E-mail: mgoldstein@proplana.com
Website: http://proplana.com

Alfred Endeio LLC
8700 Maitland Summit Blvd., Ste. 214
Orlando, FL 32810
Website: http://www.alfredeconsulting.com

Hughes Consulting Services LLC
522 Alternate 19
Palm Harbor, FL 34683
(727)631-2536
Fax: (727)474-9818
Website: http://consultinghughes.com

Strategic Business Planning Co.
PO Box 821006
South Florida, FL 33082
(954)704-9100
Fax: (888)704-3290
Free: 888-704-9100
E-mail: info@SBPlan.com
Website: http://www.ipplan.com

Cohen & Grieb, P.A.
500 N Westshore Blvd., Ste. 700
Tampa, FL 33609
(813)739-7200
Fax: (813)282-7225
E-mail: info@cohengrieb.com
Website: http://www.cohengrieb.com/
contact

Dufresne Consulting Group, Inc.
13014 N Dale Mabry, Ste. 175
Tampa, FL 33618-2808
(813)264-4775
E-mail: info@dcgconsult.com
Website: http://www.dcgconsult.com

Reliance Consulting, LLC
13940 N Dale Mabry Hwy.
Tampa, FL, 33618
(813)931-7258
Fax: (813)931-5555
Website: http://www.reliancecpa.com

Tunstall Consulting LLC
13153 N Dale Mabry Hwy., Ste. 200
Tampa, FL 33618

(813)968-4461
Fax: (813)961-2315
E-mail: info@tunstallconsulting.com
Website: http://www.tunstall
consulting.com

The Business Planning Institute, LLC.
580 Village Blvd., Ste. 150
West Palm Beach, FL 33409
(561)236-5533
Fax: (561)689-5546
E-mail: info@bpiplans.com
Website: http://www.bpiplans.com

Georgia

CHScottEnterprises
227 Sandy Springs Pl. NE, Ste. 720702
Atlanta, GA 30358-9032
(770)356-4808
E-mail: info@chscottenterprises.com
Website: http://www.chscottenterprises
.com

Fountainhead Consulting Group, Inc.
3970 Old Milton Pkwy, Ste. 210
Atlanta, GA 30005
(770)642-4220
Website: http://www.fountainhead
consultinggroup.com

PSMJ Resources Inc.
2746 Rangewood Dr.
Atlanta, GA 30345
(770)723-9651
Fax: (815)461-7478
Free: 800-537-7765
Website: http://www.psmj.com

Scullyworks, LLC
PO Box 8641
Atlanta, GA 31106-0641
(404)310-9499
Website: http://www.scullyworks.com

Theisen Consulting LLC
865 Waddington Ct.
Atlanta, GA 30350
(770)396-7344
Fax: (404)393-3527
E-mail: terri@theisenconsulting.com
Website: http://www.theisenconsulting
.com

Sterling Rose Consulting Corp.
722 Collins Hill Rd., Ste. H-307
Lawrenceville, GA 30046
(678)892-8528
E-mail: info@sterlingroseconsulting
corp.com
Website: http://www.sterlingrose
consultingcorp.com

Lemongrass Consulting, Inc.
951 Gettysburg Way
Locust Grove, GA 30248
(678)235-5901
E-mail: chamilton@lemongrass
planning.com
Website: http://lemongrassplanning.com

Samet Consulting
4672 Oxford Cir.
Macon, GA 31210
(478)757-1070
Fax:(478)757-1984
Website: http://sametconsulting.com/

Hawaii

Maui Venture Consulting LLC
PO Box 81515
Haiku, HI 96708
(808)269-1031
E-mail: df@mauiventure.net
Website: http://www.mauiventure.net

Business Plans Hawaii
3059 Maigret St.
Honolulu, HI 96816
(808)735-5597
E-mail: valerie@
businessplanshawaii.com
Website: http://www.businessplan
shawaii.com

John V. McCoy Communications Consultant
425 Ena Rd., Apt. 1204-B
Honolulu, HI 96815
(510)219-2276
E-mail: mccoy.jv@gmail.com
Website: http://www.busplan.com

Idaho

Agnew::Beck Consulting
802 W Bannock St., Ste. 803
Boise, ID 83702
(208)342-3976
E-mail: admin@agnewbeck.com
Website: http://agnewbeck.com

Kairosys
16645 Plum Rd.
Caldwell, ID 83607
(208)454-0086
E-mail: support@kairosys.net
Website: http://kairosys.net

Illinois

Midwest Business Consulting, LLC
Midway Corporate Ctr.
6640 S Cicero Ave., Ste. 204

Bedford Park, IL 60638
(708)571-3401
Fax: (708)571-3409
E-mail: inquiries@mbconsultingco.com
Website: https://www.mbconsultingco.com

Anchor Advisors, Ltd.
5366 N Elston Ave., Ste. 203
Chicago, IL 60630
(773)282-7677
Website: http://anchoradvisors.com

Brighton Windsor Group, LLC
Chicago, IL 60602
Free: 888-781-1304
E-mail: hello@brightonwindsor.com
Website: http://brightonwindsor.com

Ground Floor Partners, Inc.
150 N Michigan Ave., Ste. 2800
Chicago, IL 60601
(312)726-1981
Website: http://groundfloorpartners.com

Midwest Business Consulting, LLC
Chicago Temple Bldg.
77 W Washington, Ste. 718
Chicago, IL 60602
(312)415-0340
Fax: (312)994-8554
E-mail: inquiries@mbconsultingco.com
Website: https://www.mbconsultingco
.com

Gold Consulting, Inc.
18 Exmoor Ct.
Highwood, IL 60040
(847)433-8141
Fax: (847)433-2446
E-mail: ron@goldconsultinginc.com
Website: http://goldconsultinginc.com

Francorp
20200 Governors Dr.
Olympia Fields, IL 60461
(708)481-2900
Free: 800-372-6244
E-mail: francorp@aol.com
Website: http://www.francorp.com

MD Consultants of America, Inc.
6738 N Frostwood Pkwy.
Peoria, IL 61615
Free: 877-272-1631
Fax: (309)414-0298
E-mail: info@mdconsultantus.com
Website: http://www.mdconsultantus
.com

Quiet Storm Enterprises Ltd.
3701 Trilling Ave., Ste. 201
Rockford IL 61103-2157

(815)315-0146
Free: 877-958-0160
E-mail: info@qsenterprisesltd.net
Website: http://www.qsenterprisesltd.net

Public Sector Consulting
5718 Barlow Rd.
Sherman, IL 62684
(217)629-9869
Fax: (217)629-9732
E-mail: mail@gotopsc.com
Website: http://www.gotopsc.com

GVNW Illinois
3220 Pleasant Run, Ste. A
Springfield, IL 62711
(217)698-2700
E-mail: jushio@gvnw.com
Website: http://www.gvnw.com

Indiana

Compass CPA Group
435 Ann St.
Fort Wayne, IN 46774
(260)749-2200
Free: 866-788-9789
E-mail: information@compasscpa
group.com
Website: http://www.compasscpagroup
.com

Cox and Co.
3930 Mezzanine Dr. Ste A
Lafayette, IN, 47905
(765)449-4495
Fax: (765)449-1218
E-mail: stan@coxpa.com
Website: http://coxcpa.com

Kimmel Consulting LLC
136 S 9th St Ste 320
Noblesville, IN 46060
(317)773-3810
Fax: (317)770-8787
E-mail: info@kimmelconsultingllc.com
Website: http://www.kimmelconsulting
llc.com

Iowa

**TD&T CPAs and Advisors, P.C.
Burlington Office**
323 Jefferson St.
Burlington, IA 52601
(319)753-9877
Fax: (319)753-1156
E-mail: briani@tdtpc.com
Website: http://www.tdtpc.com/
index.php

TD&T CPAs and Advisors, P.C. Cedar Rapids Office
1700 42nd St. NE
Cedar Rapids, IA 52402
(319)393-2374
Fax: (319)393-2375
E-mail: amandal@tdtpc.com
Website: http://www.tdtpc.com/
index.php

Terry, Lockridge and Dunn
210 2nd St. SE
Cedar Rapids, IA 52407
(319)364-2945
Fax: (319)362-4487
E-mail: info@tld-inc.com
Website: http://www.tld-inc.com

TD&T CPAs and Advisors, P.C. Centerville Office
101 W Van Buren St.
Centerville, IA 52544
(641)437-4296
Fax: (641)437-1574
E-mail: markl@tdtpc.com
Website: http://www.tdtpc.com/
index.php

TD&T CPAs and Advisors, P.C. Fairfield Office
2109 W Jefferson Ave.
Fairfield, IA 52556
(641)472-6171
Fax: (641)472-6632
E-mail: jodik@tdtpc.com
Website: http://www.tdtpc.com/
index.php

Steve Meyer Consulting LLC
304 E Maple
Garrison, IA 52229
(319)477-5041
E-mail: gfdchief@netins.net
Website: http://www.stevemeyer
consulting.com/

Terry, Lockridge and Dunn
2225 Mormon Trek Blvd.
Iowa City, IA 52246
(319)339-4884
Fax: (319)358-9113
E-mail: info@tld-inc.com
Website: http://www.tld-inc.com

TD&T CPAs and Advisors, P.C. Mount Pleasant Office
204 N Main
Mount Pleasant, IA 52641
(319)385-9718
Fax: (319)385-2612
E-mail: tomh@tdtpc.com

Website: http://www.tdtpc.com/
index.php

TD&T CPAs and Advisors, P.C. Muscatine Office
500 Cedar St.
Muscatine, IA 52761
(563)264-2727
Fax: (563)263-7777
E-mail: vickib@tdtpc.com;
dennyt@tdtpc.com
Website: http://www.tdtpc.com/
index.php

TD&T CPAs and Advisors, P.C. Oskaloosa Office
317 High Ave. E
Oskaloosa, IA 52577
(641)672-2523
Fax: (641)673-7453
E-mail: joshb@tdtpc.com
Website: http://www.tdtpc.com/
index.php

TD&T CPAs and Advisors, P.C. Ottumwa Office
117 S Court
Ottumwa, IA 52501
(641)683-1823
Fax: (641)683-1868
E-mail: dougm@tdtpc.com
Website: http://www.tdtpc.com/
index.php

TD&T CPAs and Advisors, P.C. Pella Office
1108 Washington St.
Pella, IA 50219
(641)628-9411
Fax: (641)628-1321
E-mail: justinp@tdtpc.com
Website: http://www.tdtpc.com/
index.php

Murk-n-T, Inc.
209 Rose Ave. SW
Swisher, IA 52338
(319)857-4638
Fax: (319)857-4648
E-mail: info@murknt.com
Website: http://www.murknt.com/
index.php

TD&T CPAs and Advisors, P.C. West Des Moines Office
1240 Office Plaza Dr.
West Des Moines, IA 50266
(515)657-5800
Fax: (515)657-5801
E-mail: davef@tdtpc.com

Website: http://www.tdtpc.com/
index.php

Kansas

Nail CPA Firm, LLC
4901 W 136th St.
Leawood, KS 66224
(913)663-2500
E-mail: info@nailcpafirm.com
Website: http://www.nailcpafirm.com

Shockey Consulting Services, LLC
12351 W 96th Ter., Ste. 107
Lenexa, KS 66215
(913)248-9585
E-mail: solutions@shockeyconsulting
.com
Website: http://www.shockey
consulting.com/

Aspire Business Development
10955 Lowell Ave., Ste. 400
Overland Park, KS 66210
(913)660-9400
Free: 888-548-1504
Website: http://www.aspirekc.com

Wichita Technology Corp.
7829 E Rockhill Rd., Ste. 307
Wichita, KS 67206
(316)651-5900
Free: 866-810-6671
E-mail: wtc@wichitatechnology.com
Website: http://www.wichita
technology.com

Kentucky

BizFixes
277 E High St.
Lexington, KY 40507
(859)552-5151
Website: http://bizfixes.com

Louisiana

Cathy Denison, PhD & Associates Professional Services, Inc.
9655 Perkins Rd., Ste. C-123
Baton Rouge, LA 70810
(337)502-1911
E-mail: cdenison@denisonassociates.com
Website: http://www.denison
associates.com

Rabalais Business Consulting
209 Rue Louis XIV, Ste. B
Lafayette, LA 70508
(337)981-2577
Fax: (337)981-2579
Website: http://rabbiz.com

Terk Consulting Business Plans
3819A Magazine St.
New Orleans, LA 70115
(504)237-0480
E-mail: info@terkconsulting.com
Website: https://terkconsulting.com

Maine

PFBF CPAs Bath Office
259 Front St.
Bath, ME 04530
(207)371-8002
Fax: (207)877-7407
E-mail: mail@pfbf.com
Website: http://www.pfbf.com

John Rust Consulting
PO Box 459
Hampden, ME 04444
(207)337-5858
E-mail: john@johnrustconsulting.com
Website: http://www.johnrust
consulting.com

PFBF CPAs Oakland Office
46 First Park Dr.
Oakland, ME 04963
(207)873-1603
Fax: (207)877-7407
E-mail: mail@pfbf.com
Website: http://www.pfbf.com

Maryland

**Maryland Capital Enterprises, Inc.
Baltimore Area Office**
333 N Charles St.
Baltimore, MD 21201
(410)546-1900
Fax: (410)546-9718
E-mail: info@marylandcapital.org
Website: http://www.marylandcapital.org

Burdeshaw Associates Ltd.
4701 Sangamore Rd.
Bethesda, MD 20816
(301)229-5800
E-mail: jstacy@burdeshaw.com
Website: http://www.burdeshaw.com

Jacoby
2304 Frederick Rd.
Catonsville, MD 21228
(410)744-3900
Fax: (410)747-7850
Free: 877-799-GROW
E-mail: info@artjacoby.com

Black Rock Accounting & Consulting
13424 Burnt Woods Pl.
Germantown, MD 20874

(301)928-7600
Fax: (301)515-1840
E-mail: mike@blackrockaccounting.com
Website: http://www.blackrock
accounting.com

L&H Business Consulting
1212 York Rd., Ste. C-300
Lutherville, MD 21093
(410)828-4177
Fax: (410)321-1588
E-mail: info@lhbusinessconsulting.com
Website: http://www.lhbusiness
consulting.com

**Maryland Capital Enterprises, Inc.
Eastern Shore Office**
144 E Main St.
Salisbury, MD 21801
(410)546-1900
Fax: (410)546-9718
E-mail: info@marylandcapital.org
Website: http://www.marylandcapital.org

Massachusetts

The Carrot Project
89 South St.
Boston, MA 02111
(617)674-2371
E-mail: info@thecarrotproject.org
Website: http://www.thecarrotproject
.org/home

Julia Shanks Food Consulting
37 Tremont St.
Cambridge, MA 02139
(617)945-8718
E-mail: info@juliashanks.com
Website: http://www.juliashanks.com

CYTO Consulting
363 N Emerson Rd.
Lexington, MA 02420
(339)707-0767
E-mail: info@cytoconsulting.com
Website: http://www.cytoconsulting.com

Foxboro Consulting Group Inc.
36 Lancashire Dr.
Mansfield, MA 02048
(774)719-2236
E-mail: moreinfo@foxboro-consulting.com
Website: http://www.foxboro-consulting
.com

Dahn Consulting Group
Newburyport, MA 01950
(978)314-1722
E-mail: info@dahnconsulting.com
Website: http://www.dahnconsulting.com

PSMJ Resources Inc.
10 Midland Ave.
Newton, MA 02458
(617)965-0055
Fax: (617)965-5152
Free: 800-537-7765
Website: http://www.psmj.com

Spark Business Consulting
167 Washington St.
Norwell, MA 02061
(781)871-1003
Website: http://sparkbusinessconsulting
.com

Bruno P.C.
57 Obery St., Ste. 4
Plymouth, MA 02360
(508)830-0800
Fax: (508)830-0801
E-mail: info@BrunoAccountants.com
Website: https://www.brunoaccountants
.com

Non Profit Capital Management
41 Main St.
Sterling, MA 01564
(781)933-6726
Fax: (978)563-1007
E-mail: info@npcm.com
Website: http://www.npcm.com/

Michigan

Aimattech Consulting LLC
568 Woodway Ct., Ste. 1
Bloomfield Hills, MI 48302-1572
(248)540-3758
Fax: (775)305-4755
E-mail: dweaver@aimattech.com
Website: http://www.aimattech.com

**BBC Entrepreneurial Training &
Consulting LLC**
12671 E Old U.S. 12
Chelsea, MI 48118
(734)930-9741
Fax: (734)930-6629
E-mail: info@bbcetc.com
Website: http://www.bioconsultants.com

LifeLine Business Consulting
1400 Woodbridge St., 4th Fl.
Detroit, MI 48207
(313)965-3155
E-mail: hello@thelifelinenetwork.com
Website: https://thelifelinenetwork.com

TL Cramer Associates LLC
1788 Broadstone Rd.
Grosse Pointe Woods, MI 48236
(313)332-0182

E-mail: info@tlcramerassociates.com
Website: http://www.tlcramerassociates
.com

Jackson Small Business Support Center
950 W Monroe St., Ste. G-100
Jackson, MI 49202
(517)796-8151
Website: http://www.smallbusiness
supportcenter.com

Tedder Whitlock Consulting
17199 N Laurel Park Dr.
Livonia, MI 48152
(734)542-4200
Fax: (734)542-4201
E-mail: info@tedderwhitlock.com
Website: http://www.tedderwhitlock.com

MarketingHelp Inc.
6647 Riverwoods Ct. NE
Rockford, MI 49341
(616)856-0148
Website: http://www.mktghelp.com

Lucid Business Strategies
8187 Rhode Dr., Ste. D
Shelby Township, MI 48317
(586)254-0095
E-mail: results@lucidbusiness.com
Website: http://www.lucidbusiness.com

QT Business Solution
24901 Northwestern Hwy., Ste. 305
Southfield, MI 48075
(248)416-1755
Free: 877-859-6768
E-mail: info@qtbizsolutions.com
Website: http://qtbizsolutions.com

Cool & Associates Inc.
921 Village Green Ln., Ste. 1068
Waterford, MI 48328
(248)683-1130
E-mail: info@cool-associates.com
Website: http://www.cool-associates.com

Griffioen Consulting Group, Inc.
6689 Orchard Lake Rd., Ste. 295
West Bloomfield, MI 48322
Free: 888-262-5850
Fax: (248)855-4084
Website: http://www.griffioenconsulting
.com

**NooJoom Immigration Services &
Business Plan**
35253 Warren Rd.
Westland, MI 48185
(734)728-5755
E-mail: wadak@noojoom.org

Website: http://www.noojoomimmig
rationservices.com

Minnesota

Devoted Business Development
2434 E 117th St., Ste. 100
Burnsville, Minnesota
(952) 582-4669
E-mail: info@devoted-business.com
Website: http://devoted-business.com

**Community & Economic Development
Associates (CEDA)**
1500 S Hwy. 52
Chatfield, MN 55923
(507)867-3164
E-mail: ron.zeigler@cedausa.com
Website: https://www.cedausa.com

**Metropolitan Consortium of
Community Developers (MCCD)**
Open to Business Program
3137 Chicago Ave.
Minneapolis, MN 55407
(612)789-7337
Fax: (612)822-1489
E-mail: info@opentobusinessmn.org
Website: http://www.opentobusinessmn.org

**Metropolitan Economic Development
Association (MEDA)**
250 2nd Ave. S, Ste. 106
Minneapolis, MN 55401
(612)332-6332
E-mail: info@meda.net
Website: http://meda.net

WomenVenture
2021 E Hennepin Ave., Ste. 200
Minneapolis, MN 55413
(612)224-9540
Fax: (612)200-8369
E-mail: info@womenventure.org
Website: https://www.womenventure
.org/index.html

Mississippi

The IRON Network, LLC
1636 Popps Ferry Rd., Ste. 201
Biloxi, MS 39532
(412)336-8807
E-mail: sales@theironcom.com
Website: http://theironcom.com/
services/business-consulting

Richardson's Writing Service
3285 Squirrel Lake Rd.
Sledge, MS 38670
(662)326-3996
Website: http://www.richws.com

Missouri

**Taylor Management Group, LLC
(TMG)**
PO Box 50155
Clayton, MO 63015
(314)488-1566
Website: http://taymg.com

Stuff
316 W 63rd St.
Kansas City, MO 64113
(816)361-8222
E-mail: sloaneandcasey@pursuegood
stuff.com
Website: http://www.pursuegoodstuff.com

Westphal-Kelpe Consulting Inc.
4050 Broadway, Ste. 201
Kansas City, MO 64111
(816)931-7141
Fax: (816)931-7180
E-mail: info@wkcrestaurants.com
Website: http://www.westphal-kelpe.com

Shockey Consulting Services, LLC
441 Alice Ave.
Kirkwood, MO 66122
(314)497-3126
E-mail: solutions@shockeyconsulting.com
Website: http://www.shockey
consulting.com/

Sanford, Lea & Associates
1655 S Enterprise Ave., Ste. B-4
Springfield, MO 65804
(417)886-2220
Fax: (417)886-3979
E-mail: david@adifferentcpa.com
Website: https://www.adifferentcpa.com

EMD Consulting
11111 Conway Rd.
Saint Louis, MO 63131
(314)692-7551
E-mail: info@emdconsulting.com
Website: http://www.emdconsulting.com

M.A. Birsinger & Company, LLC
2464 Taylor Rd., Ste. 106
Wildwood, MO 63040
(314)249-7076
E-mail: brook@mabirsinger.com
Website: http://www.mabirsinger.com

Nebraska

McDermott & Miller, P.C.
2722 S Locust St.
Grand Island, NE 68802
(308)382-7850
Fax: (308)382-7240

E-mail: nsaale@mmcpas.com
Website: http://www.mmcpas.com

McDermott & Miller, P.C.

747 N Burlington Ave., Ste. 401
Hastings, NE 68902
(402)462-4154
Fax: (402)462-5057
E-mail: nsaale@mmcpas.com
Website: http://www.mmcpas.com

McDermott & Miller, P.C.

404 E 25th St.
Kearney, NE 68848
(308)234-5565
Fax: (308)234-2990
E-mail: nsaale@mmcpas.com
Website: http://www.mmcpas.com

Lincoln Partnership for Economic Development (LPED)

3 Landmark Centre
1128 Lincoln Mall, Ste. 100
Lincoln, NE 68508
(402)436-2350
E-mail: info@selectlincoln.org
Website: http://www.selectlincoln.org

Farm Credit Services of America

5015 S 118th St.
Omaha, NE 68137
Free: 800-884-FARM
Website: https://www.fcsamerica.com

McDermott & Miller, P.C.

11602 W Center Rd., Ste. 125
Omaha, NE 68144
(402)391-1207
Fax: (402)391-3424
E-mail: nsaale@mmcpas.com
Website: http://www.mmcpas.com

Nebraska Credit Union League (NCUL)

4885 S 118th St., Ste. 150
Omaha, NE 68137
(402)333-9331
Fax: (402)333-9431
Free: 800-950-4455
E-mail: ssullivan@nebrcul.org
Website: http://www.nebrcul.org

Steier & Prchal, Ltd.

1015 N 98th St., Ste. 100
Omaha, NE 68114
(402)390-9090
Fax: (402)505-5044
E-mail: info@steiertax.com
Website: http://www.steiertax.com/
bizplan.php

Nevada

Anderson Business Advisors, PLLC

3225 McLeod Dr., Ste. 100
Las Vegas, NV 89121
Free: 800-706-4741
Fax: (702)664-0545
E-mail: info@andersonadvisors.com
Website: https://andersonadvisors.com

Stone Law Offices, Ltd.

3295 N Fort Apache Rd., Ste. 150
Las Vegas, NV 89129
Free: 877-800-3424
Fax: (702)998-0443
Website: http://nvestateplan.com

Wise Business Plans

7251 W Lake Mead Blvd., Ste. 300
Las Vegas, NV 89128
Free: 800-496-1056 (United States)
Free: 702-562-4247 (International)
E-mail: info@wisebusinessplans.com
Website: https://wisebusinessplans.com

Drew Aguilar, CPA

1663 Hwy. 395, Ste. 201
Minden, NV 89423
(775)782-7874
Fax: (775)782-8374
E-mail: drew@carsonvalleyaccounting
.com
Website: http://www.carsonvalley
accounting.com

Thunder Vick & Co.

1325 Airmotive Way, Ste. 125
Reno, NV 89502
(775)323-4440
Fax: (775)323-8977
E-mail: admin@thunderrandcpa.com
Website: http://www.thundervickcpa.com

New Hampshire

HJ Marshall Associates

136 Sewalls Falls Rd.
Concord, NH 03301
(603)224-7073
E-mail: franmarshall@comcast.net
Website: http://www.hjmarshall
associates.com

Rodger O. Howells, LLC

6 Loudon Rd., Ste. 205
Concord, New Hampshire 03301
(603)224-3224
Free: 877-224-3224
E-mail: info@rhowellsconsulting.com
Website: http://www.rhowells
consulting.com

Nathan Wechsler & Co.

70 Commercial St., 4th Fl.
Concord, NH 03301
(603)224-5357
Fax: (603)224-3792
Website: http://www.nathanwechsler
.com

Kieschnick Consulting Services

9 Woodland Rd.
Dover, NH 03820
(603)749-2922
E-mail: peggy@kieschnickconsulting.com
Website: http://www.kieschnick
consulting.com

Trojan Consulting Group LLC

PO Box 27
Dover, NH 03821
(603)343-1707
E-mail: MNT@TrojanConsulting
Group.com
Website: http://trojanconsultinggroup
.com

Executive Service Corps (ESC)

80 Locke Rd.
Hampton, NH 03842
(603)926-0752
Website: http://www.nonprofit-
consultants.org

Hannah Grimes Center for Entrepreneurship

25 Roxbury St.
Keene, NH 03431
(603)352-5063
Fax: (603)352-5538
E-mail: info@hannahgrimes.com
Website: https://www.hannahgrimes
.com/

Nathan Wechsler & Co.

59 Emerald St.
Keene, NH 03431
(603)357-7665
Fax: (603)358-6800
Website: http://www.nathanwechsler
.com

Nathan Wechsler & Co.

44 School St.
Lebanon, NH 03766
(603)448-2650
Fax: (603)448-2476
Website: http://www.nathanwechsler
.com

Blue Ribbon Consulting, LDO, LLC

PO Box 435
New Ipswich, NH 03071
(603)878-1694

E-mail: lisa@blueribbonconsulting.com
Website: www.blueribbonconsulting.com

Dare Mighty Things, LLC
1 New Hampshire Ave., Ste. 125
Portsmouth, NH 03801
(603)431-4331
Fax: (603)431-4332
E-mail: info@daremightythings.com
Website: http://www.daremightythings
.com

New Jersey

Huffman & Huffman LLC
Changebridge Plaza
2 Changebridge Rd., Ste. 204
Montville, NJ 07045
(973)334-2600
Fax: (973)334-2627
E-mail: jhuffman@huffmancompany.com
Website: http://www.huffmancompany
.com

New Venture Design
Sperro Corporate Ctr.
2 Skyline Dr.
Montville, NJ 07045
(973)331-0022
Fax: (973)335-2656
Free: 866-639-3527
E-mail: info@newventuredesign.com
Website: http://www.newventure
design.com

Patterson & Associates LLC
Glendale Executive Campus
1000 White Horse Rd., Ste. 304
Voorhees, NJ 08043-4409
(856)435-2700
Fax: (856)435-1190
E-mail: info@pattersonassociatesllc.com
Website: http://www.patterson
associatesllc.com

New Mexico

Hinkle + Landers, P.C.
2500 9th St. NW
Albuquerque, NM 87102
(505)883-8788
Fax: (505)883-8797
E-mail: info@HL-cpas.com
Website: http://www.hl-cpas.com

Vaughn CPA
6605 Uptown Blvd., Ste. 370
Albuquerque, NM 87110
(505)828-0900
E-mail: vaughn@vaughncpa.com
Website: http://vaughncpa.com

WESST
WESST Enterprise Center
609 Broadway Blvd. NE
Albuquerque, NM 87102
(505)246-6900
Fax: (505)243-3035
Free: 800-GO-WESST
Website: https://www.wesst.org

WESST Farmington
San Juan College Quality Center for
Business
5101 College Blvd., Ste. 5060
Farmington, NM 87402
(505)566-3715
Fax: (505)566-3698
Website: https://www.wesst.org/
farmington

WESST Las Cruces
221 N Main St., #104a
Las Cruces, NM 88001
(575)541-1583
Website: https://www.wesst.org/las-cruces

WESST Rio Rancho
New Mexico Bank & Trust Bldg.
4001 Southern Blvd. SE, Ste. B
Rio Rancho, NM 87124-2069
(505)892-1238
Fax: (505)892-6157
Website: https://www.wesst.org/rio-rancho

WESST Roswell
Bank of America Bldg.
500 N Main St., Ste. 700
Roswell, NM 88201
Fax: (575)624-9850
Free: 575-624-9845
Website: https://www.wesst.org/roswell

Hinkle + Landers, P.C.
404 Brunn School Rd., Bldg. B
Santa Fe, NM 87505
(505)883-8788
Fax: (505)883-8797
E-mail: info@HL-cpas.com
Website: http://www.hl-cpas.com

WESST Santa Fe
Santa Fe Business Incubator
3900 Paseo del Sol, Ste. 351
Santa Fe, NM 87507
(505)474-6556
Fax: (505)474-6687
Website: https://www.wesst.org/santa-fe

New York

Key Accounting of New York
2488 Grand Concourse, Ste. 320B
Bronx, NY 10458

(718)584-8097
Fax: (866)496-5624
E-mail: info@keyaccnewyork.com
Website: http://keyaccnewyork.com

Soundview Business Consulting
53 Prospect Park W, Ste. 4A
Brooklyn, NY 11215
(718)499-0809
Fax: (718)499-0829
E-mail: brendan@soundviewfirm.com
Website: http://www.soundviewfirm.com

Addenda Solutions
5297 Parkside Dr., Ste. 412
Canandaigua, NY 14424
(585)394-4950
Free: 888-851-0414
Website: http://addendasolutions.com

Aspire Consulting, Ltd.
1 Horseshoe Dr.
Hyde Park, NY 12538
(845)803-0438
Fax: (845)229-8262
E-mail: info@AspireAdvantage.com
Website: http://www.aspireadvantage
.com/index.html

Capacity Business Consulting
3 Wallkill Ave.
Montgomery, NY 12549
(845)764-9484
E-mail: info@capacityconsultinginc.com
Website: http://www.capacitybusiness
consulting.com

Growthink Inc.
27 Radio Circle Dr., Ste. 202
Mount Kisco, NY 10549
Free: 800-647-6983
E-mail: services@growthink.com
Website: http://www.growthink.com

Gershon Consulting
833 Broadway, 2nd Fl.
New York, NY 10003
Free: 800-701-0176
E-mail: info@gershonconsulting.com
Website: http://www.gershonconsulting
.com

New York Business Consultants LLC
Chrysler Bldg.
405 Lexington Ave.
New York, NY 10174
(315)572-1938
Fax: (888)201-9524
Free: 800-481-2707
E-mail: info@newyorkbusiness
consultants.com

Website: http://www.newyorkbusiness
consultants.com/index.html

The Wright Consultants
394 Broadway
New York, NY 10013
(415)928-2071
Website: http://www.thewright
consultants.com

Addenda Solutions
1100 University Ave., Ste. 122
Rochester, NY 14607
(585)461-2654
Free: 888-851-0414
Website: http://addendasolutions.com

Addenda Solutions
126 Kiwassa Rd.
Saranac Lake, NY 12983
(518)891-1681
Free: 888-851-0414
Website: http://addendasolutions.com

North Carolina

Birds Eye Business Planning & Adventures
153 S Lexington Ave.
Asheville, NC 28801
(828)367-7248
E-mail: info@birdseye.info
Website: http://www.birdseye.info

Mountain BizWorks
153 S Lexington Ave.
Asheville, NC 28801
(828)253-2834
Free: 855-296-0048
E-mail: info@mountainbizworks.org
Website: https://www.mountain
bizworks.org

Allied Tax & Accounting Consultants, LLC
5550 77 Center Dr., Ste. 245
Charlotte, NC 28217
(704)676-1882
Fax: (704)676-1884
Free: 888-849-5119
E-mail: help@alliedtaxaccounting.com
Website: http://www.alliedtax
accounting.com/services/business-
consulting

Brewery Business Plan
9205 Cub Run Dr.
Concord, NC 28027
(704)960-4032
Website: https://brewerybusinessplan.com

EMD Consulting
140 Foothills Dr.
Hendersonville, NC 28792

E-mail: info@emdconsulting.com
Website: http://www.emdconsulting.com

Anagard Business Consulting, LLC
9360 Falls of Neuse Rd., Ste. 205
Raleigh, NC 27615
(919)876-1314
E-mail: info@ANAGARD.com
Website: http://www.anagard.com/
index.html

Davis Group, PA, CPAs
640 Statesville Blvd., Ste. 1
Salisbury, NC 28145-1307
(704)636-1040
Fax: (704)637-3084
E-mail: gary@dgcpa.com
Website: https://www.dgcpa.com/
business-advisory

North Dakota

Center for Innovation
Ina Mae Rude Entrepreneur Ctr.
4200 James Ray Dr.
Grand Forks, ND 58203
(701)777-3132
Fax: (701)777-2339
E-mail: info@innovators.net
Website: http://www.innovators.net

Ohio

Brown Consulting Group LLC
7965 North High St., Ste. 130
Columbus, OH 43235
(614)205-5323
E-mail: keith@browngroupcpa.com
Website: http://browngroupcpa.com

Oklahoma

Wymer Brownlee
3650 SE Camelot Dr.
Bartlesville, OK 74006
(918)333-7291
Fax: (918)333-7295
E-mail: info@wymerbrownlee.com
Website: http://www.wymerbrownlee.com

Wymer Brownlee
201 N Grand, Ste. 100
Enid, OK 73701
(580)237-0060
Fax: (580)237-0092
E-mail: info@wymerbrownlee.com
Website: http://www.wymerbrownlee.com

Wymer Brownlee
126 S Main
Fairview, OK 73737
(580)227-4709

Fax: (580)227-2166
E-mail: info@wymerbrownlee.com
Website: http://www.wymerbrownlee
.com

Entrepot
5711 E 72nd Ct.
Tulsa, Oklahoma 74136
(918)497-1748
Website: http://www.entrepotusa.com

Wymer Brownlee
7645 E 63rd St., Ste. 120
Tulsa, OK 74133
(918)392-8600
Fax: (918)392-8601
E-mail: info@wymerbrownlee.com
Website: http://www.wymerbrownlee
.com

Wymer Brownlee
10936 NW Expressway
Yukon, OK 73099
(405)283-0100
Fax: (405)283-0200
E-mail: info@wymerbrownlee.com
Website: http://www.wymerbrownlee
.com

Oregon

Timothy J. Berry
44 W Broadway Ste. 500
Eugene, OR, 97401
(541)683-6162
Website: http://timberry.com/business-
plan-expert

Advanced Trainers & Consultants, LLC (ATAC)
116 SE Hood
Gresham, OR 97080
(503)661-4013
Fax: (503)665-0775
E-mail: info@advancedtrainers.com
Website: http://www.advancedtrainers
.com

Alten Sakai & Company LLP
10260 SW Greenburg Rd., Ste. 300
Portland, OR 97223
(503)297-1072
Fax: (503)297-6634
E-mail: info@altensakai.com
Website: http://www.altensakai.com

Pointman Consulting, LLC
1130 SW Morrison
Portland, OR 97205
(503)804-2074
E-mail: noah@pointmanconsulting.com

Website: http://www.pointman
consulting.com/index.htm

GVNW Oregon
8050 SW Warm Springs St.
Tualatin, OR 97062
(503)612-4400
E-mail: jrennard@gvnw.com
Website: http://www.gvnw.com

Pennsylvania

Main Line Rail Management, Inc.
116 N Bellevue Ave., Ste. 206
Langhorne, PA 19047
(215)741-6007
Fax: (215)741-6009
E-mail: dsg@voicenet.com
Website: http://www.mlrail.com

Fairmount Ventures, Inc.
2 Penn Ctr.
1500 JFK Blvd., Ste. 1150
Philadelphia, PA 19102
(215)717-2299
E-mail: info@fairmountinc.com
Website: http://fairmountinc.com

RINK Consulting
1420 Locust St., Ste. 31N
Philadelphia, PA 19102
(215)546-5863
Website: http://www.lindarink.com

FlagShip Business Plans and Consulting
2 Gateway Ctr.
?603 Stanwix St., Ste. 1626
Pittsburgh, PA 15222
(412)219-8157
E-mail: info@flagshipbusinessplans.com
Website: http://www.flagshipbusiness
plans.com/page.html

Puerto Rico

Manuel L. Porrata & Associates
898 Muñoz Rivera Ave., Ste. 300
San Juan, PR 00927
(787)765-2140
Fax: (787)754-3285
E-mail: mporrata@manuelporrata.com
Website: http://www.manuelporrata
.com/home.html

Rhode Island

Ledoux, Petruska & Co., Inc.
1006 Charles St.
North Providence, RI 02904
(401)727-8100
Fax: (401)727-8181
E-mail: beancounter@lpcpari.com

Website: http://www.lpcpari.com/services/
business-consulting-and-solutions

South Carolina

Fluent Decisions, LLC
701 Gervais St., Ste. 150-157
Columbia, SC 29201
(803)748-2933
Website: https://www.fluentdecisions.com

South Dakota

South Dakota Enterprise Institute
Research Park at South Dakota State
University
2301 Research Park Way, Ste. 114
Brookings, SD 57006
(605)697-5015
E-mail: info@sdei.org
Website: http://www.sdei.org

Tennessee

Jackson Thorton Nashville Office
333 Commerce St., Ste. 1050
Nashville, TN 37201
(615)869-2050
Website: http://www.jacksonthornton.com

Texas

Zaetric Business Solutions LLC
27350 Blueberry Hill, Ste. 14
Conroe, TX 77385
(281)298-1878
Fax: (713)621-4885
E-mail: inquiries@zaetric.com
Website: http://www.zaetric.com

Optimus Business Plans
13355 Noel Rd., Ste. 1100
Dallas, TX 75240
(844)760-0903
Website: http://optimusbusinessplans.com

GVNW Texas
1001 Water St., Ste. A-100
Kerrville, TX 78028
(830)896-5200
E-mail: sgatto@gvnw.com
Website: http://www.gvnw.com

Butler Consultants
555 Republic Dr., Ste. 200
Plano, TX 75074
(214)491-4001
E-mail: Info@Financial-Projections.com
Website: http://contact.financial-
projections.com

Central Texas Business Consultants (CTBC)
PO Box 2213
Wimberley, TX 78676
(512)626-2938
Fax: (512)847-5541
E-mail: info@centraltexasbusiness
consulting.com
Website: http://www.centraltexas
businessconsulting.com

Utah

Vector Resources
7651 S Main St., Ste. 106
Midvale, UT 84047-7158
(801)352-8500
Fax: (801)352-8506
E-mail: info@vectorresources.com
Website: http://www.vector
resources.com

Ron Woodbury Consulting, Inc.
2899 E 3240 South St.
Saint George, UT 84790
(435)275-2978
E-mail: ron@ronwoodburyconsulting.com
Website: http://ronwoodburyconsulting.com

Vermont

CDS Consulting Co-op
659 Old Codding Rd.
Putney, VT 05346
(802)387-6013
Website: http://www.cdsconsulting.coop

Virginia

The Profit Partner, LLC
3900 Jermantown Rd., Ste. 300
Fairfax, VA 22030
(703)934-4630
Website: http://www.theprofitpartner.com

Dare Mighty Things, LLC
805 Park Ave.
Herndon, VA 20170
(703)424-3119
Fax: (603)431-4332
E-mail: info@daremightythings.com
Website: http://www.daremightythings.com

Washington

ECG Management Consultants Inc.
1111 3rd Ave., Ste. 2700
Seattle, WA 98101-3201
(206)689-2200
Fax: (206)689-2209
E-mail: ecg@ecgmc.com
Website: http://www.ecgmc.com

West Virginia

Cava & Banko, PLLC
117 E Main St.
Bridgeport, WV 26330
(304)842-4499
Fax: (304)842-4585
Website: http://cavabankocpa.com

Wisconsin

Virtual Management Solutions
959 Primrose Center Rd.
Belleville, WI 53508-9376
(608)832-8003
E-mail: davelind@chorus.net
Website: http://www.virtualmanagement
solutions.com

Wyoming

CPA Consulting Group, LLP
300 Country Club Rd., Ste. 302
Casper, WY 82609
(307)577-4040
E-mail: taxes@cpawyo.com
Website: http://www.cpacasper.com

CA Boner Business Plans
3218 Rock Springs St.
Cheyenne, WY 82001
(307)214-2043
Website: http://caboner.biz

CPA Group of Laramie, LLC
1273 N 15th St., Ste. 121
Laramie, WY 82072
(307)745-7241
Fax: (307)745-7292
Website: http://www.cpalaramie.com/
index.php

Small business administration regional offices

This section contains a listing of Small Business Administration offices arranged numerically by region. Service areas are provided. Contact the appropriate office for a referral to the nearest field office, or visit the Small Business Administration online at www.sba.gov.

Region I

**U.S. Small Business Administration
New England Office**
10 Causeway St., Ste. 265A
Boston, MA 02222
Phone: (617)565-8416
Fax: (617)565-8420
Website: http://www.sba.gov/offices/
regional/i
Serves Connecticut, Maine, Massachusetts, New Hampshire, Rhode Island, and Vermont.

Region II

**U.S. Small Business Administration
Atlantic Office**
26 Federal Plaza, Ste. 3108
New York, NY 10278
Phone: (212)264-1450
Website: http://www.sba.gov/offices/
regional/ii
Serves New Jersey, New York, Puerto Rico, and the U.S. Virgin Islands.

Region III

**U.S. Small Business Administration
Mid-Atlantic Office**
1150 1st Ave., Ste. 1001
King of Prussia, PA 19406
(610)382-3092
Website: http://www.sba.gov/offices/
regional/iii
Serves Delaware, Maryland, Pennsylvania, Virginia, Washington, DC, and West Virginia.

Region IV

**U.S. Small Business Administration
Southeast Office**
233 Peachtree St. NE, Ste. 1800
Atlanta, GA 30303
Phone: (404)331-4999
Fax: (404)331-2354
Website: http://www.sba.gov/offices/
regional/iv
Serves Alabama, Florida, Georgia, Kentucky, Mississippi, North Carolina, South Carolina, and Tennessee.

Region V

**U.S. Small Business Administration
Great Lakes Office**
500 W Madison St., Ste. 1150
Chicago, IL 60661
Phone: (312)353-0357
Fax: (312)353-3426
Website: http://www.sba.gov/offices/
regional/v
Serves Illinois, Indiana, Michigan, Minnesota, Ohio, and Wisconsin.

Region VI

**U.S. Small Business Administration
South Central Office**
4300 Amon Carter Blvd., Ste. 108
Fort Worth, TX 76155
Phone: (817)684-5581
Fax: (817)684-5588
TTY/TDD: (817)684-5552
Website: http://www.sba.gov/offices/
regional/vi
Serves Arkansas, Louisiana, New Mexico, Oklahoma, and Texas.

Region VII

**U.S. Small Business Administration
Great Plains Office**
1000 Walnut, Ste. 530
Kansas City, MO 64106
Phone: (816)426-4840
Fax: (816)426-4848
Website: http://www.sba.gov/offices/
regional/vii
Serves Iowa, Kansas, Missouri, and Nebraska.

Region VIII

**U.S. Small Business Administration
Rocky Mountains Office**
721 19th St., Ste. 400
Denver, CO 80202
Fax: (303)844-0506
Website: http://www.sba.gov/offices/
regional/viii
Serves Colorado, Montana, North Dakota, South Dakota, Utah, and Wyoming.

Region IX

**U.S. Small Business Administration
Pacific Office**
330 N Brand Blvd., Ste. 1200
Glendale, CA 91203
Phone: (818)552-3437
Fax: (202)481-0344
Website: http://www.sba.gov/offices/
regional/ix
Serves Arizona, California, Guam, Hawaii, and Nevada.

Region X

**U.S. Small Business Administration
Pacific Northwest Office**
2401 4th Ave., Ste. 400
Seattle, WA 98121
Phone: (206)553-5676
Fax: (206)553-4155
Website: http://www.sba.gov/offices/
regional/x
Serves Alaska, Idaho, Oregon, and Washington.

Small business development centers

This section contains a listing of all Small Business Development Centers, organized alphabetically by state/U.S. territory, then by city, then by agency name.

Alabama

Alabama SBDC

UNIVERSITY OF ALABAMA
2800 Milan Court Suite 124
Birmingham, AL 35211-6908
Phone: 205-943-6750
Fax: 205-943-6752
E-Mail: wcampbell@provost.uab.edu
Website: http://www.asbdc.org
Mr. William Campbell Jr, State Director

Alaska

Alaska SBDC

UNIVERSITY OF ALASKA - ANCHORAGE
430 West Seventh Avenue, Suite 110
Anchorage, AK 99501
Phone: 907-274 -7232
Fax: 907-272-0565
E-Mail: Isaac.Vanderburg@aksbdc.org
Website: http://www.aksbdc.org
Isaac Vanderburg, State Director

American Samoa

American Samoa SBDC

AMERICAN SAMOA COMMUNITY COLLEGE
P.O. Box 2609
Pago Pago, American Samoa 96799
Phone: 011-684-699-4830
Fax: 011-684-699-6132
E-Mail: hthweatt.sbdc@hotmail.com
Website: www.as-sbdc.org
Mr. Herbert Thweatt, Director

Arizona

Arizona SBDC

MARICOPA COUNTY COMMUNITY COLLEGE
2411 West 14th Street, Suite 114
Tempe, AZ 85281
Phone: (480)731-8720
Fax: (480)731-8729
E-Mail: janice.washington@domail
.maricopa.edu
Website: http://www.azsbdc.net
Janice Washington, State Director

Arkansas

Arkansas SBDC

UNIVERSITY OF ARKANSAS
2801 South University Avenue
Little Rock, AR 72204
Phone: 501-683-7700
Fax: 501-683-7720
E-Mail: jmroderick@ualr.edu
Website: http://asbtdc.org
Ms. Janet M. Roderick, State Director

California

California - Northern California Regional SBDC

Northern California SBDC

HUMBOLDT STATE UNIVERSITY
1 Harpst Street 2006A, 209 Siemens Hall
Arcata, CA, 95521
Phone: 707-826-3920
Fax: 707-826-3912
E-Mail: Kristin.Johnson@humboldt.edu
Website: https://www.norcalsbdc.org
Kristin Johnson, Regional Director

California - Northern California SBDC

CALIFORNIA STATE UNIVERSITY - CHICO
35 Main St., Rm 203rr
Chico, CA 95929-0765
Phone: 530-898-5443
Fax: 530-898-4734
E-Mail: dripke@csuchico.edu
Website: https://www.necsbdc.org
Mr. Dan Ripke, Interim Regional Director

California - San Diego and Imperial SBDC

SOUTHWESTERN COMMUNITY COLLEGE
880 National City Boulevard, Suite 103
National City, CA 91950
Phone: 619-216-6721
Fax: 619-216-6692
E-Mail: awilson@swccd.edu
Website: http://www.SBDCRegional
Network.org
Aleta Wilson, Regional Director

California - UC Merced SBDC

UC Merced Lead Center

UNIVERSITY OF CALIFORNIA - MERCED
550 East Shaw, Suite 105A
Fresno, CA 93710
Phone: 559-241-6590
Fax: 559-241-7422

E-Mail: dhowerton@ucmerced.edu
Website: http://sbdc.ucmerced.edu
Diane Howerton, State Director

California - Orange County/Inland Empire SBDC

Tri-County Lead SBDC

CALIFORNIA STATE UNIVERSITY - FULLERTON
800 North State College Boulevard,
SGMH 5313
Fullerton, CA 92834
Phone: 714-278-5168
Fax: 714-278-7101
E-Mail: kmpayne@fullerton.edu
Website: http://www.leadsbdc.org
Katrina Payne Smith, Lead Center Director

California - Los Angeles Region SBDC

LONG BEACH CITY COLLEGE
4900 E Conant Street, Building 2
Long Beach, CA 90808
Phone: 562-938-5006
Fax: 562-938-5030
E-Mail: jtorres@lbcc.edu
Website: http://www.smallbizla.org
Jesse Torres, Lead Center Director

Colorado

Colorado SBDC

COLORADO SBDC
1625 Broadway, Suite 2700
Denver, CO 80202
Phone: 303-892-3864
Fax: 303-892-3848
E-Mail: Kelly.Manning@state.co.us
Website: http://www.www.colorad
osbdc.org
Ms. Kelly Manning, State Director

Connecticut

Connecticut SBDC

UNIVERSITY OF CONNECTICUT
2100 Hillside Road, Unit 1044
Storrs, CT 06269
Phone: 855-428-7232
E-Mail: ecarter@uconn.edu
Website: www.ctsbdc.com
Emily Carter, State Director

Delaware

Delaware SBDC

DELAWARE TECHNOLOGY PARK
1 Innovation Way, Suite 301
Newark, DE 19711

Phone: 302-831-4283
Fax: 302-831-1423
E-Mail: jmbowman@udel.edu
Website: http://www.delawaresbdc.org
Mike Bowman, State Director

District of Columbia

District of Columbia SBDC

HOWARD UNIVERSITY

2600 6th Street, NW Room 128
Washington, DC 20059
Phone: 202-806-1550
Fax: 202-806-1777
E-Mail: darrell.brown@howard.edu
Website: http://www.dcsbdc.com
Darrell Brown, Executive Director

Florida

Florida SBDC

UNIVERSITY OF WEST FLORIDA

11000 University Parkway, Building 38
Pensacola, FL 32514
Phone: 850-473-7800
Fax: 850-473-7813
E-Mail: mmyhre@uwf.edu
Website: http://www.floridasbdc.com
Michael Myhre, State Director

Georgia

Georgia SBDC

UNIVERSITY OF GEORGIA

1180 East Broad Street
Athens, GA 30602
Phone: 706-542-6762
Fax: 706-542-7935
E-mail: aadams@georgiasbdc.org
Website: http://www.georgiasbdc.org
Mr. Allan Adams, State Director

Guam

Guam Small Business Development Center

UNIVERSITY OF GUAM

Pacific Islands SBDC
P.O. Box 5014 - U.O.G. Station
Mangilao, GU 96923
Phone: 671-735-2590
Fax: 671-734-2002
E-mail: casey@pacificsbdc.com
Website: http://www.uog.edu/sbdc
Mr. Casey Jeszenka, Director

Hawaii

Hawaii SBDC

UNIVERSITY OF HAWAII - HILO

200 W Kawili Street, Suite 107
Hilo, HI 96720
Phone: 808-974-7515
Fax: 808-974-7683
E-Mail: cathy.wiltse@hisbdc.org
Website: http://www.hisbdc.org
Cathy Wiltse, State Director

Idaho

Idaho SBDC

BOISE STATE UNIVERSITY

1910 University Drive
Boise, ID 83725
Phone: 208-426-3838
Fax: 208-426-3877
E-mail: ksewell@boisestate.edu
Website: http://www.idahosbdc.org
Katie Sewell, State Director

Illinois

Illinois SBDC

DEPARTMENT OF COMMERCE AND ECONOMIC OPPORTUNITY

500 E Monroe
Springfield, IL 62701
Phone: 217-524-5700
Fax: 217-524-0171
E-mail: mark.petrilli@illinois.gov
Website: http://www.ilsbdc.biz
Mr. Mark Petrilli, State Director

Indiana

Indiana SBDC

INDIANA ECONOMIC DEVELOPMENT CORPORATION

One North Capitol, Suite 700
Indianapolis, IN 46204
Phone: 317-232-8805
Fax: 317-232-8872
E-mail: JSchpok@iedc.in.gov
Website: http://www.isbdc.org
Jacob Schpok, State Director

Iowa

Iowa SBDC

IOWA STATE UNIVERSITY

2321 North Loop Drive, Suite 202
Ames, IA 50010
Phone: 515-294-2030
Fax: 515-294-6522
E-mail: lshimkat@iastate.edu

Website: http://www.iowasbdc.org
Lisa Shimkat, State Director

Kansas

Kansas SBDC

FORT HAYS STATE UNIVERSITY

214 SW Sixth Street, Suite 301
Topeka, KS 66603
Phone: 785-296-6514
Fax: 785-291-3261
E-mail: panichello@ksbdc.net
Website: http://www.fhsu.edu/ksbdc
Greg Panichello, State Director

Kentucky

Kentucky SBDC

UNIVERSITY OF KENTUCKY

One Quality Street
Lexington, KY 40507
Phone: 859-257-7668
Fax: 859-323-1907
E-mail: lrnaug0@uky.edu
Website: http://www.ksbdc.org
Becky Naugle, State Director

Louisiana

Louisiana SBDC

UNIVERSITY OF LOUISIANA - MONROE

College of Business Administration
700 University Avenue
Monroe, LA 71209
Phone: 318-342-5507
Fax: 318-342-5510
E-mail: rkessler@lsbdc.org
Website: http://www.lsbdc.org
Rande Kessler, State Director

Maine

Maine SBDC

UNIVERSITY OF SOUTHERN MAINE

96 Falmouth Street P.O. Box 9300
Portland, ME 04104
Phone: 207-780-4420
Fax: 207-780-4810
E-mail: mark.delisle@maine.edu
Website: http://www.mainesbdc.org
Mark Delisle, State Director

Maryland

Maryland SBDC

UNIVERSITY OF MARYLAND

7100 Baltimore Avenue, Suite 401
College Park, MD 20742

Phone: 301-403-8300
Fax: 301-403-8303
E-mail: rsprow@mdsbdc.umd.edu
Website: http://www.mdsbdc.umd.edu
Renee Sprow, State Director

Massachusetts

Massachusetts SBDC

UNIVERSITY OF MASSACHUSETTS
23 Tillson Farm Road
Amherst, MA 01003
Phone: 413-545-6301
Fax: 413-545-1273
E-mail: gparkin@msbdc.umass.edu
Website: http://www.www.msbdc.org
Georgianna Parkin, State Director

Michigan

Michigan SBTDC

GRAND VALLEY STATE UNIVERSITY
510 West Fulton Avenue
Grand Rapids, MI 49504
Phone: 616-331-7480
Fax: 616-331-7485
E-mail: boesen@gvsu.edu
Website: http://www.misbtdc.org
Nancy Boese, State Director

Minnesota

Minnesota SBDC

MINNESOTA SMALL BUSINESS DEVELOPMENT CENTER
1st National Bank Building
332 Minnesota Street, Suite E200
Saint Paul, MN 55101-1349
Phone: 651-259-7420
Fax: 651-296-5287
E-mail: Bruce.Strong@state.mn.us
Website: http://www.mnsbdc.com
Bruce H. Strong, State Director

Mississippi

Mississippi SBDC

UNIVERSITY OF MISSISSIPPI
122 Jeanette Phillips Drive
P.O. Box 1848
University, MS 38677
Phone: 662-915-5001
Fax: 662-915-5650
E-mail: wgurley@olemiss.edu
Website: http://www.mssbdc.org
Doug Gurley, Jr., State Director

Missouri

Missouri SBDC

UNIVERSITY OF MISSOURI
410 South 6th Street, ?200 Engineering North
Columbia, MO 65211
Phone: 573-882-9206
Fax: 573-884-4297
E-mail: bouchardc@missouri.edu
Website: http://www.missouribusiness.net
Chris Bouchard, State Director

Montana

Montana SBDC

DEPARTMENT OF COMMERCE
301 S Park Avenue, Room 114
Helena, MT 59601
Phone: 406-841-2746
Fax: 406-841-2728
E-mail: adesch@mt.gov
Website: http://www.sbdc.mt.gov
Ms. Ann Desch, State Director

Nebraska

Nebraska SBDC

UNIVERSITY OF NEBRASKA - OMAHA
200 Mammel Hall, 67th & Pine Streets
Omaha, NE 68182
Phone: 402-554-2521
Fax: 402-554-3473
E-mail: rbernier@unomaha.edu
Website: http://nbdc.unomaha.edu
Robert Bernier, State Director

Nevada

Nevada SBDC

UNIVERSITY OF NEVADA - RENO
Reno College of Business, Room 411
Reno, NV 89557-0100
Phone: 775-784-1717
Fax: 775-784-4337
E-mail: males@unr.edu
Website: http://www.nsbdc.org
Sam Males, State Director

New Hampshire

New Hampshire SBDC

UNIVERSITY OF NEW HAMPSHIRE
10 Garrison Avenue
Durham, NH 03824-3593
Phone: 603-862-2200
Fax: 603-862-4876
E-mail: Mary.Collins@unh.edu
Website: http://www.nhsbdc.org
Mary Collins, State Director

New Jersey

New Jersey SBDC

RUTGERS UNIVERSITY
1 Washington Park, 3rd Floor
Newark, NJ 07102
Phone: 973-353-1927
Fax: 973-353-1110
E-mail: bhopper@njsbdc.com
Website: http://www.njsbdc.com
Brenda Hopper, State Director

New Mexico

New Mexico SBDC

SANTA FE COMMUNITY COLLEGE
6401 Richards Avenue
Santa Fe, NM 87508
Phone: 505-428-1362
Fax: 505-428-1469
E-mail: russell.wyrick@sfcc.edu
Website: http://www.nmsbdc.org
Russell Wyrick, State Director

New York

New York SBDC

STATE UNIVERSITY OF NEW YORK
22 Corporate Woods, 3rd Floor
Albany, NY 12246
Phone: 518-443-5398
Fax: 518-443-5275
E-mail: j.king@nyssbdc.org
Website: http://www.nyssbdc.org
Jim King, State Director

North Carolina

North Carolina SBDTC

UNIVERSITY OF NORTH CAROLINA
5 West Hargett Street, Suite 600
Raleigh, NC 27601
Phone: 919-715-7272
Fax: 919-715-7777
E-mail: sdaugherty@sbtdc.org
Website: http://www.sbtdc.org
Scott Daugherty, State Director

North Dakota

North Dakota SBDC

UNIVERSITY OF NORTH DAKOTA
1200 Memorial Highway, PO Box 5509
Bismarck, ND 58506
Phone: 701-328-5375
Fax: 701-250-4304
E-mail: dkmartin@ndsbdc.org
Website: http://www.ndsbdc.org
David Martin, State Director

Ohio

Ohio SBDC

OHIO DEPARTMENT OF DEVELOPMENT
77 South High Street, 28th Floor
Columbus, OH 43216
Phone: 614-466-2711
Fax: 614-466-1789
E-mail: ezra.escudero@development
.ohio.gov
Website: http://www.ohiosbdc.org
Ezra Escudero, State Director

Oklahoma

Oklahoma SBDC

SOUTHEAST OKLAHOMA STATE UNIVERSITY
1405 N. 4th Avenue, PMB 2584
Durant, OK 74701
Phone: 580-745-2955
Fax: 580-745-7471
E-mail: wcarter@se.edu
Website: http://www.osbdc.org
Grady Pennington, State Director

Oregon

Oregon SBDC

LANE COMMUNITY COLLEGE
1445 Willamette Street, Suite 5
Eugene, OR 97401
Phone: 541-463-5250
Fax: 541-345-6006
E-mail: gregorym@lanecc.edu
Website: http://www.bizcenter.org
Mark Gregory, State Director

Pennsylvania

Pennsylvania SBDC

UNIVERSITY OF PENNSYLVANIA

The Wharton School
3819-33 Chestnut Street, Suite 325
Philadelphia, PA 19104
Phone: 215-898-1219
Fax: 215-573-2135
E-mail: cconroy@wharton.upenn.edu
Website: http://pasbdc.org
Christian Conroy, State Director

Puerto Rico

Puerto Rico SBDC

INTER-AMERICAN UNIVERSITY OF PUERTO RICO
416 Ponce de Leon Avenue, Union Plaza,
Tenth Floor

Hato Rey, PR 00918
Phone: 787-763-6811
Fax: 787-763-6875
E-mail: cmarti@prsbdc.org
Website: http://www.prsbdc.org
Carmen Marti, Executive Director

Rhode Island

Rhode Island SBDC

UNIVERSITY OF RHODE ISLAND
75 Lower College Road, 2nd Floor
Kingston, RI 02881
Phone: 401-874-4576
E-mail: gsonnenfeld@uri.edu
Website: http://www.risbdc.org
Gerald Sonnenfeld, State Director

South Carolina

South Carolina SBDC

UNIVERSITY OF SOUTH CAROLINA

Moore School of Business
1014 Greene Street
Columbia, SC 29208
Phone: 803-777-0749
Fax: 803-777-6876
E-mail: michele.abraham@moore.sc.edu
Website: http://www.scsbdc.com
Michele Abraham, State Director

South Dakota

South Dakota SBDC

UNIVERSITY OF SOUTH DAKOTA
414 East Clark Street, Patterson Hall
Vermillion, SD 57069
Phone: 605-677-5103
Fax: 605-677-5427
E-mail: jeff.eckhoff@usd.edu
Website: http://www.usd.edu/sbdc
Jeff Eckhoff, State Director

Tennessee

Tennessee SBDC

MIDDLE TENNESSEE STATE UNIVERSITY
3050 Medical Center Parkway, Ste. 200
Nashville, TN 37129
Phone: 615-849-9999
Fax: 615-893-7089
E-mail: pgeho@tsbdc.org
Website: http://www.tsbdc.org
Patrick Geho, State Director

Texas

Texas-North SBDC

DALLAS COUNTY COMMUNITY COLLEGE
1402 Corinth Street
Dallas, TX 75215
Phone: 214-860-5832
Fax: 214-860-5813
E-mail: m.langford@dcccd.edu
Website: http://www.ntsbdc.org
Mark Langford, Region Director

Texas Gulf Coast SBDC

UNIVERSITY OF HOUSTON
2302 Fannin, Suite 200
Houston, TX 77002
Phone: 713-752-8444
Fax: 713-756-1500
E-mail: fyoung@uh.edu
Website: http://sbdcnetwork.uh.edu
Mike Young, Executive Director

Texas-NW SBDC

TEXAS TECH UNIVERSITY
2579 South Loop 289, Suite 114
Lubbock, TX 79423
Phone: 806-745-3973
Fax: 806-745-6207
E-mail: c.bean@nwtsbdc.org
Website: http://www.nwtsbdc.org
Craig Bean, Executive Director

Texas-South-West Texas Border Region SBDC

UNIVERSITY OF TEXAS - SAN ANTONIO
501 West Durango Boulevard
San Antonio, TX 78207-4415
Phone: 210-458-2480
Fax: 210-458-2425
E-mail: albert.salgado@utsa.edu
Website: https://www.txsbdc.org
Alberto Salgado, Region Director

Utah

Utah SBDC

SALT LAKE COMMUNITY COLLEGE
9750 South 300 West
Salt Lake City, UT 84070
Phone: 801-957-5384
Fax: 801-985-5300
E-mail: Sherm.Wilkinson@slcc.edu
Website: http://www.utahsbdc.org
Sherm Wilkinson, State Director

Vermont

Vermont SBDC

VERMONT TECHNICAL COLLEGE
PO Box 188, 1 Main Street
Randolph Center, VT 05061-0188
Phone: 802-728-9101
Fax: 802-728-3026
E-mail: lrossi@vtsbdc.org
Website: http://www.vtsbdc.org
Linda Rossi, State Director

Virgin Islands

Virgin Islands SBDC

UNIVERSITY OF THE VIRGIN ISLANDS
8000 Nisky Center, Suite 720
Saint Thomas, VI 00802
Phone: 340-776-3206
Fax: 340-775-3756
E-mail: ldottin@uvi.edu
Website: http://www.sbdcvi.org
Leonor Dottin, State Director

Virginia

Virginia SBDC

GEORGE MASON UNIVERSITY
4031 University Drive, Suite100
Fairfax, VA 22030
Phone: 703-277-7727
Fax: 703-352-8518
E-mail: jkeenan@gmu.edu
Website: http://www.virginiasbdc.org
Jody Keenan, Director

Washington

Washington SBDC

WASHINGTON STATE UNIVERSITY
1235 N. Post Street, Suite 201
Spokane, WA 99201
Phone: 509-358-7765
Fax: 509-358-7764
E-mail: duane.fladland@wsbdc.org
Website: http://www.wsbdc.org
Duane Fladland, State Director

West Virginia

West Virginia SBDC

WEST VIRGINIA DEVELOPMENT OFFICE
Capital Complex, Building 6, Room 652
1900 Kanawha Boulevard
Charleston, WV 25305
Phone: 304-957-2087
Fax: 304-558-0127

E-mail: Kristina.J.Oliver@wv.gov
Website: http://www.wvsbdc.org
Mr. Conley Salyor, State Director

Wisconsin

Wisconsin SBDC

UNIVERSITY OF WISCONSIN
432 North Lake Street, Room 423
Madison, WI 53706
Phone: 608-263-7794
Fax: 608-263-7830
E-mail: bon.wikenheiser@uwex.edu
Website: http://www.uwex.edu/sbdc
Bon Wikenheiser, State Director

Wyoming

Wyoming SBDC

UNIVERSITY OF WYOMING
1000 E University Ave., Dept. 3922
Laramie, WY 82071-3922
Phone: (307)766-3405
Fax: (307)766-3406
E-mail: jkline@uwyo.edu
Website: http://www.wyomingentre
preneur.biz
Jill Kline, Acting State Director

Service corps of retired executives (score) offices

This section contains a listing of all SCORE offices organized alphabetically by state/U.S. territory, then by city, then by agency name.

Alabama

SCORE Office (Northeast Alabama)
1400 Commerce Blvd., Northeast
Anniston, AL 36207
(256)241-6111

SCORE Office (North Alabama)
1731 1st Ave. North, Ste. 200
Birmingham, AL 35203
(205)264-8425
Fax: (205)934-0538

SCORE Office (Baldwin County)
327 Fairhope Avenue
Fairhope, AL 36532
(251)928-6387

SCORE Office (Mobile)
451 Government Street
Mobile, AL 36652
(251)431-8614
Fax: (251)431-8646

SCORE Office (Alabama Capitol City)
600 S Court St.
Montgomery, AL 36104
(334)240-6868
Fax: (334)240-6869

SCORE Office (Tuscaloosa)
2200 University Blvd.
Tuscaloosa, AL 35402
(205)758-7588

Alaska

SCORE Office (Anchorage)
420 L St., Ste. 300
Anchorage, AK 99501
(907)271-4022
Fax: (907)271-4545

Arizona

SCORE Office (Greater Phoenix)
2828 N. Central Ave., Ste. 800
Phoenix, AZ 85004
(602)745-7250
Fax: (602)745-7210
E-mail: e-mail@SCORE-phoenix.org
Website: http://www.greaterphoenix
.score.org

SCORE Office (Northern Arizona)
1228 Willow Creek Rd., Ste. 2
Prescott, AZ 86301
(928)778-7438
Fax: (928)778-0812
Website: http://www.northernarizona
.score.org

SCORE Office (Southern Arizona)
1400 W Speedway Blvd.
Tucson, AZ 85745
(520)505-3636
Fax: (520)670-5011
Website: http://www.southernarizona
.score.org

Arkansas

SCORE Office (South Central)
201 N. Jackson Ave.
El Dorado, AR 71730-5803
(870)863-6113
Fax: (870)863-6115

SCORE Office (Northwest Arkansas)
614 E Emma St., Room M412
Springdale, AR 72764
(479)725-1809
Website: http://www.northwestarkansas
.score.org

SCORE Office (Little Rock)
2120 Riverfront Dr., Ste. 250
Little Rock, AR 72202-1747
(501)324-7379
Fax: (501)324-5199
Website: http://www.littlerock.score.org

SCORE Office (Southeast Arkansas)
P.O. Box 5069
Pine Bluff, AR 71611-5069
(870)535-0110
Fax: (870)535-1643

California

SCORE Office (Bakersfield)
P.O. Box 2426
Bakersfield, CA 93303
(661)861-9249
Fax: (661)395-4134
Website: http://www.bakersfield.score.org

SCORE Office (Santa Cruz County)
716 G Capitola Ave.
Capitola, CA 95010
(831)621-3735
Fax: (831)475-6530
Website: http://santacruzcounty.score.org

SCORE Office (Greater Chico Area)
1324 Mangrove St., Ste. 114
Chico, CA 95926
(530)342-8932
Fax: (530)342-8932
Website: http://www.greaterchicoarea
.score.org

SCORE Office (El Centro)
1850 W Main St, Ste. C
El Centro, CA 92243
(760)337-2692
Website: http://www.sandiego.score.org

SCORE Office (Central Valley)
801 R St., Ste. 201
Fresno, CA 93721
(559)487-5605
Fax: (559)487-5636
Website: http://www.centralvalley.score.org

SCORE Office (Los Angeles)
330 N. Brand Blvd., Ste. 190
Glendale, CA 91203-2304
(818)552-3206
Fax: (818)552-3323
Website: http://www.greaterlosangeles
.score.org

SCORE Office (Modesto Merced)
1880 W Wardrobe Ave.
Merced, CA 95340
(209)725-2033
Fax: (209)577-2673

Website: http://www.modestomerced
.score.org

SCORE Office (Monterey Bay)
Monterey Chamber of Commerce
30 Ragsdale Dr.
Monterey, CA 93940
(831)648-5360
Website: http://www.montereybay
.score.org

SCORE Office (East Bay)
492 9th St., Ste. 350
Oakland, CA 94607
(510)273-6611
Fax: (510)273-6015
E-mail: webmaster@eastbayscore.org
Website: http://www.eastbay.score.org

SCORE Office (Ventura County)
400 E Esplanade Dr., Ste. 301
Oxnard, CA 93036
(805)204-6022
Fax: (805)650-1414
Website: http://www.ventura.score.org

SCORE Office (Coachella)
43100 Cook St., Ste. 104
Palm Desert, CA 92211
(760)773-6507
Fax: (760)773-6514
Website: http://www.coachellavalley
.score.org

SCORE Office (Antelope Valley)
1212 E Avenue, S Ste. A3
Palmdale, CA 93550
(661)947-7679
Website: http://
www.antelopevalley.score.org

SCORE Office (Inland Empire)
11801 Pierce St., 2nd Fl.
Riverside, CA 92505
(951)-652-4390
Fax: (951)929-8543
Website: http://www.inlandempire
.score.org

SCORE Office (Sacramento)
4990 Stockton Blvd.
Sacramento, CA 95820
(916)635-9085
Fax: (916)635-9089
Website: http://www.sacramento.score.org

SCORE Office (San Diego)
550 West C. St., Ste. 550
San Diego, CA 92101-3540
(619)557-7272
Website: http://www.sandiego.score.org

SCORE Office (San Francisco)
455 Market St., 6th Fl.
San Francisco, CA 94105
(415)744-6827
Fax: (415)744-6750
E-mail: sfscore@sfscore.
Website: http://www.sanfrancisco
.score.org

SCORE Office (Silicon Valley)
234 E Gish Rd., Ste. 100
San Jose, CA 95112
(408)453-6237
Fax: (408)494-0214
E-mail: info@svscore.org
Website: http://www.siliconvalley
.score.org

SCORE Office (San Luis Obispo)
711 Tank Farm Rd., Ste. 210
San Luis Obispo, CA 93401
(805)547-0779
Website: http://www.sanluisobispo
.score.org

SCORE Office (Orange County)
200 W Santa Anna Blvd., Ste. 700
Santa Ana, CA 92701
(714)550-7369
Fax: (714)550-0191
Website: http://www.orangecounty
.score.org

SCORE Office (Santa Barbara)
924 Anacapa St.
Santa Barbara, CA 93101
(805)563-0084
Website: http://www.santabarbara
.score.org

SCORE Office (North Coast)
777 Sonoma Ave., Rm. 115E
Santa Rosa, CA 95404
(707)571-8342
Fax: (707)541-0331
Website: http://www.northcoast
.score.org

SCORE Office (Tuolumne County)
222 S Shepherd St.
Sonora, CA 95370
(209)532-4316
Fax: (209)588-0673
Website: http://www.tuolumnecounty
.score.org

Colorado

SCORE Office (Colorado Springs)
3595 E Fountain Blvd., Ste. E-1
Colorado Springs, CO 80910
(719)636-3074

Fax: (719)635-1571
Website: http://www.coloradosprings
.score.org

SCORE Office (Denver)
US Custom's House, 4th Fl.
721 19th St.
Denver, CO 80202
(303)844-3985
Fax: (303)844-6490
Website: http://www.denver.score.org

SCORE Office (Tri-River)
1102 Grand Ave.
Glenwood Springs, CO 81601
(970)945-6589

SCORE Office (Grand Junction)
2591 B & 3/4 Rd.
Grand Junction, CO 81503
(970)243-5242

SCORE Office (Gunnison)
608 N. 11th
Gunnison, CO 81230
(303)641-4422

SCORE Office (Montrose)
1214 Peppertree Dr.
Montrose, CO 81401
(970)249-6080

SCORE Office (Pagosa Springs)
PO Box 4381
Pagosa Springs, CO 81157
(970)731-4890

SCORE Office (Rifle)
0854 W Battlement Pky., Apt. C106
Parachute, CO 81635
(970)285-9390

SCORE Office (Pueblo)
302 N. Santa Fe
Pueblo, CO 81003
(719)542-1704
Fax: (719)542-1624
Website: http://www.pueblo.score.org

SCORE Office (Ridgway)
143 Poplar Pl.
Ridgway, CO 81432

SCORE Office (Silverton)
PO Box 480
Silverton, CO 81433
(303)387-5430

SCORE Office (Minturn)
PO Box 2066
Vail, CO 81658
(970)476-1224

Connecticut

SCORE Office (Greater Bridgeport)
230 Park Ave.
Bridgeport, CT 06604
(203)450-9484
Fax: (203)576-4388

SCORE Office (Western Connecticut)
155 Deer Hill Ave.
Danbury, CT 06010
(203)794-1404
Website: http://www.westernconnecticut
.score.org

SCORE Office (Greater Hartford County)
330 Main St., 2nd Fl.
Hartford, CT 06106
(860)240-4700
Fax: (860)240-4659
Website: http://www.greaterhartford
.score.org

SCORE Office (Manchester)
20 Hartford Rd.
Manchester, CT 06040
(203)646-2223
Fax: (203)646-5871

SCORE Office (New Britain)
185 Main St., Ste. 431
New Britain, CT 06051
(203)827-4492
Fax: (203)827-4480

SCORE Office (New Haven)
60 Sargent Dr.
New Haven, CT 06511
(203)865-7645
Website: http://www.newhaven.score.org

SCORE Office (Fairfield County)
111 East Ave.
Norwalk, CT 06851
(203)847-7348
Fax: (203)849-9308
Website: http://www.fairfieldcounty
.score.org

SCORE Office (Southeastern Connecticut)
665 Boston Post Rd.
Old Saybrook, CT 06475
(860)388-9508
Website: http://www.southeastern
connecticut.score.org

SCORE Office (Northwest Connecticut)
333 Kennedy Dr.
Torrington, CT 06790
(560)482-6586

Website: http://www.northwest
connecticut.score.org

Delaware

SCORE Office (Dover)
Treadway Towers
PO Box 576
Dover, DE 19903
(302)678-0892
Fax: (302)678-0189

SCORE Office (Lewes)
PO Box 1
Lewes, DE 19958
(302)645-8073
Fax: (302)645-8412

SCORE Office (Milford)
204 NE Front St.
Milford, DE 19963
(302)422-3301

SCORE Office (Wilmington)
824 Market St., Ste. 610
Wilmington, DE 19801
(302)573-6652
Fax: (302)573-6092
Website: http://www.scoredelaware.com

District of Columbia

SCORE Office (George Mason University)
409 3rd St. SW, 4th Fl.
Washington, DC 20024
800-634-0245

SCORE Office (Washington DC)
1110 Vermont Ave. NW, 9th Fl.
Washington, DC 20043
(202)606-4000
Fax: (202)606-4225
E-mail: dcscore@hotmail.com
Website: http://www.scoredc.org

Florida

SCORE Office (Desota County Chamber of Commerce)
16 South Velucia Ave.
Arcadia, FL 34266
(941)494-4033

SCORE Office (Suncoast/Pinellas)
Airport Business Ctr.
4707 - 140th Ave. N, No. 311
Clearwater, FL 33755
(813)532-6800
Fax: (813)532-6800

SCORE Office (DeLand)
336 N. Woodland Blvd.
DeLand, FL 32720

(904)734-4331
Fax: (904)734-4333

SCORE Office (South Palm Beach)
1050 S Federal Hwy., Ste. 132
Delray Beach, FL 33483
(561)278-7752
Fax: (561)278-0288

SCORE Office (Fort Lauderdale)
Federal Bldg., Ste. 123
299 E Broward Blvd.
Fort Lauderdale, FL 33301
(954)356-7263
Fax: (954)356-7145

SCORE Office (Southwest Florida)
The Renaissance
8695 College Pky., Ste. 345 & 346
Fort Myers, FL 33919
(941)489-2935
Fax: (941)489-1170

SCORE Office (Treasure Coast)
Professional Center, Ste. 2
3220 S US, No. 1
Fort Pierce, FL 34982
(561)489-0548

SCORE Office (Gainesville)
101 SE 2nd Pl., Ste. 104
Gainesville, FL 32601
(904)375-8278

SCORE Office (Hialeah Dade Chamber)
59 W 5th St.
Hialeah, FL 33010
(305)887-1515
Fax: (305)887-2453

SCORE Office (Daytona Beach)
921 Nova Rd., Ste. A
Holly Hills, FL 32117
(904)255-6889
Fax: (904)255-0229
E-mail: score87@dbeach.com

SCORE Office (South Broward)
3475 Sheridian St., Ste. 203
Hollywood, FL 33021
(305)966-8415

SCORE Office (Citrus County)
5 Poplar Ct.
Homosassa, FL 34446
(352)382-1037

SCORE Office (Jacksonville)
7825 Baymeadows Way, Ste. 100-B
Jacksonville, FL 32256
(904)443-1911
Fax: (904)443-1980
E-mail: scorejax@juno.com
Website: http://www.scorejax.org

SCORE Office (Jacksonville Satellite)
3 Independent Dr.
Jacksonville, FL 32256
(904)366-6600
Fax: (904)632-0617

SCORE Office (Central Florida)
5410 S Florida Ave., No. 3
Lakeland, FL 33801
(941)687-5783
Fax: (941)687-6225

SCORE Office (Lakeland)
100 Lake Morton Dr.
Lakeland, FL 33801
(941)686-2168

SCORE Office (Saint Petersburg)
800 W Bay Dr., Ste. 505
Largo, FL 33712
(813)585-4571

SCORE Office (Leesburg)
9501 US Hwy. 441
Leesburg, FL 34788-8751
(352)365-3556
Fax: (352)365-3501

SCORE Office (Cocoa)
1600 Farno Rd., Unit 205
Melbourne, FL 32935
(407)254-2288

SCORE Office (Melbourne)
Melbourne Professional Complex
1600 Sarno, Ste. 205
Melbourne, FL 32935
(407)254-2288
Fax: (407)245-2288

SCORE Office (Merritt Island)
1600 Sarno Rd., Ste. 205
Melbourne, FL 32935
(407)254-2288
Fax: (407)254-2288

SCORE Office (Space Coast)
Melbourn Professional Complex
1600 Sarno, Ste. 205
Melbourne, FL 32935
(407)254-2288
Fax: (407)254-2288

SCORE Office (Dade)
49 NW 5th St.
Miami, FL 33128
(305)371-6889
Fax: (305)374-1882
E-mail: score@netrox.net
Website: http://www.netrox.net/~score

SCORE Office (Naples of Collier)
International College
2654 Tamiami Trl. E

Naples, FL 34112
(941)417-1280
Fax: (941)417-1281
E-mail: score@naples.net
Website: http://www.naples.net/clubs/
score/index.htm

SCORE Office (Pasco County)
6014 US Hwy. 19, Ste. 302
New Port Richey, FL 34652
(813)842-4638

SCORE Office (Southeast Volusia)
115 Canal St.
New Smyrna Beach, FL 32168
(904)428-2449
Fax: (904)423-3512

SCORE Office (Ocala)
110 E Silver Springs Blvd.
Ocala, FL 34470
(352)629-5959

Clay County SCORE Office
Clay County Chamber of Commerce
1734 Kingsdey Ave.
PO Box 1441
Orange Park, FL 32073
(904)264-2651
Fax: (904)269-0363

SCORE Office (Orlando)
80 N. Hughey Ave.
Rm. 445 Federal Bldg.
Orlando, FL 32801
(407)648-6476
Fax: (407)648-6425

SCORE Office (Emerald Coast)
19 W Garden St., No. 325
Pensacola, FL 32501
(904)444-2060
Fax: (904)444-2070

SCORE Office (Charlotte County)
201 W Marion Ave., Ste. 211
Punta Gorda, FL 33950
(941)575-1818
E-mail: score@gls3c.com
Website: http://www.charlotte-
florida.com/business/scorepg01.htm

SCORE Office (Saint Augustine)
1 Riberia St.
Saint Augustine, FL 32084
(904)829-5681
Fax: (904)829-6477

SCORE Office (Bradenton)
2801 Fruitville, Ste. 280
Sarasota, FL 34237
(813)955-1029

SCORE Office (Manasota)
2801 Fruitville Rd., Ste. 280
Sarasota, FL 34237
(941)955-1029
Fax: (941)955-5581
E-mail: score116@gte.net
Website: http://www.score-suncoast.org

SCORE Office (Tallahassee)
200 W Park Ave.
Tallahassee, FL 32302
(850)487-2665

SCORE Office (Hillsborough)
4732 Dale Mabry Hwy. N, Ste. 400
Tampa, FL 33614-6509
(813)870-0125

SCORE Office (Lake Sumter)
122 E Main St.
Tavares, FL 32778-3810
(352)365-3556

SCORE Office (Titusville)
2000 S Washington Ave.
Titusville, FL 32780
(407)267-3036
Fax: (407)264-0127

SCORE Office (Venice)
257 N. Tamiami Trl.
Venice, FL 34285
(941)488-2236
Fax: (941)484-5903

SCORE Office (Palm Beach)
500 Australian Ave. S, Ste. 100
West Palm Beach, FL 33401
(561)833-1672
Fax: (561)833-1712

SCORE Office (Wildwood)
103 N. Webster St.
Wildwood, FL 34785

Georgia

SCORE Office (Atlanta)
Harris Tower, Suite 1900
233 Peachtree Rd., NE
Atlanta, GA 30309
(404)347-2442
Fax: (404)347-1227

SCORE Office (Augusta)
3126 Oxford Rd.
Augusta, GA 30909
(706)869-9100

SCORE Office (Columbus)
School Bldg.
PO Box 40
Columbus, GA 31901
(706)327-3654

SCORE Office (Dalton-Whitfield)
305 S Thorton Ave.
Dalton, GA 30720
(706)279-3383

SCORE Office (Gainesville)
PO Box 374
Gainesville, GA 30503
(770)532-6206
Fax: (770)535-8419

SCORE Office (Macon)
711 Grand Bldg.
Macon, GA 31201
(912)751-6160

SCORE Office (Brunswick)
4 Glen Ave.
Saint Simons Island, GA 31520
(912)265-0620
Fax: (912)265-0629

SCORE Office (Savannah)
111 E Liberty St., Ste. 103
Savannah, GA 31401
(912)652-4335
Fax: (912)652-4184
E-mail: info@scoresav.org
Website: http://www.coastalempire.com/
score/index.htm

Guam

SCORE Office (Guam)
Pacific News Bldg., Rm. 103
238 Archbishop Flores St.
Agana, GU 96910-5100
(671)472-7308

Hawaii

SCORE Office (Hawaii, Inc.)
1111 Bishop St., Ste. 204
PO Box 50207
Honolulu, HI 96813
(808)522-8132
Fax: (808)522-8135
E-mail: hnlscore@juno.com

SCORE Office (Kahului)
250 Alamaha, Unit N16A
Kahului, HI 96732
(808)871-7711

SCORE Office (Maui, Inc.)
590 E Lipoa Pkwy., Ste. 227
Kihei, HI 96753
(808)875-2380

Idaho

SCORE Office (Treasure Valley)
1020 Main St., No. 290
Boise, ID 83702

(208)334-1696
Fax: (208)334-9353

SCORE Office (Eastern Idaho)
2300 N. Yellowstone, Ste. 119
Idaho Falls, ID 83401
(208)523-1022
Fax: (208)528-7127

Illinois

SCORE Office (Fox Valley)
40 W Downer Pl.
PO Box 277
Aurora, IL 60506
(630)897-9214
Fax: (630)897-7002

SCORE Office (Greater Belvidere)
419 S State St.
Belvidere, IL 61008
(815)544-4357
Fax: (815)547-7654

SCORE Office (Bensenville)
1050 Busse Hwy. Suite 100
Bensenville, IL 60106
(708)350-2944
Fax: (708)350-2979

SCORE Office (Central Illinois)
402 N. Hershey Rd.
Bloomington, IL 61704
(309)644-0549
Fax: (309)663-8270
E-mail: webmaster@central-illinois-score.org
Website: http://www.central-illinois-score.org

SCORE Office (Southern Illinois)
150 E Pleasant Hill Rd.
Box 1
Carbondale, IL 62901
(618)453-6654
Fax: (618)453-5040

SCORE Chicago
500 W Madison St., Ste. 1150
Chicago, IL 60661
(312)353-7724
Fax: (312)886-4879
E-mail: info@scorechicago.org
Website: http://scorechicago.org

SCORE Office (Danville)
28 W N. Street
Danville, IL 61832
(217)442-7232
Fax: (217)442-6228

SCORE Office (Decatur)
Milliken University
1184 W Main St.

Decatur, IL 62522
(217)424-6297
Fax: (217)424-3993
E-mail: charding@mail.millikin.edu
Website: http://www.millikin.edu/
academics/Tabor/score.html

SCORE Office (Downers Grove)
925 Curtis
Downers Grove, IL 60515
(708)968-4050
Fax: (708)968-8368

SCORE Office (Elgin)
24 E Chicago, 3rd Fl.
PO Box 648
Elgin, IL 60120
(847)741-5660
Fax: (847)741-5677

SCORE Office (Freeport Area)
26 S Galena Ave.
Freeport, IL 61032
(815)233-1350
Fax: (815)235-4038

SCORE Office (Galesburg)
292 E Simmons St.
PO Box 749
Galesburg, IL 61401
(309)343-1194
Fax: (309)343-1195

SCORE Office (Glen Ellyn)
500 Pennsylvania
Glen Ellyn, IL 60137
(708)469-0907
Fax: (708)469-0426

SCORE Office (Greater Alton)
Alden Hall
5800 Godfrey Rd.
Godfrey, IL 62035-2466
(618)467-2280
Fax: (618)466-8289
Website: http://www.altonweb.com/score

SCORE Office (Grayslake)
19351 W Washington St.
Grayslake, IL 60030
(708)223-3633
Fax: (708)223-9371

SCORE Office (Harrisburg)
303 S Commercial
Harrisburg, IL 62946-1528
(618)252-8528
Fax: (618)252-0210

SCORE Office (Joliet)
100 N. Chicago
Joliet, IL 60432
(815)727-5371
Fax: (815)727-5374

SCORE Office (Kankakee)
101 S Schuyler Ave.
Kankakee, IL 60901
(815)933-0376
Fax: (815)933-0380

SCORE Office (Macomb)
216 Seal Hall, Rm. 214
Macomb, IL 61455
(309)298-1128
Fax: (309)298-2520

SCORE Office (Matteson)
210 Lincoln Mall
Matteson, IL 60443
(708)709-3750
Fax: (708)503-9322

SCORE Office (Mattoon)
1701 Wabash Ave.
Mattoon, IL 61938
(217)235-5661
Fax: (217)234-6544

SCORE Office (Quad Cities)
622 19th St.
Moline, IL 61265
(309)797-0082
Fax: (309)757-5435
E-mail: score@qconline.com
Website: http://www.qconline.com/
business/score

SCORE Office (Naperville)
131 W Jefferson Ave.
Naperville, IL 60540
(708)355-4141
Fax: (708)355-8355

SCORE Office (Northbrook)
2002 Walters Ave.
Northbrook, IL 60062
(847)498-5555
Fax: (847)498-5510

SCORE Office (Palos Hills)
10900 S 88th Ave.
Palos Hills, IL 60465
(847)974-5468
Fax: (847)974-0078

SCORE Office (Peoria)
124 SW Adams, Ste. 300
Peoria, IL 61602
(309)676-0755
Fax: (309)676-7534

SCORE Office (Prospect Heights)
1375 Wolf Rd.
Prospect Heights, IL 60070
(847)537-8660
Fax: (847)537-7138

SCORE Office (Quincy Tri-State)
300 Civic Center Plz., Ste. 245
Quincy, IL 62301
(217)222-8093
Fax: (217)222-3033

SCORE Office (River Grove)
2000 5th Ave.
River Grove, IL 60171
(708)456-0300
Fax: (708)583-3121

SCORE Office (Northern Illinois)
515 N. Court St.
Rockford, IL 61103
(815)962-0122
Fax: (815)962-0122

SCORE Office (Saint Charles)
103 N. 1st Ave.
Saint Charles, IL 60174-1982
(847)584-8384
Fax: (847)584-6065

SCORE Office (Springfield)
511 W Capitol Ave., Ste. 302
Springfield, IL 62704
(217)492-4416
Fax: (217)492-4867

SCORE Office (Sycamore)
112 Somunak St.
Sycamore, IL 60178
(815)895-3456
Fax: (815)895-0125

SCORE Office (University)
Hwy. 50 & Stuenkel Rd. Ste. C3305
University Park, IL 60466
(708)534-5000
Fax: (708)534-8457

Indiana

SCORE Office (Anderson)
205 W 11th St.
Anderson, IN 46015
(317)642-0264

SCORE Office (Bloomington)
Star Center
216 W Allen
Bloomington, IN 47403
(812)335-7334
E-mail: wtfische@indiana.edu
Website: http://www.brainfreezemedia
.com/score527

SCORE Office (South East Indiana)
500 Franklin St.
Box 29
Columbus, IN 47201
(812)379-4457

SCORE Office (Corydon)
310 N. Elm St.
Corydon, IN 47112
(812)738-2137
Fax: (812)738-6438

SCORE Office (Crown Point)
Old Courthouse Sq. Ste. 206
PO Box 43
Crown Point, IN 46307
(219)663-1800

SCORE Office (Elkhart)
418 S Main St.
Elkhart, IN 46515
(219)293-1531
Fax: (219)294-1859

SCORE Office (Evansville)
1100 W Lloyd Expy., Ste. 105
Evansville, IN 47708
(812)426-6144

SCORE Office (Fort Wayne)
1300 S Harrison St.
Fort Wayne, IN 46802
(219)422-2601
Fax: (219)422-2601

SCORE Office (Gary)
973 W 6th Ave., Rm. 326
Gary, IN 46402
(219)882-3918

SCORE Office (Hammond)
7034 Indianapolis Blvd.
Hammond, IN 46324
(219)931-1000
Fax: (219)845-9548

SCORE Office (Indianapolis)
429 N. Pennsylvania St., Ste. 100
Indianapolis, IN 46204-1873
(317)226-7264
Fax: (317)226-7259
E-mail: inscore@indy.net
Website: http://www.score-indiana
polis.org

SCORE Office (Jasper)
PO Box 307
Jasper, IN 47547-0307
(812)482-6866

SCORE Office (Kokomo/Howard Counties)
106 N. Washington St.
Kokomo, IN 46901
(765)457-5301
Fax: (765)452-4564

SCORE Office (Logansport)
300 E Broadway, Ste. 103

Logansport, IN 46947
(219)753-6388

SCORE Office (Madison)
301 E Main St.
Madison, IN 47250
(812)265-3135
Fax: (812)265-2923

SCORE Office (Marengo)
Rt. 1 Box 224D
Marengo, IN 47140
Fax: (812)365-2793

SCORE Office (Marion/Grant Counties)
215 S Adams
Marion, IN 46952
(765)664-5107

SCORE Office (Merrillville)
255 W 80th Pl.
Merrillville, IN 46410
(219)769-8180
Fax: (219)736-6223

SCORE Office (Michigan City)
200 E Michigan Blvd.
Michigan City, IN 46360
(219)874-6221
Fax: (219)873-1204

SCORE Office (South Central Indiana)
4100 Charleston Rd.
New Albany, IN 47150-9538
(812)945-0066

SCORE Office (Rensselaer)
104 W Washington
Rensselaer, IN 47978

SCORE Office (Salem)
210 N. Main St.
Salem, IN 47167
(812)883-4303
Fax: (812)883-1467

SCORE Office (South Bend)
300 N. Michigan St.
South Bend, IN 46601
(219)282-4350
E-mail: chair@southbend-score.org
Website: http://www.southbend-score.org

SCORE Office (Valparaiso)
150 Lincolnway
Valparaiso, IN 46383
(219)462-1105
Fax: (219)469-5710

SCORE Office (Vincennes)
27 N. 3rd
PO Box 553
Vincennes, IN 47591

(812)882-6440
Fax: (812)882-6441

SCORE Office (Wabash)
PO Box 371
Wabash, IN 46992
(219)563-1168
Fax: (219)563-6920

Iowa

SCORE Office (Burlington)
Federal Bldg.
300 N. Main St.
Burlington, IA 52601
(319)752-2967

SCORE Office (Cedar Rapids)
2750 1st Ave. NE, Ste 350
Cedar Rapids, IA 52401-1806
(319)362-6405
Fax: (319)362-7861
E:mail: score@scorecr.org
Website: http://www.scorecr.org

SCORE Office (Illowa)
333 4th Ave. S
Clinton, IA 52732
(319)242-5702

SCORE Office (Council Bluffs)
7 N. 6th St.
Council Bluffs, IA 51502
(712)325-1000

SCORE Office (Northeast Iowa)
3404 285th St.
Cresco, IA 52136
(319)547-3377

SCORE Office (Des Moines)
Federal Bldg., Rm. 749
210 Walnut St.
Des Moines, IA 50309-2186
(515)284-4760

SCORE Office (Fort Dodge)
Federal Bldg., Rm. 436
205 S 8th St.
Fort Dodge, IA 50501
(515)955-2622

SCORE Office (Independence)
110 1st. St. E
Independence, IA 50644
(319)334-7178
Fax: (319)334-7179

SCORE Office (Iowa City)
210 Federal Bldg.
PO Box 1853
Iowa City, IA 52240-1853
(319)338-1662

SCORE Office (Keokuk)
401 Main St.
Pierce Bldg., No. 1
Keokuk, IA 52632
(319)524-5055

SCORE Office (Central Iowa)
Fisher Community College
709 S Center
Marshalltown, IA 50158
(515)753-6645

SCORE Office (River City)
15 West State St.
Mason City, IA 50401
(515)423-5724

SCORE Office (South Central)
SBDC, Indian Hills Community College
525 Grandview Ave.
Ottumwa, IA 52501
(515)683-5127
Fax: (515)683-5263

SCORE Office (Dubuque)
10250 Sundown Rd.
Peosta, IA 52068
(319)556-5110

SCORE Office (Southwest Iowa)
614 W Sheridan
Shenandoah, IA 51601
(712)246-3260

SCORE Office (Sioux City)
Federal Bldg.
320 6th St.
Sioux City, IA 51101
(712)277-2324
Fax: (712)277-2325

SCORE Office (Iowa Lakes)
122 W 5th St.
Spencer, IA 51301
(712)262-3059

SCORE Office (Vista)
119 W 6th St.
Storm Lake, IA 50588
(712)732-3780

SCORE Office (Waterloo)
215 E 4th
Waterloo, IA 50703
(319)233-8431

Kansas

SCORE Office (Southwest Kansas)
501 W Spruce
Dodge City, KS 67801
(316)227-3119

SCORE Office (Emporia)
811 Homewood
Emporia, KS 66801
(316)342-1600

SCORE Office (Golden Belt)
1307 Williams
Great Bend, KS 67530
(316)792-2401

SCORE Office (Hays)
PO Box 400
Hays, KS 67601
(913)625-6595

SCORE Office (Hutchinson)
1 E 9th St.
Hutchinson, KS 67501
(316)665-8468
Fax: (316)665-7619

SCORE Office (Southeast Kansas)
404 Westminster Pl.
PO Box 886
Independence, KS 67301
(316)331-4741

SCORE Office (McPherson)
306 N. Main
PO Box 616
McPherson, KS 67460
(316)241-3303

SCORE Office (Salina)
120 Ash St.
Salina, KS 67401
(785)243-4290
Fax: (785)243-1833

SCORE Office (Topeka)
1700 College
Topeka, KS 66621
(785)231-1010

SCORE Office (Wichita)
100 E English, Ste. 510
Wichita, KS 67202
(316)269-6273
Fax: (316)269-6499

SCORE Office (Ark Valley)
205 E 9th St.
Winfield, KS 67156
(316)221-1617

Kentucky

SCORE Office (Ashland)
PO Box 830
Ashland, KY 41105
(606)329-8011
Fax: (606)325-4607

SCORE Office (Bowling Green)
812 State St.
PO Box 51
Bowling Green, KY 42101
(502)781-3200
Fax: (502)843-0458

SCORE Office (Tri-Lakes)
508 Barbee Way
Danville, KY 40422-1548
(606)231-9902

SCORE Office (Glasgow)
301 W Main St.
Glasgow, KY 42141
(502)651-3161
Fax: (502)651-3122

SCORE Office (Hazard)
B & I Technical Center
100 Airport Gardens Rd.
Hazard, KY 41701
(606)439-5856
Fax: (606)439-1808

SCORE Office (Lexington)
410 W Vine St., Ste. 290, Civic C
Lexington, KY 40507
(606)231-9902
Fax: (606)253-3190
E-mail: scorelex@uky.campus.mci.net

SCORE Office (Louisville)
188 Federal Office Bldg.
600 Dr. Martin L. King Jr. Pl.
Louisville, KY 40202
(502)582-5976

SCORE Office (Madisonville)
257 N. Main
Madisonville, KY 42431
(502)825-1399
Fax: (502)825-1396

SCORE Office (Paducah)
Federal Office Bldg.
501 Broadway, Rm. B-36
Paducah, KY 42001
(502)442-5685

Louisiana

SCORE Office (Central Louisiana)
802 3rd St.
Alexandria, LA 71309
(318)442-6671

SCORE Office (Baton Rouge)
564 Laurel St.
PO Box 3217
Baton Rouge, LA 70801
(504)381-7130
Fax: (504)336-4306

SCORE Office (North Shore)
2 W Thomas
Hammond, LA 70401
(504)345-4457
Fax: (504)345-4749

SCORE Office (Lafayette)
804 St. Mary Blvd.
Lafayette, LA 70505-1307
(318)233-2705
Fax: (318)234-8671
E-mail: score302@aol.com

SCORE Office (Lake Charles)
120 W Pujo St.
Lake Charles, LA 70601
(318)433-3632

SCORE Office (New Orleans)
365 Canal St., Ste. 3100
New Orleans, LA 70130
(504)589-2356
Fax: (504)589-2339

SCORE Office (Shreveport)
400 Edwards St.
Shreveport, LA 71101
(318)677-2536
Fax: (318)677-2541

Maine

SCORE Office (Augusta)
40 Western Ave.
Augusta, ME 04330
(207)622-8509

SCORE Office (Bangor)
Peabody Hall, Rm. 229
One College Cir.
Bangor, ME 04401
(207)941-9707

SCORE Office (Central & Northern Arroostock)
111 High St.
Caribou, ME 04736
(207)492-8010
Fax: (207)492-8010

SCORE Office (Penquis)
South St.
Dover Foxcroft, ME 04426
(207)564-7021

SCORE Office (Maine Coastal)
Mill Mall
Box 1105
Ellsworth, ME 04605-1105
(207)667-5800
E-mail: score@arcadia.net

SCORE Office (Lewiston-Auburn)
BIC of Maine-Bates Mill Complex
35 Canal St.
Lewiston, ME 04240-7764
(207)782-3708
Fax: (207)783-7745

SCORE Office (Portland)
66 Pearl St., Rm. 210
Portland, ME 04101
(207)772-1147
Fax: (207)772-5581
E-mail: Score53@score.maine.org
Website: http://www.score.maine.org/
chapter53

SCORE Office (Western Mountains)
255 River St.
PO Box 252
Rumford, ME 04257-0252
(207)369-9976

SCORE Office (Oxford Hills)
166 Main St.
South Paris, ME 04281
(207)743-0499

Maryland

SCORE Office (Southern Maryland)
2525 Riva Rd., Ste. 110
Annapolis, MD 21401
(410)266-9553
Fax: (410)573-0981
E-mail: score390@aol.com
Website: http://members.aol.com/
score390/index.htm

SCORE Office (Baltimore)
The City Crescent Bldg., 6th Fl.
10 S Howard St.
Baltimore, MD 21201
(410)962-2233
Fax: (410)962-1805

SCORE Office (Bel Air)
108 S Bond St.
Bel Air, MD 21014
(410)838-2020
Fax: (410)893-4715

SCORE Office (Bethesda)
7910 Woodmont Ave., Ste. 1204
Bethesda, MD 20814
(301)652-4900
Fax: (301)657-1973

SCORE Office (Bowie)
6670 Race Track Rd.
Bowie, MD 20715
(301)262-0920
Fax: (301)262-0921

SCORE Office (Dorchester County)
203 Sunburst Hwy.
Cambridge, MD 21613
(410)228-3575

SCORE Office (Upper Shore)
210 Marlboro Ave.
Easton, MD 21601
(410)822-4606
Fax: (410)822-7922

SCORE Office (Frederick County)
43A S Market St.
Frederick, MD 21701
(301)662-8723
Fax: (301)846-4427

SCORE Office (Gaithersburg)
9 Park Ave.
Gaithersburg, MD 20877
(301)840-1400
Fax: (301)963-3918

SCORE Office (Glen Burnie)
103 Crain Hwy. SE
Glen Burnie, MD 21061
(410)766-8282
Fax: (410)766-9722

SCORE Office (Hagerstown)
111 W Washington St.
Hagerstown, MD 21740
(301)739-2015
Fax: (301)739-1278

SCORE Office (Laurel)
7901 Sandy Spring Rd. Ste. 501
Laurel, MD 20707
(301)725-4000
Fax: (301)725-0776

SCORE Office (Salisbury)
300 E Main St.
Salisbury, MD 21801
(410)749-0185
Fax: (410)860-9925

Massachusetts

SCORE Office (NE Massachusetts)
100 Cummings Ctr., Ste. 101 K
Beverly, MA 01923
(978)922-9441
Website: http://www1.shore.net/~score

SCORE Office (Boston)
10 Causeway St., Rm. 265
Boston, MA 02222-1093
(617)565-5591
Fax: (617)565-5598
E-mail: boston-score-
20@worldnet.att.net
Website: http://www.scoreboston.org

SCORE office (Bristol/Plymouth County)
53 N. 6th St., Federal Bldg.
Bristol, MA 02740
(508)994-5093

SCORE Office (SE Massachusetts)
60 School St.
Brockton, MA 02401
(508)587-2673
Fax: (508)587-1340
Website: http://
www.metrosouthchamber.com/
score.html

SCORE Office (North Adams)
820 N. State Rd.
Cheshire, MA 01225
(413)743-5100

SCORE Office (Clinton Satellite)
1 Green St.
Clinton, MA 01510
Fax: (508)368-7689

SCORE Office (Greenfield)
PO Box 898
Greenfield, MA 01302
(413)773-5463
Fax: (413)773-7008

SCORE Office (Haverhill)
87 Winter St.
Haverhill, MA 01830
(508)373-5663
Fax: (508)373-8060

SCORE Office (Hudson Satellite)
PO Box 578
Hudson, MA 01749
(508)568-0360
Fax: (508)568-0360

SCORE Office (Cape Cod)
Independence Pk., Ste. 5B
270 Communications Way
Hyannis, MA 02601
(508)775-4884
Fax: (508)790-2540

SCORE Office (Lawrence)
264 Essex St.
Lawrence, MA 01840
(508)686-0900
Fax: (508)794-9953

SCORE Office (Leominster Satellite)
110 Erdman Way
Leominster, MA 01453
(508)840-4300
Fax: (508)840-4896

SCORE Office (Bristol/Plymouth Counties)
53 N. 6th St., Federal Bldg.
New Bedford, MA 02740
(508)994-5093

SCORE Office (Newburyport)
29 State St.
Newburyport, MA 01950
(617)462-6680

SCORE Office (Pittsfield)
66 West St.
Pittsfield, MA 01201
(413)499-2485

SCORE Office (Haverhill-Salem)
32 Derby Sq.
Salem, MA 01970
(508)745-0330
Fax: (508)745-3855

SCORE Office (Springfield)
1350 Main St.
Federal Bldg.
Springfield, MA 01103
(413)785-0314

SCORE Office (Carver)
12 Taunton Green, Ste. 201
Taunton, MA 02780
(508)824-4068
Fax: (508)824-4069

SCORE Office (Worcester)
33 Waldo St.
Worcester, MA 01608
(508)753-2929
Fax: (508)754-8560

Michigan

SCORE Office (Allegan)
PO Box 338
Allegan, MI 49010
(616)673-2479

SCORE Office (Ann Arbor)
425 S Main St., Ste. 103
Ann Arbor, MI 48104
(313)665-4433

SCORE Office (Battle Creek)
34 W Jackson Ste. 4A
Battle Creek, MI 49017-3505
(616)962-4076
Fax: (616)962-6309

SCORE Office (Cadillac)
222 Lake St.
Cadillac, MI 49601
(616)775-9776
Fax: (616)768-4255

SCORE Office (Detroit)
477 Michigan Ave., Rm. 515
Detroit, MI 48226
(313)226-7947
Fax: (313)226-3448

SCORE Office (Flint)
708 Root Rd., Rm. 308
Flint, MI 48503
(810)233-6846

SCORE Office (Grand Rapids)
111 Pearl St. NW
Grand Rapids, MI 49503-2831
(616)771-0305
Fax: (616)771-0328
E-mail: scoreone@iserv.net
Website: http://www.iserv.net/~scoreone

SCORE Office (Holland)
480 State St.
Holland, MI 49423
(616)396-9472

SCORE Office (Jackson)
209 East Washington
PO Box 80
Jackson, MI 49204
(517)782-8221
Fax: (517)782-0061

SCORE Office (Kalamazoo)
345 W Michigan Ave.
Kalamazoo, MI 49007
(616)381-5382
Fax: (616)384-0096
E-mail: score@nucleus.net

SCORE Office (Lansing)
117 E Allegan
PO Box 14030
Lansing, MI 48901
(517)487-6340
Fax: (517)484-6910

SCORE Office (Livonia)
15401 Farmington Rd.
Livonia, MI 48154
(313)427-2122
Fax: (313)427-6055

SCORE Office (Madison Heights)
26345 John R
Madison Heights, MI 48071
(810)542-5010
Fax: (810)542-6821

SCORE Office (Monroe)
111 E 1st
Monroe, MI 48161
(313)242-3366
Fax: (313)242-7253

SCORE Office (Mount Clemens)
58 S/B Gratiot
Mount Clemens, MI 48043
(810)463-1528
Fax: (810)463-6541

SCORE Office (Muskegon)
PO Box 1087
230 Terrace Plz.
Muskegon, MI 49443
(616)722-3751
Fax: (616)728-7251

SCORE Office (Petoskey)
401 E Mitchell St.
Petoskey, MI 49770
(616)347-4150

SCORE Office (Pontiac)
Executive Office Bldg.
1200 N. Telegraph Rd.
Pontiac, MI 48341
(810)975-9555

SCORE Office (Pontiac)
PO Box 430025
Pontiac, MI 48343
(810)335-9600

SCORE Office (Port Huron)
920 Pinegrove Ave.
Port Huron, MI 48060
(810)985-7101

SCORE Office (Rochester)
71 Walnut Ste. 110
Rochester, MI 48307
(810)651-6700
Fax: (810)651-5270

SCORE Office (Saginaw)
901 S Washington Ave.
Saginaw, MI 48601
(517)752-7161
Fax: (517)752-9055

SCORE Office (Upper Peninsula)
2581 I-75 Business Spur
Sault Ste. Marie, MI 49783
(906)632-3301

SCORE Office (Southfield)
21000 W 10 Mile Rd.
Southfield, MI 48075
(810)204-3050
Fax: (810)204-3099

SCORE Office (Traverse City)
202 E Grandview Pkwy.
PO Box 387
Traverse City, MI 49685
(616)947-5075
Fax: (616)946-2565

SCORE Office (Warren)
30500 Van Dyke, Ste. 118
Warren, MI 48093
(810)751-3939

Minnesota

SCORE Office (Aitkin)
Aitkin, MN 56431
(218)741-3906

SCORE Office (Albert Lea)
202 N. Broadway Ave.
Albert Lea, MN 56007
(507)373-7487

SCORE Office (Austin)
PO Box 864
Austin, MN 55912
(507)437-4561
Fax: (507)437-4869

SCORE Office (South Metro)
Ames Business Ctr.
2500 W County Rd., No. 42
Burnsville, MN 55337
(612)898-5645
Fax: (612)435-6972
E-mail: southmetro@scoreminn.org
Website: http://www.scoreminn.org/
southmetro

SCORE Office (Duluth)
1717 Minnesota Ave.
Duluth, MN 55802
(218)727-8286
Fax: (218)727-3113
E-mail: duluth@scoreminn.org
Website: http://www.scoreminn.org

SCORE Office (Fairmont)
PO Box 826
Fairmont, MN 56031
(507)235-5547
Fax: (507)235-8411

SCORE Office (Southwest Minnesota)
112 Riverfront St.
Box 999
Mankato, MN 56001
(507)345-4519
Fax: (507)345-4451
Website: http://www.scoreminn.org

SCORE Office (Minneapolis)
North Plaza Bldg., Ste. 51
5217 Wayzata Blvd.
Minneapolis, MN 55416
(612)591-0539
Fax: (612)544-0436
Website: http://www.scoreminn.org

SCORE Office (Owatonna)
PO Box 331
Owatonna, MN 55060
(507)451-7970
Fax: (507)451-7972

SCORE Office (Red Wing)
2000 W Main St., Ste. 324
Red Wing, MN 55066
(612)388-4079

SCORE Office (Southeastern Minnesota)
220 S Broadway, Ste. 100
Rochester, MN 55901
(507)288-1122
Fax: (507)282-8960
Website: http://www.scoreminn.org

SCORE Office (Brainerd)
Saint Cloud, MN 56301

SCORE Office (Central Area)
1527 Northway Dr.
Saint Cloud, MN 56301
(320)240-1332
Fax: (320)255-9050
Website: http://www.scoreminn.org

SCORE Office (Saint Paul)
350 St. Peter St., No. 295
Lowry Professional Bldg.
Saint Paul, MN 55102
(651)223-5010
Fax: (651)223-5048
Website: http://www.scoreminn.org

SCORE Office (Winona)
Box 870
Winona, MN 55987
(507)452-2272
Fax: (507)454-8814

SCORE Office (Worthington)
1121 3rd Ave.
Worthington, MN 56187
(507)372-2919
Fax: (507)372-2827

Mississippi

SCORE Office (Delta)
915 Washington Ave.
PO Box 933
Greenville, MS 38701
(601)378-3141

SCORE Office (Gulfcoast)
1 Government Plaza
2909 13th St., Ste. 203
Gulfport, MS 39501
(228)863-0054

SCORE Office (Jackson)
1st Jackson Center, Ste. 400
101 W Capitol St.
Jackson, MS 39201
(601)965-5533

SCORE Office (Meridian)
5220 16th Ave.
Meridian, MS 39305
(601)482-4412

Missouri

SCORE Office (Lake of the Ozark)
University Extension
113 Kansas St.
PO Box 1405
Camdenton, MO 65020
(573)346-2644
Fax: (573)346-2694
E-mail: score@cdoc.net
Website: http://sites.cdoc.net/score

Chamber of Commerce (Cape Girardeau)
PO Box 98
Cape Girardeau, MO 63702-0098
(314)335-3312

SCORE Office (Mid-Missouri)
1705 Halstead Ct.
Columbia, MO 65203
(573)874-1132

SCORE Office (Ozark-Gateway)
1486 Glassy Rd.
Cuba, MO 65453-1640
(573)885-4954

SCORE Office (Kansas City)
323 W 8th St., Ste. 104
Kansas City, MO 64105
(816)374-6675
Fax: (816)374-6692
E-mail: SCOREBIC@AOL.COM
Website: http://www.crn.org/score

SCORE Office (Sedalia)
Lucas Place
323 W 8th St., Ste.104
Kansas City, MO 64105
(816)374-6675

SCORE office (Tri-Lakes)
PO Box 1148
Kimberling, MO 65686
(417)739-3041

SCORE Office (Tri-Lakes)
HCR1 Box 85
Lampe, MO 65681
(417)858-6798

SCORE Office (Mexico)
111 N. Washington St.
Mexico, MO 65265
(314)581-2765

SCORE Office (Southeast Missouri)
Rte. 1, Box 280
Neelyville, MO 63954
(573)989-3577

SCORE office (Poplar Bluff Area)
806 Emma St.
Poplar Bluff, MO 63901
(573)686-8892

SCORE Office (Saint Joseph)
3003 Frederick Ave.
Saint Joseph, MO 64506
(816)232-4461

SCORE Office (Saint Louis)
815 Olive St., Rm. 242
Saint Louis, MO 63101-1569
(314)539-6970
Fax: (314)539-3785
E-mail: info@stlscore.org
Website: http://www.stlscore.org

SCORE Office (Lewis & Clark)
425 Spencer Rd.
Saint Peters, MO 63376
(314)928-2900
Fax: (314)928-2900
E-mail: score01@mail.win.org

SCORE Office (Springfield)
620 S Glenstone, Ste. 110
Springfield, MO 65802-3200
(417)864-7670
Fax: (417)864-4108

SCORE office (Southeast Kansas)
1206 W First St.
Webb City, MO 64870
(417)673-3984

Montana

SCORE Office (Billings)
815 S 27th St.
Billings, MT 59101
(406)245-4111

SCORE Office (Bozeman)
1205 E Main St.
Bozeman, MT 59715
(406)586-5421

SCORE Office (Butte)
1000 George St.
Butte, MT 59701
(406)723-3177

SCORE Office (Great Falls)
710 First Ave. N
Great Falls, MT 59401
(406)761-4434
E-mail: scoregtf@in.tch.com

SCORE Office (Havre, Montana)
518 First St.
Havre, MT 59501
(406)265-4383

SCORE Office (Helena)
Federal Bldg.
301 S Park
Helena, MT 59626-0054
(406)441-1081

SCORE Office (Kalispell)
2 Main St.
Kalispell, MT 59901
(406)756-5271
Fax: (406)752-6665

SCORE Office (Missoula)
723 Ronan
Missoula, MT 59806
(406)327-8806
E-mail: score@safeshop.com
Website: http://missoula.bigsky.net/score

Nebraska

SCORE Office (Columbus)
Columbus, NE 68601
(402)564-2769

SCORE Office (Fremont)
92 W 5th St.
Fremont, NE 68025
(402)721-2641

SCORE Office (Hastings)
Hastings, NE 68901
(402)463-3447

SCORE Office (Lincoln)
8800 O St.
Lincoln, NE 68520
(402)437-2409

SCORE Office (Panhandle)
150549 CR 30
Minatare, NE 69356
(308)632-2133
Website: http://www.tandt.com/SCORE

SCORE Office (Norfolk)
3209 S 48th Ave.
Norfolk, NE 68106
(402)564-2769

SCORE Office (North Platte)
3301 W 2nd St.
North Platte, NE 69101
(308)532-4466

SCORE Office (Omaha)
11145 Mill Valley Rd.
Omaha, NE 68154
(402)221-3606
Fax: (402)221-3680
E-mail: infoctr@ne.uswest.net
Website: http://www.tandt.com/score

Nevada

SCORE Office (Incline Village)
969 Tahoe Blvd.
Incline Village, NV 89451
(702)831-7327
Fax: (702)832-1605

SCORE Office (Carson City)
301 E Stewart
PO Box 7527
Las Vegas, NV 89125
(702)388-6104

SCORE Office (Las Vegas)
300 Las Vegas Blvd. S, Ste. 1100
Las Vegas, NV 89101
(702)388-6104

SCORE Office (Northern Nevada)
SBDC, College of Business Administration
Univ. of Nevada
Reno, NV 89557-0100
(702)784-4436
Fax: (702)784-4337

New Hampshire

SCORE Office (North Country)
PO Box 34
Berlin, NH 03570
(603)752-1090

SCORE Office (Concord)
143 N. Main St., Rm. 202A
PO Box 1258
Concord, NH 03301
(603)225-1400
Fax: (603)225-1409

SCORE Office (Dover)
299 Central Ave.
Dover, NH 03820
(603)742-2218
Fax: (603)749-6317

SCORE Office (Monadnock)
34 Mechanic St.
Keene, NH 03431-3421
(603)352-0320

SCORE Office (Lakes Region)
67 Water St., Ste. 105
Laconia, NH 03246
(603)524-9168

SCORE Office (Upper Valley)
Citizens Bank Bldg., Rm. 310
20 W Park St.
Lebanon, NH 03766
(603)448-3491
Fax: (603)448-1908
E-mail: billt@valley.net
Website: http://www.valley.net/~score

SCORE Office (Merrimack Valley)
275 Chestnut St., Rm. 618
Manchester, NH 03103
(603)666-7561
Fax: (603)666-7925

SCORE Office (Mount Washington Valley)
PO Box 1066
North Conway, NH 03818
(603)383-0800

SCORE Office (Seacoast)
195 Commerce Way, Unit-A
Portsmouth, NH 03801-3251
(603)433-0575

New Jersey

SCORE Office (Somerset)
Paritan Valley Community College,
Rte. 28
Branchburg, NJ 08807
(908)218-8874
E-mail: nj-score@grizbiz.com.
Website: http://www.nj-score.org

SCORE Office (Chester)
5 Old Mill Rd.
Chester, NJ 07930
(908)879-7080

SCORE Office (Greater Princeton)
4 A George Washington Dr.
Cranbury, NJ 08512
(609)520-1776

SCORE Office (Freehold)
36 W Main St.
Freehold, NJ 07728
(908)462-3030
Fax: (908)462-2123

SCORE Office (North West)
Picantinny Innovation Ctr.
3159 Schrader Rd.
Hamburg, NJ 07419
(973)209-8525
Fax: (973)209-7252

E-mail: nj-score@grizbiz.com
Website: http://www.nj-score.org

SCORE Office (Monmouth)
765 Newman Springs Rd.
Lincroft, NJ 07738
(908)224-2573
E-mail: nj-score@grizbiz.com
Website: http://www.nj-score.org

SCORE Office (Manalapan)
125 Symmes Dr.
Manalapan, NJ 07726
(908)431-7220

SCORE Office (Jersey City)
2 Gateway Ctr., 4th Fl.
Newark, NJ 07102
(973)645-3982
Fax: (973)645-2375

SCORE Office (Newark)
2 Gateway Center, 15th Fl.
Newark, NJ 07102-5553
(973)645-3982
Fax: (973)645-2375
E-mail: nj-score@grizbiz.com
Website: http://www.nj-score.org

SCORE Office (Bergen County)
327 E Ridgewood Ave.
Paramus, NJ 07652
(201)599-6090
E-mail: nj-score@grizbiz.com
Website: http://www.nj-score.org

SCORE Office (Pennsauken)
4900 Rte. 70
Pennsauken, NJ 08109
(609)486-3421

SCORE Office (Southern New Jersey)
4900 Rte. 70
Pennsauken, NJ 08109
(609)486-3421
E-mail: nj-score@grizbiz.com
Website: http://www.nj-score.org

SCORE Office (Greater Princeton)
216 Rockingham Row
Princeton Forrestal Village
Princeton, NJ 08540
(609)520-1776
Fax: (609)520-9107
E-mail: nj-score@grizbiz.com
Website: http://www.nj-score.org

SCORE Office (Shrewsbury)
Hwy. 35
Shrewsbury, NJ 07702
(908)842-5995
Fax: (908)219-6140

SCORE Office (Ocean County)

33 Washington St.
Toms River, NJ 08754
(732)505-6033
E-mail: nj-score@grizbiz.com
Website: http://www.nj-score.org

SCORE Office (Wall)

2700 Allaire Rd.
Wall, NJ 07719
(908)449-8877

SCORE Office (Wayne)

2055 Hamburg Tpke.
Wayne, NJ 07470
(201)831-7788
Fax: (201)831-9112

New Mexico

SCORE Office (Albuquerque)

525 Buena Vista, SE
Albuquerque, NM 87106
(505)272-7999
Fax: (505)272-7963

SCORE Office (Las Cruces)

Loretto Towne Center
505 S Main St., Ste. 125
Las Cruces, NM 88001
(505)523-5627
Fax: (505)524-2101
E-mail: score.397@zianet.com

SCORE Office (Roswell)

Federal Bldg., Rm. 237
Roswell, NM 88201
(505)625-2112
Fax: (505)623-2545

SCORE Office (Santa Fe)

Montoya Federal Bldg.
120 Federal Place, Rm. 307
Santa Fe, NM 87501
(505)988-6302
Fax: (505)988-6300

New York

SCORE Office (Northeast)

1 Computer Dr. S
Albany, NY 12205
(518)446-1118
Fax: (518)446-1228

SCORE Office (Auburn)

30 South St.
PO Box 675
Auburn, NY 13021
(315)252-7291

SCORE Office (South Tier Binghamton)

Metro Center, 2nd Fl.
49 Court St.
PO Box 995
Binghamton, NY 13902
(607)772-8860

SCORE Office (Queens County City)

12055 Queens Blvd., Rm. 333
Borough Hall, NY 11424
(718)263-8961

SCORE Office (Buffalo)

Federal Bldg., Rm. 1311
111 W Huron St.
Buffalo, NY 14202
(716)551-4301
Website: http://www2.pcom.net/score/buf45.html

SCORE Office (Canandaigua)

Chamber of Commerce Bldg.
113 S Main St.
Canandaigua, NY 14424
(716)394-4400
Fax: (716)394-4546

SCORE Office (Chemung)

333 E Water St., 4th Fl.
Elmira, NY 14901
(607)734-3358

SCORE Office (Geneva)

Chamber of Commerce Bldg.
PO Box 587
Geneva, NY 14456
(315)789-1776
Fax: (315)789-3993

SCORE Office (Glens Falls)

84 Broad St.
Glens Falls, NY 12801
(518)798-8463
Fax: (518)745-1433

SCORE Office (Orange County)

40 Matthews St.
Goshen, NY 10924
(914)294-8080
Fax: (914)294-6121

SCORE Office (Huntington Area)

151 W Carver St.
Huntington, NY 11743
(516)423-6100

SCORE Office (Tompkins County)

904 E Shore Dr.
Ithaca, NY 14850
(607)273-7080

SCORE Office (Long Island City)

120-55 Queens Blvd.
Jamaica, NY 11424
(718)263-8961
Fax: (718)263-9032

SCORE Office (Chatauqua)

101 W 5th St.
Jamestown, NY 14701
(716)484-1103

SCORE Office (Westchester)

2 Caradon Ln.
Katonah, NY 10536
(914)948-3907
Fax: (914)948-4645
E-mail: score@w-w-w.com
Website: http://w-w-w.com/score

SCORE Office (Queens County)

Queens Borough Hall
120-55 Queens Blvd. Rm. 333
Kew Gardens, NY 11424
(718)263-8961
Fax: (718)263-9032

SCORE Office (Brookhaven)

3233 Rte. 112
Medford, NY 11763
(516)451-6563
Fax: (516)451-6925

SCORE Office (Melville)

35 Pinelawn Rd., Rm. 207-W
Melville, NY 11747
(516)454-0771

SCORE Office (Nassau County)

400 County Seat Dr., No. 140
Mineola, NY 11501
(516)571-3303
E-mail: Counse1998@aol.com
Website: http://members.aol.com/Counse1998/Default.htm

SCORE Office (Mount Vernon)

4 N. 7th Ave.
Mount Vernon, NY 10550
(914)667-7500

SCORE Office (New York)

26 Federal Plz., Rm. 3100
New York, NY 10278
(212)264-4507
Fax: (212)264-4963
E-mail: score1000@erols.com
Website: http://users.erols.com/score-nyc

SCORE Office (Newburgh)

47 Grand St.
Newburgh, NY 12550
(914)562-5100

SCORE Office (Owego)
188 Front St.
Owego, NY 13827
(607)687-2020

SCORE Office (Peekskill)
1 S Division St.
Peekskill, NY 10566
(914)737-3600
Fax: (914)737-0541

SCORE Office (Penn Yan)
2375 Rte. 14A
Penn Yan, NY 14527
(315)536-3111

SCORE Office (Dutchess)
110 Main St.
Poughkeepsie, NY 12601
(914)454-1700

SCORE Office (Rochester)
601 Keating Federal Bldg., Rm. 410
100 State St.
Rochester, NY 14614
(716)263-6473
Fax: (716)263-3146
Website: http://www.ggw.org/score

SCORE Office (Saranac Lake)
30 Main St.
Saranac Lake, NY 12983
(315)448-0415

SCORE Office (Suffolk)
286 Main St.
Setauket, NY 11733
(516)751-3886

SCORE Office (Staten Island)
130 Bay St.
Staten Island, NY 10301
(718)727-1221

SCORE Office (Ulster)
Clinton Bldg., Rm. 107
Stone Ridge, NY 12484
(914)687-5035
Fax: (914)687-5015
Website: http://www.scoreulster.org

SCORE Office (Syracuse)
401 S Salina, 5th Fl.
Syracuse, NY 13202
(315)471-9393

SCORE Office (Utica)
SUNY Institute of Technology, Route 12
Utica, NY 13504-3050
(315)792-7553

SCORE Office (Watertown)
518 Davidson St.
Watertown, NY 13601

(315)788-1200
Fax: (315)788-8251

North Carolina

SCORE office (Asheboro)
317 E Dixie Dr.
Asheboro, NC 27203
(336)626-2626
Fax: (336)626-7077

SCORE Office (Asheville)
Federal Bldg., Rm. 259
151 Patton
Asheville, NC 28801-5770
(828)271-4786
Fax: (828)271-4009

SCORE Office (Chapel Hill)
104 S Estes Dr.
PO Box 2897
Chapel Hill, NC 27514
(919)967-7075

SCORE Office (Coastal Plains)
PO Box 2897
Chapel Hill, NC 27515
(919)967-7075
Fax: (919)968-6874

SCORE Office (Charlotte)
200 N. College St., Ste. A-2015
Charlotte, NC 28202
(704)344-6576
Fax: (704)344-6769
E-mail: CharlotteSCORE47@AOL.com
Website: http://www.charweb.org/
business/score

SCORE Office (Durham)
411 W Chapel Hill St.
Durham, NC 27707
(919)541-2171

SCORE Office (Gastonia)
PO Box 2168
Gastonia, NC 28053
(704)864-2621
Fax: (704)854-8723

SCORE Office (Greensboro)
400 W Market St., Ste. 103
Greensboro, NC 27401-2241
(910)333-5399

SCORE Office (Henderson)
PO Box 917
Henderson, NC 27536
(919)492-2061
Fax: (919)430-0460

SCORE Office (Hendersonville)
Federal Bldg., Rm. 108
W 4th Ave. & Church St.

Hendersonville, NC 28792
(828)693-8702
E-mail: score@circle.net
Website: http://www.wncguide.com/
score/Welcome.html

SCORE Office (Unifour)
PO Box 1828
Hickory, NC 28603
(704)328-6111

SCORE Office (High Point)
1101 N. Main St.
High Point, NC 27262
(336)882-8625
Fax: (336)889-9499

SCORE Office (Outer Banks)
Collington Rd. and Mustain
Kill Devil Hills, NC 27948
(252)441-8144

SCORE Office (Down East)
312 S Front St., Ste. 6
New Bern, NC 28560
(252)633-6688
Fax: (252)633-9608

SCORE Office (Kinston)
PO Box 95
New Bern, NC 28561
(919)633-6688

SCORE Office (Raleigh)
Century Post Office Bldg., Ste. 306
300 Federal St. Mall
Raleigh, NC 27601
(919)856-4739
E-mail: jendres@ibm.net
Website: http://www.intrex.net/score96/
score96.htm

SCORE Office (Sanford)
1801 Nash St.
Sanford, NC 27330
(919)774-6442
Fax: (919)776-8739

SCORE Office (Sandhills Area)
1480 Hwy. 15-501
PO Box 458
Southern Pines, NC 28387
(910)692-3926

SCORE Office (Wilmington)
Corps of Engineers Bldg.
96 Darlington Ave., Ste. 207
Wilmington, NC 28403
(910)815-4576
Fax: (910)815-4658

North Dakota

SCORE Office (Bismarck-Mandan)
700 E Main Ave., 2nd Fl.
PO Box 5509
Bismarck, ND 58506-5509
(701)250-4303

SCORE Office (Fargo)
657 2nd Ave., Rm. 225
Fargo, ND 58108-3083
(701)239-5677

SCORE Office (Upper Red River)
4275 Technology Dr., Rm. 156
Grand Forks, ND 58202-8372
(701)777-3051

SCORE Office (Minot)
100 1st St. SW
Minot, ND 58701-3846
(701)852-6883
Fax: (701)852-6905

Ohio

SCORE Office (Akron)
1 Cascade Plz., 7th Fl.
Akron, OH 44308
(330)379-3163
Fax: (330)379-3164

SCORE Office (Ashland)
Gill Center
47 W Main St.
Ashland, OH 44805
(419)281-4584

SCORE Office (Canton)
116 Cleveland Ave. NW, Ste. 601
Canton, OH 44702-1720
(330)453-6047

SCORE Office (Chillicothe)
165 S Paint St.
Chillicothe, OH 45601
(614)772-4530

SCORE Office (Cincinnati)
Ameritrust Bldg., Rm. 850
525 Vine St.
Cincinnati, OH 45202
(513)684-2812
Fax: (513)684-3251
Website: http://www.score.chapter34.org

SCORE Office (Cleveland)
Eaton Center, Ste. 620
1100 Superior Ave.
Cleveland, OH 44114-2507
(216)522-4194
Fax: (216)522-4844

SCORE Office (Columbus)
2 Nationwide Plz., Ste. 1400
Columbus, OH 43215-2542
(614)469-2357
Fax: (614)469-2391
E-mail: info@scorecolumbus.org
Website: http://www.scorecolumbus.org

SCORE Office (Dayton)
Dayton Federal Bldg., Rm. 505
200 W Second St.
Dayton, OH 45402-1430
(513)225-2887
Fax: (513)225-7667

SCORE Office (Defiance)
615 W 3rd St.
PO Box 130
Defiance, OH 43512
(419)782-7946

SCORE Office (Findlay)
123 E Main Cross St.
PO Box 923
Findlay, OH 45840
(419)422-3314

SCORE Office (Lima)
147 N. Main St.
Lima, OH 45801
(419)222-6045
Fax: (419)229-0266

SCORE Office (Mansfield)
55 N. Mulberry St.
Mansfield, OH 44902
(419)522-3211

SCORE Office (Marietta)
Thomas Hall
Marietta, OH 45750
(614)373-0268

SCORE Office (Medina)
County Administrative Bldg.
144 N. Broadway
Medina, OH 44256
(216)764-8650

SCORE Office (Licking County)
50 W Locust St.
Newark, OH 43055
(614)345-7458

SCORE Office (Salem)
2491 State Rte. 45 S
Salem, OH 44460
(216)332-0361

SCORE Office (Tiffin)
62 S Washington St.
Tiffin, OH 44883
(419)447-4141
Fax: (419)447-5141

SCORE Office (Toledo)
608 Madison Ave., Ste. 910
Toledo, OH 43624
(419)259-7598
Fax: (419)259-6460

SCORE Office (Heart of Ohio)
377 W Liberty St.
Wooster, OH 44691
(330)262-5735
Fax: (330)262-5745

SCORE Office (Youngstown)
306 Williamson Hall
Youngstown, OH 44555
(330)746-2687

Oklahoma

SCORE Office (Anadarko)
PO Box 366
Anadarko, OK 73005
(405)247-6651

SCORE Office (Ardmore)
410 W Main
Ardmore, OK 73401
(580)226-2620

SCORE Office (Northeast Oklahoma)
210 S Main
Grove, OK 74344
(918)787-2796
Fax: (918)787-2796
E-mail: Score595@greencis.net

SCORE Office (Lawton)
4500 W Lee Blvd., Bldg. 100, Ste. 107
Lawton, OK 73505
(580)353-8727
Fax: (580)250-5677

SCORE Office (Oklahoma City)
210 Park Ave., No. 1300
Oklahoma City, OK 73102
(405)231-5163
Fax: (405)231-4876
E-mail: score212@usa.net

SCORE Office (Stillwater)
439 S Main
Stillwater, OK 74074
(405)372-5573
Fax: (405)372-4316

SCORE Office (Tulsa)
616 S Boston, Ste. 406
Tulsa, OK 74119
(918)581-7462
Fax: (918)581-6908
Website: http://www.ionet.net/~tulscore

Oregon

SCORE Office (Bend)
63085 N. Hwy. 97
Bend, OR 97701
(541)923-2849
Fax: (541)330-6900

SCORE Office (Willamette)
1401 Willamette St.
PO Box 1107
Eugene, OR 97401-4003
(541)465-6600
Fax: (541)484-4942

SCORE Office (Florence)
3149 Oak St.
Florence, OR 97439
(503)997-8444
Fax: (503)997-8448

SCORE Office (Southern Oregon)
33 N. Central Ave., Ste. 216
Medford, OR 97501
(541)776-4220
E-mail: pgr134f@prodigy.com

SCORE Office (Portland)
1515 SW 5th Ave., Ste. 1050
Portland, OR 97201
(503)326-3441
Fax: (503)326-2808
E-mail: gr134@prodigy.com

SCORE Office (Salem)
416 State St. (corner of Liberty)
Salem, OR 97301
(503)370-2896

Pennsylvania

SCORE Office (Altoona-Blair)
1212 12th Ave.
Altoona, PA 16601-3493
(814)943-8151

SCORE Office (Lehigh Valley)
Rauch Bldg. 37
Lehigh University
621 Taylor St.
Bethlehem, PA 18015
(610)758-4496
Fax: (610)758-5205

SCORE Office (Butler County)
100 N. Main St.
PO Box 1082
Butler, PA 16003
(412)283-2222
Fax: (412)283-0224

SCORE Office (Harrisburg)
4211 Trindle Rd.
Camp Hill, PA 17011

(717)761-4304
Fax: (717)761-4315

SCORE Office (Cumberland Valley)
75 S 2nd St.
Chambersburg, PA 17201
(717)264-2935

SCORE Office (Monroe County-Stroudsburg)
556 Main St.
East Stroudsburg, PA 18301
(717)421-4433

SCORE Office (Erie)
120 W 9th St.
Erie, PA 16501
(814)871-5650
Fax: (814)871-7530

SCORE Office (Bucks County)
409 Hood Blvd.
Fairless Hills, PA 19030
(215)943-8850
Fax: (215)943-7404

SCORE Office (Hanover)
146 Broadway
Hanover, PA 17331
(717)637-6130
Fax: (717)637-9127

SCORE Office (Harrisburg)
100 Chestnut, Ste. 309
Harrisburg, PA 17101
(717)782-3874

SCORE Office (East Montgomery County)
Baederwood Shopping Center
1653 The Fairways, Ste. 204
Jenkintown, PA 19046
(215)885-3027

SCORE Office (Kittanning)
2 Butler Rd.
Kittanning, PA 16201
(412)543-1305
Fax: (412)543-6206

SCORE Office (Lancaster)
118 W Chestnut St.
Lancaster, PA 17603
(717)397-3092

SCORE Office (Westmoreland County)
300 Fraser Purchase Rd.
Latrobe, PA 15650-2690
(412)539-7505
Fax: (412)539-1850

SCORE Office (Lebanon)
252 N. 8th St.
PO Box 899

Lebanon, PA 17042-0899
(717)273-3727
Fax: (717)273-7940

SCORE Office (Lewistown)
3 W Monument Sq., Ste. 204
Lewistown, PA 17044
(717)248-6713
Fax: (717)248-6714

SCORE Office (Delaware County)
602 E Baltimore Pike
Media, PA 19063
(610)565-3677
Fax: (610)565-1606

SCORE Office (Milton Area)
112 S Front St.
Milton, PA 17847
(717)742-7341
Fax: (717)792-2008

SCORE Office (Mon-Valley)
435 Donner Ave.
Monessen, PA 15062
(412)684-4277
Fax: (412)684-7688

SCORE Office (Monroeville)
William Penn Plaza
2790 Mosside Blvd., Ste. 295
Monroeville, PA 15146
(412)856-0622
Fax: (412)856-1030

SCORE Office (Airport Area)
986 Brodhead Rd.
Moon Township, PA 15108-2398
(412)264-6270
Fax: (412)264-1575

SCORE Office (Northeast)
8601 E Roosevelt Blvd.
Philadelphia, PA 19152
(215)332-3400
Fax: (215)332-6050

SCORE Office (Philadelphia)
1315 Walnut St., Ste. 500
Philadelphia, PA 19107
(215)790-5050
Fax: (215)790-5057
E-mail: score46@bellatlantic.net
Website: http://www.pgweb.net/score46

SCORE Office (Pittsburgh)
1000 Liberty Ave., Rm. 1122
Pittsburgh, PA 15222
(412)395-6560
Fax: (412)395-6562

SCORE Office (Tri-County)
801 N. Charlotte St.
Pottstown, PA 19464
(610)327-2673

SCORE Office (Reading)
601 Penn St.
Reading, PA 19601
(610)376-3497

SCORE Office (Scranton)
Oppenheim Bldg.
116 N. Washington Ave., Ste. 650
Scranton, PA 18503
(717)347-4611
Fax: (717)347-4611

SCORE Office (Central Pennsylvania)
200 Innovation Blvd., Ste. 242-B
State College, PA 16803
(814)234-9415
Fax: (814)238-9686
Website: http://countrystore.org/
business/score.htm

SCORE Office (Monroe-Stroudsburg)
556 Main St.
Stroudsburg, PA 18360
(717)421-4433

SCORE Office (Uniontown)
Federal Bldg.
Pittsburg St.
PO Box 2065 DTS
Uniontown, PA 15401
(412)437-4222
E-mail: uniontownscore@lcsys.net

SCORE Office (Warren County)
315 2nd Ave.
Warren, PA 16365
(814)723-9017

SCORE Office (Waynesboro)
323 E Main St.
Waynesboro, PA 17268
(717)762-7123
Fax: (717)962-7124

SCORE Office (Chester County)
Government Service Center, Ste. 281
601 Westtown Rd.
West Chester, PA 19382-4538
(610)344-6910
Fax: (610)344-6919
E-mail: score@locke.ccil.org

SCORE Office (Wilkes-Barre)
7 N. Wilkes-Barre Blvd.
Wilkes Barre, PA 18702-5241
(717)826-6502
Fax: (717)826-6287

SCORE Office (North Central Pennsylvania)
240 W 3rd St., Rm. 227
PO Box 725

Williamsport, PA 17703
(717)322-3720
Fax: (717)322-1607
E-mail: score234@mail.csrlink.net
Website: http://www.lycoming.org/score

SCORE Office (York)
Cyber Center
2101 Pennsylvania Ave.
York, PA 17404
(717)845-8830
Fax: (717)854-9333

Puerto Rico

SCORE Office (Puerto Rico & Virgin Islands)
PO Box 12383-96
San Juan, PR 00914-0383
(787)726-8040
Fax: (787)726-8135

Rhode Island

SCORE Office (Barrington)
281 County Rd.
Barrington, RI 02806
(401)247-1920
Fax: (401)247-3763

SCORE Office (Woonsocket)
640 Washington Hwy.
Lincoln, RI 02865
(401)334-1000
Fax: (401)334-1009

SCORE Office (Wickford)
8045 Post Rd.
North Kingstown, RI 02852
(401)295-5566
Fax: (401)295-8987

SCORE Office (J.G.E. Knight)
380 Westminster St.
Providence, RI 02903
(401)528-4571
Fax: (401)528-4539
Website: http://www.riscore.org

SCORE Office (Warwick)
3288 Post Rd.
Warwick, RI 02886
(401)732-1100
Fax: (401)732-1101

SCORE Office (Westerly)
74 Post Rd.
Westerly, RI 02891
(401)596-7761
800-732-7636
Fax: (401)596-2190

South Carolina

SCORE Office (Aiken)
PO Box 892
Aiken, SC 29802
(803)641-1111
800-542-4536
Fax: (803)641-4174

SCORE Office (Anderson)
Anderson Mall
3130 N. Main St.
Anderson, SC 29621
(864)224-0453

SCORE Office (Coastal)
284 King St.
Charleston, SC 29401
(803)727-4778
Fax: (803)853-2529

SCORE Office (Midlands)
Strom Thurmond Bldg., Rm. 358
1835 Assembly St., Rm 358
Columbia, SC 29201
(803)765-5131
Fax: (803)765-5962
Website: http://www.scoremidlands.org

SCORE Office (Piedmont)
Federal Bldg., Rm. B-02
300 E Washington St.
Greenville, SC 29601
(864)271-3638

SCORE Office (Greenwood)
PO Drawer 1467
Greenwood, SC 29648
(864)223-8357

SCORE Office (Hilton Head Island)
52 Savannah Trail
Hilton Head, SC 29926
(803)785-7107
Fax: (803)785-7110

SCORE Office (Grand Strand)
937 Broadway
Myrtle Beach, SC 29577
(803)918-1079
Fax: (803)918-1083
E-mail: score381@aol.com

SCORE Office (Spartanburg)
PO Box 1636
Spartanburg, SC 29304
(864)594-5000
Fax: (864)594-5055

South Dakota

SCORE Office (West River)
Rushmore Plz. Civic Ctr.
444 Mount Rushmore Rd., No. 209

Rapid City, SD 57701
(605)394-5311
E-mail: score@gwtc.net

SCORE Office (Sioux Falls)
First Financial Center
110 S Phillips Ave., Ste. 200
Sioux Falls, SD 57104-6727
(605)330-4231
Fax: (605)330-4231

Tennessee

SCORE Office (Chattanooga)
Federal Bldg., Rm. 26
900 Georgia Ave.
Chattanooga, TN 37402
(423)752-5190
Fax: (423)752-5335

SCORE Office (Cleveland)
PO Box 2275
Cleveland, TN 37320
(423)472-6587
Fax: (423)472-2019

SCORE Office (Upper Cumberland Center)
1225 S Willow Ave.
Cookeville, TN 38501
(615)432-4111
Fax: (615)432-6010

SCORE Office (Unicoi County)
PO Box 713
Erwin, TN 37650
(423)743-3000
Fax: (423)743-0942

SCORE Office (Greeneville)
115 Academy St.
Greeneville, TN 37743
(423)638-4111
Fax: (423)638-5345

SCORE Office (Jackson)
194 Auditorium St.
Jackson, TN 38301
(901)423-2200

SCORE Office (Northeast Tennessee)
1st Tennessee Bank Bldg.
2710 S Roan St., Ste. 584
Johnson City, TN 37601
(423)929-7686
Fax: (423)461-8052

SCORE Office (Kingsport)
151 E Main St.
Kingsport, TN 37662
(423)392-8805

SCORE Office (Greater Knoxville)
Farragot Bldg., Ste. 224
530 S Gay St.
Knoxville, TN 37902
(423)545-4203
E-mail: scoreknox@ntown.com
Website: http://www.scoreknox.org

SCORE Office (Maryville)
201 S Washington St.
Maryville, TN 37804-5728
(423)983-2241
800-525-6834
Fax: (423)984-1386

SCORE Office (Memphis)
Federal Bldg., Ste. 390
167 N. Main St.
Memphis, TN 38103
(901)544-3588

SCORE Office (Nashville)
50 Vantage Way, Ste. 201
Nashville, TN 37228-1500
(615)736-7621

Texas

SCORE Office (Abilene)
2106 Federal Post Office and
Court Bldg.
Abilene, TX 79601
(915)677-1857

SCORE Office (Austin)
2501 S Congress
Austin, TX 78701
(512)442-7235
Fax: (512)442-7528

**SCORE Office
(Golden Triangle)**
450 Boyd St.
Beaumont, TX 77704
(409)838-6581
Fax: (409)833-6718

SCORE Office (Brownsville)
3505 Boca Chica Blvd., Ste. 305
Brownsville, TX 78521
(210)541-4508

SCORE Office (Brazos Valley)
3000 Briarcrest, Ste. 302
Bryan, TX 77802
(409)776-8876
E-mail: 102633.2612@compuserve.com

SCORE Office (Cleburne)
Watergarden Pl., 9th Fl., Ste. 400
Cleburne, TX 76031
(817)871-6002

SCORE Office (Corpus Christi)
651 Upper North Broadway, Ste. 654
Corpus Christi, TX 78477
(512)888-4322
Fax: (512)888-3418

SCORE Office (Dallas)
6260 E Mockingbird
Dallas, TX 75214-2619
(214)828-2471
Fax: (214)821-8033

SCORE Office (El Paso)
10 Civic Center Plaza
El Paso, TX 79901
(915)534-0541
Fax: (915)534-0513

SCORE Office (Bedford)
100 E 15th St., Ste. 400
Fort Worth, TX 76102
(817)871-6002

SCORE Office (Fort Worth)
100 E 15th St., No. 24
Fort Worth, TX 76102
(817)871-6002
Fax: (817)871-6031
E-mail: fwbac@onramp.net

SCORE Office (Garland)
2734 W Kingsley Rd.
Garland, TX 75041
(214)271-9224

SCORE Office (Granbury Chamber of Commerce)
416 S Morgan
Granbury, TX 76048
(817)573-1622
Fax: (817)573-0805

SCORE Office (Lower Rio Grande Valley)
222 E Van Buren, Ste. 500
Harlingen, TX 78550
(956)427-8533
Fax: (956)427-8537

SCORE Office (Houston)
9301 Southwest Fwy., Ste. 550
Houston, TX 77074
(713)773-6565
Fax: (713)773-6550

SCORE Office (Irving)
3333 N. MacArthur Blvd., Ste. 100
Irving, TX 75062
(214)252-8484
Fax: (214)252-6710

SCORE Office (Lubbock)
1205 Texas Ave., Rm. 411D
Lubbock, TX 79401

(806)472-7462
Fax: (806)472-7487

SCORE Office (Midland)
Post Office Annex
200 E Wall St., Rm. P121
Midland, TX 79701
(915)687-2649

SCORE Office (Orange)
1012 Green Ave.
Orange, TX 77630-5620
(409)883-3536
800-528-4906
Fax: (409)886-3247

SCORE Office (Plano)
1200 E 15th St.
PO Drawer 940287
Plano, TX 75094-0287
(214)424-7547
Fax: (214)422-5182

SCORE Office (Port Arthur)
4749 Twin City Hwy., Ste. 300
Port Arthur, TX 77642
(409)963-1107
Fax: (409)963-3322

SCORE Office (Richardson)
411 Belle Grove
Richardson, TX 75080
(214)234-4141
800-777-8001
Fax: (214)680-9103

SCORE Office (San Antonio)
Federal Bldg., Rm. A527
727 E Durango
San Antonio, TX 78206
(210)472-5931
Fax: (210)472-5935

SCORE Office (Texarkana State College)
819 State Line Ave.
Texarkana, TX 75501
(903)792-7191
Fax: (903)793-4304

SCORE Office (East Texas)
RTDC
1530 SSW Loop 323, Ste. 100
Tyler, TX 75701
(903)510-2975
Fax: (903)510-2978

SCORE Office (Waco)
401 Franklin Ave.
Waco, TX 76701
(817)754-8898
Fax: (817)756-0776
Website: http://www.brc-waco.com

SCORE Office (Wichita Falls)
Hamilton Bldg.
900 8th St.
Wichita Falls, TX 76307
(940)723-2741
Fax: (940)723-8773

Utah

SCORE Office (Northern Utah)
160 N. Main
Logan, UT 84321
(435)746-2269

SCORE Office (Ogden)
1701 E Windsor Dr.
Ogden, UT 84604
(801)629-8613
E-mail: score158@netscape.net

SCORE Office (Central Utah)
1071 E Windsor Dr.
Provo, UT 84604
(801)373-8660

SCORE Office (Southern Utah)
225 South 700 East
Saint George, UT 84770
(435)652-7751

SCORE Office (Salt Lake)
310 S Main St.
Salt Lake City, UT 84101
(801)746-2269
Fax: (801)746-2273

Vermont

SCORE Office (Champlain Valley)
Winston Prouty Federal Bldg.
11 Lincoln St., Rm. 106
Essex Junction, VT 05452
(802)951-6762

SCORE Office (Montpelier)
87 State St., Rm. 205
PO Box 605
Montpelier, VT 05601
(802)828-4422
Fax: (802)828-4485

SCORE Office (Marble Valley)
256 N. Main St.
Rutland, VT 05701-2413
(802)773-9147

SCORE Office (Northeast Kingdom)
20 Main St.
PO Box 904
Saint Johnsbury, VT 05819
(802)748-5101

Virgin Islands

SCORE Office (Saint Croix)
United Plaza Shopping Center
PO Box 4010, Christiansted
Saint Croix, VI 00822
(809)778-5380

SCORE Office (Saint Thomas-Saint John)
Federal Bldg., Rm. 21
Veterans Dr.
Saint Thomas, VI 00801
(809)774-8530

Virginia

SCORE Office (Arlington)
2009 N. 14th St., Ste. 111
Arlington, VA 22201
(703)525-2400

SCORE Office (Blacksburg)
141 Jackson St.
Blacksburg, VA 24060
(540)552-4061

SCORE Office (Bristol)
20 Volunteer Pkwy.
Bristol, VA 24203
(540)989-4850

SCORE Office (Central Virginia)
1001 E Market St., Ste. 101
Charlottesville, VA 22902
(804)295-6712
Fax: (804)295-7066

SCORE Office (Alleghany Satellite)
241 W Main St.
Covington, VA 24426
(540)962-2178
Fax: (540)962-2179

SCORE Office (Central Fairfax)
3975 University Dr., Ste. 350
Fairfax, VA 22030
(703)591-2450

SCORE Office (Falls Church)
PO Box 491
Falls Church, VA 22040
(703)532-1050
Fax: (703)237-7904

SCORE Office (Glenns)
Glenns Campus
Box 287
Glenns, VA 23149
(804)693-9650

SCORE Office (Peninsula)
6 Manhattan Sq.
PO Box 7269

Hampton, VA 23666
(757)766-2000
Fax: (757)865-0339
E-mail: score100@seva.net

SCORE Office (Tri-Cities)
108 N. Main St.
Hopewell, VA 23860
(804)458-5536

SCORE Office (Lynchburg)
Federal Bldg.
1100 Main St.
Lynchburg, VA 24504-1714
(804)846-3235

SCORE Office (Greater Prince William)
8963 Center St
Manassas, VA 20110
(703)368-4813
Fax: (703)368-4733

SCORE Office (Martinsville)
115 Broad St.
Martinsville, VA 24112-0709
(540)632-6401
Fax: (540)632-5059

SCORE Office (Hampton Roads)
Federal Bldg., Rm. 737
200 Grandby St.
Norfolk, VA 23510
(757)441-3733
Fax: (757)441-3733
E-mail: scorehr60@juno.com

SCORE Office (Norfolk)
Federal Bldg., Rm. 737
200 Granby St.
Norfolk, VA 23510
(757)441-3733
Fax: (757)441-3733

SCORE Office (Virginia Beach)
Chamber of Commerce
200 Grandby St., Rm 737
Norfolk, VA 23510
(804)441-3733

SCORE Office (Radford)
1126 Norwood St.
Radford, VA 24141
(540)639-2202

SCORE Office (Richmond)
Federal Bldg.
400 N. 8th St., Ste. 1150
PO Box 10126
Richmond, VA 23240-0126
(804)771-2400
Fax: (804)771-8018
E-mail: scorechapter12@yahoo.com
Website: http://www.cvco.org/score

SCORE Office (Roanoke)
Federal Bldg., Rm. 716
250 Franklin Rd.
Roanoke, VA 24011
(540)857-2834
Fax: (540)857-2043
E-mail: scorerva@juno.com
Website: http://hometown.aol.com/
scorerv/Index.html

SCORE Office (Fairfax)
8391 Old Courthouse Rd., Ste. 300
Vienna, VA 22182
(703)749-0400

SCORE Office (Greater Vienna)
513 Maple Ave. West
Vienna, VA 22180
(703)281-1333
Fax: (703)242-1482

SCORE Office (Shenandoah Valley)
301 W Main St.
Waynesboro, VA 22980
(540)949-8203
Fax: (540)949-7740
E-mail: score427@intelos.net

SCORE Office (Williamsburg)
201 Penniman Rd.
Williamsburg, VA 23185
(757)229-6511
E-mail: wacc@williamsburgcc.com

SCORE Office (Northern Virginia)
1360 S Pleasant Valley Rd.
Winchester, VA 22601
(540)662-4118

Washington

SCORE Office (Gray's Harbor)
506 Duffy St.
Aberdeen, WA 98520
(360)532-1924
Fax: (360)533-7945

SCORE Office (Bellingham)
101 E Holly St.
Bellingham, WA 98225
(360)676-3307

SCORE Office (Everett)
2702 Hoyt Ave.
Everett, WA 98201-3556
(206)259-8000

SCORE Office (Gig Harbor)
3125 Judson St.
Gig Harbor, WA 98335
(206)851-6865

SCORE Office (Kennewick)
PO Box 6986
Kennewick, WA 99336
(509)736-0510

SCORE Office (Puyallup)
322 2nd St. SW
PO Box 1298
Puyallup, WA 98371
(206)845-6755
Fax: (206)848-6164

SCORE Office (Seattle)
1200 6th Ave., Ste. 1700
Seattle, WA 98101
(206)553-7320
Fax: (206)553-7044
E-mail: score55@aol.com
Website: http://www.scn.org/civic/score-
online/index55.html

SCORE Office (Spokane)
801 W Riverside Ave., No. 240
Spokane, WA 99201
(509)353-2820
Fax: (509)353-2600
E-mail: score@dmi.net
Website: http://www.dmi.net/score

SCORE Office (Clover Park)
PO Box 1933
Tacoma, WA 98401-1933
(206)627-2175

SCORE Office (Tacoma)
1101 Pacific Ave.
Tacoma, WA 98402
(253)274-1288
Fax: (253)274-1289

SCORE Office (Fort Vancouver)
1701 Broadway, S-1
Vancouver, WA 98663
(360)699-1079

SCORE Office (Walla Walla)
500 Tausick Way
Walla Walla, WA 99362
(509)527-4681

SCORE Office (Mid-Columbia)
1113 S 14th Ave.
Yakima, WA 98907
(509)574-4944
Fax: (509)574-2943
Website: http://www.ellensburg.com/
~score

West Virginia

SCORE Office (Charleston)
1116 Smith St.
Charleston, WV 25301

(304)347-5463
E-mail: score256@juno.com

SCORE Office (Virginia Street)
1116 Smith St., Ste. 302
Charleston, WV 25301
(304)347-5463

SCORE Office (Marion County)
PO Box 208
Fairmont, WV 26555-0208
(304)363-0486

SCORE Office (Upper Monongahela Valley)
1000 Technology Dr., Ste. 1111
Fairmont, WV 26555
(304)363-0486
E-mail: score537@hotmail.com

SCORE Office (Huntington)
1101 6th Ave., Ste. 220
Huntington, WV 25701-2309
(304)523-4092

SCORE Office (Wheeling)
1310 Market St.
Wheeling, WV 26003
(304)233-2575
Fax: (304)233-1320

Wisconsin

SCORE Office (Fox Cities)
227 S Walnut St.
Appleton, WI 54913
(920)734-7101
Fax: (920)734-7161

SCORE Office (Beloit)
136 W Grand Ave., Ste. 100
PO Box 717
Beloit, WI 53511
(608)365-8835
Fax: (608)365-9170

SCORE Office (Eau Claire)
Federal Bldg., Rm. B11
510 S Barstow St.
Eau Claire, WI 54701
(715)834-1573
E-mail: score@ecol.net
Website: http://www.ecol.net/~score

SCORE Office (Fond du Lac)
207 N. Main St.
Fond du Lac, WI 54935
(414)921-9500
Fax: (414)921-9559

SCORE Office (Green Bay)
835 Potts Ave.
Green Bay, WI 54304

(414)496-8930
Fax: (414)496-6009

SCORE Office (Janesville)
20 S Main St., Ste. 11
PO Box 8008
Janesville, WI 53547
(608)757-3160
Fax: (608)757-3170

SCORE Office (La Crosse)
712 Main St.
La Crosse, WI 54602-0219
(608)784-4880

SCORE Office (Madison)
505 S Rosa Rd.
Madison, WI 53719
(608)441-2820

SCORE Office (Manitowoc)
1515 Memorial Dr.
PO Box 903
Manitowoc, WI 54221-0903
(414)684-5575
Fax: (414)684-1915

SCORE Office (Milwaukee)
310 W Wisconsin Ave., Ste. 425
Milwaukee, WI 53203
(414)297-3942
Fax: (414)297-1377

SCORE Office (Central Wisconsin)
1224 Lindbergh Ave.
Stevens Point, WI 54481
(715)344-7729

SCORE Office (Superior)
Superior Business Center Inc.
1423 N. 8th St.
Superior, WI 54880
(715)394-7388
Fax: (715)393-7414

SCORE Office (Waukesha)
223 Wisconsin Ave.
Waukesha, WI 53186-4926
(414)542-4249

SCORE Office (Wausau)
300 3rd St., Ste. 200
Wausau, WI 54402-6190
(715)845-6231

SCORE Office (Wisconsin Rapids)
2240 Kingston Rd.
Wisconsin Rapids, WI 54494
(715)423-1830

Wyoming

SCORE Office (Casper)
Federal Bldg., No. 2215
100 East B St.

Casper, WY 82602
(307)261-6529
Fax: (307)261-6530

Venture capital & financing companies

This section contains a listing of financing and loan companies in the United States and Canada. These listing are arranged alphabetically by country, then by state or province, then by city, then by organization name.

Canada

Alberta

Launchworks Inc.
1902J 11th St., SE
Calgary, AB, Canada T2G 3G2
(403)269-1119
Fax: (403)269-1141
Website: http://www.launchworks.com

Native Venture Capital Company, Inc.
21 Artist View Point, Box 7
Site 25, RR 12
Calgary, AB, Canada T3E 6W3
(903)208-5380

Miralta Capital Inc.
4445 Calgary Trail South
888 Terrace Plaza Alberta
Edmonton, AB, Canada T6H 5R7
(780)438-3535
Fax: (780)438-3129

Vencap Equities Alberta Ltd.
10180-101st St., Ste. 1980
Edmonton, AB, Canada T5J 3S4
(403)420-1171
Fax: (403)429-2541

British Columbia

Discovery Capital
5th Fl., 1199 West Hastings
Vancouver, BC, Canada V6E 3T5
(604)683-3000
Fax: (604)662-3457
E-mail: info@discoverycapital.com
Website: http://www.discoverycapital
.com

Greenstone Venture Partners
1177 West Hastings St.
Ste. 400
Vancouver, BC, Canada V6E 2K3
(604)717-1977
Fax: (604)717-1976
Website: http://www.greenstonevc.com

Growthworks Capital
2600-1055 West Georgia St.
Box 11170 Royal Centre
Vancouver, BC, Canada V6E 3R5
(604)895-7259
Fax: (604)669-7605
Website: http://www.wofund.com

MDS Discovery Venture Management, Inc.
555 W Eighth Ave., Ste. 305
Vancouver, BC, Canada V5Z 1C6
(604)872-8464
Fax: (604)872-2977
E-mail: info@mds-ventures.com

Ventures West Management Inc.
1285 W Pender St., Ste. 280
Vancouver, BC, Canada V6E 4B1
(604)688-9495
Fax: (604)687-2145
Website: http://www.ventureswest.com

Nova Scotia

ACF Equity Atlantic Inc.
Purdy's Wharf Tower II
Ste. 2106
Halifax, NS, Canada B3J 3R7
(902)421-1965
Fax: (902)421-1808

Montgomerie, Huck & Co.
146 Bluenose Dr.
PO Box 538
Lunenburg, NS, Canada B0J 2C0
(902)634-7125
Fax: (902)634-7130

Ontario

IPS Industrial Promotion Services Ltd.
60 Columbia Way, Ste. 720
Markham, ON, Canada L3R 0C9
(905)475-9400
Fax: (905)475-5003

Betwin Investments Inc.
Box 23110
Sault Ste. Marie, ON, Canada P6A 6W6
(705)253-0744
Fax: (705)253-0744

Bailey & Company, Inc.
594 Spadina Ave.
Toronto, ON, Canada M5S 2H4
(416)921-6930
Fax: (416)925-4670

BCE Capital
200 Bay St.
South Tower, Ste. 3120
Toronto, ON, Canada M5J 2J2

(416)815-0078
Fax: (416)941-1073
Website: http://www.bcecapital.com

Castlehill Ventures
55 University Ave., Ste. 500
Toronto, ON, Canada M5J 2H7
(416)862-8574
Fax: (416)862-8875

CCFL Mezzanine Partners of Canada
70 University Ave.
Ste. 1450
Toronto, ON, Canada M5J 2M4
(416)977-1450
Fax: (416)977-6764
E-mail: info@ccfl.com
Website: http://www.ccfl.com

Celtic House International
100 Simcoe St., Ste. 100
Toronto, ON, Canada M5H 3G2
(416)542-2436
Fax: (416)542-2435
Website: http://www.celtic-house.com

Clairvest Group Inc.
22 St. Clair Ave. East
Ste. 1700
Toronto, ON, Canada M4T 2S3
(416)925-9270
Fax: (416)925-5753

Crosbie & Co., Inc.
One First Canadian Place
9th Fl.
PO Box 116
Toronto, ON, Canada M5X 1A4
(416)362-7726
Fax: (416)362-3447
E-mail: info@crosbieco.com
Website: http://www.crosbieco.com

Drug Royalty Corp.
Eight King St. East
Ste. 202
Toronto, ON, Canada M5C 1B5
(416)863-1865
Fax: (416)863-5161

Grieve, Horner, Brown & Asculai
8 King St. E, Ste. 1704
Toronto, ON, Canada M5C 1B5
(416)362-7668
Fax: (416)362-7660

Jefferson Partners
77 King St. West
Ste. 4010
PO Box 136
Toronto, ON, Canada M5K 1H1
(416)367-1533

Fax: (416)367-5827
Website: http://www.jefferson.com

J.L. Albright Venture Partners
Canada Trust Tower, 161 Bay St.
Ste. 4440
PO Box 215
Toronto, ON, Canada M5J 2S1
(416)367-2440
Fax: (416)367-4604
Website: http://www.jlaventures.com

McLean Watson Capital Inc.
One First Canadian Place
Ste. 1410
PO Box 129
Toronto, ON, Canada M5X 1A4
(416)363-2000
Fax: (416)363-2010
Website: http://www.mcleanwatson.com

Middlefield Capital Fund
One First Canadian Place
85th Fl.
PO Box 192
Toronto, ON, Canada M5X 1A6
(416)362-0714
Fax: (416)362-7925
Website: http://www.middlefield.com

Mosaic Venture Partners
24 Duncan St.
Ste. 300
Toronto, ON, Canada M5V 3M6
(416)597-8889
Fax: (416)597-2345

Onex Corp.
161 Bay St.
PO Box 700
Toronto, ON, Canada M5J 2S1
(416)362-7711
Fax: (416)362-5765

Penfund Partners Inc.
145 King St. West
Ste. 1920
Toronto, ON, Canada M5H 1J8
(416)865-0300
Fax: (416)364-6912
Website: http://www.penfund.com

Primaxis Technology Ventures Inc.
1 Richmond St. West, 8th Fl.
Toronto, ON, Canada M5H 3W4
(416)313-5210
Fax: (416)313-5218
Website: http://www.primaxis.com

Priveq Capital Funds
240 Duncan Mill Rd., Ste. 602
Toronto, ON, Canada M3B 3P1

(416)447-3330
Fax: (416)447-3331
E-mail: priveq@sympatico.ca

Roynat Ventures
40 King St. West, 26th Fl.
Toronto, ON, Canada M5H 1H1
(416)933-2667
Fax: (416)933-2783
Website: http://www.roynatcapital.com

Tera Capital Corp.
366 Adelaide St. East, Ste. 337
Toronto, ON, Canada M5A 3X9
(416)368-1024
Fax: (416)368-1427

Working Ventures Canadian Fund Inc.
250 Bloor St. East, Ste. 1600
Toronto, ON, Canada M4W 1E6
(416)934-7718
Fax: (416)929-0901
Website: http://www.workingventures.ca

Quebec

Altamira Capital Corp.
202 University
Niveau de Maisoneuve, Bur. 201
Montreal, QC, Canada H3A 2A5
(514)499-1656
Fax: (514)499-9570

Federal Business Development Bank
Venture Capital Division
Five Place Ville Marie, Ste. 600
Montreal, QC, Canada H3B 5E7
(514)283-1896
Fax: (514)283-5455

Hydro-Quebec Capitech Inc.
75 Boul, Rene Levesque Quest
Montreal, QC, Canada H2Z 1A4
(514)289-4783
Fax: (514)289-5420
Website: http://www.hqcapitech.com

Investissement Desjardins
2 complexe Desjardins
C.P. 760
Montreal, QC, Canada H5B 1B8
(514)281-7131
Fax: (514)281-7808
Website: http://www.desjardins.com/id

Marleau Lemire Inc.
One Place Ville-Marie, Ste. 3601
Montreal, QC, Canada H3B 3P2
(514)877-3800
Fax: (514)875-6415

Speirs Consultants Inc.
365 Stanstead

Montreal, QC, Canada H3R 1X5
(514)342-3858
Fax: (514)342-1977

Tecnocap Inc.
4028 Marlowe
Montreal, QC, Canada H4A 3M2
(514)483-6009
Fax: (514)483-6045
Website: http://www.technocap.com

Telsoft Ventures
1000, Rue de la Gauchetiere
Quest, 25eme Etage
Montreal, QC, Canada H3B 4W5
(514)397-8450
Fax: (514)397-8451

Saskatchewan

Saskatchewan Government Growth Fund
1801 Hamilton St., Ste. 1210
Canada Trust Tower
Regina, SK, Canada S4P 4B4
(306)787-2994
Fax: (306)787-2086

United states

Alabama

FHL Capital Corp.
600 20th Street North
Suite 350
Birmingham, AL 35203
(205)328-3098
Fax: (205)323-0001

Harbert Management Corp.
One Riverchase Pkwy. South
Birmingham, AL 35244
(205)987-5500
Fax: (205)987-5707
Website: http://www.harbert.net

Jefferson Capital Fund
PO Box 13129
Birmingham, AL 35213
(205)324-7709

Private Capital Corp.
100 Brookwood Pl., 4th Fl.
Birmingham, AL 35209
(205)879-2722
Fax: (205)879-5121

21st Century Health Ventures
One Health South Pkwy.
Birmingham, AL 35243
(256)268-6250
Fax: (256)970-8928

FJC Growth Capital Corp.
200 Westside Sq., Ste. 340
Huntsville, AL 35801
(256)922-2918
Fax: (256)922-2909

Hickory Venture Capital Corp.
301 Washington St. NW
Suite 301
Huntsville, AL 35801
(256)539-1931
Fax: (256)539-5130
E-mail: hvcc@hvcc.com
Website: http://www.hvcc.com

Southeastern Technology Fund
7910 South Memorial Pkwy., Ste. F
Huntsville, AL 35802
(256)883-8711
Fax: (256)883-8558

Cordova Ventures
4121 Carmichael Rd., Ste. 301
Montgomery, AL 36106
(334)271-6011
Fax: (334)260-0120
Website: http://www.cordovaventures.com

Small Business Clinic of Alabama/AG Bartholomew & Associates
PO Box 231074
Montgomery, AL 36123-1074
(334)284-3640

Arizona

Miller Capital Corp.
4909 E McDowell Rd.
Phoenix, AZ 85008
(602)225-0504
Fax: (602)225-9024
Website: http://www.themillergroup.com

The Columbine Venture Funds
9449 North 90th St., Ste. 200
Scottsdale, AZ 85258
(602)661-9222
Fax: (602)661-6262

Koch Ventures
17767 N. Perimeter Dr., Ste. 101
Scottsdale, AZ 85255
(480)419-3600
Fax: (480)419-3606
Website: http://www.kochventures.com

McKee & Co.
7702 E Doubletree Ranch Rd.
Suite 230
Scottsdale, AZ 85258
(480)368-0333
Fax: (480)607-7446

Merita Capital Ltd.
7350 E Stetson Dr., Ste. 108-A
Scottsdale, AZ 85251
(480)947-8700
Fax: (480)947-8766

Valley Ventures / Arizona Growth Partners L.P.
6720 N. Scottsdale Rd., Ste. 208
Scottsdale, AZ 85253
(480)661-6600
Fax: (480)661-6262

Estreetcapital.com
660 South Mill Ave., Ste. 315
Tempe, AZ 85281
(480)968-8400
Fax: (480)968-8480
Website: http://www.estreet
capital.com

Coronado Venture Fund
PO Box 65420
Tucson, AZ 85728-5420
(520)577-3764
Fax: (520)299-8491

Arkansas

Arkansas Capital Corp.
225 South Pulaski St.
Little Rock, AR 72201
(501)374-9247
Fax: (501)374-9425
Website: http://www.arcapital.com

California

Sundance Venture Partners, L.P.
100 Clocktower Place, Ste. 130
Carmel, CA 93923
(831)625-6500
Fax: (831)625-6590

Westar Capital (Costa Mesa)
949 South Coast Dr., Ste. 650
Costa Mesa, CA 92626
(714)481-5160
Fax: (714)481-5166
E-mail: mailbox@westarcapital.com
Website: http://www.westarcapital.com

Alpine Technology Ventures
20300 Stevens Creek Boulevard, Ste. 495
Cupertino, CA 95014
(408)725-1810
Fax: (408)725-1207
Website: http://www.alpineventures.com

Bay Partners
10600 N. De Anza Blvd.
Cupertino, CA 95014-2031
(408)725-2444

Fax: (408)446-4502
Website: http://www.baypartners.com

Novus Ventures
20111 Stevens Creek Blvd., Ste. 130
Cupertino, CA 95014
(408)252-3900
Fax: (408)252-1713
Website: http://www.novusventures.com

Triune Capital
19925 Stevens Creek Blvd., Ste. 200
Cupertino, CA 95014
(310)284-6800
Fax: (310)284-3290

Acorn Ventures
268 Bush St., Ste. 2829
Daly City, CA 94014
(650)994-7801
Fax: (650)994-3305
Website: http://www.acornventures.com

Digital Media Campus
2221 Park Place
El Segundo, CA 90245
(310)426-8000
Fax: (310)426-8010
E-mail: info@thecampus.com
Website: http://www.digitalmedia
campus.com

BankAmerica Ventures / BA Venture Partners
950 Tower Ln., Ste. 700
Foster City, CA 94404
(650)378-6000
Fax: (650)378-6040
Website: http://www.baventure
partners.com

Starting Point Partners
666 Portofino Lane
Foster City, CA 94404
(650)722-1035
Website: http://www.startingpoint
partners.com

Opportunity Capital Partners
2201 Walnut Ave., Ste. 210
Fremont, CA 94538
(510)795-7000
Fax: (510)494-5439
Website: http://www.ocpcapital.com

Imperial Ventures Inc.
9920 S La Cienega Boulevar, 14th Fl.
Inglewood, CA 90301
(310)417-5409
Fax: (310)338-6115

Ventana Global (Irvine)
18881 Von Karman Ave., Ste. 1150
Irvine, CA 92612

(949)476-2204
Fax: (949)752-0223
Website: http://www.ventanaglobal.com

Integrated Consortium Inc.
50 Ridgecrest Rd.
Kentfield, CA 94904
(415)925-0386
Fax: (415)461-2726

Enterprise Partners
979 Ivanhoe Ave., Ste. 550
La Jolla, CA 92037
(858)454-8833
Fax: (858)454-2489
Website: http://www.epvc.com

Domain Associates
28202 Cabot Rd., Ste. 200
Laguna Niguel, CA 92677
(949)347-2446
Fax: (949)347-9720
Website: http://www.domainvc.com

Cascade Communications Ventures
60 E Sir Francis Drake Blvd., Ste. 300
Larkspur, CA 94939
(415)925-6500
Fax: (415)925-6501

Allegis Capital
One First St., Ste. Two
Los Altos, CA 94022
(650)917-5900
Fax: (650)917-5901
Website: http://www.allegiscapital.com

Aspen Ventures
1000 Fremont Ave., Ste. 200
Los Altos, CA 94024
(650)917-5670
Fax: (650)917-5677
Website: http://www.aspenventures.com

AVI Capital L.P.
1 First St., Ste. 2
Los Altos, CA 94022
(650)949-9862
Fax: (650)949-8510
Website: http://www.avicapital.com

Bastion Capital Corp.
1999 Avenue of the Stars, Ste. 2960
Los Angeles, CA 90067
(310)788-5700
Fax: (310)277-7582
E-mail: ga@bastioncapital.com
Website: http://www.bastioncapital.com

Davis Group
PO Box 69953
Los Angeles, CA 90069-0953

(310)659-6327
Fax: (310)659-6337

Developers Equity Corp.
1880 Century Park East, Ste. 211
Los Angeles, CA 90067
(213)277-0300

Far East Capital Corp.
350 S Grand Ave., Ste. 4100
Los Angeles, CA 90071
(213)687-1361
Fax: (213)617-7939
E-mail: free@fareastnationalbank.com

Kline Hawkes & Co.
11726 San Vicente Blvd., Ste. 300
Los Angeles, CA 90049
(310)442-4700
Fax: (310)442-4707
Website: http://www.klinehawkes.com

Lawrence Financial Group
701 Teakwood
PO Box 491773
Los Angeles, CA 90049
(310)471-4060
Fax: (310)472-3155

Riordan Lewis & Haden
300 S Grand Ave., 29th Fl.
Los Angeles, CA 90071
(213)229-8500
Fax: (213)229-8597

Union Venture Corp.
445 S Figueroa St., 9th Fl.
Los Angeles, CA 90071
(213)236-4092
Fax: (213)236-6329

Wedbush Capital Partners
1000 Wilshire Blvd.
Los Angeles, CA 90017
(213)688-4545
Fax: (213)688-6642
Website: http://www.wedbush.com

Advent International Corp.
2180 Sand Hill Rd., Ste. 420
Menlo Park, CA 94025
(650)233-7500
Fax: (650)233-7515
Website: http://www.adventinternational
.com

Altos Ventures
2882 Sand Hill Rd., Ste. 100
Menlo Park, CA 94025
(650)234-9771
Fax: (650)233-9821
Website: http://www.altosvc.com

Applied Technology
1010 El Camino Real, Ste. 300
Menlo Park, CA 94025
(415)326-8622
Fax: (415)326-8163

APV Technology Partners
535 Middlefield, Ste. 150
Menlo Park, CA 94025
(650)327-7871
Fax: (650)327-7631
Website: http://www.apvtp.com

August Capital Management
2480 Sand Hill Rd., Ste. 101
Menlo Park, CA 94025
(650)234-9900
Fax: (650)234-9910
Website: http://www.augustcap.com

Baccharis Capital Inc.
2420 Sand Hill Rd., Ste. 100
Menlo Park, CA 94025
(650)324-6844
Fax: (650)854-3025

Benchmark Capital
2480 Sand Hill Rd., Ste. 200
Menlo Park, CA 94025
(650)854-8180
Fax: (650)854-8183
E-mail: info@benchmark.com
Website: http://www.benchmark.com

Bessemer Venture Partners (Menlo Park)
535 Middlefield Rd., Ste. 245
Menlo Park, CA 94025
(650)853-7000
Fax: (650)853-7001
Website: http://www.bvp.com

The Cambria Group
1600 El Camino Real Rd., Ste. 155
Menlo Park, CA 94025
(650)329-8600
Fax: (650)329-8601
Website: http://www.cambriagroup.com

Canaan Partners
2884 Sand Hill Rd., Ste. 115
Menlo Park, CA 94025
(650)854-8092
Fax: (650)854-8127
Website: http://www.canaan.com

Capstone Ventures
3000 Sand Hill Rd., Bldg. One, Ste. 290
Menlo Park, CA 94025
(650)854-2523
Fax: (650)854-9010
Website: http://www.capstonevc.com

Comdisco Venture Group (Silicon Valley)
3000 Sand Hill Rd., Bldg. 1, Ste. 155
Menlo Park, CA 94025
(650)854-9484
Fax: (650)854-4026

Commtech International
535 Middlefield Rd., Ste. 200
Menlo Park, CA 94025
(650)328-0190
Fax: (650)328-6442

Compass Technology Partners
1550 El Camino Real, Ste. 275
Menlo Park, CA 94025-4111
(650)322-7595
Fax: (650)322-0588
Website: http://www.compasstech
partners.com

Convergence Partners
3000 Sand Hill Rd., Ste. 235
Menlo Park, CA 94025
(650)854-3010
Fax: (650)854-3015
Website: http://www.convergence
partners.com

The Dakota Group
PO Box 1025
Menlo Park, CA 94025
(650)853-0600
Fax: (650)851-4899
E-mail: info@dakota.com

Delphi Ventures
3000 Sand Hill Rd.
Bldg. One, Ste. 135
Menlo Park, CA 94025
(650)854-9650
Fax: (650)854-2961
Website: http://www.delphiventures.com

El Dorado Ventures
2884 Sand Hill Rd., Ste. 121
Menlo Park, CA 94025
(650)854-1200
Fax: (650)854-1202
Website: http://www.eldoradoventures
.com

Glynn Ventures
3000 Sand Hill Rd., Bldg. 4, Ste. 235
Menlo Park, CA 94025
(650)854-2215

Indosuez Ventures
2180 Sand Hill Rd., Ste. 450
Menlo Park, CA 94025
(650)854-0587

Fax: (650)323-5561
Website: http://www.indosuezventures
.com

Institutional Venture Partners
3000 Sand Hill Rd., Bldg. 2, Ste. 290
Menlo Park, CA 94025
(650)854-0132
Fax: (650)854-5762
Website: http://www.ivp.com

Interwest Partners (Menlo Park)
3000 Sand Hill Rd., Bldg. 3, Ste. 255
Menlo Park, CA 94025-7112
(650)854-8585
Fax: (650)854-4706
Website: http://www.interwest.com

**Kleiner Perkins Caufield & Byers
(Menlo Park)**
2750 Sand Hill Rd.
Menlo Park, CA 94025
(650)233-2750
Fax: (650)233-0300
Website: http://www.kpcb.com

Magic Venture Capital LLC
1010 El Camino Real, Ste. 300
Menlo Park, CA 94025
(650)325-4149

Matrix Partners
2500 Sand Hill Rd., Ste. 113
Menlo Park, CA 94025
(650)854-3131
Fax: (650)854-3296
Website: http://www.matrixpartners.com

Mayfield Fund
2800 Sand Hill Rd.
Menlo Park, CA 94025
(650)854-5560
Fax: (650)854-5712
Website: http://www.mayfield.com

**McCown De Leeuw and Co. (Menlo
Park)**
3000 Sand Hill Rd., Bldg. 3, Ste. 290
Menlo Park, CA 94025-7111
(650)854-6000
Fax: (650)854-0853
Website: http://www.mdcpartners.com

Menlo Ventures
3000 Sand Hill Rd., Bldg. 4, Ste. 100
Menlo Park, CA 94025
(650)854-8540
Fax: (650)854-7059
Website: http://www.menloventures.com

Merrill Pickard Anderson & Eyre
2480 Sand Hill Rd., Ste. 200
Menlo Park, CA 94025

(650)854-8600
Fax: (650)854-0345

New Enterprise Associates (Menlo Park)
2490 Sand Hill Rd.
Menlo Park, CA 94025
(650)854-9499
Fax: (650)854-9397
Website: http://www.nea.com

Onset Ventures
2400 Sand Hill Rd., Ste. 150
Menlo Park, CA 94025
(650)529-0700
Fax: (650)529-0777
Website: http://www.onset.com

Paragon Venture Partners
3000 Sand Hill Rd., Bldg. 1, Ste. 275
Menlo Park, CA 94025
(650)854-8000
Fax: (650)854-7260

**Pathfinder Venture Capital Funds
(Menlo Park)**
3000 Sand Hill Rd., Bldg. 3, Ste. 255
Menlo Park, CA 94025
(650)854-0650
Fax: (650)854-4706

Rocket Ventures
3000 Sandhill Rd., Bldg. 1, Ste. 170
Menlo Park, CA 94025
(650)561-9100
Fax: (650)561-9183
Website: http://www.rocketventures.com

Sequoia Capital
3000 Sand Hill Rd., Bldg. 4, Ste. 280
Menlo Park, CA 94025
(650)854-3927
Fax: (650)854-2977
E-mail: sequoia@sequioacap.com
Website: http://www.sequoiacap.com

Sierra Ventures
3000 Sand Hill Rd., Bldg. 4, Ste. 210
Menlo Park, CA 94025
(650)854-1000
Fax: (650)854-5593
Website: http://www.sierraventures.com

Sigma Partners
2884 Sand Hill Rd., Ste. 121
Menlo Park, CA 94025-7022
(650)853-1700
Fax: (650)853-1717
E-mail: info@sigmapartners.com
Website: http://www.sigmapartners.com

Sprout Group (Menlo Park)
3000 Sand Hill Rd.
Bldg. 3, Ste. 170

Menlo Park, CA 94025
(650)234-2700
Fax: (650)234-2779
Website: http://www.sproutgroup.com

TA Associates (Menlo Park)
70 Willow Rd., Ste. 100
Menlo Park, CA 94025
(650)328-1210
Fax: (650)326-4933
Website: http://www.ta.com

Thompson Clive & Partners Ltd.
3000 Sand Hill Rd., Bldg. 1, Ste. 185
Menlo Park, CA 94025-7102
(650)854-0314
Fax: (650)854-0670
E-mail: mail@tcvc.com
Website: http://www.tcvc.com

Trinity Ventures Ltd.
3000 Sand Hill Rd., Bldg. 1, Ste. 240
Menlo Park, CA 94025
(650)854-9500
Fax: (650)854-9501
Website: http://www.trinityventures.com

U.S. Venture Partners
2180 Sand Hill Rd., Ste. 300
Menlo Park, CA 94025
(650)854-9080
Fax: (650)854-3018
Website: http://www.usvp.com

USVP-Schlein Marketing Fund
2180 Sand Hill Rd., Ste. 300
Menlo Park, CA 94025
(415)854-9080
Fax: (415)854-3018
Website: http://www.usvp.com

Venrock Associates
2494 Sand Hill Rd., Ste. 200
Menlo Park, CA 94025
(650)561-9580
Fax: (650)561-9180
Website: http://www.venrock.com

Brad Peery Capital Inc.
145 Chapel Pkwy.
Mill Valley, CA 94941
(415)389-0625
Fax: (415)389-1336

Dot Edu Ventures
650 Castro St., Ste. 270
Mountain View, CA 94041
(650)575-5638
Fax: (650)325-5247
Website: http://www.doteduventures
.com

Forrest, Binkley & Brown
840 Newport Ctr. Dr., Ste. 480
Newport Beach, CA 92660
(949)729-3222
Fax: (949)729-3226
Website: http://www.fbbvc.com

Marwit Capital LLC
180 Newport Center Dr., Ste. 200
Newport Beach, CA 92660
(949)640-6234
Fax: (949)720-8077
Website: http://www.marwit.com

Kaiser Permanente / National Venture Development
1800 Harrison St., 22nd Fl.
Oakland, CA 94612
(510)267-4010
Fax: (510)267-4036
Website: http://www.kpventures.com

Nu Capital Access Group, Ltd.
7677 Oakport St., Ste. 105
Oakland, CA 94621
(510)635-7345
Fax: (510)635-7068

Inman and Bowman
4 Orinda Way, Bldg. D, Ste. 150
Orinda, CA 94563
(510)253-1611
Fax: (510)253-9037

Accel Partners (San Francisco)
428 University Ave.
Palo Alto, CA 94301
(650)614-4800
Fax: (650)614-4880
Website: http://www.accel.com

Advanced Technology Ventures
485 Ramona St., Ste. 200
Palo Alto, CA 94301
(650)321-8601
Fax: (650)321-0934
Website: http://www.atvcapital.com

Anila Fund
400 Channing Ave.
Palo Alto, CA 94301
(650)833-5790
Fax: (650)833-0590
Website: http://www.anila.com

Asset Management Company Venture Capital
2275 E Bayshore, Ste. 150
Palo Alto, CA 94303
(650)494-7400
Fax: (650)856-1826
E-mail: postmaster@assetman.com
Website: http://www.assetman.com

BancBoston Capital / BancBoston Ventures
435 Tasso St., Ste. 250
Palo Alto, CA 94305
(650)470-4100
Fax: (650)853-1425
Website: http://www.bancbostoncapital.com

Charter Ventures
525 University Ave., Ste. 1400
Palo Alto, CA 94301
(650)325-6953
Fax: (650)325-4762
Website: http://www.charterventures.com

Communications Ventures
505 Hamilton Avenue, Ste. 305
Palo Alto, CA 94301
(650)325-9600
Fax: (650)325-9608
Website: http://www.comven.com

HMS Group
2468 Embarcadero Way
Palo Alto, CA 94303-3313
(650)856-9862
Fax: (650)856-9864

Jafco America Ventures, Inc.
505 Hamilton Ste. 310
Palto Alto, CA 94301
(650)463-8800
Fax: (650)463-8801
Website: http://www.jafco.com

New Vista Capital
540 Cowper St., Ste. 200
Palo Alto, CA 94301
(650)329-9333
Fax: (650)328-9434
E-mail: fgreene@nvcap.com
Website: http://www.nvcap.com

Norwest Equity Partners (Palo Alto)
245 Lytton Ave., Ste. 250
Palo Alto, CA 94301-1426
(650)321-8000
Fax: (650)321-8010
Website: http://www.norwestvp.com

Oak Investment Partners
525 University Ave., Ste. 1300
Palo Alto, CA 94301
(650)614-3700
Fax: (650)328-6345
Website: http://www.oakinv.com

Patricof & Co. Ventures, Inc. (Palo Alto)
2100 Geng Rd., Ste. 150
Palo Alto, CA 94303

(650)494-9944
Fax: (650)494-6751
Website: http://www.patricof.com

RWI Group
835 Page Mill Rd.
Palo Alto, CA 94304
(650)251-1800
Fax: (650)213-8660
Website: http://www.rwigroup.com

Summit Partners (Palo Alto)
499 Hamilton Ave., Ste. 200
Palo Alto, CA 94301
(650)321-1166
Fax: (650)321-1188
Website: http://www.summitpartners.com

Sutter Hill Ventures
755 Page Mill Rd., Ste. A-200
Palo Alto, CA 94304
(650)493-5600
Fax: (650)858-1854
E-mail: shv@shv.com

Vanguard Venture Partners
525 University Ave., Ste. 600
Palo Alto, CA 94301
(650)321-2900
Fax: (650)321-2902
Website: http://www.vanguardventures.com

Venture Growth Associates
2479 East Bayshore St., Ste. 710
Palo Alto, CA 94303
(650)855-9100
Fax: (650)855-9104

Worldview Technology Partners
435 Tasso St., Ste. 120
Palo Alto, CA 94301
(650)322-3800
Fax: (650)322-3880
Website: http://www.worldview.com

Draper, Fisher, Jurvetson / Draper Associates
400 Seaport Ct., Ste.250
Redwood City, CA 94063
(415)599-9000
Fax: (415)599-9726
Website: http://www.dfj.com

Gabriel Venture Partners
350 Marine Pkwy., Ste. 200
Redwood Shores, CA 94065
(650)551-5000
Fax: (650)551-5001
Website: http://www.gabrielvp.com

Hallador Venture Partners, L.L.C.
740 University Ave., Ste. 110
Sacramento, CA 95825-6710
(916)920-0191
Fax: (916)920-5188
E-mail: chris@hallador.com

Emerald Venture Group
12396 World Trade Dr., Ste. 116
San Diego, CA 92128
(858)451-1001
Fax: (858)451-1003
Website: http://www.emeraldventure
.com

Forward Ventures
9255 Towne Centre Dr.
San Diego, CA 92121
(858)677-6077
Fax: (858)452-8799
E-mail: info@forwardventure.com
Website: http://www.forwardventure
.com

Idanta Partners Ltd.
4660 La Jolla Village Dr., Ste. 850
San Diego, CA 92122
(619)452-9690
Fax: (619)452-2013
Website: http://www.idanta.com

Kingsbury Associates
3655 Nobel Dr., Ste. 490
San Diego, CA 92122
(858)677-0600
Fax: (858)677-0800

Kyocera International Inc.
Corporate Development
8611 Balboa Ave.
San Diego, CA 92123
(858)576-2600
Fax: (858)492-1456

Sorrento Associates, Inc.
4370 LaJolla Village Dr., Ste. 1040
San Diego, CA 92122
(619)452-3100
Fax: (619)452-7607
Website: http://www.sorrentoventures
.com

Western States Investment Group
9191 Towne Ctr. Dr., Ste. 310
San Diego, CA 92122
(619)678-0800
Fax: (619)678-0900

Aberdare Ventures
One Embarcadero Center, Ste. 4000
San Francisco, CA 94111
(415)392-7442

Fax: (415)392-4264
Website: http://www.aberdare.com

Acacia Venture Partners
101 California St., Ste. 3160
San Francisco, CA 94111
(415)433-4200
Fax: (415)433-4250
Website: http://www.acaciavp.com

Access Venture Partners
319 Laidley St.
San Francisco, CA 94131
(415)586-0132
Fax: (415)392-6310
Website: http://www.accessventure
partners.com

Alta Partners
One Embarcadero Center, Ste. 4050
San Francisco, CA 94111
(415)362-4022
Fax: (415)362-6178
E-mail: alta@altapartners.com
Website: http://www.altapartners.com

Bangert Dawes Reade Davis & Thom
220 Montgomery St., Ste. 424
San Francisco, CA 94104
(415)954-9900
Fax: (415)954-9901
E-mail: bdrdt@pacbell.net

Berkeley International Capital Corp.
650 California St., Ste. 2800
San Francisco, CA 94108-2609
(415)249-0450
Fax: (415)392-3929
Website: http://www.berkeleyvc.com

Blueprint Ventures LLC
456 Montgomery St., 22nd Fl.
San Francisco, CA 94104
(415)901-4000
Fax: (415)901-4035
Website: http://www.blueprintventures
.com

Blumberg Capital Ventures
580 Howard St., Ste. 401
San Francisco, CA 94105
(415)905-5007
Fax: (415)357-5027
Website: http://www.blumberg-
capital.com

**Burr, Egan, Deleage, and Co.
(San Francisco)**
1 Embarcadero Center, Ste. 4050
San Francisco, CA 94111
(415)362-4022
Fax: (415)362-6178

Burrill & Company
120 Montgomery St., Ste. 1370
San Francisco, CA 94104
(415)743-3160
Fax: (415)743-3161
Website: http://www.burrillandco.com

CMEA Ventures
235 Montgomery St., Ste. 920
San Francisco, CA 94401
(415)352-1520
Fax: (415)352-1524
Website: http://www.cmeaventures.com

Crocker Capital
1 Post St., Ste. 2500
San Francisco, CA 94101
(415)956-5250
Fax: (415)959-5710

Dominion Ventures, Inc.
44 Montgomery St., Ste. 4200
San Francisco, CA 94104
(415)362-4890
Fax: (415)394-9245

Dorset Capital
Pier 1
Bay 2
San Francisco, CA 94111
(415)398-7101
Fax: (415)398-7141
Website: http://www.dorsetcapital.com

Gatx Capital
Four Embarcadero Center, Ste. 2200
San Francisco, CA 94904
(415)955-3200
Fax: (415)955-3449

IMinds
135 Main St., Ste. 1350
San Francisco, CA 94105
(415)547-0000
Fax: (415)227-0300
Website: http://www.iminds.com

LF International Inc.
360 Post St., Ste. 705
San Francisco, CA 94108
(415)399-0110
Fax: (415)399-9222
Website: http://www.lfvc.com

Newbury Ventures
535 Pacific Ave., 2nd Fl.
San Francisco, CA 94133
(415)296-7408
Fax: (415)296-7416
Website: http://www.newburyven.com

Quest Ventures (San Francisco)
333 Bush St., Ste. 1750
San Francisco, CA 94104

(415)782-1414
Fax: (415)782-1415

Robertson-Stephens Co.
555 California St., Ste. 2600
San Francisco, CA 94104
(415)781-9700
Fax: (415)781-2556
Website: http://www.omegaadventures
.com

Rosewood Capital, L.P.
One Maritime Plaza, Ste. 1330
San Francisco, CA 94111-3503
(415)362-5526
Fax: (415)362-1192
Website: http://www.rosewoodvc.com

Ticonderoga Capital Inc.
555 California St., No. 4950
San Francisco, CA 94104
(415)296-7900
Fax: (415)296-8956

21st Century Internet Venture Partners
Two South Park
2nd Floor
San Francisco, CA 94107
(415)512-1221
Fax: (415)512-2650
Website: http://www.21vc.com

VK Ventures
600 California St., Ste.1700
San Francisco, CA 94111
(415)391-5600
Fax: (415)397-2744

Walden Group of Venture Capital Funds
750 Battery St., Seventh Floor
San Francisco, CA 94111
(415)391-7225
Fax: (415)391-7262

Acer Technology Ventures
2641 Orchard Pkwy.
San Jose, CA 95134
(408)433-4945
Fax: (408)433-5230

Authosis
226 Airport Pkwy., Ste. 405
San Jose, CA 95110
(650)814-3603
Website: http://www.authosis.com

Western Technology Investment
2010 N. First St., Ste. 310
San Jose, CA 95131
(408)436-8577
Fax: (408)436-8625
E-mail: mktg@westerntech.com

Drysdale Enterprises
177 Bovet Rd., Ste. 600
San Mateo, CA 94402
(650)341-6336
Fax: (650)341-1329
E-mail: drysdale@aol.com

Greylock
2929 Campus Dr., Ste. 400
San Mateo, CA 94401
(650)493-5525
Fax: (650)493-5575
Website: http://www.greylock.com

Technology Funding
2000 Alameda de las Pulgas, Ste. 250
San Mateo, CA 94403
(415)345-2200
Fax: (415)345-1797

2M Invest Inc.
1875 S Grant St.
Suite 750
San Mateo, CA 94402
(650)655-3765
Fax: (650)372-9107
E-mail: 2minfo@2minvest.com
Website: http://www.2minvest.com

Phoenix Growth Capital Corp.
2401 Kerner Blvd.
San Rafael, CA 94901
(415)485-4569
Fax: (415)485-4663

NextGen Partners LLC
1705 East Valley Rd.
Santa Barbara, CA 93108
(805)969-8540
Fax: (805)969-8542
Website: http://www.nextgenpartners.com

Denali Venture Capital
1925 Woodland Ave.
Santa Clara, CA 95050
(408)690-4838
Fax: (408)247-6979
E-mail: wael@denaliventurecapital.com
Website: http://www.denaliventure
capital.com

Dotcom Ventures LP
3945 Freedom Circle, Ste. 740
Santa Clara, CA 95045
(408)919-9855
Fax: (408)919-9857
Website: http://www.dotcomventuresatl
.com

Silicon Valley Bank
3003 Tasman
Santa Clara, CA 95054

(408)654-7400
Fax: (408)727-8728

Al Shugart International
920 41st Ave.
Santa Cruz, CA 95062
(831)479-7852
Fax: (831)479-7852
Website: http://www.alshugart.com

Leonard Mautner Associates
1434 Sixth St.
Santa Monica, CA 90401
(213)393-9788
Fax: (310)459-9918

Palomar Ventures
100 Wilshire Blvd., Ste. 450
Santa Monica, CA 90401
(310)260-6050
Fax: (310)656-4150
Website: http://www.palomarventures
.com

Medicus Venture Partners
12930 Saratoga Ave., Ste. D8
Saratoga, CA 95070
(408)447-8600
Fax: (408)447-8599
Website: http://www.medicusvc.com

Redleaf Venture Management
14395 Saratoga Ave., Ste. 130
Saratoga, CA 95070
(408)868-0800
Fax: (408)868-0810
E-mail: nancy@redleaf.com
Website: http://www.redleaf.com

Artemis Ventures
207 Second St., Ste. E
3rd Fl.
Sausalito, CA 94965
(415)289-2500
Fax: (415)289-1789
Website: http://www.artemisventures
.com

Deucalion Venture Partners
19501 Brooklime
Sonoma, CA 95476
(707)938-4974
Fax: (707)938-8921

Windward Ventures
PO Box 7688
Thousand Oaks, CA 91359-7688
(805)497-3332
Fax: (805)497-9331

National Investment Management, Inc.
2601 Airport Dr., Ste.210
Torrance, CA 90505

(310)784-7600
Fax: (310)784-7605

Southern California Ventures
406 Amapola Ave. Ste. 125
Torrance, CA 90501
(310)787-4381
Fax: (310)787-4382

Sandton Financial Group
21550 Oxnard St., Ste. 300
Woodland Hills, CA 91367
(818)702-9283

Woodside Fund
850 Woodside Dr.
Woodside, CA 94062
(650)368-5545
Fax: (650)368-2416
Website: http://www.woodsidefund.com

Colorado

Colorado Venture Management
Ste. 300
Boulder, CO 80301
(303)440-4055
Fax: (303)440-4636

Dean & Associates
4362 Apple Way
Boulder, CO 80301
Fax: (303)473-9900

Roser Ventures LLC
1105 Spruce St.
Boulder, CO 80302
(303)443-6436
Fax: (303)443-1885
Website: http://www.roserventures.com

Sequel Venture Partners
4430 Arapahoe Ave., Ste. 220
Boulder, CO 80303
(303)546-0400
Fax: (303)546-9728
E-mail: tom@sequelvc.com
Website: http://www.sequelvc.com

New Venture Resources
445C E Cheyenne Mtn. Blvd.
Colorado Springs, CO 80906-4570
(719)598-9272
Fax: (719)598-9272

The Centennial Funds
1428 15th St.
Denver, CO 80202-1318
(303)405-7500
Fax: (303)405-7575
Website: http://www.centennial.com

Rocky Mountain Capital Partners
1125 17th St., Ste. 2260
Denver, CO 80202
(303)291-5200
Fax: (303)291-5327

Sandlot Capital LLC
600 South Cherry St., Ste. 525
Denver, CO 80246
(303)893-3400
Fax: (303)893-3403
Website: http://www.sandlotcapital.com

Wolf Ventures
50 South Steele St., Ste. 777
Denver, CO 80209
(303)321-4800
Fax: (303)321-4848
E-mail: businessplan@wolfventures.com
Website: http://www.wolfventures.com

The Columbine Venture Funds
5460 S Quebec St., Ste. 270
Englewood, CO 80111
(303)694-3222
Fax: (303)694-9007

Investment Securities of Colorado, Inc.
4605 Denice Dr.
Englewood, CO 80111
(303)796-9192

Kinship Partners
6300 S Syracuse Way, Ste. 484
Englewood, CO 80111
(303)694-0268
Fax: (303)694-1707
E-mail: block@vailsys.com

Boranco Management, L.L.C.
1528 Hillside Dr.
Fort Collins, CO 80524-1969
(970)221-2297
Fax: (970)221-4787

Aweida Ventures
890 West Cherry St., Ste. 220
Louisville, CO 80027
(303)664-9520
Fax: (303)664-9530
Website: http://www.aweida.com

Access Venture Partners
8787 Turnpike Dr., Ste. 260
Westminster, CO 80030
(303)426-8899
Fax: (303)426-8828

Connecticut

Medmax Ventures, LP
1 Northwestern Dr., Ste. 203
Bloomfield, CT 06002

(860)286-2960
Fax: (860)286-9960

James B. Kobak & Co.
Four Mansfield Place
Darien, CT 06820
(203)656-3471
Fax: (203)655-2905

Orien Ventures
1 Post Rd.
Fairfield, CT 06430
(203)259-9933
Fax: (203)259-5288

ABP Acquisition Corporation
115 Maple Ave.
Greenwich, CT 06830
(203)625-8287
Fax: (203)447-6187

Catterton Partners
9 Greenwich Office Park
Greenwich, CT 06830
(203)629-4901
Fax: (203)629-4903
Website: http://www.cpequity.com

Consumer Venture Partners
3 Pickwick Plz.
Greenwich, CT 06830
(203)629-8800
Fax: (203)629-2019

Insurance Venture Partners
31 Brookside Dr., Ste. 211
Greenwich, CT 06830
(203)861-0030
Fax: (203)861-2745

The NTC Group
Three Pickwick Plaza
Ste. 200
Greenwich, CT 06830
(203)862-2800
Fax: (203)622-6538

**Regulus International
Capital Co., Inc.**
140 Greenwich Ave.
Greenwich, CT 06830
(203)625-9700
Fax: (203)625-9706

Axiom Venture Partners
City Place II
185 Asylum St., 17th Fl.
Hartford, CT 06103
(860)548-7799
Fax: (860)548-7797
Website: http://www.axiomventures
.com

Conning Capital Partners
City Place II
185 Asylum St.
Hartford, CT 06103-4105
(860)520-1289
Fax: (860)520-1299
E-mail: pe@conning.com
Website: http://www.conning.com

First New England Capital L.P.
100 Pearl St.
Hartford, CT 06103
(860)293-3333
Fax: (860)293-3338
E-mail: info@firstnewenglandcapital.com
Website: http://www.firstnewengland
capital.com

Northeast Ventures
One State St., Ste. 1720
Hartford, CT 06103
(860)547-1414
Fax: (860)246-8755

Windward Holdings
38 Sylvan Rd.
Madison, CT 06443
(203)245-6870
Fax: (203)245-6865

Advanced Materials Partners, Inc.
45 Pine St.
PO Box 1022
New Canaan, CT 06840
(203)966-6415
Fax: (203)966-8448
E-mail: wkb@amplink.com

RFE Investment Partners
36 Grove St.
New Canaan, CT 06840
(203)966-2800
Fax: (203)966-3109
Website: http://www.rfeip.com

Connecticut Innovations, Inc.
999 West St.
Rocky Hill, CT 06067
(860)563-5851
Fax: (860)563-4877
E-mail: pamela.hartley@ctinnovations
.com
Website: http://www.ctinnovations.com

Canaan Partners
105 Rowayton Ave.
Rowayton, CT 06853
(203)855-0400
Fax: (203)854-9117
Website: http://www.canaan.com

Landmark Partners, Inc.
10 Mill Pond Ln.
Simsbury, CT 06070
(860)651-9760
Fax: (860)651-8890
Website: http://www.landmarkpartners
.com

Sweeney & Company
PO Box 567
Southport, CT 06490
(203)255-0220
Fax: (203)255-0220
E-mail: sweeney@connix.com

Baxter Associates, Inc.
PO Box 1333
Stamford, CT 06904
(203)323-3143
Fax: (203)348-0622

Beacon Partners Inc.
6 Landmark Sq., 4th Fl.
Stamford, CT 06901-2792
(203)359-5776
Fax: (203)359-5876

Collinson, Howe, and Lennox, LLC
1055 Washington Blvd., 5th Fl.
Stamford, CT 06901
(203)324-7700
Fax: (203)324-3636
E-mail: info@chlmedical.com
Website: http://www.chlmedical.com

Prime Capital Management Co.
550 West Ave.
Stamford, CT 06902
(203)964-0642
Fax: (203)964-0862

Saugatuck Capital Co.
1 Canterbury Green
Stamford, CT 06901
(203)348-6669
Fax: (203)324-6995
Website: http://www.saugatuckcapital
.com

Soundview Financial Group Inc.
22 Gatehouse Rd.
Stamford, CT 06902
(203)462-7200
Fax: (203)462-7350
Website: http://www.sndv.com

TSG Ventures, L.L.C.
177 Broad St., 12th Fl.
Stamford, CT 06901
(203)406-1500
Fax: (203)406-1590

Whitney & Company
177 Broad St.
Stamford, CT 06901
(203)973-1400
Fax: (203)973-1422
Website: http://www.jhwhitney.com

**Cullinane & Donnelly Venture
Partners L.P.**
970 Farmington Ave.
West Hartford, CT 06107
(860)521-7811

**The Crestview Investment and
Financial Group**
431 Post Rd. E, Ste. 1
Westport, CT 06880-4403
(203)222-0333
Fax: (203)222-0000

**Marketcorp Venture Associates, L.P.
(MCV)**
274 Riverside Ave.
Westport, CT 06880
(203)222-3030
Fax: (203)222-3033

Oak Investment Partners (Westport)
1 Gorham Island
Westport, CT 06880
(203)226-8346
Fax: (203)227-0372
Website: http://www.oakinv.com

Oxford Bioscience Partners
315 Post Rd. W
Westport, CT 06880-5200
(203)341-3300
Fax: (203)341-3309
Website: http://www.oxbio.com

Prince Ventures (Westport)
25 Ford Rd.
Westport, CT 06880
(203)227-8332
Fax: (203)226-5302

LTI Venture Leasing Corp.
221 Danbury Rd.
Wilton, CT 06897
(203)563-1100
Fax: (203)563-1111
Website: http://www.ltileasing.com

Delaware

Blue Rock Capital
5803 Kennett Pike, Ste. A
Wilmington, DE 19807
(302)426-0981
Fax: (302)426-0982
Website: http://www.bluerockcapital
.com

District of Columbia

Allied Capital Corp.
1919 Pennsylvania Ave. NW
Washington, DC 20006-3434
(202)331-2444
Fax: (202)659-2053
Website: http://www.alliedcapital.com

Atlantic Coastal Ventures, L.P.
3101 South St. NW
Washington, DC 20007
(202)293-1166
Fax: (202)293-1181
Website: http://www.atlanticcv.com

Columbia Capital Group, Inc.
1660 L St. NW, Ste. 308
Washington, DC 20036
(202)775-8815
Fax: (202)223-0544

Core Capital Partners
901 15th St., NW
9th Fl.
Washington,
DC 20005
(202)589-0090
Fax: (202)589-0091
Website: http://www.core-capital.com

Next Point Partners
701 Pennsylvania Ave. NW, Ste. 900
Washington, DC 20004
(202)661-8703
Fax: (202)434-7400
E-mail: mf@nextpoint.vc
Website: http://www.nextpointvc.com

Telecommunications Development Fund
2020 K. St. NW
Ste. 375
Washington, DC 20006
(202)293-8840
Fax: (202)293-8850
Website: http://www.tdfund.com

Wachtel & Co., Inc.
1101 4th St. NW
Washington, DC 20005-5680
(202)898-1144

Winslow Partners LLC
1300 Connecticut Ave. NW
Washington, DC 20036-1703
(202)530-5000
Fax: (202)530-5010
E-mail: winslow@winslowpartners.com

Women's Growth Capital Fund
1054 31st St., NW
Ste. 110
Washington, DC 20007

(202)342-1431
Fax: (202)341-1203
Website: http://www.wgcf.com

Florida

Sigma Capital Corp.
22668 Caravelle Circle
Boca Raton, FL 33433
(561)368-9783

North American Business Development Co., L.L.C.
111 East Las Olas Blvd.
Fort Lauderdale, FL 33301
(305)463-0681
Fax: (305)527-0904
Website: http://
www.northamericanfund.com

Chartwell Capital Management Co. Inc.
1 Independent Dr., Ste. 3120
Jacksonville, FL 32202
(904)355-3519
Fax: (904)353-5833
E-mail: info@chartwellcap.com

CEO Advisors
1061 Maitland Center Commons
Ste. 209
Maitland, FL 32751
(407)660-9327
Fax: (407)660-2109

Henry & Co.
8201 Peters Rd., Ste. 1000
Plantation, FL 33324
(954)797-7400

Avery Business Development Services
2506 St. Michel Ct.
Ponte Vedra, FL 32082
(904)285-6033

New South Ventures
5053 Ocean Blvd.
Sarasota, FL 34242
(941)358-6000
Fax: (941)358-6078
Website: http://
www.newsouthventures.com

Venture Capital Management Corp.
PO Box 2626
Satellite Beach, FL 32937
(407)777-1969

Florida Capital Venture Ltd.
325 Florida Bank Plaza
100 W Kennedy Blvd.
Tampa, FL 33602
(813)229-2294
Fax: (813)229-2028

Quantum Capital Partners
339 South Plant Ave.
Tampa, FL 33606
(813)250-1999
Fax: (813)250-1998
Website: http://www.quantumcapital
partners.com

South Atlantic Venture Fund
614 W Bay St.
Tampa, FL 33606-2704
(813)253-2500
Fax: (813)253-2360
E-mail: venture@southatlantic.com
Website: http://www.southatlantic.com

LM Capital Corp.
120 S Olive, Ste. 400
West Palm Beach, FL 33401
(561)833-9700
Fax: (561)655-6587
Website: http://www.lmcapitalsecurities
.com

Georgia

Venture First Associates
4811 Thornwood Dr.
Acworth, GA 30102
(770)928-3733
Fax: (770)928-6455

Alliance Technology Ventures
8995 Westside Pkwy., Ste. 200
Alpharetta, GA 30004
(678)336-2000
Fax: (678)336-2001
E-mail: info@atv.com
Website: http://www.atv.com

Cordova Ventures
2500 North Winds Pkwy., Ste. 475
Alpharetta, GA 30004
(678)942-0300
Fax: (678)942-0301
Website: http://www.cordovaventures
.com

Advanced Technology Development Fund
1000 Abernathy, Ste. 1420
Atlanta, GA 30328-5614
(404)668-2333
Fax: (404)668-2333

CGW Southeast Partners
12 Piedmont Center, Ste. 210
Atlanta, GA 30305
(404)816-3255
Fax: (404)816-3258
Website: http://www.cgwlp.com

Cyberstarts
1900 Emery St., NW
3rd Fl.
Atlanta, GA 30318
(404)267-5000
Fax: (404)267-5200
Website: http://www.cyberstarts.com

EGL Holdings, Inc.
10 Piedmont Center, Ste. 412
Atlanta, GA 30305
(404)949-8300
Fax: (404)949-8311

Equity South
1790 The Lenox Bldg.
3399 Peachtree Rd. NE
Atlanta, GA 30326
(404)237-6222
Fax: (404)261-1578

Five Paces
3400 Peachtree Rd., Ste. 200
Atlanta, GA 30326
(404)439-8300
Fax: (404)439-8301
Website: http://www.fivepaces.com

Frontline Capital, Inc.
3475 Lenox Rd., Ste. 400
Atlanta, GA 30326
(404)240-7280
Fax: (404)240-7281

Fuqua Ventures LLC
1201 W Peachtree St. NW, Ste. 5000
Atlanta, GA 30309
(404)815-4500
Fax: (404)815-4528
Website: http://www.fuquaventures.com

Noro-Moseley Partners
4200 Northside Pkwy., Bldg. 9
Atlanta, GA 30327
(404)233-1966
Fax: (404)239-9280
Website: http://www.noro-moseley.com

Renaissance Capital Corp.
34 Peachtree St. NW, Ste. 2230
Atlanta, GA 30303
(404)658-9061
Fax: (404)658-9064

River Capital, Inc.
Two Midtown Plaza
1360 Peachtree St. NE, Ste. 1430
Atlanta, GA 30309
(404)873-2166
Fax: (404)873-2158

State Street Bank & Trust Co.
3414 Peachtree Rd. NE, Ste. 1010
Atlanta, GA 30326

(404)364-9500
Fax: (404)261-4469

UPS Strategic Enterprise Fund
55 Glenlake Pkwy. NE
Atlanta, GA 30328
(404)828-8814
Fax: (404)828-8088
E-mail: jcacyce@ups.com
Website: http://www.ups.com/sef/
sef_home

Wachovia
191 Peachtree St. NE, 26th Fl.
Atlanta, GA 30303
(404)332-1000
Fax: (404)332-1392
Website: http://www.wachovia.com/wca

Brainworks Ventures
4243 Dunwoody Club Dr.
Chamblee, GA 30341
(770)239-7447

First Growth Capital Inc.
Best Western Plaza, Ste. 105
PO Box 815
Forsyth, GA 31029
(912)781-7131

Financial Capital Resources, Inc.
21 Eastbrook Bend, Ste. 116
Peachtree City, GA 30269
(404)487-6650

Hawaii

HMS Hawaii Management Partners
Davies Pacific Center
841 Bishop St., Ste. 860
Honolulu, HI 96813
(808)545-3755
Fax: (808)531-2611

Idaho

Sun Valley Ventures
160 Second St.
Ketchum, ID 83340
(208)726-5005
Fax: (208)726-5094

Illinois

Open Prairie Ventures
115 N. Neil St., Ste. 209
Champaign, IL 61820
(217)351-7000
Fax: (217)351-7051
E-mail: inquire@openprairie.com
Website: http://www.openprairie.com

ABN AMRO Private Equity
208 S La Salle St., 10th Fl.
Chicago, IL 60604
(312)855-7079
Fax: (312)553-6648
Website: http://www.abnequity.com

Alpha Capital Partners, Ltd.
122 S Michigan Ave., Ste. 1700
Chicago, IL 60603
(312)322-9800
Fax: (312)322-9808
E-mail: acp@alphacapital.com

Ameritech Development Corp.
30 S Wacker Dr., 37th Fl.
Chicago, IL 60606
(312)750-5083
Fax: (312)609-0244

**Apex Investment
Partners**
225 W Washington, Ste. 1450
Chicago, IL 60606
(312)857-2800
Fax: (312)857-1800
E-mail: apex@apexvc.com
Website: http://www.apexvc.com

Arch Venture Partners
8725 W Higgins Rd., Ste. 290
Chicago, IL 60631
(773)380-6600
Fax: (773)380-6606
Website: http://www.archventure.com

The Bank Funds
208 South LaSalle St., Ste. 1680
Chicago, IL 60604
(312)855-6020
Fax: (312)855-8910

Batterson Venture Partners
303 W Madison St., Ste. 1110
Chicago, IL 60606-3309
(312)269-0300
Fax: (312)269-0021
Website: http://www.battersonvp.com

**William Blair Capital Partners,
L.L.C.**
222 W Adams St., Ste. 1300
Chicago, IL 60606
(312)364-8250
Fax: (312)236-1042
E-mail: privateequity@wmblair.com
Website: http://www.wmblair.com

Bluestar Ventures
208 South LaSalle St., Ste. 1020
Chicago, IL 60604
(312)384-5000

Fax: (312)384-5005
Website: http://www.bluestarventures
.com

The Capital Strategy Management Co.
233 S Wacker Dr.
Box 06334
Chicago, IL 60606
(312)444-1170

DN Partners
77 West Wacker Dr., Ste. 4550
Chicago, IL 60601
(312)332-7960
Fax: (312)332-7979

Dresner Capital Inc.
29 South LaSalle St., Ste. 310
Chicago, IL 60603
(312)726-3600
Fax: (312)726-7448

Eblast Ventures LLC
11 South LaSalle St., 5th Fl.
Chicago, IL 60603
(312)372-2600
Fax: (312)372-5621
Website: http://www.eblastventures.com

Essex Woodlands Health Ventures, L.P.
190 S LaSalle St., Ste. 2800
Chicago, IL 60603
(312)444-6040
Fax: (312)444-6034
Website: http://www.essexwoodlands.com

First Analysis Venture Capital
233 S Wacker Dr., Ste. 9500
Chicago, IL 60606
(312)258-1400
Fax: (312)258-0334
Website: http://www.firstanalysis.com

Frontenac Co.
135 S LaSalle St., Ste.3800
Chicago, IL 60603
(312)368-0044
Fax: (312)368-9520
Website: http://www.frontenac.com

GTCR Golder Rauner, LLC
6100 Sears Tower
Chicago, IL 60606
(312)382-2200
Fax: (312)382-2201
Website: http://www.gtcr.com

High Street Capital LLC
311 South Wacker Dr., Ste. 4550
Chicago, IL 60606
(312)697-4990
Fax: (312)697-4994
Website: http://www.highstr.com

IEG Venture Management, Inc.
70 West Madison
Chicago, IL 60602
(312)644-0890
Fax: (312)454-0369
Website: http://www.iegventure.com

JK&B Capital
180 North Stetson, Ste. 4500
Chicago, IL 60601
(312)946-1200
Fax: (312)946-1103
E-mail: gspencer@jkbcapital.com
Website: http://www.jkbcapital.com

Kettle Partners L.P.
350 W Hubbard, Ste. 350
Chicago, IL 60610
(312)329-9300
Fax: (312)527-4519
Website: http://www.kettlevc.com

Lake Shore Capital Partners
20 N. Wacker Dr., Ste. 2807
Chicago, IL 60606
(312)803-3536
Fax: (312)803-3534

LaSalle Capital Group Inc.
70 W Madison St., Ste. 5710
Chicago, IL 60602
(312)236-7041
Fax: (312)236-0720

Linc Capital, Inc.
303 E Wacker Pkwy., Ste. 1000
Chicago, IL 60601
(312)946-2670
Fax: (312)938-4290
E-mail: bdemars@linccap.com

Madison Dearborn Partners, Inc.
3 First National Plz., Ste. 3800
Chicago, IL 60602
(312)895-1000
Fax: (312)895-1001
E-mail: invest@mdcp.com
Website: http://www.mdcp.com

Mesirow Private Equity Investments Inc.
350 N. Clark St.
Chicago, IL 60610
(312)595-6950
Fax: (312)595-6211
Website: http://
www.meisrowfinancial.com

Mosaix Ventures LLC
1822 North Mohawk
Chicago, IL 60614
(312)274-0988

Fax: (312)274-0989
Website: http://www.mosaixventures.com

Nesbitt Burns
111 West Monroe St.
Chicago, IL 60603
(312)416-3855
Fax: (312)765-8000
Website: http://www.harrisbank.com

Polestar Capital, Inc.
180 N. Michigan Ave., Ste. 1905
Chicago, IL 60601
(312)984-9090
Fax: (312)984-9877
E-mail: wl@polestarvc.com
Website: http://www.polestarvc.com

Prince Ventures (Chicago)
10 S Wacker Dr., Ste. 2575
Chicago, IL 60606-7407
(312)454-1408
Fax: (312)454-9125

Prism Capital
444 N. Michigan Ave.
Chicago, IL 60611
(312)464-7900
Fax: (312)464-7915
Website: http://www.prismfund.com

Third Coast Capital
900 N. Franklin St., Ste. 700
Chicago, IL 60610
(312)337-3303
Fax: (312)337-2567
E-mail: manic@earthlink.com
Website: http://www.thirdcoastcapital.com

Thoma Cressey Equity Partners
4460 Sears Tower, 92nd Fl.
233 S Wacker Dr.
Chicago, IL 60606
(312)777-4444
Fax: (312)777-4445
Website: http://www.thomacressey.com

Tribune Ventures
435 N. Michigan Ave., Ste. 600
Chicago, IL 60611
(312)527-8797
Fax: (312)222-5993
Website: http://www.tribuneventures.com

Wind Point Partners (Chicago)
676 N. Michigan Ave., Ste. 330
Chicago, IL 60611
(312)649-4000
Website: http://www.wppartners.com

Marquette Venture Partners
520 Lake Cook Rd., Ste. 450
Deerfield, IL 60015

(847)940-1700
Fax: (847)940-1724
Website: http://www.marquett
eventures.com

Duchossois Investments Limited, LLC
845 Larch Ave.
Elmhurst, IL 60126
(630)530-6105
Fax: (630)993-8644
Website: http://www.duchtec.com

Evanston Business Investment Corp.
1840 Oak Ave.
Evanston, IL 60201
(847)866-1840
Fax: (847)866-1808
E-mail: t-parkinson@nwu.com
Website: http://www.ebic.com

Inroads Capital Partners L.P.
1603 Orrington Ave., Ste. 2050
Evanston, IL 60201-3841
(847)864-2000
Fax: (847)864-9692

The Cerulean Fund/WGC Enterprises
1701 E Lake Ave., Ste. 170
Glenview, IL 60025
(847)657-8002
Fax: (847)657-8168

Ventana Financial Resources, Inc.
249 Market Sq.
Lake Forest, IL 60045
(847)234-3434

Beecken, Petty & Co.
901 Warrenville Rd., Ste. 205
Lisle, IL 60532
(630)435-0300
Fax: (630)435-0370
E-mail: hep@bpcompany.com
Website: http://www.bpcompany.com

Allstate Private Equity
3075 Sanders Rd., Ste. G5D
Northbrook, IL 60062-7127
(847)402-8247
Fax: (847)402-0880

KB Partners
1101 Skokie Blvd., Ste. 260
Northbrook, IL 60062-2856
(847)714-0444
Fax: (847)714-0445
E-mail: keith@kbpartners.com
Website: http://www.kbpartners.com

Transcap Associates Inc.
900 Skokie Blvd., Ste. 210
Northbrook, IL 60062

(847)753-9600
Fax: (847)753-9090

Graystone Venture Partners, L.L.C. / Portage Venture Partners
One Northfield Plaza, Ste. 530
Northfield, IL 60093
(847)446-9460
Fax: (847)446-9470
Website: http://www.portageventures
.com

Motorola Inc.
1303 E Algonquin Rd.
Schaumburg, IL 60196-1065
(847)576-4929
Fax: (847)538-2250
Website: http://www.mot.com/mne

Indiana

Irwin Ventures LLC
500 Washington St.
Columbus, IN 47202
(812)373-1434
Fax: (812)376-1709
Website: http://www.irwinventures.com

Cambridge Venture Partners
4181 East 96th St., Ste. 200
Indianapolis, IN 46240
(317)814-6192
Fax: (317)944-9815

CID Equity Partners
One American Square, Ste. 2850
Box 82074
Indianapolis, IN 46282
(317)269-2350
Fax: (317)269-2355
Website: http://www.cidequity.com

Gazelle Techventures
6325 Digital Way, Ste. 460
Indianapolis, IN 46278
(317)275-6800
Fax: (317)275-1101
Website: http://www.gazellevc.com

Monument Advisors Inc.
Bank One Center/Circle
111 Monument Circle, Ste. 600
Indianapolis, IN 46204-5172
(317)656-5065
Fax: (317)656-5060
Website: http://www.monumentadv.com

MWV Capital Partners
201 N. Illinois St., Ste. 300
Indianapolis, IN 46204
(317)237-2323
Fax: (317)237-2325
Website: http://www.mwvcapital.com

First Source Capital Corp.
100 North Michigan St.
PO Box 1602
South Bend, IN 46601
(219)235-2180
Fax: (219)235-2227

Iowa

Allsop Venture Partners
118 Third Ave. SE, Ste. 837
Cedar Rapids, IA 52401
(319)368-6675
Fax: (319)363-9515

InvestAmerica Investment Advisors, Inc.
101 2nd St. SE, Ste. 800
Cedar Rapids, IA 52401
(319)363-8249
Fax: (319)363-9683

Pappajohn Capital Resources
2116 Financial Center
Des Moines, IA 50309
(515)244-5746
Fax: (515)244-2346
Website: http://www.pappajohn.com

Berthel Fisher & Company Planning Inc.
701 Tama St.
PO Box 609
Marion, IA 52302
(319)497-5700
Fax: (319)497-4244

Kansas

Enterprise Merchant Bank
7400 West 110th St., Ste. 560
Overland Park, KS 66210
(913)327-8500
Fax: (913)327-8505

Kansas Venture Capital, Inc. (Overland Park)
6700 Antioch Plz., Ste. 460
Overland Park, KS 66204
(913)262-7117
Fax: (913)262-3509
E-mail: jdalton@kvci.com

Child Health Investment Corp.
6803 W 64th St., Ste. 208
Shawnee Mission, KS 66202
(913)262-1436
Fax: (913)262-1575
Website: http://www.chca.com

Kansas Technology Enterprise Corp.
214 SW 6th, 1st Fl.
Topeka, KS 66603-3719

(785)296-5272
Fax: (785)296-1160
E-mail: ktec@ktec.com
Website: http://www.ktec.com

Kentucky

**Kentucky Highlands
Investment Corp.**
362 Old Whitley Rd.
London, KY 40741
(606)864-5175
Fax: (606)864-5194
Website: http://www.khic.org

Chrysalis Ventures, L.L.C.
1850 National City Tower
Louisville, KY 40202
(502)583-7644
Fax: (502)583-7648
E-mail: bobsany@chrysalisventures.com
Website: http://www.chrysalis
ventures.com

Humana Venture Capital
500 West Main St.
Louisville, KY 40202
(502)580-3922
Fax: (502)580-2051
E-mail: gemont@humana.com
George Emont, Director

Summit Capital Group, Inc.
6510 Glenridge Park Pl., Ste. 8
Louisville, KY 40222
(502)332-2700

Louisiana

Bank One Equity Investors, Inc.
451 Florida St.
Baton Rouge, LA 70801
(504)332-4421
Fax: (504)332-7377

Advantage Capital Partners
LLE Tower
909 Poydras St., Ste. 2230
New Orleans, LA 70112
(504)522-4850
Fax: (504)522-4950
Website: http://www.advantagecap.com

Maine

CEI Ventures / Coastal Ventures LP
2 Portland Fish Pier, Ste. 201
Portland, ME 04101
(207)772-5356
Fax: (207)772-5503
Website: http://www.ceiventures.com

Commwealth Bioventures, Inc.
4 Milk St.
Portland, ME 04101
(207)780-0904
Fax: (207)780-0913

Maryland

Annapolis Ventures LLC
151 West St., Ste. 302
Annapolis, MD 21401
(443)482-9555
Fax: (443)482-9565
Website: http://www.annapolisventures
.com

Delmag Ventures
220 Wardour Dr.
Annapolis, MD 21401
(410)267-8196
Fax: (410)267-8017
Website: http://
www.delmagventures.com

Abell Venture Fund
111 S Calvert St., Ste. 2300
Baltimore, MD 21202
(410)547-1300
Fax: (410)539-6579
Website: http://www.abell.org

ABS Ventures (Baltimore)
1 South St., Ste. 2150
Baltimore, MD 21202
(410)895-3895
Fax: (410)895-3899
Website: http://www.absventures.com

Anthem Capital, L.P.
16 S Calvert St., Ste. 800
Baltimore, MD 21202-1305
(410)625-1510
Fax: (410)625-1735
Website: http://www.anthemcapital.com

Catalyst Ventures
1119 St. Paul St.
Baltimore, MD 21202
(410)244-0123
Fax: (410)752-7721

Maryland Venture Capital Trust
217 E Redwood St., Ste. 2200
Baltimore, MD 21202
(410)767-6361
Fax: (410)333-6931

New Enterprise Associates (Baltimore)
1119 St. Paul St.
Baltimore, MD 21202
(410)244-0115
Fax: (410)752-7721
Website: http://www.nea.com

T. Rowe Price Threshold Partnerships
100 E Pratt St., 8th Fl.
Baltimore, MD 21202
(410)345-2000
Fax: (410)345-2800

Spring Capital Partners
16 W Madison St.
Baltimore, MD 21201
(410)685-8000
Fax: (410)727-1436
E-mail: mailbox@springcap.com

Arete Corporation
3 Bethesda Metro Ctr., Ste. 770
Bethesda, MD 20814
(301)657-6268
Fax: (301)657-6254
Website: http://www.arete-microgen.com

Embryon Capital
7903 Sleaford Place
Bethesda, MD 20814
(301)656-6837
Fax: (301)656-8056

Potomac Ventures
7920 Norfolk Ave., Ste. 1100
Bethesda, MD 20814
(301)215-9240
Website: http://www.potomac
ventures.com

Toucan Capital Corp.
3 Bethesda Metro Center, Ste. 700
Bethesda, MD 20814
(301)961-1970
Fax: (301)961-1969
Website: http://www.toucancapital.com

Kinetic Ventures LLC
2 Wisconsin Cir., Ste. 620
Chevy Chase, MD 20815
(301)652-8066
Fax: (301)652-8310
Website: http://www.kineticventures
.com

Boulder Ventures Ltd.
4750 Owings Mills Blvd.
Owings Mills, MD 21117
(410)998-3114
Fax: (410)356-5492
Website: http://www.boulderventures
.com

Grotech Capital Group
9690 Deereco Rd., Ste. 800
Timonium, MD 21093
(410)560-2000
Fax: (410)560-1910
Website: http://www.grotech.com

Massachusetts

Adams, Harkness & Hill, Inc.
60 State St.
Boston, MA 02109
(617)371-3900

Advent International
75 State St., 29th Fl.
Boston, MA 02109
(617)951-9400
Fax: (617)951-0566
Website: http://www.adventinternational.com

American Research and Development
30 Federal St.
Boston, MA 02110-2508
(617)423-7500
Fax: (617)423-9655

Ascent Venture Partners
255 State St., 5th Fl.
Boston, MA 02109
(617)270-9400
Fax: (617)270-9401
E-mail: info@ascentvp.com
Website: http://www.ascentvp.com

Atlas Venture
222 Berkeley St.
Boston, MA 02116
(617)488-2200
Fax: (617)859-9292
Website: http://www.atlasventure.com

Axxon Capital
28 State St., 37th Fl.
Boston, MA 02109
(617)722-0980
Fax: (617)557-6014
Website: http://www.axxoncapital.com

BancBoston Capital/BancBoston Ventures
175 Federal St., 10th Fl.
Boston, MA 02110
(617)434-2509
Fax: (617)434-6175
Website: http://www.bancboston
capital.com

Boston Capital Ventures
Old City Hall
45 School St.
Boston, MA 02108
(617)227-6550
Fax: (617)227-3847
E-mail: info@bcv.com
Website: http://www.bcv.com

Boston Financial & Equity Corp.
20 Overland St.
PO Box 15071

Boston, MA 02215
(617)267-2900
Fax: (617)437-7601
E-mail: debbie@bfec.com

Boston Millennia Partners
30 Rowes Wharf
Boston, MA 02110
(617)428-5150
Fax: (617)428-5160
Website: http://www.millennia
partners.com

Bristol Investment Trust
842A Beacon St.
Boston, MA 02215-3199
(617)566-5212
Fax: (617)267-0932

Brook Venture Management LLC
50 Federal St., 5th Fl.
Boston, MA 02110
(617)451-8989
Fax: (617)451-2369
Website: http://www.brookventure.com

Burr, Egan, Deleage, and Co. (Boston)
200 Clarendon St., Ste. 3800
Boston, MA 02116
(617)262-7770
Fax: (617)262-9779

Cambridge/Samsung Partners
One Exeter Plaza
Ninth Fl.
Boston, MA 02116
(617)262-4440
Fax: (617)262-5562

Chestnut Street Partners, Inc.
75 State St., Ste. 2500
Boston, MA 02109
(617)345-7220
Fax: (617)345-7201
E-mail: chestnut@chestnutp.com

Claflin Capital Management, Inc.
10 Liberty Sq., Ste. 300
Boston, MA 02109
(617)426-6505
Fax: (617)482-0016
Website: http://www.claflincapital.com

Copley Venture Partners
99 Summer St., Ste. 1720
Boston, MA 02110
(617)737-1253
Fax: (617)439-0699

Corning Capital / Corning Technology Ventures
121 High Street, Ste. 400
Boston, MA 02110

(617)338-2656
Fax: (617)261-3864
Website: http://www.corningventures
.com

Downer & Co.
211 Congress St.
Boston, MA 02110
(617)482-6200
Fax: (617)482-6201
E-mail: cdowner@downer.com
Website: http://www.downer.com

Fidelity Ventures
82 Devonshire St.
Boston, MA 02109
(617)563-6370
Fax: (617)476-9023
Website: http://www.fidelityventures
.com

Greylock Management Corp. (Boston)
1 Federal St.
Boston, MA 02110-2065
(617)423-5525
Fax: (617)482-0059

Gryphon Ventures
222 Berkeley St., Ste.1600
Boston, MA 02116
(617)267-9191
Fax: (617)267-4293
E-mail: all@gryphoninc.com

Halpern, Denny & Co.
500 Boylston St.
Boston, MA 02116
(617)536-6602
Fax: (617)536-8535

Harbourvest Partners, LLC
1 Financial Center, 44th Fl.
Boston, MA 02111
(617)348-3707
Fax: (617)350-0305
Website: http://www.hvpllc.com

Highland Capital Partners
2 International Pl.
Boston, MA 02110
(617)981-1500
Fax: (617)531-1550
E-mail: info@hcp.com
Website: http://www.hcp.com

Lee Munder Venture Partners
John Hancock Tower T-53
200 Clarendon St.
Boston, MA 02103
(617)380-5600
Fax: (617)380-5601
Website: http://www.leemunder.com

M/C Venture Partners
75 State St., Ste. 2500
Boston, MA 02109
(617)345-7200
Fax: (617)345-7201
Website: http://www.mcventure
partners.com

Massachusetts Capital Resources Co.
420 Boylston St.
Boston, MA 02116
(617)536-3900
Fax: (617)536-7930

**Massachusetts Technology
Development Corp. (MTDC)**
148 State St.
Boston, MA 02109
(617)723-4920
Fax: (617)723-5983
E-mail: jhodgman@mtdc.com
Website: http://www.mtdc.com

New England Partners
One Boston Place, Ste. 2100
Boston, MA 02108
(617)624-8400
Fax: (617)624-8999
Website: http://www.nepartners.com

North Hill Ventures
Ten Post Office Square
11th Fl.
Boston, MA 02109
(617)788-2112
Fax: (617)788-2152
Website: http://www.northhill
ventures.com

OneLiberty Ventures
150 Cambridge Park Dr.
Boston, MA 02140
(617)492-7280
Fax: (617)492-7290
Website: http://www.oneliberty.com

Schroder Ventures
Life Sciences
60 State St., Ste. 3650
Boston, MA 02109
(617)367-8100
Fax: (617)367-1590
Website: http://www.shroder
ventures.com

Shawmut Capital Partners
75 Federal St., 18th Fl.
Boston, MA 02110
(617)368-4900
Fax: (617)368-4910
Website: http://www.shawmut
capital.com

Solstice Capital LLC
15 Broad St., 3rd Fl.
Boston, MA 02109
(617)523-7733
Fax: (617)523-5827
E-mail: solticecapital@solcap.com

Spectrum Equity Investors
One International Pl., 29th Fl.
Boston, MA 02110
(617)464-4600
Fax: (617)464-4601
Website: http://www.spectrumequity.com

Spray Venture Partners
One Walnut St.
Boston, MA 02108
(617)305-4140
Fax: (617)305-4144
Website: http://www.sprayventure.com

The Still River Fund
100 Federal St., 29th Fl.
Boston, MA 02110
(617)348-2327
Fax: (617)348-2371
Website: http://www.stillriverfund.com

Summit Partners
600 Atlantic Ave., Ste. 2800
Boston, MA 02210-2227
(617)824-1000
Fax: (617)824-1159
Website: http://www.summitpartners.com

TA Associates, Inc. (Boston)
High Street Tower
125 High St., Ste. 2500
Boston, MA 02110
(617)574-6700
Fax: (617)574-6728
Website: http://www.ta.com

TVM Techno Venture Management
101 Arch St., Ste. 1950
Boston, MA 02110
(617)345-9320
Fax: (617)345-9377
E-mail: info@tvmvc.com
Website: http://www.tvmvc.com

UNC Ventures
64 Burough St.
Boston, MA 02130-4017
(617)482-7070
Fax: (617)522-2176

**Venture Investment Management
Company (VIMAC)**
177 Milk St.
Boston, MA 02190-3410
(617)292-3300

Fax: (617)292-7979
E-mail: bzeisig@vimac.com
Website: http://www.vimac.com

MDT Advisers, Inc.
125 Cambridge Park Dr.
Cambridge, MA 02140-2314
(617)234-2200
Fax: (617)234-2210
Website: http://www.mdtai.com

TTC Ventures
One Main St., 6th Fl.
Cambridge, MA 02142
(617)528-3137
Fax: (617)577-1715
E-mail: info@ttcventures.com

Zero Stage Capital Co. Inc.
101 Main St., 17th Fl.
Cambridge, MA 02142
(617)876-5355
Fax: (617)876-1248
Website: http://www.zerostage.com

Atlantic Capital
164 Cushing Hwy.
Cohasset, MA 02025
(617)383-9449
Fax: (617)383-6040
E-mail: info@atlanticcap.com
Website: http://www.atlanticcap.com

Seacoast Capital Partners
55 Ferncroft Rd.
Danvers, MA 01923
(978)750-1300
Fax: (978)750-1301
E-mail: gdeli@seacoastcapital.com
Website: http://www.seacoastcapital.com

Sage Management Group
44 South Street
PO Box 2026
East Dennis, MA 02641
(508)385-7172
Fax: (508)385-7272
E-mail: sagemgt@capecod.net

Applied Technology
1 Cranberry Hill
Lexington, MA 02421-7397
(617)862-8622
Fax: (617)862-8367

Royalty Capital Management
5 Downing Rd.
Lexington, MA 02421-6918
(781)861-8490

Argo Global Capital
210 Broadway, Ste. 101
Lynnfield, MA 01940

(781)592-5250
Fax: (781)592-5230
Website: http://www.gsmcapital.com

Industry Ventures
6 Bayne Lane
Newburyport, MA 01950
(978)499-7606
Fax: (978)499-0686
Website: http://www.industryventures.com

Softbank Capital Partners
10 Langley Rd., Ste. 202
Newton Center, MA 02459
(617)928-9300
Fax: (617)928-9305
E-mail: clax@bvc.com

Advanced Technology Ventures (Boston)
281 Winter St., Ste. 350
Waltham, MA 02451
(781)290-0707
Fax: (781)684-0045
E-mail: info@atvcapital.com
Website: http://www.atvcapital.com

Castile Ventures
890 Winter St., Ste. 140
Waltham, MA 02451
(781)890-0060
Fax: (781)890-0065
Website: http://www.castileventures.com

Charles River Ventures
1000 Winter St., Ste. 3300
Waltham, MA 02451
(781)487-7060
Fax: (781)487-7065
Website: http://www.crv.com

Comdisco Venture Group (Waltham)
Totton Pond Office Center
400-1 Totten Pond Rd.
Waltham, MA 02451
(617)672-0250
Fax: (617)398-8099

Marconi Ventures
890 Winter St., Ste. 310
Waltham, MA 02451
(781)839-7177
Fax: (781)522-7477
Website: http://www.marconi.com

Matrix Partners
Bay Colony Corporate Center
1000 Winter St., Ste.4500
Waltham, MA 02451
(781)890-2244
Fax: (781)890-2288
Website: http://www.matrixpartners.com

North Bridge Venture Partners
950 Winter St. Ste. 4600
Waltham, MA 02451
(781)290-0004
Fax: (781)290-0999
E-mail: eta@nbvp.com

Polaris Venture Partners
Bay Colony Corporate Ctr.
1000 Winter St., Ste. 3500
Waltham, MA 02451
(781)290-0770
Fax: (781)290-0880
E-mail: partners@polarisventures.com
Website: http://www.polarisventures
.com

Seaflower Ventures
Bay Colony Corporate Ctr.
1000 Winter St. Ste. 1000
Waltham, MA 02451
(781)466-9552
Fax: (781)466-9553
E-mail: moot@seaflower.com
Website: http://www.seaflower.com

Ampersand Ventures
55 William St., Ste. 240
Wellesley, MA 02481
(617)239-0700
Fax: (617)239-0824
E-mail: info@ampersandventures.com
Website: http://www.ampersand
ventures.com

Battery Ventures (Boston)
20 William St., Ste. 200
Wellesley, MA 02481
(781)577-1000
Fax: (781)577-1001
Website: http://www.battery.com

Commonwealth Capital Ventures, L.P.
20 William St., Ste.225
Wellesley, MA 02481
(781)237-7373
Fax: (781)235-8627
Website: http://www.ccvlp.com

Fowler, Anthony & Company
20 Walnut St.
Wellesley, MA 02481
(781)237-4201
Fax: (781)237-7718

Gemini Investors
20 William St.
Wellesley, MA 02481
(781)237-7001
Fax: (781)237-7233

Grove Street Advisors Inc.
20 William St., Ste. 230
Wellesley, MA 02481
(781)263-6100
Fax: (781)263-6101
Website: http://www.grovestreetadvisors
.com

Mees Pierson Investeringsmaat B.V.
20 William St., Ste. 210
Wellesley, MA 02482
(781)239-7600
Fax: (781)239-0377

Norwest Equity Partners
40 William St., Ste. 305
Wellesley, MA 02481-3902
(781)237-5870
Fax: (781)237-6270
Website: http://www.norwestvp.com

Bessemer Venture Partners (Wellesley Hills)
83 Walnut St.
Wellesley Hills, MA 02481
(781)237-6050
Fax: (781)235-7576
E-mail: travis@bvpny.com
Website: http://www.bvp.com

Venture Capital Fund of New England
20 Walnut St., Ste. 120
Wellesley Hills, MA 02481-2175
(781)239-8262
Fax: (781)239-8263

Prism Venture Partners
100 Lowder Brook Dr., Ste. 2500
Westwood, MA 02090
(781)302-4000
Fax: (781)302-4040
E-mail: dwbaum@prismventure.com

Palmer Partners LP
200 Unicorn Park Dr.
Woburn, MA 01801
(781)933-5445
Fax: (781)933-0698

Michigan

Arbor Partners, L.L.C.
130 South First St.
Ann Arbor, MI 48104
(734)668-9000
Fax: (734)669-4195
Website: http://www.arborpartners.com

EDF Ventures
425 N. Main St.
Ann Arbor, MI 48104
(734)663-3213
Fax: (734)663-7358

E-mail: edf@edfvc.com
Website: http://www.edfvc.com

White Pines Management, L.L.C.
2401 Plymouth Rd., Ste. B
Ann Arbor, MI 48105
(734)747-9401
Fax: (734)747-9704
E-mail: ibund@whitepines.com
Website: http://www.whitepines.com

Wellmax, Inc.
3541 Bendway Blvd., Ste. 100
Bloomfield Hills, MI 48301
(248)646-3554
Fax: (248)646-6220

Venture Funding, Ltd.
Fisher Bldg.
3011 West Grand Blvd., Ste. 321
Detroit, MI 48202
(313)871-3606
Fax: (313)873-4935

Investcare Partners L.P. / GMA Capital LLC
32330 W Twelve Mile Rd.
Farmington Hills, MI 48334
(248)489-9000
Fax: (248)489-8819
E-mail: gma@gmacapital.com
Website: http://www.gmacapital.com

Liberty Bidco Investment Corp.
30833 Northwestern Highway, Ste. 211
Farmington Hills, MI 48334
(248)626-6070
Fax: (248)626-6072

Seaflower Ventures
5170 Nicholson Rd.
PO Box 474
Fowlerville, MI 48836
(517)223-3335
Fax: (517)223-3337
E-mail: gibbons@seaflower.com
Website: http://www.seaflower.com

Ralph Wilson Equity Fund LLC
15400 E Jefferson Ave.
Gross Pointe Park, MI 48230
(313)821-9122
Fax: (313)821-9101
Website: http://www.RalphWilson
EquityFund.com
J. Skip Simms, President

Minnesota

Development Corp. of Austin
1900 Eighth Ave., NW
Austin, MN 55912
(507)433-0346

Fax: (507)433-0361
E-mail: dca@smig.net
Website: http://www.spamtownusa.com

Northeast Ventures Corp.
802 Alworth Bldg.
Duluth, MN 55802
(218)722-9915
Fax: (218)722-9871

Medical Innovation Partners, Inc.
6450 City West Pkwy.
Eden Prairie, MN 55344-3245
(612)828-9616
Fax: (612)828-9596

St. Paul Venture Capital, Inc.
10400 Vicking Dr., Ste. 550
Eden Prairie, MN 55344
(612)995-7474
Fax: (612)995-7475
Website: http://www.stpaulvc.com

Cherry Tree Investments, Inc.
7601 France Ave. S, Ste. 150
Edina, MN 55435
(612)893-9012
Fax: (612)893-9036
Website: http://www.cherrytree.com

Shared Ventures, Inc.
6550 York Ave. S
Edina, MN 55435
(612)925-3411

Sherpa Partners LLC
5050 Lincoln Dr., Ste. 490
Edina, MN 55436
(952)942-1070
Fax: (952)942-1071
Website: http://www.sherpapartners.com

Affinity Capital Management
901 Marquette Ave., Ste. 1810
Minneapolis, MN 55402
(612)252-9900
Fax: (612)252-9911
Website: http://www.affinitycapital.com

Artesian Capital
1700 Foshay Tower
821 Marquette Ave.
Minneapolis, MN 55402
(612)334-5600
Fax: (612)334-5601
E-mail: artesian@artesian.com

Coral Ventures
60 S 6th St., Ste. 3510
Minneapolis, MN 55402
(612)335-8666
Fax: (612)335-8668
Website: http://www.coralventures.com

Crescendo Venture Management, L.L.C.
800 LaSalle Ave., Ste. 2250
Minneapolis, MN 55402
(612)607-2800
Fax: (612)607-2801
Website: http://www.crescendo
ventures.com

Gideon Hixon Venture
1900 Foshay Tower
821 Marquette Ave.
Minneapolis, MN 55402
(612)904-2314
Fax: (612)204-0913

Norwest Equity Partners
3600 IDS Center
80 S 8th St.
Minneapolis, MN 55402
(612)215-1600
Fax: (612)215-1601
Website: http://www.norwestvp.com

Oak Investment Partners (Minneapolis)
4550 Norwest Center
90 S 7th St.
Minneapolis, MN 55402
(612)339-9322
Fax: (612)337-8017
Website: http://www.oakinv.com

Pathfinder Venture Capital Funds (Minneapolis)
7300 Metro Blvd., Ste. 585
Minneapolis, MN 55439
(612)835-1121
Fax: (612)835-8389
E-mail: jahrens620@aol.com

U.S. Bancorp Piper Jaffray Ventures, Inc.
800 Nicollet Mall, Ste. 800
Minneapolis, MN 55402
(612)303-5686
Fax: (612)303-1350
Website: http://www.paperjaffrey
ventures.com

The Food Fund, Ltd. Partnership
5720 Smatana Dr., Ste. 300
Minnetonka, MN 55343
(612)939-3950
Fax: (612)939-8106

Mayo Medical Ventures
200 First St. SW
Rochester, MN 55905
(507)266-4586
Fax: (507)284-5410
Website: http://www.mayo.edu

Missouri

Bankers Capital Corp.
3100 Gillham Rd.
Kansas City, MO 64109
(816)531-1600
Fax: (816)531-1334

Capital for Business, Inc. (Kansas City)
1000 Walnut St., 18th Fl.
Kansas City, MO 64106
(816)234-2357
Fax: (816)234-2952
Website: http://www.capitalfor
business.com

De Vries & Co. Inc.
800 West 47th St.
Kansas City, MO 64112
(816)756-0055
Fax: (816)756-0061

InvestAmerica Venture Group Inc. (Kansas City)
Commerce Tower
911 Main St., Ste. 2424
Kansas City, MO 64105
(816)842-0114
Fax: (816)471-7339

Kansas City Equity Partners
233 W 47th St.
Kansas City, MO 64112
(816)960-1771
Fax: (816)960-1777
Website: http://www.kcep.com

Bome Investors, Inc.
8000 Maryland Ave., Ste. 1190
Saint Louis, MO 63105
(314)721-5707
Fax: (314)721-5135
Website: http://www.gatewayventures
.com

Capital for Business, Inc. (Saint Louis)
11 S Meramac St., Ste. 1430
Saint Louis, MO 63105
(314)746-7427
Fax: (314)746-8739
Website: http://www.capitalforbusiness
.com

Crown Capital Corp.
540 Maryville Centre Dr., Ste. 120
Saint Louis, MO 63141
(314)576-1201
Fax: (314)576-1525
Website: http://www.crown-cap.com

Gateway Associates L.P.
8000 Maryland Ave., Ste. 1190
Saint Louis, MO 63105

(314)721-5707
Fax: (314)721-5135

Harbison Corp.
8112 Maryland Ave., Ste. 250
Saint Louis, MO 63105
(314)727-8200
Fax: (314)727-0249

Nebraska

Heartland Capital Fund, Ltd.
PO Box 642117
Omaha, NE 68154
(402)778-5124
Fax: (402)445-2370
Website: http://
www.heartlandcapitalfund.com

Odin Capital Group
1625 Farnam St., Ste. 700
Omaha, NE 68102
(402)346-6200
Fax: (402)342-9311
Website: http://www.odincapital.com

Nevada

Edge Capital Investment Co. LLC
1350 E Flamingo Rd., Ste. 3000
Las Vegas, NV 89119
(702)438-3343
E-mail: info@edgecapital.net
Website: http://www.edgecapital.net

The Benefit Capital Companies Inc.
PO Box 542
Logandale, NV 89021
(702)398-3222
Fax: (702)398-3700

Millennium Three Venture Group LLC
6880 South McCarran Blvd., Ste. A-11
Reno, NV 89509
(775)954-2020
Fax: (775)954-2023
Website: http://www.m3vg.com

New Jersey

Alan I. Goldman & Associates
497 Ridgewood Ave.
Glen Ridge, NJ 07028
(973)857-5680
Fax: (973)509-8856

CS Capital Partners LLC
328 Second St., Ste. 200
Lakewood, NJ 08701
(732)901-1111
Fax: (212)202-5071
Website: http://www.cs-capital.com

Edison Venture Fund
1009 Lenox Dr., Ste. 4
Lawrenceville, NJ 08648
(609)896-1900
Fax: (609)896-0066
E-mail: info@edisonventure.com
Website: http://www.edisonventure.com

Tappan Zee Capital Corp. (New Jersey)
201 Lower Notch Rd.
PO Box 416
Little Falls, NJ 07424
(973)256-8280
Fax: (973)256-2841

The CIT Group/Venture Capital, Inc.
650 CIT Dr.
Livingston, NJ 07039
(973)740-5429
Fax: (973)740-5555
Website: http://www.cit.com

Capital Express, L.L.C.
1100 Valleybrook Ave.
Lyndhurst, NJ 07071
(201)438-8228
Fax: (201)438-5131
E-mail: niles@capitalexpress.com
Website: http://www.capitalexpress.com

Westford Technology Ventures, L.P.
17 Academy St.
Newark, NJ 07102
(973)624-2131
Fax: (973)624-2008

Accel Partners
1 Palmer Sq.
Princeton, NJ 08542
(609)683-4500
Fax: (609)683-4880
Website: http://www.accel.com

Cardinal Partners
221 Nassau St.
Princeton, NJ 08542
(609)924-6452
Fax: (609)683-0174
Website: http://www.cardinalhealth
partners.com

Domain Associates L.L.C.
One Palmer Sq., Ste. 515
Princeton, NJ 08542
(609)683-5656
Fax: (609)683-9789
Website: http://www.domainvc.com

Johnston Associates, Inc.
181 Cherry Valley Rd.
Princeton, NJ 08540
(609)924-3131

Fax: (609)683-7524
E-mail: jaincorp@aol.com

Kemper Ventures
Princeton Forrestal Village
155 Village Blvd.
Princeton, NJ 08540
(609)936-3035
Fax: (609)936-3051

Penny Lane Parnters
One Palmer Sq., Ste. 309
Princeton, NJ 08542
(609)497-4646
Fax: (609)497-0611

Early Stage Enterprises L.P.
995 Route 518
Skillman, NJ 08558
(609)921-8896
Fax: (609)921-8703
Website: http://www.esevc.com

MBW Management Inc.
1 Springfield Ave.
Summit, NJ 07901
(908)273-4060
Fax: (908)273-4430

BCI Advisors, Inc.
Glenpointe Center W.
Teaneck, NJ 07666
(201)836-3900
Fax: (201)836-6368
E-mail: info@bciadvisors.com
Website: http://www.bcipartners.com

**Demuth, Folger & Wetherill / DFW
Capital Partners**
Glenpointe Center E., 5th Fl.
300 Frank W. Burr Blvd.
Teaneck, NJ 07666
(201)836-2233
Fax: (201)836-5666
Website: http://www.dfwcapital.com

First Princeton Capital Corp.
189 Berdan Ave., No. 131
Wayne, NJ 07470-3233
(973)278-3233
Fax: (973)278-4290
Website: http://www.lytellcatt.net

**Edelson Technology
Partners**
300 Tice Blvd.
Woodcliff Lake, NJ 07675
(201)930-9898
Fax: (201)930-8899
Website: http://www.edelsontech.com

New Mexico

Bruce F. Glaspell & Associates
10400 Academy Rd. NE, Ste. 313
Albuquerque, NM 87111
(505)292-4505
Fax: (505)292-4258

High Desert Ventures, Inc.
6101 Imparata St. NE, Ste. 1721
Albuquerque, NM 87111
(505)797-3330
Fax: (505)338-5147

**New Business Capital
Fund, Ltd.**
5805 Torreon NE
Albuquerque, NM 87109
(505)822-8445

SBC Ventures
10400 Academy Rd. NE, Ste. 313
Albuquerque, NM 87111
(505)292-4505
Fax: (505)292-4528

Technology Ventures Corp.
1155 University Blvd. SE
Albuquerque, NM 87106
(505)246-2882
Fax: (505)246-2891

New York

**Small Business Technology
Investment Fund**
99 Washington Ave., Ste. 1731
Albany, NY 12210
(518)473-9741
Fax: (518)473-6876

Rand Capital Corp.
2200 Rand Bldg.
Buffalo, NY 14203
(716)853-0802
Fax: (716)854-8480
Website: http://www.randcapital.com

Seed Capital Partners
620 Main St.
Buffalo, NY 14202
(716)845-7520
Fax: (716)845-7539
Website: http://www.seedcp.com

Coleman Venture Group
5909 Northern Blvd.
PO Box 224
East Norwich, NY 11732
(516)626-3642
Fax: (516)626-9722

Vega Capital Corp.
45 Knollwood Rd.
Elmsford, NY 10523
(914)345-9500
Fax: (914)345-9505

Herbert Young Securities, Inc.
98 Cuttermill Rd.
Great Neck, NY 11021
(516)487-8300
Fax: (516)487-8319

Sterling/Carl Marks Capital, Inc.
175 Great Neck Rd., Ste. 408
Great Neck, NY 11021
(516)482-7374
Fax: (516)487-0781
E-mail: stercrlmar@aol.com
Website: http://www.serlingcarlmarks.com

Impex Venture Management Co.
PO Box 1570
Green Island, NY 12183
(518)271-8008
Fax: (518)271-9101

Corporate Venture Partners L.P.
200 Sunset Park
Ithaca, NY 14850
(607)257-6323
Fax: (607)257-6128

Arthur P. Gould & Co.
One Wilshire Dr.
Lake Success, NY 11020
(516)773-3000
Fax: (516)773-3289

Dauphin Capital Partners
108 Forest Ave.
Locust Valley, NY 11560
(516)759-3339
Fax: (516)759-3322
Website: http://www.dauphincapital.com

550 Digital Media Ventures
555 Madison Ave., 10th Fl.
New York, NY 10022
Website: http://www.550dmv.com

Aberlyn Capital Management Co., Inc.
500 Fifth Ave.
New York, NY 10110
(212)391-7750
Fax: (212)391-7762

Adler & Company
342 Madison Ave., Ste. 807
New York, NY 10173
(212)599-2535
Fax: (212)599-2526

Alimansky Capital Group, Inc.
605 Madison Ave., Ste. 300
New York, NY 10022-1901
(212)832-7300
Fax: (212)832-7338

Allegra Partners
515 Madison Ave., 29th Fl.
New York, NY 10022
(212)826-9080
Fax: (212)759-2561

The Argentum Group
The Chyrsler Bldg.
405 Lexington Ave.
New York, NY 10174
(212)949-6262
Fax: (212)949-8294
Website: http://www.argentumgroup.com

Axavision Inc.
14 Wall St., 26th Fl.
New York, NY 10005
(212)619-4000
Fax: (212)619-7202

Bedford Capital Corp.
18 East 48th St., Ste. 1800
New York, NY 10017
(212)688-5700
Fax: (212)754-4699
E-mail: info@bedfordnyc.com
Website: http://www.bedfordnyc.com

Bloom & Co.
950 Third Ave.
New York, NY 10022
(212)838-1858
Fax: (212)838-1843

Bristol Capital Management
300 Park Ave., 17th Fl.
New York, NY 10022
(212)572-6306
Fax: (212)705-4292

Citicorp Venture Capital Ltd.
(New York City)
399 Park Ave., 14th Fl.
Zone 4
New York, NY 10043
(212)559-1127
Fax: (212)888-2940

CM Equity Partners
135 E 57th St.
New York, NY 10022
(212)909-8428
Fax: (212)980-2630

Cohen & Co., L.L.C.
800 Third Ave.
New York, NY 10022

(212)317-2250
Fax: (212)317-2255
E-mail: nlcohen@aol.com

**Cornerstone Equity
Investors, L.L.C.**
717 5th Ave., Ste. 1100
New York, NY 10022
(212)753-0901
Fax: (212)826-6798
Website: http://www.cornerstone-equity.com

CW Group, Inc.
1041 3rd Ave., 2nd fl.
New York, NY 10021
(212)308-5266
Fax: (212)644-0354
Website: http://www.cwventures.com

DH Blair Investment Banking Corp.
44 Wall St., 2nd Fl.
New York, NY 10005
(212)495-5000
Fax: (212)269-1438

Dresdner Kleinwort Capital
75 Wall St.
New York, NY 10005
(212)429-3131
Fax: (212)429-3139
Website: http://www.dresdnerkb.com

East River Ventures, L.P.
645 Madison Ave., 22nd Fl.
New York, NY 10022
(212)644-2322
Fax: (212)644-5498

Easton Hunt Capital Partners
641 Lexington Ave., 21st Fl.
New York, NY 10017
(212)702-0950
Fax: (212)702-0952
Website: http://www.eastoncapital.com

Elk Associates Funding Corp.
747 3rd Ave., Ste. 4C
New York, NY 10017
(212)355-2449
Fax: (212)759-3338

EOS Partners, L.P.
320 Park Ave., 22nd Fl.
New York, NY 10022
(212)832-5800
Fax: (212)832-5815
E-mail: mfirst@eospartners.com
Website: http://www.eospartners.com

Euclid Partners
45 Rockefeller Plaza, Ste. 3240
New York, NY 10111

(212)218-6880
Fax: (212)218-6877
E-mail: graham@euclidpartners.com
Website: http://www.euclidpartners.com

Evergreen Capital Partners, Inc.
150 East 58th St.
New York, NY 10155
(212)813-0758
Fax: (212)813-0754

Exeter Capital L.P.
10 E 53rd St.
New York, NY 10022
(212)872-1172
Fax: (212)872-1198
E-mail: exeter@usa.net

Financial Technology Research Corp.
518 Broadway
Penthouse
New York, NY 10012
(212)625-9100
Fax: (212)431-0300
E-mail: fintek@financier.com

4C Ventures
237 Park Ave., Ste. 801
New York, NY 10017
(212)692-3680
Fax: (212)692-3685
Website: http://www.4cventures.com

Fusient Ventures
99 Park Ave., 20th Fl.
New York, NY 10016
(212)972-8999
Fax: (212)972-9876
E-mail: info@fusient.com
Website: http://www.fusient.com

Generation Capital Partners
551 Fifth Ave., Ste. 3100
New York, NY 10176
(212)450-8507
Fax: (212)450-8550
Website: http://www.genpartners.com

Golub Associates, Inc.
555 Madison Ave.
New York, NY 10022
(212)750-6060
Fax: (212)750-5505

Hambro America Biosciences Inc.
650 Madison Ave., 21st Floor
New York, NY 10022
(212)223-7400
Fax: (212)223-0305

Hanover Capital Corp.
505 Park Ave., 15th Fl.
New York, NY 10022

(212)755-1222
Fax: (212)935-1787

Harvest Partners, Inc.
280 Park Ave., 33rd Fl.
New York, NY 10017
(212)559-6300
Fax: (212)812-0100
Website: http://www.harvpart.com

Holding Capital Group, Inc.
10 E 53rd St., 30th Fl.
New York, NY 10022
(212)486-6670
Fax: (212)486-0843

Hudson Venture Partners
660 Madison Ave., 14th Fl.
New York, NY 10021-8405
(212)644-9797
Fax: (212)644-7430
Website: http://www.hudsonptr.com

IBJS Capital Corp.
1 State St., 9th Fl.
New York, NY 10004
(212)858-2018
Fax: (212)858-2768

InterEquity Capital Partners, L.P.
220 5th Ave.
New York, NY 10001
(212)779-2022
Fax: (212)779-2103
Website: http://www.interequity-capital.com

The Jordan Edmiston Group Inc.
150 East 52nd St., 18th Fl.
New York, NY 10022
(212)754-0710
Fax: (212)754-0337

Josephberg, Grosz and Co., Inc.
633 3rd Ave., 13th Fl.
New York, NY 10017
(212)974-9926
Fax: (212)397-5832

J.P. Morgan Capital Corp.
60 Wall St.
New York, NY 10260-0060
(212)648-9000
Fax: (212)648-5002
Website: http://www.jpmorgan.com

The Lambda Funds
380 Lexington Ave., 54th Fl.
New York, NY 10168
(212)682-3454
Fax: (212)682-9231

Lepercq Capital Management Inc.
1675 Broadway
New York, NY 10019
(212)698-0795
Fax: (212)262-0155

Loeb Partners Corp.
61 Broadway, Ste. 2400
New York, NY 10006
(212)483-7000
Fax: (212)574-2001

Madison Investment Partners
660 Madison Ave.
New York, NY 10021
(212)223-2600
Fax: (212)223-8208

MC Capital Inc.
520 Madison Ave., 16th Fl.
New York, NY 10022
(212)644-0841
Fax: (212)644-2926

McCown, De Leeuw and Co. (New York)
65 E 55th St., 36th Fl.
New York, NY 10022
(212)355-5500
Fax: (212)355-6283
Website: http://www.mdcpartners.com

Morgan Stanley Venture Partners
1221 Avenue of the Americas, 33rd Fl.
New York, NY 10020
(212)762-7900
Fax: (212)762-8424
E-mail: msventures@ms.com
Website: http://www.msvp.com

Nazem and Co.
645 Madison Ave., 12th Fl.
New York, NY 10022
(212)371-7900
Fax: (212)371-2150

Needham Capital Management, L.L.C.
445 Park Ave.
New York, NY 10022
(212)371-8300
Fax: (212)705-0299
Website: http://www.needhamco.com

Norwood Venture Corp.
1430 Broadway, Ste. 1607
New York, NY 10018
(212)869-5075
Fax: (212)869-5331
E-mail: nvc@mail.idt.net
Website: http://www.norven.com

Noveltek Venture Corp.
521 Fifth Ave., Ste. 1700
New York, NY 10175
(212)286-1963

Paribas Principal, Inc.
787 7th Ave.
New York, NY 10019
(212)841-2005
Fax: (212)841-3558

Patricof & Co. Ventures, Inc. (New York)
445 Park Ave.
New York, NY 10022
(212)753-6300
Fax: (212)319-6155
Website: http://www.patricof.com

The Platinum Group, Inc.
350 Fifth Ave, Ste. 7113
New York, NY 10118
(212)736-4300
Fax: (212)736-6086
Website: http://www.platinumgroup.com

Pomona Capital
780 Third Ave., 28th Fl.
New York, NY 10017
(212)593-3639
Fax: (212)593-3987
Website: http://www.pomonacapital.com

Prospect Street Ventures
10 East 40th St., 44th Fl.
New York, NY 10016
(212)448-0702
Fax: (212)448-9652
E-mail: wkohler@prospectstreet.com
Website: http://www.prospectstreet.com

Regent Capital Management
505 Park Ave., Ste. 1700
New York, NY 10022
(212)735-9900
Fax: (212)735-9908

Rothschild Ventures, Inc.
1251 Avenue of the Americas, 51st Fl.
New York, NY 10020
(212)403-3500
Fax: (212)403-3652
Website: http://www.nmrothschild.com

Sandler Capital Management
767 Fifth Ave., 45th Fl.
New York, NY 10153
(212)754-8100
Fax: (212)826-0280

Siguler Guff & Company
630 Fifth Ave., 16th Fl.
New York, NY 10111
(212)332-5100
Fax: (212)332-5120

Spencer Trask Ventures Inc.
535 Madison Ave.
New York, NY 10022

(212)355-5565
Fax: (212)751-3362
Website: http://www.spencertrask.com

Sprout Group (New York City)
277 Park Ave.
New York, NY 10172
(212)892-3600
Fax: (212)892-3444
E-mail: info@sproutgroup.com
Website: http://www.sproutgroup.com

US Trust Private Equity
114 W.47th St.
New York, NY 10036
(212)852-3949
Fax: (212)852-3759
Website: http://www.ustrust.com/
privateequity

Vencon Management Inc.
301 West 53rd St., Ste. 10F
New York, NY 10019
(212)581-8787
Fax: (212)397-4126
Website: http://www.venconinc.com

Venrock Associates
30 Rockefeller Plaza, Ste. 5508
New York, NY 10112
(212)649-5600
Fax: (212)649-5788
Website: http://www.venrock.com

Venture Capital Fund of America, Inc.
509 Madison Ave., Ste. 812
New York, NY 10022
(212)838-5577
Fax: (212)838-7614
E-mail: mail@vcfa.com
Website: http://www.vcfa.com

Venture Opportunities Corp.
150 E 58th St.
New York, NY 10155
(212)832-3737
Fax: (212)980-6603

Warburg Pincus Ventures, Inc.
466 Lexington Ave., 11th Fl.
New York, NY 10017
(212)878-9309
Fax: (212)878-9200
Website: http://www.warburgpincus.com

Wasserstein, Perella & Co. Inc.
31 W 52nd St., 27th Fl.
New York, NY 10019
(212)702-5691
Fax: (212)969-7879

Welsh, Carson, Anderson, & Stowe
320 Park Ave., Ste. 2500
New York, NY 10022-6815

(212)893-9500
Fax: (212)893-9575

Whitney and Co. (New York)
630 Fifth Ave. Ste. 3225
New York, NY 10111
(212)332-2400
Fax: (212)332-2422
Website: http://www.jhwitney.com

Winthrop Ventures
74 Trinity Place, Ste. 600
New York, NY 10006
(212)422-0100

The Pittsford Group
8 Lodge Pole Rd.
Pittsford, NY 14534
(716)223-3523

Genesee Funding
70 Linden Oaks, 3rd Fl.
Rochester, NY 14625
(716)383-5550
Fax: (716)383-5305

Gabelli Multimedia Partners
One Corporate Center
Rye, NY 10580
(914)921-5395
Fax: (914)921-5031

Stamford Financial
108 Main St.
Stamford, NY 12167
(607)652-3311
Fax: (607)652-6301
Website: http://www.stamfordfinancial
.com

Northwood Ventures LLC
485 Underhill Blvd., Ste. 205
Syosset, NY 11791
(516)364-5544
Fax: (516)364-0879
E-mail: northwood@northwood.com
Website: http://www.northwoodventures
.com

Exponential Business Development Co.
216 Walton St.
Syracuse, NY 13202-1227
(315)474-4500
Fax: (315)474-4682
E-mail: dirksonn@aol.com
Website: http://www.exponential-ny.com

Onondaga Venture Capital Fund Inc.
714 State Tower Bldg.
Syracuse, NY 13202
(315)478-0157
Fax: (315)478-0158

Bessemer Venture Partners (Westbury)
1400 Old Country Rd., Ste. 109
Westbury, NY 11590
(516)997-2300
Fax: (516)997-2371
E-mail: bob@bvpny.com
Website: http://www.bvp.com

Ovation Capital Partners
120 Bloomingdale Rd., 4th Fl.
White Plains, NY 10605
(914)258-0011
Fax: (914)684-0848
Website: http://www.ovationcapital.com

North Carolina

Carolinas Capital Investment Corp.
1408 Biltmore Dr.
Charlotte, NC 28207
(704)375-3888
Fax: (704)375-6226

First Union Capital Partners
1st Union Center, 12th Fl.
301 S College St.
Charlotte, NC 28288-0732
(704)383-0000
Fax: (704)374-6711
Website: http://www.fucp.com

Frontier Capital LLC
525 North Tryon St., Ste. 1700
Charlotte, NC 28202
(704)414-2880
Fax: (704)414-2881
Website: http://www.frontierfunds.com

Kitty Hawk Capital
2700 Coltsgate Rd., Ste. 202
Charlotte, NC 28211
(704)362-3909
Fax: (704)362-2774
Website: http://www.kittyhawkcapital
.com

Piedmont Venture Partners
One Morrocroft Centre
6805 Morisson Blvd., Ste. 380
Charlotte, NC 28211
(704)731-5200
Fax: (704)365-9733
Website: http://www.piedmontvp.com

Ruddick Investment Co.
1800 Two First Union Center
Charlotte, NC 28282
(704)372-5404
Fax: (704)372-6409

The Shelton Companies Inc.
3600 One First Union Center
301 S College St.

Charlotte, NC 28202
(704)348-2200
Fax: (704)348-2260

Wakefield Group
1110 E Morehead St.
PO Box 36329
Charlotte, NC 28236
(704)372-0355
Fax: (704)372-8216
Website: http://www.wakefieldgroup.com

Aurora Funds, Inc.
2525 Meridian Pkwy., Ste. 220
Durham, NC 27713
(919)484-0400
Fax: (919)484-0444
Website: http://www.aurorafunds.com

Intersouth Partners
3211 Shannon Rd., Ste. 610
Durham, NC 27707
(919)493-6640
Fax: (919)493-6649
E-mail: info@intersouth.com
Website: http://www.intersouth.com

Geneva Merchant Banking Partners
PO Box 21962
Greensboro, NC 27420
(336)275-7002
Fax: (336)275-9155
Website: http://www.genevamerchant
bank.com

The North Carolina Enterprise Fund, L.P.
3600 Glenwood Ave., Ste. 107
Raleigh, NC 27612
(919)781-2691
Fax: (919)783-9195
Website: http://www.ncef.com

Ohio

Senmend Medical Ventures
4445 Lake Forest Dr., Ste. 600
Cincinnati, OH 45242
(513)563-3264
Fax: (513)563-3261

The Walnut Group
312 Walnut St., Ste. 1151
Cincinnati, OH 45202
(513)651-3300
Fax: (513)929-4441
Website: http://www.thewalnutgroup.com

Brantley Venture Partners
20600 Chagrin Blvd., Ste. 1150
Cleveland, OH 44122
(216)283-4800
Fax: (216)283-5324

Clarion Capital Corp.
1801 E 9th St., Ste. 1120
Cleveland, OH 44114
(216)687-1096
Fax: (216)694-3545

Crystal Internet Venture Fund, L.P.
1120 Chester Ave., Ste. 418
Cleveland, OH 44114
(216)263-5515
Fax: (216)263-5518
E-mail: jf@crystalventure.com
Website: http://www.crystalventure.com

Key Equity Capital Corp.
127 Public Sq., 28th Fl.
Cleveland, OH 44114
(216)689-3000
Fax: (216)689-3204
Website: http://www.keybank.com

Morgenthaler Ventures
Terminal Tower
50 Public Square, Ste. 2700
Cleveland, OH 44113
(216)416-7500
Fax: (216)416-7501
Website: http://www.morgenthaler.com

National City Equity Partners Inc.
1965 E 6th St.
Cleveland, OH 44114
(216)575-2491
Fax: (216)575-9965
E-mail: nccap@aol.com
Website: http://www.nccapital.com

Primus Venture Partners, Inc.
5900 LanderBrook Dr., Ste. 2000
Cleveland, OH 44124-4020
(440)684-7300
Fax: (440)684-7342
E-mail: info@primusventure.com
Website: http://www.primusventure.com

Banc One Capital Partners (Columbus)
150 East Gay St., 24th Fl.
Columbus, OH 43215
(614)217-1100
Fax: (614)217-1217

Battelle Venture Partners
505 King Ave.
Columbus, OH 43201
(614)424-7005
Fax: (614)424-4874

Ohio Partners
62 E Board St., 3rd Fl.
Columbus, OH 43215
(614)621-1210
Fax: (614)621-1240

Capital Technology Group, L.L.C.
400 Metro Place North, Ste. 300
Dublin, OH 43017
(614)792-6066
Fax: (614)792-6036
E-mail: info@capitaltech.com
Website: http://www.capitaltech.com

Northwest Ohio Venture Fund
4159 Holland-Sylvania R., Ste. 202
Toledo, OH 43623
(419)824-8144
Fax: (419)882-2035
E-mail: bwalsh@novf.com

Oklahoma

Moore & Associates
1000 W Wilshire Blvd., Ste. 370
Oklahoma City, OK 73116
(405)842-3660
Fax: (405)842-3763

Chisholm Private Capital Partners
100 West 5th St., Ste. 805
Tulsa, OK 74103
(918)584-0440
Fax: (918)584-0441
Website: http://www.chisholmvc.com

Davis, Tuttle Venture Partners (Tulsa)
320 S Boston, Ste. 1000
Tulsa, OK 74103-3703
(918)584-7272
Fax: (918)582-3404
Website: http://www.davistuttle.com

RBC Ventures
2627 E 21st St.
Tulsa, OK 74114
(918)744-5607
Fax: (918)743-8630

Oregon

Utah Ventures II LP
10700 SW Beaverton-Hillsdale Hwy., Ste. 548
Beaverton, OR 97005
(503)574-4125
E-mail: adishlip@uven.com
Website: http://www.uven.com

Orien Ventures
14523 SW Westlake Dr.
Lake Oswego, OR 97035
(503)699-1680
Fax: (503)699-1681

OVP Venture Partners (Lake Oswego)
340 Oswego Pointe Dr., Ste. 200
Lake Oswego, OR 97034
(503)697-8766

Fax: (503)697-8863
E-mail: info@ovp.com
Website: http://www.ovp.com

Oregon Resource and Technology Development Fund
4370 NE Halsey St., Ste. 233
Portland, OR 97213-1566
(503)282-4462
Fax: (503)282-2976

Shaw Venture Partners
400 SW 6th Ave., Ste. 1100
Portland, OR 97204-1636
(503)228-4884
Fax: (503)227-2471
Website: http://www.shawventures.com

Pennsylvania

Mid-Atlantic Venture Funds
125 Goodman Dr.
Bethlehem, PA 18015
(610)865-6550
Fax: (610)865-6427
Website: http://www.mavf.com

Newspring Ventures
100 W Elm St., Ste. 101
Conshohocken, PA 19428
(610)567-2380
Fax: (610)567-2388
Website: http://www.newsprintventures.com

Patricof & Co. Ventures, Inc.
455 S Gulph Rd., Ste. 410
King of Prussia, PA 19406
(610)265-0286
Fax: (610)265-4959
Website: http://www.patricof.com

Loyalhanna Venture Fund
527 Cedar Way, Ste. 104
Oakmont, PA 15139
(412)820-7035
Fax: (412)820-7036

Innovest Group Inc.
2000 Market St., Ste. 1400
Philadelphia, PA 19103
(215)564-3960
Fax: (215)569-3272

Keystone Venture Capital Management Co.
1601 Market St., Ste. 2500
Philadelphia, PA 19103
(215)241-1200
Fax: (215)241-1211
Website: http://www.keystonevc.com

Liberty Venture Partners
2005 Market St., Ste. 200
Philadelphia, PA 19103
(215)282-4484
Fax: (215)282-4485
E-mail: info@libertyvp.com
Website: http://www.libertyvp.com

Penn Janney Fund, Inc.
1801 Market St., 11th Fl.
Philadelphia, PA 19103
(215)665-4447
Fax: (215)557-0820

Philadelphia Ventures, Inc.
The Bellevue
200 S Broad St.
Philadelphia, PA 19102
(215)732-4445
Fax: (215)732-4644

Birchmere Ventures Inc.
2000 Technology Dr.
Pittsburgh, PA 15219-3109
(412)803-8000
Fax: (412)687-8139
Website: http://www.birchmerevc.com

CEO Venture Fund
2000 Technology Dr., Ste. 160
Pittsburgh, PA 15219-3109
(412)687-3451
Fax: (412)687-8139
E-mail: ceofund@aol.com
Website: http://www.ceoventurefund.com

Innovation Works Inc.
2000 Technology Dr., Ste. 250
Pittsburgh, PA 15219
(412)681-1520
Fax: (412)681-2625
Website: http://www.innovationworks.org

Keystone Minority Capital Fund L.P.
1801 Centre Ave., Ste. 201
Williams Sq.
Pittsburgh, PA 15219
(412)338-2230
Fax: (412)338-2224

Mellon Ventures, Inc.
One Mellon Bank Ctr., Rm. 3500
Pittsburgh, PA 15258
(412)236-3594
Fax: (412)236-3593
Website: http://www.mellonventures.com

Pennsylvania Growth Fund
5850 Ellsworth Ave., Ste. 303
Pittsburgh, PA 15232
(412)661-1000
Fax: (412)361-0676

Point Venture Partners
The Century Bldg.
130 Seventh St., 7th Fl.
Pittsburgh, PA 15222
(412)261-1966
Fax: (412)261-1718

Cross Atlantic Capital Partners
5 Radnor Corporate Center, Ste. 555
Radnor, PA 19087
(610)995-2650
Fax: (610)971-2062
Website: http://www.xacp.com

Meridian Venture Partners (Radnor)
The Radnor Court Bldg., Ste. 140
259 Radnor-Chester Rd.
Radnor, PA 19087
(610)254-2999
Fax: (610)254-2996
E-mail: mvpart@ix.netcom.com

TDH
919 Conestoga Rd., Bldg. 1, Ste. 301
Rosemont, PA 19010
(610)526-9970
Fax: (610)526-9971

Adams Capital Management
500 Blackburn Ave.
Sewickley, PA 15143
(412)749-9454
Fax: (412)749-9459
Website: http://www.acm.com

S.R. One, Ltd.
Four Tower Bridge
200 Barr Harbor Dr., Ste. 250
W Conshohocken, PA 19428
(610)567-1000
Fax: (610)567-1039

Greater Philadelphia Venture Capital Corp.
351 East Conestoga Rd.
Wayne, PA 19087
(610)688-6829
Fax: (610)254-8958

PA Early Stage
435 Devon Park Dr., Bldg. 500, Ste. 510
Wayne, PA 19087
(610)293-4075
Fax: (610)254-4240
Website: http://www.paearlystage.com

The Sandhurst Venture Fund, L.P.
351 E Constoga Rd.
Wayne, PA 19087
(610)254-8900
Fax: (610)254-8958

TL Ventures

700 Bldg.

435 Devon Park Dr.

Wayne, PA 19087-1990

(610)975-3765

Fax: (610)254-4210

Website: http://www.tlventures.com

Rockhill Ventures, Inc.

100 Front St., Ste. 1350

West Conshohocken, PA 19428

(610)940-0300

Fax: (610)940-0301

Puerto Rico

Advent-Morro Equity Partners

Banco Popular Bldg.

206 Tetuan St., Ste. 903

San Juan, PR 00902

(787)725-5285

Fax: (787)721-1735

North America Investment Corp.

Mercantil Plaza, Ste. 813

PO Box 191831

San Juan, PR 00919

(787)754-6178

Fax: (787)754-6181

Rhode Island

Manchester Humphreys, Inc.

40 Westminster St., Ste. 900

Providence, RI 02903

(401)454-0400

Fax: (401)454-0403

Navis Partners

50 Kennedy Plaza, 12th Fl.

Providence, RI 02903

(401)278-6770

Fax: (401)278-6387

Website: http://www.navispartners.com

South Carolina

Capital Insights, L.L.C.

PO Box 27162

Greenville, SC 29616-2162

(864)242-6832

Fax: (864)242-6755

E-mail: jwarner@capitalinsights.com

Website: http://www.capitalinsights.com

Transamerica Mezzanine Financing

7 N. Laurens St., Ste. 603

Greenville, SC 29601

(864)232-6198

Fax: (864)241-4444

Tennessee

Valley Capital Corp.

Krystal Bldg.

100 W Martin Luther King Blvd., Ste. 212

Chattanooga, TN 37402

(423)265-1557

Fax: (423)265-1588

Coleman Swenson Booth Inc.

237 2nd Ave. S

Franklin, TN 37064-2649

(615)791-9462

Fax: (615)791-9636

Website: http://www.colemanswenson.com

Capital Services & Resources, Inc.

5159 Wheelis Dr., Ste. 106

Memphis, TN 38117

(901)761-2156

Fax: (907)767-0060

Paradigm Capital Partners LLC

6410 Poplar Ave., Ste. 395

Memphis, TN 38119

(901)682-6060

Fax: (901)328-3061

SSM Ventures

845 Crossover Ln., Ste. 140

Memphis, TN 38117

(901)767-1131

Fax: (901)767-1135

Website: http://www.ssmventures.com

Capital Across America L.P.

501 Union St., Ste. 201

Nashville, TN 37219

(615)254-1414

Fax: (615)254-1856

Website: http://www.capitalacrossamerica
.com

Equitas L.P.

2000 Glen Echo Rd., Ste. 101

PO Box 158838

Nashville, TN 37215-8838

(615)383-8673

Fax: (615)383-8693

Massey Burch Capital Corp.

One Burton Hills Blvd., Ste. 350

Nashville, TN 37215

(615)665-3221

Fax: (615)665-3240

E-mail: tcalton@masseyburch.com

Website: http://www.masseyburch.com

Nelson Capital Corp.

3401 West End Ave., Ste. 300

Nashville, TN 37203

(615)292-8787

Fax: (615)385-3150

Texas

Phillips-Smith Specialty Retail Group

5080 Spectrum Dr., Ste. 805 W

Addison, TX 75001

(972)387-0725

Fax: (972)458-2560

E-mail: pssrg@aol.com

Website: http://www.phillips-smith.com

Austin Ventures, L.P.

701 Brazos St., Ste. 1400

Austin, TX 78701

(512)485-1900

Fax: (512)476-3952

E-mail: info@ausven.com

Website: http://www.austinventures.com

The Capital Network

3925 West Braker Lane, Ste. 406

Austin, TX 78759-5321

(512)305-0826

Fax: (512)305-0836

Techxas Ventures LLC

5000 Plaza on the Lake

Austin, TX 78746

(512)343-0118

Fax: (512)343-1879

E-mail: bruce@techxas.com

Website: http://www.techxas.com

Alliance Financial of Houston

218 Heather Ln.

Conroe, TX 77385-9013

(936)447-3300

Fax: (936)447-4222

Amerimark Capital Corp.

1111 W Mockingbird, Ste. 1111

Dallas, TX 75247

(214)638-7878

Fax: (214)638-7612

E-mail: amerimark@amcapital.com

Website: http://www.amcapital.com

**AMT Venture Partners / AMT
Capital Ltd.**

5220 Spring Valley Rd., Ste. 600

Dallas, TX 75240

(214)905-9757

Fax: (214)905-9761

Website: http://www.amtcapital.com

Arkoma Venture Partners

5950 Berkshire Lane, Ste. 1400

Dallas, TX 75225

(214)739-3515

Fax: (214)739-3572

E-mail: joelf@arkomavp.com

Capital Southwest Corp.

12900 Preston Rd., Ste. 700

Dallas, TX 75230

(972)233-8242
Fax: (972)233-7362
Website: http://www.capitalsouthwest.com

Dali, Hook Partners
One Lincoln Center, Ste. 1550
5400 LBJ Freeway
Dallas, TX 75240
(972)991-5457
Fax: (972)991-5458
E-mail: dhook@hookpartners.com
Website: http://www.hookpartners.com

HO2 Partners
Two Galleria Tower
13455 Noel Rd., Ste. 1670
Dallas, TX 75240
(972)702-1144
Fax: (972)702-8234
Website: http://www.ho2.com

Interwest Partners (Dallas)
2 Galleria Tower
13455 Noel Rd., Ste. 1670
Dallas, TX 75240
(972)392-7279
Fax: (972)490-6348
Website: http://www.interwest.com

Kahala Investments, Inc.
8214 Westchester Dr., Ste. 715
Dallas, TX 75225
(214)987-0077
Fax: (214)987-2332

MESBIC Ventures Holding Co.
2435 North Central Expressway, Ste. 200
Dallas, TX 75080
(972)991-1597
Fax: (972)991-4770
Website: http://www.mvhc.com

North Texas MESBIC, Inc.
9500 Forest Lane, Ste. 430
Dallas, TX 75243
(214)221-3565
Fax: (214)221-3566

Richard Jaffe & Company, Inc,
7318 Royal Cir.
Dallas, TX 75230
(214)265-9397
Fax: (214)739-1845

Sevin Rosen Management Co.
13455 Noel Rd., Ste. 1670
Dallas, TX 75240
(972)702-1100
Fax: (972)702-1103
E-mail: info@srfunds.com
Website: http://www.srfunds.com

Stratford Capital Partners, L.P.
300 Crescent Ct., Ste. 500
Dallas, TX 75201
(214)740-7377
Fax: (214)720-7393
E-mail: stratcap@hmtf.com

Sunwestern Investment Group
12221 Merit Dr., Ste. 935
Dallas, TX 75251
(972)239-5650
Fax: (972)701-0024

Wingate Partners
750 N St. Paul St., Ste. 1200
Dallas, TX 75201
(214)720-1313
Fax: (214)871-8799

Buena Venture Associates
201 Main St., 32nd Fl.
Fort Worth, TX 76102
(817)339-7400
Fax: (817)390-8408
Website: http://www.buenaventure.com

The Catalyst Group
3 Riverway, Ste. 770
Houston, TX 77056
(713)623-8133
Fax: (713)623-0473
E-mail: herman@thecatalystgroup.net
Website: http://www.thecatalystgroup.net

Cureton & Co., Inc.
1100 Louisiana, Ste. 3250
Houston, TX 77002
(713)658-9806
Fax: (713)658-0476

Davis, Tuttle Venture Partners (Dallas)
8 Greenway Plaza, Ste. 1020
Houston, TX 77046
(713)993-0440
Fax: (713)621-2297
Website: http://www.davistuttle.com

Houston Partners
401 Louisiana, 8th Fl.
Houston, TX 77002
(713)222-8600
Fax: (713)222-8932

Southwest Venture Group
10878 Westheimer, Ste. 178
Houston, TX 77042
(713)827-8947
(713)461-1470

AM Fund
4600 Post Oak Place, Ste. 100
Houston, TX 77027
(713)627-9111
Fax: (713)627-9119

Ventex Management, Inc.
3417 Milam St.
Houston, TX 77002-9531
(713)659-7870
Fax: (713)659-7855

MBA Venture Group
1004 Olde Town Rd., Ste. 102
Irving, TX 75061
(972)986-6703

First Capital Group Management Co.
750 East Mulberry St., Ste. 305
PO Box 15616
San Antonio, TX 78212
(210)736-4233
Fax: (210)736-5449

The Southwest Venture Partnerships
16414 San Pedro, Ste. 345
San Antonio, TX 78232
(210)402-1200
Fax: (210)402-1221
E-mail: swvp@aol.com

Medtech International Inc.
1742 Carriageway
Sugarland, TX 77478
(713)980-8474
Fax: (713)980-6343

Utah

First Security Business Investment Corp.
15 East 100 South, Ste. 100
Salt Lake City, UT 84111
(801)246-5737
Fax: (801)246-5740

Utah Ventures II, L.P.
423 Wakara Way, Ste. 206
Salt Lake City, UT 84108
(801)583-5922
Fax: (801)583-4105
Website: http://www.uven.com

Wasatch Venture Corp.
1 S Main St., Ste. 1400
Salt Lake City, UT 84133
(801)524-8939
Fax: (801)524-8941
E-mail: mail@wasatchvc.com

Vermont

North Atlantic Capital Corp.
76 Saint Paul St., Ste. 600
Burlington, VT 05401
(802)658-7820
Fax: (802)658-5757
Website: http://www.northatlanticcapital
.com

Green Mountain Advisors Inc.
PO Box 1230
Quechee, VT 05059
(802)296-7800
Fax: (802)296-6012
Website: http://www.gmtcap.com

Virginia

Oxford Financial Services Corp.
Alexandria, VA 22314
(703)519-4900
Fax: (703)519-4910
E-mail: oxford133@aol.com

Continental SBIC
4141 N. Henderson Rd.
Arlington, VA 22203
(703)527-5200
Fax: (703)527-3700

Novak Biddle Venture Partners
1750 Tysons Blvd., Ste. 1190
McLean, VA 22102
(703)847-3770
Fax: (703)847-3771
E-mail: roger@novakbiddle.com
Website: http://www.novakbiddle.com

Spacevest
11911 Freedom Dr., Ste. 500
Reston, VA 20190
(703)904-9800
Fax: (703)904-0571
E-mail: spacevest@spacevest.com
Website: http://www.spacevest.com

Virginia Capital
1801 Libbie Ave., Ste. 201
Richmond, VA 23226
(804)648-4802
Fax: (804)648-4809
E-mail: webmaster@vacapital.com
Website: http://www.vacapital.com

Calvert Social Venture Partners
402 Maple Ave. W
Vienna, VA 22180
(703)255-4930
Fax: (703)255-4931
E-mail: calven2000@aol.com

Fairfax Partners
8000 Towers Crescent Dr., Ste. 940
Vienna, VA 22182
(703)847-9486
Fax: (703)847-0911

Global Internet Ventures
8150 Leesburg Pike, Ste. 1210
Vienna, VA 22182
(703)442-3300
Fax: (703)442-3388
Website: http://www.givinc.com

Walnut Capital Corp. (Vienna)
8000 Towers Crescent Dr., Ste. 1070
Vienna, VA 22182
(703)448-3771
Fax: (703)448-7751

Washington

Encompass Ventures
777 108th Ave. NE, Ste. 2300
Bellevue, WA 98004
(425)486-3900
Fax: (425)486-3901
E-mail: info@evpartners.com
Website: http://www.encompassventures
.com

Fluke Venture Partners
11400 SE Sixth St., Ste. 230
Bellevue, WA 98004
(425)453-4590
Fax: (425)453-4675
E-mail: gabelein@flukeventures.com
Website: http://www.flukeventures.com

Pacific Northwest Partners SBIC, L.P.
15352 SE 53rd St.
Bellevue, WA 98006
(425)455-9967
Fax: (425)455-9404

Materia Venture Associates, L.P.
3435 Carillon Pointe
Kirkland, WA 98033-7354
(425)822-4100
Fax: (425)827-4086

OVP Venture Partners (Kirkland)
2420 Carillon Pt.
Kirkland, WA 98033
(425)889-9192
Fax: (425)889-0152
E-mail: info@ovp.com
Website: http://www.ovp.com

Digital Partners
999 3rd Ave., Ste. 1610
Seattle, WA 98104
(206)405-3607
Fax: (206)405-3617
Website: http://www.digitalpartners.com

Frazier & Company
601 Union St., Ste. 3300
Seattle, WA 98101
(206)621-7200
Fax: (206)621-1848
E-mail: jon@frazierco.com

Kirlan Venture Capital, Inc.
221 First Ave. W, Ste. 108
Seattle, WA 98119-4223
(206)281-8610

Fax: (206)285-3451
Website: http://www.kirlanventure.com

Phoenix Partners
1000 2nd Ave., Ste. 3600
Seattle, WA 98104
(206)624-8968
Fax: (206)624-1907

Voyager Capital
800 5th St., Ste. 4100
Seattle, WA 98103
(206)470-1180
Fax: (206)470-1185
E-mail: info@voyagercap.com
Website: http://www.voyagercap.com

Northwest Venture Associates
221 N. Wall St., Ste. 628
Spokane, WA 99201
(509)747-0728
Fax: (509)747-0758
Website: http://www.nwva.com

Wisconsin

Venture Investors Management, L.L.C.
University Research Park
505 S Rosa Rd.
Madison, WI 53719
(608)441-2700
Fax: (608)441-2727
E-mail: roger@ventureinvestors.com
Website: http://www.venture
investers.com

Capital Investments, Inc.
1009 West Glen Oaks Lane, Ste. 103
Mequon, WI 53092
(414)241-0303
Fax: (414)241-8451
Website: http://www.capitalinvestment
sinc.com

Future Value Venture, Inc.
2745 N. Martin Luther King Dr., Ste. 204
Milwaukee, WI 53212-2300
(414)264-2252
Fax: (414)264-2253
E-mail: fvvventures@aol.com
William Beckett, President

Lubar and Co., Inc.
700 N. Water St., Ste. 1200
Milwaukee, WI 53202
(414)291-9000
Fax: (414)291-9061

GCI
20875 Crossroads Cir., Ste. 100
Waukesha, WI 53186
(262)798-5080
Fax: (262)798-5087

Glossary of Small Business Terms

Absolute liability
Liability that is incurred due to product defects or negligent actions. Manufacturers or retail establishments are held responsible, even though the defect or action may not have been intentional or negligent.

ACE
See Active Corps of Executives

Accident and health benefits
Benefits offered to employees and their families in order to offset the costs associated with accidental death, accidental injury, or sickness.

Account statement
A record of transactions, including payments, new debt, and deposits, incurred during a defined period of time.

Accounting system
System capturing the costs of all employees and/or machinery included in business expenses.

Accounts payable
See Trade credit

Accounts receivable
Unpaid accounts which arise from unsettled claims and transactions from the sale of a company's products or services to its customers.

Active Corps of Executives (ACE)
A group of volunteers for a management assistance program of the U.S. Small Business Administration; volunteers provide one-on-one counseling and teach workshops and seminars for small firms.

ADA
See Americans with Disabilities Act

Adaptation
The process whereby an invention is modified to meet the needs of users.

Adaptive engineering
The process whereby an invention is modified to meet the manufacturing and commercial requirements of a targeted market.

Adverse selection
The tendency for higher-risk individuals to purchase health care and more comprehensive plans, resulting in increased costs.

Advertising
A marketing tool used to capture public attention and influence purchasing decisions for a product or service. Utilizes various forms of media to generate consumer response, such as flyers, magazines, newspapers, radio, and television.

Age discrimination
The denial of the rights and privileges of employment based solely on the age of an individual.

Agency costs
Costs incurred to insure that the lender or investor maintains control over assets while allowing the borrower or entrepreneur to use them. Monitoring and information costs are the two major types of agency costs.

Agribusiness
The production and sale of commodities and products from the commercial farming industry.

Americans with Disabilities Act (ADA)
Law designed to ensure equal access and opportunity to handicapped persons.

Annual report
Yearly financial report prepared by a business that adheres to the requirements set forth by the Securities and Exchange Commission (SEC).

Antitrust immunity
Exemption from prosecution under antitrust laws. In the transportation industry, firms with antitrust immunity are permitted under certain conditions to set schedules and sometimes prices for the public benefit.

Applied research
Scientific study targeted for use in a product or process.

Assets
Anything of value owned by a company.

Audit
The verification of accounting records and business procedures conducted by an outside accounting service.

Average cost
Total production costs divided by the quantity produced.

Balance Sheet
A financial statement listing the total assets and liabilities of a company at a given time.

Bankruptcy
The condition in which a business cannot meet its debt obligations and petitions a federal district court either for reorganization of its debts (Chapter 11) or for liquidation of its assets (Chapter 7).

Basket clause
A provision specifying the amount of public pension funds that may be placed in investments not included on a state's legal list (see separate citation).

BDC
See Business development corporation

Benefit
Various services, such as health care, flextime, day care, insurance, and vacation, offered to employees as part of a hiring package. Typically subsidized in whole or in part by the business.

BIDCO
See Business and industrial development company

Billing cycle
A system designed to evenly distribute customer billing throughout the month, preventing clerical backlogs.

Blue chip security
A low-risk, low-yield security representing an interest in a very stable company.

Blue sky laws
A general term that denotes various states' laws regulating securities.

Bond
A written instrument executed by a bidder or contractor (the principal) and a second party (the surety or sureties) to assure fulfillment of the principal's obligations to a third party (the obligee or government) identified in the bond. If the principal's obligations are not met, the bond assures payment to the extent stipulated of any loss sustained by the obligee.

Bonding requirements
Terms contained in a bond (see separate citation).

Bonus
An amount of money paid to an employee as a reward for achieving certain business goals or objectives.

Brainstorming
A group session where employees contribute their ideas for solving a problem or meeting a company objective without fear of retribution or ridicule.

Brand name
The part of a brand, trademark, or service mark that can be spoken. It can be a word, letter, or group of words or letters.

Bridge financing
A short-term loan made in expectation of intermediateterm or long-term financing. Can be used when a company plans to go public in the near future.

Broker
One who matches resources available for innovation with those who need them.

Budget
An estimate of the spending necessary to complete a project or offer a service in comparison to cash-on-hand and expected earnings for the coming year, with an emphasis on cost control.

Business and industrial development company (BIDCO)
A private, for-profit financing corporation chartered by the state to provide both equity and long-term debt capital to small business owners (see separate citations for equity and debt capital).

Business birth

The formation of a new establishment or enterprise. The appearance of a new establishment or enterprise in the Small Business Data Base (see separate citation).

Business conditions

Outside factors that can affect the financial performance of a business.

Business contractions

The number of establishments that have decreased in employment during a specified time.

Business cycle

A period of economic recession and recovery. These cycles vary in duration.

Business death

The voluntary or involuntary closure of a firm or establishment. The disappearance of an establishment or enterprise from the Small Business Data Base (see separate citation).

Business development corporation (BDC)

A business financing agency, usually composed of the financial institutions in an area or state, organized to assist in financing businesses unable to obtain assistance through normal channels; the risk is spread among various members of the business development corporation, and interest rates may vary somewhat from those charged by member institutions. A venture capital firm in which shares of ownership are publicly held and to which the Investment Act of 1940 applies.

Business dissolution

For enumeration purposes, the absence of a business that was present in the prior time period from any current record.

Business entry

See Business birth

Business ethics

Moral values and principles espoused by members of the business community as a guide to fair and honest business practices.

Business exit

See Business death

Business expansions

The number of establishments that added employees during a specified time.

Business failure

Closure of a business causing a loss to at least one creditor.

Business format franchising

The purchase of the name, trademark, and an ongoing business plan of the parent corporation or franchisor by the franchisee.

Business license

A legal authorization issued by municipal and state governments and required for business operations.

Business name

Enterprises must register their business names with local governments usually on a "doing business as" (DBA) form. (This name is sometimes referred to as a "fictional name.") The procedure is part of the business licensing process and prevents any other business from using that same name for a similar business in the same locality.

Business norms

See Financial ratios

Business permit

See Business license

Business plan

A document that spells out a company's expected course of action for a specified period, usually including a detailed listing and analysis of risks and uncertainties. For the small business, it should examine the proposed products, the market, the industry, the management policies, the marketing policies, production needs, and financial needs. Frequently, it is used as a prospectus for potential investors and lenders.

Business proposal

See Business plan

Business service firm

An establishment primarily engaged in rendering services to other business organizations on a fee or contract basis.

Business start

For enumeration purposes, a business with a name or similar designation that did not exist in a prior time period.

Cafeteria plan
See Flexible benefit plan

Capacity
Level of a firm's, industry's, or nation's output corresponding to full practical utilization of available resources.

Capital
Assets less liabilities, representing the ownership interest in a business. A stock of accumulated goods, especially at a specified time and in contrast to income received during a specified time period. Accumulated goods devoted to production. Accumulated possessions calculated to bring income.

Capital expenditure
Expenses incurred by a business for improvements that will depreciate over time.

Capital gain
The monetary difference between the purchase price and the selling price of capital. Capital gains are taxed at a rate of 28% by the federal government.

Capital intensity
The relative importance of capital in the production process, usually expressed as the ratio of capital to labor but also sometimes as the ratio of capital to output.

Capital resource
The equipment, facilities and labor used to create products and services.

Catastrophic care
Medical and other services for acute and long-term illnesses that cost more than insurance coverage limits or that cost the amount most families may be expected to pay with their own resources.

CDC
See Certified development corporation

Certified development corporation (CDC)
A local area or statewide corporation or authority (for profit or nonprofit) that packages U.S. Small Business Administration (SBA), bank, state, and/or private money into financial assistance for existing business capital improvements. The SBA holds the second lien on its maximum share of 40 percent involvement. Each

state has at least one certified development corporation. This program is called the SBA 504 Program.

Certified lenders
Banks that participate in the SBA guaranteed loan program (see separate citation). Such banks must have a good track record with the U.S. Small Business Administration (SBA) and must agree to certain conditions set forth by the agency. In return, the SBA agrees to process any guaranteed loan application within three business days.

Channel of distribution
The means used to transport merchandise from the manufacturer to the consumer.

Chapter 7 of the 1978 Bankruptcy Act
Provides for a court-appointed trustee who is responsible for liquidating a company's assets in order to settle outstanding debts.

Chapter 11 of the 1978 Bankruptcy Act
Allows the business owners to retain control of the company while working with their creditors to reorganize their finances and establish better business practices to prevent liquidation of assets.

Closely held corporation
A corporation in which the shares are held by a few persons, usually officers, employees, or others close to the management; these shares are rarely offered to the public.

Code of Federal Regulations
Codification of general and permanent rules of the federal government published in the Federal Register.

Code sharing
See Computer code sharing

Coinsurance
Upon meeting the deductible payment, health insurance participants may be required to make additional health care cost-sharing payments. Coinsurance is a payment of a fixed percentage of the cost of each service; copayment is usually a fixed amount to be paid with each service.

Collateral
Securities, evidence of deposit, or other property pledged by a borrower to secure repayment of a loan.

Collective ratemaking
The establishment of uniform charges for services by a group of businesses in the same industry.

Commercial insurance plan
See Underwriting

Commercial loans
Short-term renewable loans used to finance specific capital needs of a business.

Commercialization
The final stage of the innovation process, including production and distribution.

Common stock
The most frequently used instrument for purchasing ownership in private or public companies. Common stock generally carries the right to vote on certain corporate actions and may pay dividends, although it rarely does in venture investments. In liquidation, common stockholders are the last to share in the proceeds from the sale of a corporation's assets; bondholders and preferred shareholders have priority. Common stock is often used in firstround start-up financing.

Community development corporation
A corporation established to develop economic programs for a community and, in most cases, to provide financial support for such development.

Competitor
A business whose product or service is marketed for the same purpose/use and to the same consumer group as the product or service of another.

Consignment
A merchandising agreement, usually referring to secondhand shops, where the dealer pays the owner of an item a percentage of the profit when the item is sold.

Consortium
A coalition of organizations such as banks and corporations for ventures requiring large capital resources.

Consultant
An individual that is paid by a business to provide advice and expertise in a particular area.

Consumer price index
A measure of the fluctuation in prices between two points in time.

Consumer research
Research conducted by a business to obtain information about existing or potential consumer markets.

Continuation coverage
Health coverage offered for a specified period of time to employees who leave their jobs and to their widows, divorced spouses, or dependents.

Contractions
See Business contractions

Convertible preferred stock
A class of stock that pays a reasonable dividend and is convertible into common stock (see separate citation). Generally the convertible feature may only be exercised after being held for a stated period of time. This arrangement is usually considered second-round financing when a company needs equity to maintain its cash flow.

Convertible securities
A feature of certain bonds, debentures, or preferred stocks that allows them to be exchanged by the owner for another class of securities at a future date and in accordance with any other terms of the issue.

Copayment
See Coinsurance

Copyright
A legal form of protection available to creators and authors to safeguard their works from unlawful use or claim of ownership by others. Copyrights may be acquired for works of art, sculpture, music, and published or unpublished manuscripts. All copyrights should be registered at the Copyright Office of the Library of Congress.

Corporate financial ratios
The relationship between key figures found in a company's financial statement expressed as a numeric value. Used to evaluate risk and company performance. Also known as Financial averages, Operating ratios, and Business ratios.

Corporation
A legal entity, chartered by a state or the federal government, recognized as a separate entity having its own rights, privileges, and liabilities distinct from those of its members.

Cost containment
Actions taken by employers and insurers to curtail rising health care costs; for example, increasing employee cost sharing (see separate citation), requiring second opinions, or preadmission screening.

Cost sharing
The requirement that health care consumers contribute to their own medical care costs through deductibles and coinsurance (see separate citations). Cost sharing does not include the amounts paid in premiums. It is used to control utilization of services; for example, requiring a fixed amount to be paid with each health care service.

Cottage industry
Businesses based in the home in which the family members are the labor force and family-owned equipment is used to process the goods.

Credit Rating
A letter or number calculated by an organization (such as Dun & Bradstreet) to represent the ability and disposition of a business to meet its financial obligations.

Customer service
Various techniques used to ensure the satisfaction of a customer.

Cyclical peak
The upper turning point in a business cycle.

Cyclical trough
The lower turning point in a business cycle.

DBA (Doing business as)
See Business name

Death
See Business death

Debenture
A certificate given as acknowledgment of a debt (see separate citation) secured by the general credit of the issuing corporation. A bond, usually without security, issued by a corporation and sometimes convertible to common stock.

Debt
Something owed by one person to another. Financing in which a company receives capital that must be repaid; no ownership is transferred.

Debt capital
Business financing that normally requires periodic interest payments and repayment of the principal within a specified time.

Debt financing
See Debt capital

Debt securities
Loans such as bonds and notes that provide a specified rate of return for a specified period of time.

Deductible
A set amount that an individual must pay before any benefits are received.

Demand shock absorbers
A term used to describe the role that some small firms play by expanding their output levels to accommodate a transient surge in demand.

Demographics
Statistics on various markets, including age, income, and education, used to target specific products or services to appropriate consumer groups.

Demonstration
Showing that a product or process has been modified sufficiently to meet the needs of users.

Deregulation
The lifting of government restrictions; for example, the lifting of government restrictions on the entry of new businesses, the expansion of services, and the setting of prices in particular industries.

Disaster loans
Various types of physical and economic assistance available to individuals and businesses through the U.S. Small Business Administration (SBA). This is the only SBA loan program available for residential purposes.

Discrimination
The denial of the rights and privileges of employment based on factors such as age, race, religion, or gender.

Diseconomies of scale
The condition in which the costs of production increase faster than the volume of production.

Dissolution
See Business dissolution

Distribution
Delivering a product or process to the user.

Distributor
One who delivers merchandise to the user.

Diversified company
A company whose products and services are used by several different markets.

Doing business as (DBA)
See Business name

Dow Jones
An information services company that publishes the Wall Street Journal and other sources of financial information.

Dow Jones Industrial Average
An indicator of stock market performance.

Earned income
A tax term that refers to wages and salaries earned by the recipient, as opposed to monies earned through interest and dividends.

Economic efficiency
The use of productive resources to the fullest practical extent in the provision of the set of goods and services that is most preferred by purchasers in the economy.

Economic indicators
Statistics used to express the state of the economy. These include the length of the average work week, the rate of unemployment, and stock prices.

Economically disadvantaged
See Socially and economically disadvantaged

Economies of scale
See Scale economies

EEOC
See Equal Employment Opportunity Commission

8(a) Program
A program authorized by the Small Business Act that directs federal contracts to small businesses owned and operated by socially and economically disadvantaged individuals.

Electronic mail (e-mail)
The electronic transmission of mail via phone lines.

E-mail
See Electronic mail

Employee leasing
A contract by which employers arrange to have their workers hired by a leasing company and then leased back to them for a management fee. The leasing company typically assumes the administrative burden of payroll and provides a benefit package to the workers.

Employee tenure
The length of time an employee works for a particular employer.

Employer identification number
The business equivalent of a social security number. Assigned by the U.S. Internal Revenue Service.

Enterprise
An aggregation of all establishments owned by a parent company. An enterprise may consist of a single, independent establishment or include subsidiaries and other branches under the same ownership and control.

Enterprise zone
A designated area, usually found in inner cities and other areas with significant unemployment, where businesses receive tax credits and other incentives to entice them to establish operations there.

Entrepreneur
A person who takes the risk of organizing and operating a new business venture.

Entry
See Business entry

Equal Employment Opportunity Commission (EEOC)
A federal agency that ensures nondiscrimination in the hiring and firing practices of a business.

Equal opportunity employer
An employer who adheres to the standards set by the Equal Employment Opportunity Commission (see separate citation).

Equity
The ownership interest. Financing in which partial or total ownership of a company is surrendered in exchange for capital. An investor's financial return comes from dividend payments and from growth in the net worth of the business.

Equity capital
See Equity; Equity midrisk venture capital

Equity financing
See Equity; Equity midrisk venture capital

Equity midrisk venture capital
An unsecured investment in a company. Usually a purchase of ownership interest in a company that occurs in the later stages of a company's development.

Equity partnership
A limited partnership arrangement for providing start-up and seed capital to businesses.

Equity securities
See Equity

Equity-type
Debt financing subordinated to conventional debt.

Establishment
A single-location business unit that may be independent (a single-establishment enterprise) or owned by a parent enterprise.

Establishment and Enterprise Microdata File
See U.S. Establishment and Enterprise Microdata File

Establishment birth
See Business birth

Establishment Longitudinal Microdata File
See U.S. Establishment Longitudinal Microdata File

Ethics
See Business ethics

Evaluation
Determining the potential success of translating an invention into a product or process.

Exit
See Business exit

Experience rating
See Underwriting

Export
A product sold outside of the country.

Export license
A general or specific license granted by the U.S. Department of Commerce required of anyone wishing to export goods. Some restricted articles need approval from the U.S. Departments of State, Defense, or Energy.

Failure
See Business failure

Fair share agreement
An agreement reached between a franchisor and a minority business organization to extend business ownership to minorities by either reducing the amount of capital required or by setting aside certain marketing areas for minority business owners.

Feasibility study
A study to determine the likelihood that a proposed product or development will fulfill the objectives of a particular investor.

Federal Trade Commission (FTC)
Federal agency that promotes free enterprise and competition within the U.S.

Federal Trade Mark Act of 1946
See Lanham Act

Fictional name
See Business name

Fiduciary
An individual or group that hold assets in trust for a beneficiary.

Financial analysis
The techniques used to determine money needs in a business. Techniques include ratio analysis, calculation of return on investment, guides for measuring profitability, and break-even analysis to determine ultimate success.

Financial intermediary

A financial institution that acts as the intermediary between borrowers and lenders. Banks, savings and loan associations, finance companies, and venture capital companies are major financial intermediaries in the United States.

Financial ratios

See Corporate financial ratios; Industry financial ratios

Financial statement

A written record of business finances, including balance sheets and profit and loss statements.

Financing

See First-stage financing; Second-stage financing; Thirdstage financing

First-stage financing

Financing provided to companies that have expended their initial capital, and require funds to start full-scale manufacturing and sales. Also known as First-round financing.

Fiscal year

Any twelve-month period used by businesses for accounting purposes.

504 Program

See Certified development corporation

Flexible benefit plan

A plan that offers a choice among cash and/or qualified benefits such as group term life insurance, accident and health insurance, group legal services, dependent care assistance, and vacations.

FOB

See Free on board

Format franchising

See Business format franchising; Franchising

401(k) plan

A financial plan where employees contribute a percentage of their earnings to a fund that is invested in stocks, bonds, or money markets for the purpose of saving money for retirement.

Four Ps

Marketing terms referring to Product, Price, Place, and Promotion.

Franchising

A form of licensing by which the owner-the franchisor- distributes or markets a product, method, or service through affiliated dealers called franchisees. The product, method, or service being marketed is identified by a brand name, and the franchisor maintains control over the marketing methods employed. The franchisee is often given exclusive access to a defined geographic area.

Free on board (FOB)

A pricing term indicating that the quoted price includes the cost of loading goods into transport vessels at a specified place.

Frictional unemployment

See Unemployment

FTC

See Federal Trade Commission

Fulfillment

The systems necessary for accurate delivery of an ordered item, including subscriptions and direct marketing.

Full-time workers

Generally, those who work a regular schedule of more than 35 hours per week.

Garment registration number

A number that must appear on every garment sold in the U.S. to indicate the manufacturer of the garment, which may or may not be the same as the label under which the garment is sold. The U.S. Federal Trade Commission assigns and regulates garment registration numbers.

Gatekeeper

A key contact point for entry into a network.

GDP

See Gross domestic product

General obligation bond

A municipal bond secured by the taxing power of the municipality. The Tax Reform Act of 1986 limits the purposes for which such bonds may be issued and establishes volume limits on the extent of their issuance.

GLOSSARY OF SMALL BUSINESS TERMS

GNP
See Gross national product

Good Housekeeping Seal
Seal appearing on products that signifies the fulfillment of the standards set by the Good Housekeeping Institute to protect consumer interests.

Goods sector
All businesses producing tangible goods, including agriculture, mining, construction, and manufacturing businesses.

GPO
See Gross product originating

Gross domestic product (GDP)
The part of the nation's gross national product (see separate citation) generated by private business using resources from within the country.

Gross national product (GNP)
The most comprehensive single measure of aggregate economic output. Represents the market value of the total output of goods and services produced by a nation's economy.

Gross product originating (GPO)
A measure of business output estimated from the income or production side using employee compensation, profit income, net interest, capital consumption, and indirect business taxes.

HAL
See Handicapped assistance loan program

Handicapped assistance loan program (HAL)
Low-interest direct loan program through the U.S. Small Business Administration (SBA) for handicapped persons. The SBA requires that these persons demonstrate that their disability is such that it is impossible for them to secure employment, thus making it necessary to go into their own business to make a living.

Health maintenance organization (HMO)
Organization of physicians and other health care professionals that provides health services to subscribers and their dependents on a prepaid basis.

Health provider
An individual or institution that gives medical care. Under Medicare, an institutional provider is a hospital, skilled nursing facility, home health agency, or provider of certain physical therapy services.

Hispanic
A person of Cuban, Mexican, Puerto Rican, Latin American (Central or South American), European Spanish, or other Spanish-speaking origin or ancestry.

HMO
See Health maintenance organization

Home-based business
A business with an operating address that is also a residential address (usually the residential address of the proprietor).

Hub-and-spoke system
A system in which flights of an airline from many different cities (the spokes) converge at a single airport (the hub). After allowing passengers sufficient time to make connections, planes then depart for different cities.

Human Resources Management
A business program designed to oversee recruiting, pay, benefits, and other issues related to the company's work force, including planning to determine the optimal use of labor to increase production, thereby increasing profit.

Idea
An original concept for a new product or process.

Import
Products produced outside the country in which they are consumed.

Income
Money or its equivalent, earned or accrued, resulting from the sale of goods and services.

Income statement
A financial statement that lists the profits and losses of a company at a given time.

Incorporation
The filing of a certificate of incorporation with a state's secretary of state, thereby limiting the business owner's liability.

Incubator
A facility designed to encourage entrepreneurship and minimize obstacles to new business formation and growth, particularly for high-technology firms, by housing a number of fledgling enterprises that share an array of services, such as meeting areas, secretarial services, accounting, research library, on-site financial and management counseling, and word processing facilities.

Independent contractor
An individual considered self-employed (see separate citation) and responsible for paying Social Security taxes and income taxes on earnings.

Indirect health coverage
Health insurance obtained through another individual's health care plan; for example, a spouse's employersponsored plan.

Industrial development authority
The financial arm of a state or other political subdivision established for the purpose of financing economic development in an area, usually through loans to nonprofit organizations, which in turn provide facilities for manufacturing and other industrial operations.

Industry financial ratios
Corporate financial ratios averaged for a specified industry. These are used for comparison purposes and reveal industry trends and identify differences between the performance of a specific company and the performance of its industry. Also known as Industrial averages, Industry ratios, Financial averages, and Business or Industrial norms.

Inflation
Increases in volume of currency and credit, generally resulting in a sharp and continuing rise in price levels.

Informal capital
Financing from informal, unorganized sources; includes informal debt capital such as trade credit or loans from friends and relatives and equity capital from informal investors.

Initial public offering (IPO)
A corporation's first offering of stock to the public.

Innovation
The introduction of a new idea into the marketplace in the form of a new product or service or an improvement in organization or process.

Intellectual property
Any idea or work that can be considered proprietary in nature and is thus protected from infringement by others.

Internal capital
Debt or equity financing obtained from the owner or through retained business earnings.

Internet
A government-designed computer network that contains large amounts of information and is accessible through various vendors for a fee.

Intrapreneurship
The state of employing entrepreneurial principles to nonentrepreneurial situations.

Invention
The tangible form of a technological idea, which could include a laboratory prototype, drawings, formulas, etc.

IPO
See Initial public offering

Job description
The duties and responsibilities required in a particular position.

Job tenure
A period of time during which an individual is continuously employed in the same job.

Joint marketing agreements
Agreements between regional and major airlines, often involving the coordination of flight schedules, fares, and baggage transfer. These agreements help regional carriers operate at lower cost.

Joint venture
Venture in which two or more people combine efforts in a particular business enterprise, usually a single transaction or a limited activity, and agree to share the profits and losses jointly or in proportion to their contributions.

Keogh plan
Designed for self-employed persons and unincorporated businesses as a tax-deferred pension account.

Labor force
Civilians considered eligible for employment who are also willing and able to work.

Labor force participation rate
The civilian labor force as a percentage of the civilian population.

Labor intensity
The relative importance of labor in the production process, usually measured as the capital-labor ratio; i.e., the ratio of units of capital (typically, dollars of tangible assets) to the number of employees. The higher the capital-labor ratio exhibited by a firm or industry, the lower the capital intensity of that firm or industry is said to be.

Labor surplus area
An area in which there exists a high unemployment rate. In procurement (see separate citation), extra points are given to firms in counties that are designated a labor surplus area; this information is requested on procurement bid sheets.

Labor union
An organization of similarly-skilled workers who collectively bargain with management over the conditions of employment.

Laboratory prototype
See Prototype

LAN
See Local Area Network

Lanham Act
Refers to the Federal Trade Mark Act of 1946. Protects registered trademarks, trade names, and other service marks used in commerce.

Large business-dominated industry
Industry in which a minimum of 60 percent of employment or sales is in firms with more than 500 workers.

LBO
See Leveraged buy-out

Leader pricing
A reduction in the price of a good or service in order to generate more sales of that good or service.

Legal list
A list of securities selected by a state in which certain institutions and fiduciaries (such as pension funds, insurance companies, and banks) may invest. Securities not on the list are not eligible for investment. Legal lists typically restrict investments to high quality securities meeting certain specifications. Generally, investment is limited to U.S. securities and investment-grade blue chip securities (see separate citation).

Leveraged buy-out (LBO)
The purchase of a business or a division of a corporation through a highly leveraged financing package.

Liability
An obligation or duty to perform a service or an act. Also defined as money owed.

License
A legal agreement granting to another the right to use a technological innovation.

Limited Liability Company
A hybrid type of legal structure that provides the limited liability features of a corporation and the tax efficiencies and operational flexibility of a partnership. Depending on the state, the members can consist of a single individual (one owner), two or more individuals, corporations or other LLCs.

Limited liability partnerships
A business organization that allows limited partners to enjoy limited personal liability while general partners have unlimited personal liability

Liquidity
The ability to convert a security into cash promptly.

Loans
See Commercial loans; Disaster loans; SBA direct loans; SBA guaranteed loans; SBA special lending institution categories Local Area Network (LAN) Computer networks contained within a single building or small area; used to facilitate the sharing of information.

Local development corporation

An organization, usually made up of local citizens of a community, designed to improve the economy of the area by inducing business and industry to locate and expand there. A local development corporation establishes a capability to finance local growth.

Long-haul rates

Rates charged by a transporter in which the distance traveled is more than 800 miles.

Long-term debt

An obligation that matures in a period that exceeds five years.

Low-grade bond

A corporate bond that is rated below investment grade by the major rating agencies (Standard and Poor's, Moody's).

Macro-efficiency

Efficiency as it pertains to the operation of markets and market systems.

Managed care

A cost-effective health care program initiated by employers whereby low-cost health care is made available to the employees in return for exclusive patronage to program doctors.

Management Assistance Programs

See SBA Management Assistance Programs

Management and technical assistance

A term used by many programs to mean business (as opposed to technological) assistance.

Mandated benefits

Specific treatments, providers, or individuals required by law to be included in commercial health plans.

Market evaluation

The use of market information to determine the sales potential of a specific product or process.

Market failure

The situation in which the workings of a competitive market do not produce the best results from the point of view of the entire society.

Market information

Data of any type that can be used for market evaluation, which could include demographic data, technology forecasting, regulatory changes, etc.

Market research

A systematic collection, analysis, and reporting of data about the market and its preferences, opinions, trends, and plans; used for corporate decision-making.

Market share

In a particular market, the percentage of sales of a specific product.

Marketing

Promotion of goods or services through various media.

Master Establishment List (MEL)

A list of firms in the United States developed by the U.S. Small Business Administration; firms can be selected by industry, region, state, standard metropolitan statistical area (see separate citation), county, and zip code.

Maturity

The date upon which the principal or stated value of a bond or other indebtedness becomes due and payable.

Medicaid (Title XIX)

A federally aided, state-operated and administered program that provides medical benefits for certain low income persons in need of health and medical care who are eligible for one of the government's welfare cash payment programs, including the aged, the blind, the disabled, and members of families with dependent children where one parent is absent, incapacitated, or unemployed.

Medicare (Title XVIII)

A nationwide health insurance program for disabled and aged persons. Health insurance is available to insured persons without regard to income. Monies from payroll taxes cover hospital insurance and monies from general revenues and beneficiary premiums pay for supplementary medical insurance.

MEL

See Master Establishment List

Merchant Status
The relationship between a company and a bank or credit card company allowing the company to accept credit card payments

MESBIC
See Minority enterprise small business investment corporation

MET
See Multiple employer trust

Metropolitan statistical area (MSA)
A means used by the government to define large population centers that may transverse different governmental jurisdictions. For example, the Washington, D.C. MSA includes the District of Columbia and contiguous parts of Maryland and Virginia because all of these geopolitical areas comprise one population and economic operating unit.

Mezzanine financing
See Third-stage financing

Micro-efficiency
Efficiency as it pertains to the operation of individual firms.

Microdata
Information on the characteristics of an individual business firm.

Microloan
An SBA loan program that helps entrepreneurs obtain loans from less than $100 to $25,000.

Mid-term debt
An obligation that matures within one to five years.

Midrisk venture capital
See Equity midrisk venture capital

Minimum premium plan
A combination approach to funding an insurance plan aimed primarily at premium tax savings. The employer self-funds a fixed percentage of estimated monthly claims and the insurance company insures the excess.

Minimum wage
The lowest hourly wage allowed by the federal government.

Minority Business Development Agency
Contracts with private firms throughout the nation to sponsor Minority Business Development Centers which provide minority firms with advice and technical assistance on a fee basis.

Minority Enterprise Small Business Investment Corporation (MESBIC)
A federally funded private venture capital firm licensed by the U.S. Small Business Administration to provide capital to minority-owned businesses (see separate citation).

Minority-owned business
Businesses owned by those who are socially or economically disadvantaged (see separate citation).

Mission statement
A short statement describing a company's function, markets and competitive advantages.

Mom and Pop business
A small store or enterprise having limited capital, principally employing family members.

Multi-employer plan
A health plan to which more than one employer is required to contribute and that may be maintained through a collective bargaining agreement and required to meet standards prescribed by the U.S. Department of Labor.

Multi-level marketing
A system of selling in which you sign up other people to assist you and they, in turn, recruit others to help them. Some entrepreneurs have built successful companies on this concept because the main focus of their activities is their product and product sales.

Multiple employer trust (MET)
A self-funded benefit plan generally geared toward small employers sharing a common interest.

NASDAQ
See National Association of Securities Dealers Automated Quotations

National Association of Securities Dealers Automated Quotations
Provides price quotes on over-the-counter securities as well as securities listed on the New York Stock Exchange.

National income
Aggregate earnings of labor and property arising from the production of goods and services in a nation's economy.

Net assets
See Net worth

Net income
The amount remaining from earnings and profits after all expenses and costs have been met or deducted. Also known as Net earnings.

Net profit
Money earned after production and overhead expenses (see separate citations) have been deducted.

Net worth
The difference between a company's total assets and its total liabilities.

Network
A chain of interconnected individuals or organizations sharing information and/or services.

New York Stock Exchange (NYSE)
The oldest stock exchange in the U.S. Allows for trading in stocks, bonds, warrants, options, and rights that meet listing requirements.

Niche
A career or business for which a person is well-suited. Also, a product which fulfills one need of a particular market segment, often with little or no competition.

Nodes
One workstation in a network, either local area or wide area (see separate citations).

Nonbank bank
A bank that either accepts deposits or makes loans, but not both. Used to create many new branch banks.

Noncompetitive awards
A method of contracting whereby the federal government negotiates with only one contractor to supply a product or service.

Nonmember bank
A state-regulated bank that does not belong to the federal bank system.

Nonprofit
An organization that has no shareholders, does not distribute profits, and is without federal and state tax liabilities.

Norms
See Financial ratios

North American Free Trade Agreement (NAFTA)
Passed in 1993, NAFTA eliminates trade barriers among businesses in the U.S., Canada, and Mexico.

NYSE
See New York Stock Exchange

Occupational Safety & Health Administration (OSHA)
Federal agency that regulates health and safety standards within the workplace.

Operating Expenses
Business expenditures not directly associated with the production of goods or services.

Optimal firm size
The business size at which the production cost per unit of output (average cost) is, in the long run, at its minimum.

Organizational chart
A hierarchical chart tracking the chain of command within an organization.

OSHA
See Occupational Safety & Health Administration

Overhead
Expenses, such as employee benefits and building utilities, incurred by a business that are unrelated to the actual product or service sold.

Owner's capital
Debt or equity funds provided by the owner(s) of a business; sources of owner's capital are personal savings, sales of assets, or loans from financial institutions.

P & L
See Profit and loss statement

Part-time workers
Normally, those who work less than 35 hours per week. The Tax Reform Act indicated that part-time

workers who work less than 17.5 hours per week may be excluded from health plans for purposes of complying with federal nondiscrimination rules.

Part-year workers
Those who work less than 50 weeks per year.

Partnership
Two or more parties who enter into a legal relationship to conduct business for profit. Defined by the U.S. Internal Revenue Code as joint ventures, syndicates, groups, pools, and other associations of two or more persons organized for profit that are not specifically classified in the IRS code as corporations or proprietorships.

Patent
A grant made by the government assuring an inventor the sole right to make, use, and sell an invention for a period of 17 years.

PC
See Professional corporation

Peak
See Cyclical peak

Pension
A series of payments made monthly, semiannually, annually, or at other specified intervals during the lifetime of the pensioner for distribution upon retirement. The term is sometimes used to denote the portion of the retirement allowance financed by the employer's contributions.

Pension fund
A fund established to provide for the payment of pension benefits; the collective contributions made by all of the parties to the pension plan.

Performance appraisal
An established set of objective criteria, based on job description and requirements, that is used to evaluate the performance of an employee in a specific job.

Permit
See Business license

Plan
See Business plan

Pooling
An arrangement for employers to achieve efficiencies and lower health costs by joining together to purchase group health insurance or self-insurance.

PPO
See Preferred provider organization

Preferred lenders program
See SBA special lending institution categories

Preferred provider organization (PPO)
A contractual arrangement with a health care services organization that agrees to discount its health care rates in return for faster payment and/or a patient base.

Premiums
The amount of money paid to an insurer for health insurance under a policy. The premium is generally paid periodically (e.g., monthly), and often is split between the employer and the employee. Unlike deductibles and coinsurance or copayments, premiums are paid for coverage whether or not benefits are actually used.

Prime-age workers
Employees 25 to 54 years of age.

Prime contract
A contract awarded directly by the U.S. Federal Government.

Private company
See Closely held corporation

Private placement
A method of raising capital by offering for sale an investment or business to a small group of investors (generally avoiding registration with the Securities and Exchange Commission or state securities registration agencies). Also known as Private financing or Private offering.

Pro forma
The use of hypothetical figures in financial statements to represent future expenditures, debts, and other potential financial expenses.

Proactive
Taking the initiative to solve problems and anticipate future events before they happen, instead of reacting

to an already existing problem or waiting for a difficult situation to occur.

Procurement
A contract from an agency of the federal government for goods or services from a small business.

Product development
The stage of the innovation process where research is translated into a product or process through evaluation, adaptation, and demonstration.

Product franchising
An arrangement for a franchisee to use the name and to produce the product line of the franchisor or parent corporation.

Production
The manufacture of a product.

Production prototype
See Prototype

Productivity
A measurement of the number of goods produced during a specific amount of time.

Professional corporation (PC)
Organized by members of a profession such as medicine, dentistry, or law for the purpose of conducting their professional activities as a corporation. Liability of a member or shareholder is limited in the same manner as in a business corporation.

Profit and loss statement (P & L)
The summary of the incomes (total revenues) and costs of a company's operation during a specific period of time. Also known as Income and expense statement.

Proposal
See Business plan

Proprietorship
The most common legal form of business ownership; about 85 percent of all small businesses are proprietorships. The liability of the owner is unlimited in this form of ownership.

Prospective payment system
A cost-containment measure included in the Social Security Amendments of 1983 whereby Medicare payments to hospitals are based on established prices, rather than on cost reimbursement.

Prototype
A model that demonstrates the validity of the concept of an invention (laboratory prototype); a model that meets the needs of the manufacturing process and the user (production prototype).

Prudent investor rule or standard
A legal doctrine that requires fiduciaries to make investments using the prudence, diligence, and intelligence that would be used by a prudent person in making similar investments. Because fiduciaries make investments on behalf of third-party beneficiaries, the standard results in very conservative investments. Until recently, most state regulations required the fiduciary to apply this standard to each investment. Newer, more progressive regulations permit fiduciaries to apply this standard to the portfolio taken as a whole, thereby allowing a fiduciary to balance a portfolio with higher-yield, higher-risk investments. In states with more progressive regulations, practically every type of security is eligible for inclusion in the portfolio of investments made by a fiduciary, provided that the portfolio investments, in their totality, are those of a prudent person.

Public equity markets
Organized markets for trading in equity shares such as common stocks, preferred stocks, and warrants. Includes markets for both regularly traded and nonregularly traded securities.

Public offering
General solicitation for participation in an investment opportunity. Interstate public offerings are supervised by the U.S. Securities and Exchange Commission (see separate citation).

Quality control
The process by which a product is checked and tested to ensure consistent standards of high quality.

Rate of return
The yield obtained on a security or other investment based on its purchase price or its current market price. The total rate of return is current income plus or minus capital appreciation or depreciation.

Real property
Includes the land and all that is contained on it.

Realignment
See Resource realignment

Recession
Contraction of economic activity occurring between the peak and trough (see separate citations) of a business cycle.

Regulated market
A market in which the government controls the forces of supply and demand, such as who may enter and what price may be charged.

Regulation D
A vehicle by which small businesses make small offerings and private placements of securities with limited disclosure requirements. It was designed to ease the burdens imposed on small businesses utilizing this method of capital formation.

Regulatory Flexibility Act
An act requiring federal agencies to evaluate the impact of their regulations on small businesses before the regulations are issued and to consider less burdensome alternatives.

Research
The initial stage of the innovation process, which includes idea generation and invention.

Research and development financing
A tax-advantaged partnership set up to finance product development for start-ups as well as more mature companies.

Resource mobility
The ease with which labor and capital move from firm to firm or from industry to industry.

Resource realignment
The adjustment of productive resources to interindustry changes in demand.

Resources
The sources of support or help in the innovation process, including sources of financing, technical evaluation, market evaluation, management and business assistance, etc.

Retained business earnings
Business profits that are retained by the business rather than being distributed to the shareholders as dividends.

Return on investment
A profitability measure that evaluates the performance of a business by dividing net profit by net worth.

Revolving credit
An agreement with a lending institution for an amount of money, which cannot exceed a set maximum, over a specified period of time. Each time the borrower repays a portion of the loan, the amount of the repayment may be borrowed yet again.

Risk capital
See Venture capital

Risk management
The act of identifying potential sources of financial loss and taking action to minimize their negative impact.

Routing
The sequence of steps necessary to complete a product during production.

S corporations
See Sub chapter S corporations

SBA
See Small Business Administration

SBA direct loans
Loans made directly by the U.S. Small Business Administration (SBA); monies come from funds appropriated specifically for this purpose. In general, SBA direct loans carry interest rates slightly lower than those in the private financial markets and are available only to applicants unable to secure private financing or an SBA guaranteed loan.

SBA 504 Program
See Certified development corporation

SBA guaranteed loans
Loans made by lending institutions in which the U.S. Small Business Administration (SBA) will pay a prior agreed-upon percentage of the outstanding principal in the event the borrower of the loan

defaults. The terms of the loan and the interest rate are negotiated between theborrower and the lending institution, within set parameters.

SBA loans
See Disaster loans; SBA direct loans; SBA guaranteed loans; SBA special lending institution categories

SBA Management Assistance Programs
Classes, workshops, counseling, and publications offered by the U.S. Small Business Administration.

SBA special lending institution categories
U.S. Small Business Administration (SBA) loan program in which the SBA promises certified banks a 72-hour turnaround period in giving its approval for a loan, and in which preferred lenders in a pilot program are allowed to write SBA loans without seeking prior SBA approval.

SBDB
See Small Business Data Base

SBDC
See Small business development centers

SBI
See Small business institutes program

SBIC
See Small business investment corporation

SBIR Program
See Small Business Innovation Development Act of 1982

Scale economies
The decline of the production cost per unit of output (average cost) as the volume of output increases.

Scale efficiency
The reduction in unit cost available to a firm when producing at a higher output volume.

SCORE
See Service Corps of Retired Executives

SEC
See Securities and Exchange Commission

SECA
See Self-Employment Contributions Act

Second-stage financing
Working capital for the initial expansion of a company that is producing, shipping, and has growing accounts receivable and inventories. Also known as Second-round financing.

Secondary market
A market established for the purchase and sale of outstanding securities following their initial distribution.

Secondary worker
Any worker in a family other than the person who is the primary source of income for the family.

Secondhand capital
Previously used and subsequently resold capital equipment (e.g., buildings and machinery).

Securities and Exchange Commission (SEC)
Federal agency charged with regulating the trade of securities to prevent unethical practices in the investor market.

Securitized debt
A marketing technique that converts long-term loans to marketable securities.

Seed capital
Venture financing provided in the early stages of the innovation process, usually during product development.

Self-employed person
One who works for a profit or fees in his or her own business, profession, or trade, or who operates a farm.

Self-Employment Contributions Act (SECA)
Federal law that governs the self-employment tax (see separate citation).

Self-employment income
Income covered by Social Security if a business earns a net income of at least $400.00 during the year. Taxes are paid on earnings that exceed $400.00.

Self-employment retirement plan
See Keogh plan

Self-employment tax
Required tax imposed on self-employed individuals for the provision of Social Security and Medicare. The tax must be paid quarterly with estimated income tax statements.

Self-funding
A health benefit plan in which a firm uses its own funds to pay claims, rather than transferring the financial risks of paying claims to an outside insurer in exchange for premium payments.

Service Corps of Retired Executives (SCORE)
Volunteers for the SBA Management Assistance Program who provide one-on-one counseling and teach workshops and seminars for small firms.

Service firm
See Business service firm

Service sector
Broadly defined, all U.S. industries that produce intangibles, including the five major industry divisions of transportation, communications, and utilities; wholesale trade; retail trade; finance, insurance, and real estate; and services.

Set asides
See Small business set asides

Short-haul service
A type of transportation service in which the transporter supplies service between cities where the maximum distance is no more than 200 miles.

Short-term debt
An obligation that matures in one year.

SIC codes
See Standard Industrial Classification codes

Single-establishment enterprise
See Establishment

Small business
An enterprise that is independently owned and operated, is not dominant in its field, and employs fewer than 500 people. For SBA purposes, the U.S. Small Business Administration (SBA) considers various other factors (such as gross annual sales) in determining size of a business.

Small Business Administration (SBA)
An independent federal agency that provides assistance with loans, management, and advocating interests before other federal agencies.

Small Business Data Base
A collection of microdata (see separate citation) files on individual firms developed and maintained by the U.S. Small Business Administration.

Small business development centers (SBDC)
Centers that provide support services to small businesses, such as individual counseling, SBA advice, seminars and conferences, and other learning center activities. Most services are free of charge, or available at minimal cost.

Small business development corporation
See Certified development corporation

Small business-dominated industry
Industry in which a minimum of 60 percent of employment or sales is in firms with fewer than 500 employees.

Small Business Innovation Development Act of 1982
Federal statute requiring federal agencies with large extramural research and development budgets to allocate a certain percentage of these funds to small research and development firms. The program, called the Small Business Innovation Research (SBIR) Program, is designed to stimulate technological innovation and make greater use of small businesses in meeting national innovation needs.

Small business institutes (SBI) program
Cooperative arrangements made by U.S. Small Business Administration district offices and local colleges and universities to provide small business firms with graduate students to counsel them without charge.

Small business investment corporation (SBIC)
A privately owned company licensed and funded through the U.S. Small Business Administration and private sector sources to provide equity or debt capital to small businesses.

Small business set asides
Procurement (see separate citation) opportunities required by law to be on all contracts under $10,000 or a certain percentage of an agency's total procurement expenditure.

Smaller firms
For U.S. Department of Commerce purposes, those firms not included in the Fortune 1000.

SMSA
See Metropolitan statistical area

Socially and economically disadvantaged
Individuals who have been subjected to racial or ethnic prejudice or cultural bias without regard to their qualities as individuals, and whose abilities to compete are impaired because of diminished opportunities to obtain capital and credit.

Sole proprietorship
An unincorporated, one-owner business, farm, or professional practice.

Special lending institution categories
See SBA special lending institution categories

Standard Industrial Classification (SIC) codes
Four-digit codes established by the U.S. Federal Government to categorize businesses by type of economic activity; the first two digits correspond to major groups such as construction and manufacturing, while the last two digits correspond to subgroups such as home construction or highway construction.

Start-up
A new business, at the earliest stages of development and financing.

Start-up costs
Costs incurred before a business can commence operations.

Start-up financing
Financing provided to companies that have either completed product development and initial marketing or have been in business for less than one year but have not yet sold their product commercially.

Stock
A certificate of equity ownership in a business.

Stop-loss coverage
Insurance for a self-insured plan that reimburses the company for any losses it might incur in its health claims beyond a specified amount.

Strategic planning
Projected growth and development of a business to establish a guiding direction for the future. Also used to determine which market segments to explore for optimal sales of products or services.

Structural unemployment
See Unemployment

Sub chapter S corporations
Corporations that are considered noncorporate for tax purposes but legally remain corporations.

Subcontract
A contract between a prime contractor and a subcontractor, or between subcontractors, to furnish supplies or services for performance of a prime contract (see separate citation) or a subcontract.

Surety bonds
Bonds providing reimbursement to an individual, company, or the government if a firm fails to complete a contract. The U.S. Small Business Administration guarantees surety bonds in a program much like the SBA guaranteed loan program (see separate citation).

Swing loan
See Bridge financing

Target market
The clients or customers sought for a business' product or service.

Targeted Jobs Tax Credit
Federal legislation enacted in 1978 that provides a tax credit to an employer who hires structurally unemployed individuals.

Tax number
A number assigned to a business by a state revenue department that enables the business to buy goods without paying sales tax.

Taxable bonds
An interest-bearing certificate of public or private indebtedness. Bonds are issued by public agencies to finance economic development.

Technical assistance
See Management and technical assistance

Technical evaluation
Assessment of technological feasibility.

Technology
The method in which a firm combines and utilizes labor and capital resources to produce goods or services; the application of science for commercial or industrial purposes.

Technology transfer
The movement of information about a technology or intellectual property from one party to another for use.

Tenure
See Employee tenure

Term
The length of time for which a loan is made.

Terms of a note
The conditions or limits of a note; includes the interest rate per annum, the due date, and transferability and convertibility features, if any.

Third-party administrator
An outside company responsible for handling claims and performing administrative tasks associated with health insurance plan maintenance.

Third-stage financing
Financing provided for the major expansion of a company whose sales volume is increasing and that is breaking even or profitable. These funds are used for further plant expansion, marketing, working capital, or development of an improved product. Also known as Third-round or Mezzanine financing.

Time management
Skills and scheduling techniques used to maximize productivity.

Trade credit
Credit extended by suppliers of raw materials or finished products. In an accounting statement, trade credit is referred to as "accounts payable."

Trade name
The name under which a company conducts business, or by which its business, goods, or services are identified. It may or may not be registered as a trademark.

Trade periodical
A publication with a specific focus on one or more aspects of business and industry.

Trade secret
Competitive advantage gained by a business through the use of a unique manufacturing process or formula.

Trade show
An exhibition of goods or services used in a particular industry. Typically held in exhibition centers where exhibitors rent space to display their merchandise.

Trademark
A graphic symbol, device, or slogan that identifies a business. A business has property rights to its trademark from the inception of its use, but it is still prudent to register all trademarks with the Trademark Office of the U.S. Department of Commerce.

Trend
A statistical measurement used to track changes that occur over time.

Trough
See Cyclical trough

UCC
See Uniform Commercial Code

UL
See Underwriters Laboratories

Underwriters Laboratories (UL)
One of several private firms that tests products and processes to determine their safety. Although various firms can provide this kind of testing service, many local and insurance codes specify UL certification.

Underwriting
A process by which an insurer determines whether or not and on what basis it will accept an application for insurance. In an experience-rated plan, premiums are based on a firm's or group's past claims; factors other than prior claims are used for community-rated or manually rated plans.

Unfair competition
Refers to business practices, usually unethical, such as using unlicensed products, pirating merchandise, or misleading the public through false advertising, which

give the offending business an unequitable advantage over others.

Unfunded accrued liability
The excess of total liabilities, both present and prospective, over present and prospective assets.

Unemployment
The joblessness of individuals who are willing to work, who are legally and physically able to work, and who are seeking work. Unemployment may represent the temporary joblessness of a worker between jobs (frictional unemployment) or the joblessness of a worker whose skills are not suitable for jobs available in the labor market (structural unemployment).

Uniform Commercial Code (UCC)
A code of laws governing commercial transactions across the U.S., except Louisiana. Their purpose is to bring uniformity to financial transactions.

Uniform product code (UPC symbol)
A computer-readable label comprised of ten digits and stripes that encodes what a product is and how much it costs. The first five digits are assigned by the Uniform Product Code Council, and the last five digits by the individual manufacturer.

Unit cost
See Average cost

UPC symbol
See Uniform product code

U.S. Establishment and Enterprise Microdata (USEEM) File
A cross-sectional database containing information on employment, sales, and location for individual enterprises and establishments with employees that have a Dun & Bradstreet credit rating.

U.S. Establishment Longitudinal Microdata (USELM) File
A database containing longitudinally linked sample microdata on establishments drawn from the U.S. Establishment and Enterprise Microdata file (see separate citation).

U.S. Small Business Administration 504 Program
See Certified development corporation

USEEM
See U.S. Establishment and Enterprise Microdata File

USELM
See U.S. Establishment Longitudinal Microdata File

VCN
See Venture capital network

Venture capital
Money used to support new or unusual business ventures that exhibit above-average growth rates, significant potential for market expansion, and are in need of additional financing to sustain growth or further research and development; equity or equity-type financing traditionally provided at the commercialization stage, increasingly available prior to commercialization.

Venture capital company
A company organized to provide seed capital to a business in its formation stage, or in its first or second stage of expansion. Funding is obtained through public or private pension funds, commercial banks and bank holding companies, small business investment corporations licensed by the U.S. Small Business Administration, private venture capital firms, insurance companies, investment management companies, bank trust departments, industrial companies seeking to diversify their investment, and investment bankers acting as intermediaries for other investors or directly investing on their own behalf.

Venture capital limited partnerships
Designed for business development, these partnerships are an institutional mechanism for providing capital for young, technology-oriented businesses. The investors' money is pooled and invested in money market assets until venture investments have been selected. The general partners are experienced investment managers who select and invest the equity and debt securities of firms with high growth potential and the ability to go public in the near future.

Venture capital network (VCN)
A computer database that matches investors with entrepreneurs.

WAN
See Wide Area Network

Wide Area Network (WAN)
Computer networks linking systems throughout a state or around the world in order to facilitate the sharing of information.

Withholding
Federal, state, social security, and unemployment taxes withheld by the employer from employees' wages; employers are liable for these taxes and the corporate umbrella and bankruptcy will not exonerate an employer from paying back payroll withholding. Employers should escrow these funds in a separate account and disperse them quarterly to withholding authorities.

Workers' compensation
A state-mandated form of insurance covering workers injured in job-related accidents. In some states, the state is the insurer; in other states, insurance must be acquired from commercial insurance firms. Insurance rates are based on a number of factors, including salaries, firm history, and risk of occupation.

Working capital
Refers to a firm's short-term investment of current assets, including cash, short-term securities, accounts receivable, and inventories.

Yield
The rate of income returned on an investment, expressed as a percentage. Income yield is obtained by dividing the current dollar income by the current market price of the security. Net yield or yield to maturity is the current income yield minus any premium above par or plus any discount from par in purchase price, with the adjustment spread over the period from the date of purchase to the date of maturity.

Index

Listings in this index are arranged alphabetically by business plan type, then alphabetically by business plan name. Users are provided with the volume number in which the plan appears.

Index

Index

Index

Index